S0-BJK-337

Job the Silent

JOB

THE SILENT

A Study in Historical Counterpoint

BRUCE ZUCKERMAN

New York   Oxford

OXFORD UNIVERSITY PRESS

Oxford University Press

Oxford New York

Athens Auckland Bangkok Bogotá Bombay
Buenos Aires Calcutta Cape Town Dar es Salaam
Delhi Florence Hong Kong Istanbul Karachi
Kuala Lumpur Madras Madrid Melbourne
Mexico City Nairobi Paris Singapore
Taipei Tokyo Toronto Warsaw

and associated companies in
Berlin Ibadan

Library of Congress Cataloging-in-Publication Data
Zuckerman, Bruce.
Job the silent : a study in historical counterpoint /
Bruce Zuckerman.
p. cm. Bibliography: p. Includes index.
ISBN 0-19-505896-8; ISBN 0-19-512127-9 (pbk.)
1. Bible. O.T. Job—Criticism, interpretation, etc.
2. Job (Biblical figure) I. Title.
BS1415.2.Z83 1990 223'.106—dc19
89-9340

1 3 5 7 9 8 6 4 2

For my teacher Marvin H. Pope,
who, above all else,
taught us not to be afraid
to use our imagination

Acknowledgments

There are many who have made this book possible. Those who in classroom and conversation helped me shape the ideas behind this book: my teachers, especially R. B. Y. Scott, who first introduced me to Job; Judah Goldin, who introduced me to the thought of Shalom Spiegel; my friends Joel Manon, who first led me to "Bontsye Shvayg," and Hugh Miller, who forced me to think hard about Job in some of the most important conversations of my life. A special thanks must go to Ruth Hirshman, General Manager of radio station KCRW, whose creative programing gave me the germ of the idea to combine a study of Job and Perets' Bontsye.

Many colleagues gave me constructive advice and criticism while this book was still in various stages of manuscript. Foremost among them are my colleagues in the School of Religion at the University of Southern California and at the Hebrew Union College campus in Los Angeles. I must single out Ronald Hock of the former and William Cutter of the latter, both of whom plowed through several incarnations of my manuscript and offered crucial advice at crucial times. A special acknowledgment also must go to Abraham Zygielbaum of HUC, who was my first Yiddish advisor and who sensitized me to how important a figure Bontsye was to the Holocaust generation. I also must mention Arnold Dunn, a molecular biologist at USC, who has somehow managed to master the field of Judaic studies in his spare time, and who was kind enough to impart so many wonderful insights to me. Jerry Frakes of the USC department of German also spent some time looking over my translations of "Bontsye Shvayg" and made a number of valuable suggestions. Arguably, I owe my academic life to the Dean of Letters, Arts and Sciences at USC, William Spitzer. He gave me the most valuable gift he could give—the time to show what I could do—and did so when a more prudent administrator might well have done otherwise. Most especially, I must mention Steven Fine, friend and curator, who did so much to help me sharpen my thoughts through his gentle but firm criticisms.

Many colleagues from other institutions labored under the weight of my manuscript: Noel Freedman did everything down to correcting my spelling and showed me why he is commonly acknowledged to be the finest editor there is in the field of biblical studies. Judy Baskin seemed to understand more than anyone else what I was trying to do and gave me advice and encouragement to see the work through. Janet Hadda somehow managed to find time in her astonishing schedule to help me feel my way through Yiddish and to give me confidence that I was not so far off the beaten path with my approach to this field. Dina Abramowicz, the librarian at YIVO, did for me as she has done for so many others—find the books and articles that no one else could seem to find and offer cogent advice as well. Jeffrey Shandler worked unstintingly on my behalf at YIVO and was my final arbiter on all things

Yiddish. Without him, the Yiddish sections of this book would have been simply impossible.

Finally, I must turn to those who had to live with me through the creation of this book and who have born the brunt of the burden. Sharon Brown has kept my life in order for so long now that I can hardly imagine how I managed before she brought order to my inherent chaos. Only she knows how much she has done to keep the world at bay and me in front of the word processor. My children Katie, Peter and Ellen saw less of me than they should have during the last year I worked on this book. They still managed to make me feel that I was loved and I was missed. The greatest burden fell upon my wife Elizabeth who understood what I needed to do and what I could not do. She was so busy, she never *did* have time to read this book.

I leave the last word for my editor at Oxford, Cynthia Read. She understood this book even before she saw it, and we have been on the same wavelength ever since. Besides, Cynthia is the only editor to whom I can talk to about my (and her) true passion—fishing.

Palos Verdes, California   B. Z.
October 1990

Contents

Job the Silent

Introduction

The point of departure for this study is, in essence, a simple question: Why do we think of the biblical Job as patient Job; indeed, why is this such a fixed concept in the popular consciousness that the "patience of Job" has been elevated to the level of a nearly universal cultural proverb, if not cliché? This question is easy to pose, but—as this study will endeavor to demonstrate—the answer is not so easily framed. In fact, in the course of trying to formulate an answer, one is naturally led to consider further questions about the book and tradition of Job that are equally challenging to answer, if not more so.

None of this is surprising. Whenever one considers critical problems that have anything to do with the Bible, two things are usually sure to happen. First, one problem will lead to another. Second, the lack of concrete evidence will be so overwhelming that no sure explanation will be found; or to put this more practically, no explanation will be found that all scholars are likely to rally around.

I do not expect my study to change this picture very much. It seems to me that of necessity, any theory that purports to explain how the Bible works in its own time is, as the rabbis liked to say, "a mountain suspended by a hair." Like everyone else, I want to spin my web of theoretical insights, which, of course, I tend to believe are insightful. Still it gives me pause—and should give any serious biblical exegete pause—to consider how slender the strands of evidence are that hold one's theoretical superstructures together, how easily the merest breath of new evidence or fresh critical insight can rend one's carefully constructed complex of elegant ideas to tatters. Still, there is no harm and perhaps some good in trying to theorize about the Bible in general and the patience of Job in particular, as long as one begins with the recognition that any theory proposed is no more than the last, best hope against chaos.

In actuality, though, I must admit that the leading element in this inquiry into the patience of Job is not a theory at all. Instead, it is a metaphor; that is, in trying to sort out the problem I have posed for myself, I have found it better, or perhaps I should say more comfortable, to reach for a metaphor and then array my theoretical prognostications according to its dictates rather than to work in the opposite direction (as is usually done).

What I like about metaphors is that they are, by their very nature, more malleable than theories. A good metaphor has a certain undefined but concrete quality about it by which it can even transcend the words used to bring it to life. It might

3

even be said that the words used to compose a metaphor really only approximate what it actually means; that one can sense the reality in a metaphor, but, in the final analysis, one cannot completely define what makes it seem more tangible than a theory and therefore more real.

I often feel the same way about biblical texts—that I can better sense what they mean than say what they mean. I therefore find the use of metaphor felicitous, since it allows me at least to start my analysis with something a little more tangible and flexible than a theory. Also it allows me to begin my thinking with a freer play of imagination; and considering the lack of specific evidence, which so severely handicaps scholarly research into the Bible, imagination must always be an essential ingredient in one's analysis, whether this be manifest in metaphor, theory or anything else.

The substance of my metaphor, in this particular case, is this: that a biblical text, especially the text of the book of Job, is a composition in counterpoint. What I actually mean by counterpoint will be made clearer as this study unfolds, but for the present purpose let us say that counterpoint involves the playing off of distinct but related themes, one against the other. Sometimes this counterpoint manifests itself in sharp oppositions as one finds in the point-counterpoint of debate; at other times it seems more harmonious, like the interwoven melodic lines that one hears in polyphonic music. For my purposes, this sort of counterplay and interplay must also have a wide ranging, historical dimension; hence, this study will follow the metaphor of what I will call "historical counterpoint," not only where it leads among the textual strands that have finally come together in the book of Job but also among traditions, legends, stories and interpretations that stretch across long periods of time, even millennia.

To a very large extent, I have let my metaphor not only determine the focus of my inquiry but have also allowed it to shape the manner in which the inquiry is conducted. Hence, the reader will find that this study does not proceed directly towards its goal. Rather, it constantly veers off in one direction and then another for the express purpose of playing one idea against another until a whole complex of harmonies and variations is built up around the main theme.

It must be admitted that in some instances the tangents followed in this study may seem rather extensive, and the reader (although perhaps finding a given tangent intrinsically interesting) may begin to wonder how this material links up to the main themes. I can only appeal to the reader to have faith that what may not seem relevant at first will be shown to be relevant later; in this discussion meanings only become clear in the light of other meanings. To put this in terms of yet another metaphor, my study is a kind of Chinese puzzle—composed of odd pieces that may at first seem unrelated to one another but that, when finally put together in the right order, really do endeavor to make up a coherent whole.

For readers who always like to know where they are going and when they are going to get there, following the ins and outs of this study may well be a disconcerting experience; and it may not be much consolation to know that they have been subjected to what may seem an intellectual obstacle course with malice aforethought. Still, in my view, the form of this critical analysis is just as important as its substance (perhaps even more so). For the structure serves the metaphor, and in order to understand the metaphor the reader must not only be told about it but must experience it as well.

The most prominent play of theme against theme in this work involves considering the book of Job over against a very famous Yiddish short story, written late in the nineteenth century: Y. L. Perets' "Bontsye Shvayg" or—as it is usually translated—"Bontsye the Silent." This will naturally seem quite a drastic juxtaposition since it endeavors to bring together, for purposes of comparison, the literature of two quite distinct (although distantly related) worlds chronologically and culturally remote from one another. There are obvious risks involved in such a procedure, and the prudent reader might wonder whether it is reasonable to assume that a story from Yiddish literature could say anything insightful about a book in the Bible or vice versa.

The case in favor of this contention will, of course, be made as this study develops, and the reader will be able to judge whether the comparison has real value. But a short discussion of the rationale behind playing Job against "Bontsye Shvayg" may be appropriate here. The dynamic that shaped the book of Job into its canonical form is, in my view, rather complicated—some might even say perverse; for it is based upon the assumption that at one time or another, various contributors to the biblical tradition of Job either willfully or accidentally misapprehended the intentions of earlier contributors and often even interpreted the tradition in a manner entirely opposite to the desires of those who preceded them.

While such a scenario may seem theoretically possible, a reasonable objection might be raised: How likely is it that the Joban texts and traditions would develop in such a contrary fashion in *real life*? It would be difficult to overcome this objection were I to confine my inquiry to the ancient world in which the book of Job was written. One can speculate about what this world was like and what the Joban writers and editors intended, but we really cannot know very much about any of this. Beyond the internal evidence of the book of Job itself, a few stray references in Ezekiel, one pseudepigraphical story, a scattering of rabbinical comments, a few Dead Sea Scroll manuscripts and a single reference in the New Testament, Job and its tradition in antiquity are almost a total unknown.

So to make a credible case, I must look elsewhere for evidence—and it is to the world of Yiddish culture, tradition and literature, beginning in the late nineteenth century, that I have chosen to look. My argument is essentially by analogy: If I can reasonably demonstrate that a process has acted on a Yiddish story very much like the process I have proposed to have worked upon the book of Job, perhaps the historical reality of the former can give historical credibility to the latter.

But, the reader may query, why turn to this particular Yiddish story and this particular milieu as opposed to something or someplace else? The truth of the matter is this: "Bontsye Shvayg" and its cultural history have proven to be the key to interpretation for me: That is to say, through looking at this story and what happened to it I first began to see a pattern for understanding the growth and development of the book of Job. Especially, by looking at Perets' story and how its hero was appreciated within the Yiddish environment, I began to see why Job had to become the paragon of patience that he now is. It might well be possible to choose another subject to play against the book of Job to equal or even better effect. But I started with "Bontsye"; in fact, it would be fairer to say that it chose me rather than the other way around.

Besides, as it turns out, this story, although one of the most popular works from the "big three" of Yiddish literature (Sholom Aleichem, Mendele and Perets), has never really been the subject of a detailed literary analysis—or at least one I have found to be altogether satisfactory. So I have decided to rush in where others have not yet bothered to tread in the hope that my analysis, especially as it relates "Bontsye Shvayg" to the Joban tradition, may offer a few new insights on a story that has seemed so familiar to its Yiddish audience as to require little or no explanation.

Since "Bontsye Shvayg" is not easily available in English translation, and because translations that are available are not, in my view, entirely satisfactory, the original Yiddish version and its translation have been added in an appendix. Readers unfamiliar with "Bontsye Shvayg" should take the few minutes required to go over this story before beginning chapter 1.

Biblical and Semitic scholars may find themselves growing a little impatient as they are asked to consider in some fair detail the cultural history of "Bontsye Shvayg." On the other hand, Yiddish scholars who find their way to this study may chafe that they have to be subjected to so much biblical criticism. Still, if those interested in the Bible learn a bit more than they planned about Yiddish or those interested in Yiddish learn more about the Bible, especially Job, than they might have liked, I cannot say that I will be sorry. This study, quite intentionally, is neither fish nor fowl. Like the title, *Job the Silent*, it is a hybrid; I can only hope that the result of this cross-pollination will be something more than the sum of its antecedents.

Before I conclude this introductory *apologia*, there are a few more points to be noted. First, while this study is not necessarily intended to be an "easy read," it is meant to be accessible to those interested in the book of Job and Y. L. Perets beyond professional scholars in the fields of biblical, Semitic, and Yiddish studies. This includes individuals who do not know the original languages of the texts considered, especially biblical Hebrew, Greek and Yiddish. While some technical, philological discussion is inevitable, I have tried to keep all such discussions within reasonable bounds and to relegate them as much as possible to the endnotes. When it has been essential to consider a passage, phrase or word in the original languages, the terms are translated into English so that the nonspecialist can follow along without too much difficulty.

I hope that this study will be of some use to the "informed layperson," to individuals who have a reasonably good familiarity with biblical and/or Yiddish literature—especially with the book of Job and/or the writings of Perets—but who do not necessarily make their living off the Bible or the study of Yiddish. While I would not necessarily recommend this study as a first introduction to the book of Job or to Yiddish literature, I hope it will serve those who have read and admired Job but have always had trouble coming to grips with its various levels of meaning, levels that may even seem to contradict one another. Also, I hope it will be insightful for lovers of Yiddish who are familiar with Perets' stories but who may have never looked at his work in a critically analytical fashion.

The professional scholar may find it trying here and there to have to sit through some explanations and clarifications that seem too elementary and self-evident or at least are well known to the specialist. Still, I have no intention of writing a study with such a narrow focus that only professors (or future professors) of biblical or Yiddish literature can appreciate (or castigate) what is going on. Instead, I have tried to keep the language clear—as free of specialized jargon as possible—and have tried to lay out the arguments in a fashion that my hypothetical "informed layperson" can follow. Besides, I have always suspected that, if I cannot present an argument so that any reasonably intelligent person can understand it, then perhaps the argument itself is not reasonably intelligent. So, at the very least, it may be hoped that my effort to communicate to the nonprofessional will have helped make this study more interesting, entertaining and, above all, lucid—even for the professional.

I should also confess at this point that I am not a Yiddish specialist, so this study probably suffers as a result of my naiveté in regard to this field. I beg the indulgence of any who feel that I have not only poached on territory that is not my own but have also done so with less sophistication than they might have liked. I have had the good sense to seek out the counsel and advice of some fine and generous colleagues in the field of Yiddish studies, and they will be acknowledged where their aid has been essential and their influence has been felt. Without their patient support, this study would have been impossible. On the other hand, in the final analysis, the opinions expressed here are my own, and sometimes I have decided respectfully to disagree with one opinion or another that my colleagues in Yiddish studies have voiced to me.

Like Elihu in Job (at least as I see him), I have felt compelled to break into an ongoing debate that is not my own and where, by rights, I have no recognized standing. Whether my views are any more (or any less) insightful than Elihu's remains to be seen. Still, I believe in pursuing a line of interpretation wherever it leads; and if it leads me into foreign waters, as it has in this instance, I am willing to take the risk and suffer the consequences. I have certainly been grateful to critics from outside my field who have entered into my academic territory and proceeded to enrich my understanding of the Bible with critical insights that never would have occurred to me. In taking the risks I am taking, I am trying in a small way to acknowledge the debt I owe to them.

Another point that will become quite obvious to anyone who has followed Job criticism over any length of time is that by and large, this is a study that aligns itself more with the "Old Guard" of Job critics, as opposed to the "Young Turks." This is particularly true in several, related respects.

First, this study generally accepts the long-established scholarly view that the book of Job has a complicated textual history involving multiple authorship—this as opposed to the recent trend to read the book of Job as a unified work from a single hand. Of course, if this study were written two or three centuries ago, I could turn the critical tables and group myself with the iconoclasts of Job criticism rather than with the conservatives. For certainly the dominant view before the rise of biblical criticism in the nineteenth century was that Job (like everything else in the Bible) was the work of a single author (usually assumed to be the Author of All). Today, the critical pendulum seems to be swinging back in this direction (although for quite different reasons than before). Still, I find the arguments made in defense of the single-author approach to Job completely unconvincing; and perhaps this study can do its small part to help shove the pendulum back in what I, at least, think is the right direction.

No thoroughgoing effort will be made to combat the single-author theory, point by point, in the main text of this study. However, the various issues will be engaged and discussed as they become relevant, and some special arguments will also be considered in greater detail in the endnotes. For the moment, let me just say this: All in all, I strongly believe that the case in favor of the composite authorship of Job has never been stronger. In light of what we now know about how ancient texts evolved (especially Mesopotamian traditions that we can now track through recension after recension) it seems fair to state that in the Ancient Near East multiple authorship of traditional works was more the rule than the exception. In fact, I would argue that, *prima facie*, we should assume that biblical texts were almost always the product of multiple hands and that the burden of proof is on those who would try to prove otherwise.

Another point, related to this issue of authorship, merits some consideration: To what extent can one speak in all seriousness of a given "author" of Job (or some part thereof) as though this "author" were a "real" person? To put this in more specific terms, how can one claim any ability to affirm that thus-and-so were the "author's" intentions or that the literary-religious-cultural environment that formed the context for this "author's" work were as follows? Of course, the only proper answer is that one cannot do this with any confidence at all. For example, one would have to be naive indeed to claim authoritatively: the "Poet" of the main body of the Job-Poem knew this or the "Elihu-author" reacted to that. After all, even in the case of a "real" author such as Y. L. Perets we cannot always be *sure* what his intentions were, even though the evidence available to help us is vastly more extensive.

Despite this, I feel inclined to cling to the somewhat romantic notion that it is still worthwhile to imagine what an author intended or to speculate on the environment that served as the context for his or her work. In the case of so ancient a text as Job, one must be particularly aware of how vulnerable such efforts are to the criticism that they are built upon aesthetic judgments and little else. Nonetheless, it is my belief that one must make these judgments and come to appropriate conclusions, however hypothetical. This is our only recourse if we are to have any hope of catching a glimpse of the ancient writers of Job.

To be sure, we might very well go in the other direction: admit the task is hopeless, the speculations inadequate if not simplistic, and the result—no matter how "ingenious"—more or less irrelevant. But I believe in the reality of the Joban authors and that we can come to some comprehension of how and why they wrote what they wrote. And even if we cannot, I would still argue that we should try; for only when we place ourselves in the mind-set of the creative artist (even if that author is our own fiction) do we have a hope of gaining insight into so creative a literary work of art as the book of Job.

Yet another question relevant to the issue of authorship should be aired here— and this the most serious of all. Namely, is an historical reconstruction of the evolution of Job necessary if we are to understand the book of Job? Or to put this another way, does it really make any difference how people in the past interpreted or misinterpreted Job? Should meaning be tied to history at all? Edwin M. Good, has articulated this concern as well as anyone, and he bears careful consideration:

> We in Old Testament studies have been for so long so thoroughly brainwashed to believe that to study a book means to study its "author" that we usually don't know what to do with ourselves if the question of authorship is removed from consideration. . . .I do not mean that removing the question of authorship from consideration solves the question the way fundamentalists solve it, which is finally a dogmatic cop-out. I mean really to *remove* the question, not to ask it, not to wonder (at the outset anyway) whether one is dealing with one mind or several, not to be trapped into the intentional fallacy. That fallacy, and I truly accept that word for it, holds that the meaning of a piece of literature is identical with the author's intended meaning.*

This point cannot be lightly dismissed, and one must take very seriously the efforts that discerning and sensitive critics have invested into reading the book of Job (regardless of its history) as a text that has come down to the modern world in its current form. There is sound justification in such an approach if for no other reason than that it is the canonical form of Job that has had the decisive influence upon western civilization. Hence, if one is going to understand how this influence has been felt, one must also interpret Job according to that dominant view and read it as a unified work.

Beyond this, there are intrinsic reasons for reading a work "as is" rather than according to what its author or authors intended. Good is quite right to say that one should not fall into the false assumption that meaning is only to be found in the creator's perspective rather than in that of the audience. The audience is always the final arbiter; like the marketplace in commerce. It is the audience who decide what is of value and what is not; what exactly makes something precious or valueless; and especially, it is they who cause these evaluations to rise and fall as the times change.

Nonetheless, there is another point to be noted. The reason the interpretations of a literary work evolve and change over time is because those who read it also evolve and change throughout history; that is, the meaning of a given work is dynamic because the audience is dynamic. It is this dynamic that particularly interests me, and I certainly believe that we can gain as much critical insight by tracking the movement of interpretation as we can by looking critically at its beginning point or its end.

This study pays great attention to origins, and to that extent it is very much the successor of the historical-critical approach to the Bible that has dominated the field since the mid-nineteenth century. On the other hand, it is also concerned with how things ended up, and in this regard it acknowledges concerns of the type Good, among others has shown to be so important. Thus, there is a good deal of "straight" literary criticism in this volume that could be judged on its merits without reference to an historical perspective.** But more than anything else, this study wishes to consider the how and why of the dynamic that formed the book of Job and its surrounding traditions, and for that matter "Bontsye Shvayg" and its surrounding traditions: it is, first and foremost, a study of change.

Therefore, neither historical nor literary criticism will dominate this study; instead they will be made to play off one another as the argument develops. This interplay of criticisms will be especially prominent when focused on the early Christian epistle writer who, if he did not invent the phrase "the patience of Job," certainly made it stick. In one respect he will be seen in an historical dimension as the end point of a long interpretive tradition; but in another respect he will be seen as an early literary critic who listens to all the harmonies within the Joban tradition and finally hears what he wishes to hear. Appropriately, this study will begin by looking at him in the one way and end by seeing him in the other.

One final observation: if one takes the arguments made here individually, especially insofar as they apply to Job, very little that is original will be found. The road of Job-criticism is well traveled; and as Qoheleth, the author of Ecclesiastes, would say, "What has been is what will be, and what has been done is what will be done."

There are many scholars whose work has both directly and indirectly informed my own: The aforementioned Prof. Good who was one of the first modern scholars to consider looking at Job in an ironic fashion; the great commentators of the past like Dhorme, Beer, Driver and Gray; the more recent commentators such as Tur-Sinai, Fohrer, Gordis, Westermann, Pope and now most recently Habel; scholars such as Kramer, Jacobsen and Lambert, who have done so much to put Ancient Near Eastern literature, especially Mesopotamian Wisdom writings, in a proper perspective; MacDonald, Ginsberg and Hurvitz, who anticipate many of the arguments I make about Job; discerning Yiddish critics from Waxman and Wiener through Miron, Roskies and Mintz; Sanders and Childs, the critics who pioneered the analysis of biblical texts in their canonical form; and Bolle, Limburg, Dick and Scholnick, whose fine dissertations made my work so much easier. Especially to be acknowledged is Shalom Spiegel, whose work has been a particular inspiration to me. As will soon be clear, the first part of this study depends on Spiegel and should be considered as no less than my homage to him.

In the critical shadow of such as these, one comes very soon to recognize that it is just about impossible to say something new—especially about the book of Job. Still, it may be possible to say something different; that is, by assembling the various arguments in a different order, and playing them against one another in a different way, one may perhaps be able to come to a different sort of critical insight. In any case, while the questions posed at the beginning of this study will all be answered by the time it concludes, no answers are final. My voice is but one of many engaging in the point and counterpoint that is the continuing Joban debate. Or to put it another way: mine is but the latest critical line of argument scored over the lines that have proceeded it; another variation on the theme. The Joban counterpoint continues and will continue.

PART I

1

The "Patience" Problem

tēn hupomonēn Iōb ēkousate, kai to telos kuriou eidete, hoti polusplagkhnos estin ho kurios kai oiktirmōn.

You have heard of the patience of Job, and the purpose of the Lord you have seen: that the Lord is compassionate and merciful.

This quotation comes from the Epistle of James 5:11,[1] and is, of course, the source of the cliché that has fixed the dominant view of Job for us: *ten hupomonēn Iōb*, the proverbial "patience of Job." The term *hupomonē* has remained tied to the biblical figure; for when Job penetrates our consciousness it is always in this particular manner—as a paragon of patience. Yet, as Marvin H. Pope has commented, this "is, however, scarcely a balanced view, since it ignores the thrust of more than nine tenths of the book and appears to take account only of the beginning and end of the story."[2]

In fact, there are many ways in which one might characterize Job; one might view him as righteous, forthright, sincere, perhaps a bit prideful; but "patience" is not the most obvious of his personality traits.[3] The term used in the Epistle of James to describe Job therefore seems out of place. Note that *hupomonē* not only connotes patience, but more specifically an unquestioning, unresisting fortitude and endurance in the face of suffering. Thus, in Luke 21:19 Jesus tells his disciples that it is through their patience (*hupomonē*) that they will be able to survive the horrible persecutions that will befall them (cf. 21:10–18). Similarly, Paul informs the Romans that followers of Christ must rejoice in their sufferings, persecutions that lead naturally to patience (*hupomonēn*; Rom. 5:3).[4]

Such forbearance might fairly be said to describe the Job in the Prologue of the biblical book (chaps. 1–2), but it strains credulity to argue that Job holds on to his fortitude beyond the beginning of chapter 3. At this point, Job clearly abandons his unquestioning patience and becomes a most impatient man. He no longer quietly endures his sufferings but instead vocally chronicles them and vociferously demands, first from his Friends and then ultimately from God Himself, a reason why he has been so greatly persecuted.

Presumably, the author of the Epistle of James knew of the book of Job in something resembling the form we have it today.[5] Moreover, it is not unreasonable to assume that the audience to whom the letter is addressed, had read (or at least had

13

been read) the biblical Job as well. So why does he speak to them so highly of the "patience of Job," as though this were the one, enduring quality that should be associated with the Joban figure? Why single out Job as the unquestioning and steadfast sufferer, when one could certainly find a more appropriate biblical model—for example, Isaiah's suffering servant (cf., e.g., Isa. 53)? Why invoke Job, of all people, as *the* example of patience for all good Christians to follow when the biblical evidence clearly shows that Job is, by and large, just the opposite of this?

Perhaps, though, we are not reading James quite closely enough. Notice that he states, "you have *heard* of the patience of Job," using the verb *akouō*. This is not quite the same thing as saying "you have *read* [in the Bible] of the patience of Job." If the latter phrase were used, presumably with a Greek verb such as *anaginōskō* taking the place of *akouō*, one would have a highly circumscribed and narrow statement definitely focused upon precisely the Job one finds in the Bible.[6] However, because the operative verb is *akouō*, a good deal more flexibility in interpretation is possible. What one hears is not necessarily the same thing as what one reads. After all, there can be no doubt that the Scriptures themselves represent but a fraction of the traditions clustered around biblical figures. The abundance and considerable variety of Jewish legends preserved and discussed by the early rabbis—not to mention the numerous writings of a similar vein in the Pseudepigrapha and the Dead Sea Scrolls—amply attest to this. Could it be, then, that the author of James is not speaking so much of the Job one reads about in the Bible, but rather of the Job one *hears* about in the traditions?[7]

Perhaps so; but if this is true, it does not really solve our problem regarding why James invokes the example of "the patience of Job." In fact, just the opposite is the case: the problem becomes even more acute. For how could one have a circumstance in which an oral tradition about the "patience of Job" takes precedence over the picture of Job one unquestionably finds in the Bible, that of a man who may begin patiently but who loses his patience very quickly? Indeed, there is an even deeper problem lurking beneath this question. If the tradition knows of a forbearing Job, while the Bible essentially attests a contrary view of him, how can these opposing pictures be allowed to coexist?

In a way, though, this has always been one of the most difficult problems that inhibits interpretation of the biblical book of Job itself. For the components of the book's Prose Frame Story, that is, the Prologue (chaps. 1–2) and the Epilogue (42:7–17), have always seemed to go together and to support the view of the Epistle of James: Job, the Patient. But these brackets at the beginning and end of the book clash dramatically with the Job one finds throughout the Poem (3–42:6): Job, the Impatient. The book of Job therefore appears to be at odds with itself; and however one may attempt to resolve its contradictory picture, the result never seems to be quite successful. Like oil and water, the Prose Frame Story and the Poem naturally tend to disengage from one another despite all efforts to homogenize them. So we can add to the set of questions posed above yet another question both closely related and equally as serious: How can it be that the Prologue/Epilogue and the Poem have been joined together in the same book of Job when everything suggests that the union is forced? Or to put this another way: How can one make sense of the literary structure of Job when it actually seems to be strained by its thematic contraries to the point of collapse?

But in order to answer this latter question, our best course may be to go back to the first set of questions posed, regarding how the Epistle of James can speak of a patient Job about whom one has heard and give him precedence over the impatient Job about whom one has read. For if this question is, as I suggested, closely related to the question of how we explain the literary structure of the book of Job, the answers may be related as well. Indeed, if we can find a way to answer our first group of queries, perhaps they may forge for us the tools with which to answer the second.

2

The *Akedah* Model

Fortunately, there is an important precedent to which we can turn for guidance. The situation noted above for Job is not an isolated case: There is another righteous biblical figure, tested by God, whose circumstance is relevant to our inquiry—the Abraham of Genesis 22, the *Akedah*.[8] For here, too, we find a similar curious situation: The biblical account makes an emphatic point of telling us that although God commanded Abraham to sacrifice his son, He dispatched—just in time—an angel to stay the patriarch from his dreadful deed. In fact, the countermanding charge constitutes the climax of the biblical story: "Do not lay your hand on the boy, and do not do anything to him!" (Gen. 22:12).

Yet though this is unquestionably the story of the *Akedah* as one reads it in the Bible, there also appear to be other traditions which were heard that give quite a different account of the story. Thus, in a twelfth century poem Rabbi Ephraim ben Jacob from Bonn describes the climactic scene of Abraham and Isaac in this manner:

He [Abraham] made haste, he pinned him [Isaac] down with his knees
He made his two arms strong.
With steady hands he slaughtered him according to the rite,
Full right was the slaughter.

Down upon him fell the resurrecting dew, and he revived.
(The father) seized him (then) to slaughter him once more.
Scripture bear witness! Well grounded is the fact:
And the Lord called Abraham, even a second time from heaven.

* * *

The pure one thought: The child is free of guilt,
Now I, whither shall I go?
Then he heard: Your son was found an acceptable sacrifice,
By Myself have I sworn it, saith the Lord.

And Rabbi Ephraim's poem is not the only attestation to a tradition that speaks of the death of Isaac. The renowned Jewish sage Abraham ibn Ezra (d. 1167) is so concerned about this version of the *Akedah* that he feels constrained to emphasize that it is contrary to what the Bible clearly states to be so: "But he who asserts that Abraham slew Isaac and abandoned him and that afterwards Isaac came to life

16

again, is speaking contrary to Writ." The very zealous nature of ibn Ezra's denial of this unauthorized version of the *Akedah* probably indicates the extent to which this tradition was viable in Jewish legend. In any case, many similar remarks about the death of Isaac may be cited, focusing, for example, on the ashes or the blood of his sacrifice. These traditions are especially well known today thanks to Shalom Spiegel, who collected and analyzed them in his celebrated book, *The Last Trial*.[9]

What Spiegel reveals for us is a picture that looks familiar. We find authorities who give precedence to traditions they have heard—even though they must know that these traditions run counter to what the text of the Bible plainly says. And once again the serious question arises: how are we to explain these circumstances? But it is precisely here where we can at last begin to receive some aid; for Spiegel not only collected these traditions on the death of Isaac, he also formulated a rationale for their presence within the rabbinic legends. Thus, thanks to his remarkably original insights, we may begin to grasp why they managed to retain so solid a foothold within Jewish consciousness.

Spiegel argues that if these contrary legends about the *Akedah* are given precedence over the authorized version, then that precedence is deserved. For the traditions they preserve do not supersede the biblical tradition; rather, it is the other way around: It is the biblical account that is trying to push out a much more ancient story of sacrifice not almost committed but sacrifice fulfilled. Thus, for example, if the traditions speak—even figuratively—of "the blood of Isaac," Spiegel contends that they do so because in more ancient times there was a firm belief that such blood was shed.

> It may be that here are the last and faint echoes of some primitive pagan or prebiblical version of the Akedah story. Possibly too, "the blood of Isaac's Akedah" may be a fossil expression from the world of idolatry, some tiny stone fragment from pagan ruins sunk into the edifice of the talmudic haggadah—and therefore we would have here, as occasionally also elsewhere in the Midrashim of early generations, some leftovers of belief before the beliefs of Israel.[10]

If Spiegel is correct in the way he interprets the legends surrounding the *Akedah* that conflict with what the text of the Bible says, then we must look at the biblical account itself in a somewhat unaccustomed manner. We tend to assume that this and all other traditions found in the Bible must be seen as the *Authority*: the point of reference from which all discussion of Judaeo-Christian religion must begin and to which all interpretation must refer. But in doing so, we can forget that in more ancient times the Bible also had a point of reference to which it had to refer, namely, the dominant authority of those times: the Canaanite, Mesopotamian and other "pagan" religions and cultures of the Ancient Near East. And if the formulators of the biblical religion were inspired to construct and defend a religious world-view at odds with this "pagan" standard, then, in contemporary terms, their version of events is best seen not as the point of reference but rather as the counterpoint.

But if this is true, we have to readjust somewhat the manner in which we are used to thinking about "authorized," biblical traditions such as that in Genesis 22. Spiegel reminds us that the authority of these traditions was once quite fragile, since they stood at first in the shadow of much more ancient beliefs and practices.

Moreover, it was no small thing for the writers, editors and religious leaders who formulated the Bible to set their versions of the traditions up against the precedent of ancient authority, even though that authority might be of a distasteful, "pagan" nature. They could not have done so with ease and confidence, no matter how certain they were of the rightness and righteousness of their stand. More likely, they brought forward their countervailing versions of the traditions with considerable difficulty and trepidation. Indeed, even as they endeavored to separate themselves from the dominant cultures, the separation must have been wrenching, if not painful. Thus, though we know that the Bible reflects a break with the authorities of the past which was decisive, we should not further assume that this schism was necessarily complete. Rather, it is to be expected that vestiges from the more ancient religions and cultures would remain embedded in the biblical traditions, reminders that beneath the new authorities, older authorities still maintained their hold. In fact, we should recognize that there was considerable advantage to be derived from tying new traditions (at least in part) to the old; for then ancient authorities could serve to legitimize the modern by giving them a patina of venerability that they would not otherwise have had.

Spiegel notes that the story we find in the *Akedah* has very ancient reverberations.[11] It has been played out many times with many variations by many cultures, though the theme is basically the same: the hero faced with the awesome dilemma owing to an inexorable set of circumstances, the demand from an authority, not to be refused, for the child of the hero, his most precious possession—all leading to the decisive moment when the hero must deliver what is required, or if not that, perhaps a suitable substitute. Often, the story ends as a tragedy—and a bloody one at that.

The authority of such venerable traditions could be denied, if this were deemed necessary on theological grounds. But the traditions *themselves* could not be so easily ignored. Certainly, their continued presence in the Jewish haggadic literature demonstrates that this is so. How else can one explain the otherwise inexplicable presence of "Isaac's blood" on the altar of sacrifice, despite what the Bible says? This blood calls to mind the older stories found not only in the *Akedah* but also in other legends of like genre, for example, in the Paschal ceremony and its later refiguring as Easter. Thus Spiegel notes:

> It may well be that "the blood of Isaac's Akedah" surviving in our sources is nothing other than an archaic cliché in origin probably a pagan figure of speech whose pagan soul has left it. And yet this relic of an archaic manner of speaking— emptied though it be of its original idolatrous substance—is a distinct echo of those early times when the expression was first coined and believed in, literally, actually. If in the haggadic lore it was possible to pour together the paschal blood with the blood of Isaac's Akedah, this is a sign that once upon a time they did imagine that the hand was laid on the lad, the knife did make contact with the throat, and did what it did *contrary* to what is written in the Torah.[12]

But the matter does not end here. For Spiegel notes that the ancient story of Isaac's sacrifice not only reveals its presence in the legends one hears but also left its mark, if ever so slightly, on the biblical text itself. The key passage, in this respect, is the last one in the story (Gen. 22:19): *wyšb ʾbrhm ʾl-nʿryw wyqmw wylkw yḥdw ʾl-bʾr šbʿ wyšb ʾbrhm bbʾr šbʿ*[13] "And Abraham returned to his lads and they continued on together to Beer Sheva and Abraham dwelt in Beer Sheva." Spiegel comments, ". . .in connection with the descent from the mountain, it does not say, 'So *they* returned to the young men,' but 'So *Abraham returned* [in the singular!] to the young men' (vs. 19). One would think it was only the father who returned, and his son was not with him." The question Spiegel poses for us cannot be ignored: "Where was Isaac?"[14] His unexpected absence from the story is striking; and in light of the traditions we have considered above, it cannot be easily dismissed as simply an accidental oversight. Furthermore, the issue of the absent Isaac does not rest on an ambiguous and subtle nuance in the text. Rather, verse 19 seems particularly designed to draw attention to itself—to make sure that we do not ignore the point that Abraham's son now is missing from the scene. We therefore find a singular verb, connected only with Abraham as he descends Mount Moriah (*wyšb*), "and (Abraham) returned." Then, lest we think the verb is a collective that might include both father and son under the rubric "Abraham," this is immediately belied by the use of two plural verbs (*wyqmw wylkw* lit. "and they arose and went"—to make it clear that Abraham and his servants go on "together" (*yḥdw*). Moreover, this last *yḥdw* also drives home the point of Isaac's absence. Previously in vs. 6 it was emphasized that going up Mount Moriah, Abraham and Isaac—the two of them— went *together* (*wylkw šnyhm yḥdw*); and to make the point even more prominent, the phrase was repeated again in vs. 7. Thus, in vs. 19, when we see that now Abraham and only the lads are going together, this serves to remind us that the special one, the only one (*yḥyd*, cf. 22:12, 12; note the word play, *yaḥīd*, "only one" versus *yaḥdāw*, "together"), is nowhere to be found. Finally, the last phrase again underscores Abraham's singular presence by again using a singular verb: He and the lads went together, but Abraham alone "dwelt" (*wyšb*) in Beer Sheva.[15]

Seen from this perspective, vs. 16 also begins to assume darker connotations— especially when it is juxtaposed to vs. 12. In vs. 12, God affirms his approval of Abraham *ky ʿth ydʿty ky-yrʾ ʾlhym ʾth wlʾ ḥśkt ʾt-bnk ʾt-yḥydk mmny*, "for now I know that you fear God since you have not withheld your son, your only one from me." The key verb here is *ḥśk* "to withhold, restrain." Abraham would not withhold his son but was willing to let him go, that is, to deliver him over to sacrifice. But what God approves of here is not Abraham's action but rather his passive willingness to accept an action. The utilization of *ḥśk* in the verse suggests that when Abraham was faced with the *Akedah*, he was willing to let the worst happen. However, no emphasis is placed on anything that Abraham actually *did* because, in the final analysis, he never did anything.[16]

But vs. 16, though in many ways a close parallel to 12, adds a crucial phrase that, like vs. 19, cannot help but draw attention to itself. For when the LORD calls to Abraham a second time, His approval comes *ky yʿn ʾšr ʿśyt ʾt-hdbr hzh wlʾ ḥśkt ʾt-bnk ʾt-yḥydk* "because you have done this thing and have not withheld your son, your only one." Again the verb *ḥśk* is employed, but before it is interposed a phrase that clearly connotes action—not merely contemplated but action completed: "because you have done this thing." Not only did Abraham not withhold his son, but he also did "this thing" (*hdbr hzh*) as well.

It is certainly possible that the distinction between vs. 12 and 16 reflects the interweaving of different textual sources. Note, in this regard, that *Elohim* (God) speaks in the former case and *YHWH* (the LORD) in the latter. Moreover, the phrase *wyqr' ml'k yhwh 'l-'brhm šnyt* "And the angel of the LORD called to Abraham a second time. . ." (22:15) seems to invite one to see it as introducing an interpolated, secondary textual strain into the biblical text. Naturally, many scholars have developed arguments along this line.[17] Thus, for example, one might see two stories being joined together here—one that speaks of the near sacrifice of Isaac, another that evokes an earlier version where the "thing" itself is done. But whether this text-critical interpretation of the biblical version of the *Akedah* is correct or not is largely a side issue. The point is, the writer(s) and/or editor(s) of Genesis 22 in some manner or form felt compelled to leave traces of the older story within the biblical text itself—despite their undeniable wish to affirm that the older story was definitely wrong.

We have suggested already that a respect for, or perhaps an awe of, the ancient traditions is reason enough for finding Isaac missing when we arrive at Gen. 22:19. Yet there may still be another factor playing a role in the preservation of the bloody traces we find in Gen. 22:16, 19: The biblically authorized version—despite its being so finely told—is nonetheless a somewhat anticlimactic story. Everything leads to the crucial moment of sacrifice in Genesis 22; but at the last instant, this denouement is scuttled, and a less climactic moment is substituted in its place. Theologically, of course, this may be necessary; and because the story is so masterfully structured, we hardly notice. Still, it should be recognized that when the story shows us Isaac being spared rather than killed, the story as a *story* has been robbed of its tragic dimension.

Compare, in this connection, the somewhat similar account of Jephthah and his daughter in Judges 11. Jephthah, seeking victory over Israel's Ammonite enemies, vows to sacrifice whomsoever first comes forth from his door on his return from battle, if God will allow him to triumph (11:29–31). But after he achieves his victory, it is his only daughter (like Isaac, termed a *yhyd*, "only one"; cf. 11:34)[18] who comes out of the door to meet him. Thus, he must fulfill upon her his dreadful vow. Thereupon, 11:39 reports *wy'š lh 't-ndrw 'šr ndr*, "and he enacted on her his vow that he had vowed."

It is interesting to note that in medieval times the rabbis sought to blunt the force of Jephthah's vow. The interpretation was brought forward that his daughter did not really die but rather lived in seclusion as a virgin, devoting herself entirely to God's service.[19] This of course, relieves the story of any perceived theological problems; but as a colleague once commented to me regarding this interpretation, "If Jephthah's daughter doesn't die, doesn't this ruin the story?"[20]

The observation is astute; for if Jephthah's daughter does not die, there is nothing really at stake, no tragic dimension that makes the legend memorable and thus worthy of preservation. It would be like the version of *Hamlet* that sometimes used to be played out in the Victorian era, where Hamlet and Ophelia miraculously revive at the conclusion of the "drama" to live happily ever after. The tragedy then becomes a comedy which no doubt makes the more squeamish and sentimental in the audience feel relieved and happy. But the play is no longer Shakespearean.

One may therefore ask the same question in respect to the *Akedah*: If Isaac does not die, doesn't it ruin that story as well? The answer here, though, must be more equivocal; for "ruin" is far too harsh a characterization. Unquestionably, the authorized story succeeds quite well as a drama and has succeeded for generations. There is a palpable tension in a heinous act contemplated, dangled (as it were) before the reader, and then snatched back at the last possible moment. Because the horror of the potential deed is kept offstage, like the violence in a Greek tragedy (or the sacrifice of Jephthah's daughter), it is therefore not constrained by the action of the story. Thus, it can be shaped by the reader's imagination and becomes all the more horrific as a result. The drama engendered by this imagined sacrifice of son by father is what gives the authorized *Akedah* much of its force as a great story.

Yet if one cannot fault the *Akedah*—at least not entirely—on dramatic grounds, there is nonetheless a sense of incompleteness or imperfection about the authorized version. One is left with a feeling that however harrowing his ordeal, Abraham has not been tested to the limit. Consider, in this respect, the famous outcry of mother Hannah when her seven children were taken and murdered during the persecutions of Hadrian: "Their mother wept and said to them: Children, do not be distressed, for to this end were you created—to sanctify in the world the Name of the Holy One, blessed be He. Go and tell Father Abraham: Let not your heart swell with pride! You built one altar, but I have built seven altars and on them have offered up my seven sons. What is more: Yours was a trial, mine was an accomplished fact!"[21] Implicit in this statement is a rebuke of sorts to the authorized version of the *Akedah*, as if to say, it is admirable to see an Abraham hold fast to his faith in God when sorely tested; but this is *nothing* when compared to one who keeps faith when the test is no longer merely a trial but rather an accomplished fact.[22] Indeed, how can one call Abraham's action truly heroic if that heroism is not tested to the full extent? It is one thing to accept God's will before the fact, but acceptance after the fact—after no angel has come forward to stay the sacrificial knife—*that* is a far greater thing.

Perhaps one reason we find the vestiges of an accomplished sacrifice in the biblical version of the *Akedah* is because its writers and/or editors are sensitive to the criticism that their version is not as complete as the version heard in more ancient traditions. Perhaps, too, these traces remain for an even more basic reason: because they allow the writers/editors to allude to that aspect of the ancient story that is its most dramatic and miraculous point—the point upon which all the action *really* turns—even if they dare not bring this directly into the authorized story itself.

In actuality, it is not the sacrifice that should be seen as the great moment—at least in the unauthorized *Akedah*—but rather what happens *after* the sacrifice, after Abraham has gone back to Beer Sheva alone. For the story cannot end as a tragedy. One cannot have a loyal Abraham left with a sacrificed son and no one to carry on the chosen line thereafter. Promises have been made by God to Abraham, covenants have been cut; and these promises and covenants must be kept. Indeed, if they were not kept, there could be no Jacob nor the sons of Jacob and thus no Bible at all. Consequently, if Isaac has died by the hand of his father, then, for the sake of his father, he must be restored again. As Rabbi Ephraim and ibn Ezra have already shown us, the legend speaks not only of the death of the son but of his resurrection.

Of course, one might reasonably argue that any story of the death of Isaac that also includes his subsequent resurrection might best be seen as a Jewish apologetic in the face of the Christian *mythos*. But Spiegel refrains from taking so obvious a line of interpretation. He comments:

> You might be inclined to say that all this encomium on the righteousness, yea sanctity too, of the son who is to be the offering, comes as the result of Christian influence—or to *dispute* the Christian claim. Maybe; and again, maybe not. For Judaism had to contend not only with Christianity but with all the religions and civilizations of the ancient Near East. Against them too Judaism entered the lists, them too it sought to refute; and it happened that wittingly and unwittingly it borrowed from them too. Jews, Christians—neither escaped pagan influences. Pagan legends and fancies regarding gods who died and from death rose again to life shaped the redemption *mythos* of the Christians. Is it conceivable that nothing of this ancient heritage or of the pagan milieu survived and settled in Judaism as well?[23]

Moreover, an *Akedah* story that ends in the resurrection of the son satisfies all requirements and silences all criticisms of the nature alluded to above. No longer can any mother of a martyred child say of Abraham, "Yours was only a trial, mine was an accomplished fact. You were tested only partially, I was tested to the full extent." For Abraham, too, has been tried to the limit: he has suffered, has lost completely and has gone on *alone* without his son—but with his unquestioning loyalty to God still intact.[24] Only thereafter comes the miraculous restoration. This is not tragedy superficially turned into comedy like a Victorian *Hamlet*. Rather, it is tragedy transformed into triumph. It has taken its hero to depths from which there seemed to be no escape only to change things in a moment into a stunning victory over death. The climax one finds in this version of the *Akedah* is of the highest dramatic sort—and it may be argued that the climax one finds in the authorized version of the story (Gen. 22:12) pales by comparison.

If Spiegel's interpretation is valid, the *Akedah* of both Scripture and legend proves to be a most complicated story—one that says one thing but also says quite another. And this leaves us with one other question to consider. If we grant that two countervailing traditions are tied together in the same legend—indeed, that both contrasting perspectives are manifest in the text of Genesis 22 itself—how are we to understand their relationship best—especially their relationship within the biblical text? How are we to characterize a biblical narrative that shows us a sacrificial knife deflected, but also depicts an Abraham returning alone to Beer Sheva after having done "this thing"?

One might speak of such a narrative as being at odds with itself, as being contradictory or paradoxical. One might even try to ignore the issue entirely and chalk up everything to grammatical peculiarity, scribal error or simply a mechanical editing of textual sources. But none of these recourses seems, at least to me, satisfactory. As I have suggested above, the traces of a more ancient story beneath our authorized version of the *Akedah* appear to be intentional in Genesis 22. Verses 16 and 19 are not "out of place"; they have to be there if the story is not to be robbed of a good deal of its legitimacy for its ancient audience. But it would be wrong simply to describe the manifest contrasts as merely contradictory or paradoxical.

Rather, they have a special *relationship* to one another. Even as they contrast, they also complement.

Maybe the best way to describe this relationship is in terms of counterpoint. We have already utilized this term above in reference to the biblical tradition being more the counterpoint than the point of reference in its ancient Near Eastern context.[25] But this is not the nuance of counterpoint I wish to emphasize here, i.e., counterpoint strictly in the forensic sense, connoting the contrary point, the exact opposite, the antithesis. Instead, I am thinking more of counterpoint in the musical sense.

Musical counterpoint, as the *Oxford English Dictionary* notes, is "the art of adding one or more melodies to a given melody or 'plain song' according to certain fixed rules."[26] What these "rules" are is a most complicated and variable thing— better left for detailed discussion in a course on musicology. But good counterpoint, in general, involves both an harmonious relationship between lines of melody as well as a degree of independence that separates these lines from one another.[27] The relationship of melodic lines may, for example, involve an inversion of chords or intervals or of a given musical phrase itself; or a contrast of rhythms, as in syncopation; or successive repetitions of a theme to make a canon or fugue. Perhaps the term in its original sense catches best the spirit of what a contrapuntal composition involves: *punctus contra punctum*, point-against-point, note-against-note;[28] that is, the notes of one melody mark a distinction from the notes of the other melody (or melodies). But that distinction is not haphazard. Although the relationship is often both subtle and intricate, it also involves definable patterns that make musical sense. Thus, the harmonies and dissonances join together, even as the individual notes of the respective melodic lines stand against one another; and the total polyphonic composition is greater than the sum of its parts: a celebration of the musical interweaving of disparate but related elements.

Of course, the kind of counterpoint that occurs among the various strands of a biblical narrative like the *Akedah* is a good deal different from that which a composer scores among the various lines of a polyphonic composition. In the latter case a creative artist develops all the voices of his musical composition more or less simultaneously as formal structures that work against one another.[29] Thus, the counterpoint is essentially synchronic. But the joining of the contrasting harmonies in ancient biblical traditions has a diachronic dimension: rather like a musical composition that has been progressively supplemented and rescored by one composer after another across often large spans of time—an historical counterpoint. Yet even though the overall composition is typically built up over the centuries, the result is not to be seen—or, to keep within our metaphor, heard—as a haphazard cacophony of clashing dissonances. The successive layers of traditions maintain a relationship to one another just like the levels of contrapuntal music. And like music in counterpoint, the traditions that ultimately form a biblical narrative are best understood when heard *together* rather than when merely isolated and analyzed as discrete entities.

It is very hard to make "logical" sense of the *Akedah* as found in Scripture and legend. Logical analysis tends to abhor contrast and contradiction and to concentrate its rational arsenal of interpretive approaches on their resolution. But were one to "rationalize" the *Akedah* in this manner, one would do so only at the expense of what the story or stories really mean. However, one can make "musical sense" of the *Akedah* very well. For music, especially contrapuntal music, not only tolerates contrast and contradiction but depends on this playing of one theme against another for its artistry.

In the *Akedah* there is a primary theme that tells of a son almost sacrificed but who was saved by a merciful God at the last moment. But beneath this theme another older theme plays an harmonic inversion that tells not only of the son's death but of his subsequent resurrection. For the most part, it is the first theme that takes the dominant role and is the one that we seem to hear. But the other is always there, contrapuntally contrasting with and complementing the leading melody, giving it a depth and texture that it otherwise would not have. Moreover, occasionally this bass theme rises to dominance; then, it is the usually dominant theme that drifts into the background of contrapuntal harmony—only to reassert itself and force the darker theme back into its secondary role. The *Akedah* moves to this contrapuntal rhythm and lives by the complicated harmonies that play within its verses and between its verses, between what is written and what is heard. And it is not the only contrapuntal story to be found in the Bible. As we suggested above, the *Akedah*—especially as it is interpreted by Spiegel—supplies a crucial precedent—or perhaps we should say model—that will help us understand the book of Job. For Job, too, perhaps is best seen as a study in historical counterpoint.

3

The Case against a Linear Reading

I previously emphasized that the Prologue/Epilogue of Job and the Poem[30] do not seem to coalesce. Instead we took the view that there is a decisive, thematic break between the end of the Prologue (2:13) and the beginning of the Poem (3:1 ff.) and an equally wide thematic gap between the end of the Poem (42:6) and the beginning of the Epilogue (42:7 ff.) However, it could be argued that the dramatic contrast proposed here has been overdrawn, that there is no real justification for seeing a conflict between the two pictures of Job we respectively see in the Prologue/ Epilogue and the Poem. Rather, they follow in a logical progression. After all, a linear reading of the Joban story line can make excellent sense of Job's change of moods.

One might simply propose the direct and obvious interpretation mentioned at the beginning of this study: Job is patient through the first two chapters but very shortly gets quite angry and impatient due to his increasingly deplorable circumstances. In chapters 3 and following Job's impatient anger builds in intensity, goaded, no doubt, by the tediously pious arguments of his Three Friends. Finally (chaps. 29–31), Job can restrain himself no longer; he throws all caution to the winds and directs a long and dreadful oath toward God Himself—challenging the Almighty, demanding an explanation.[31] This challenge is accepted by God, who confronts Job from out of the whirlwind and then proceeds to overwhelm him with the enormity of the divine power and majesty (chaps. 38–41). This encounter with God has a profound effect on Job, and it literally shocks him out of his self-centered impatience. Job is then overcome by humility and therefore submits to God's will (42:5–6). Nonetheless, although God has certainly rebuked Job for questioning His wisdom and power, He also grants that the issues Job raised during his period of impatient anger were valid issues. Thus, God rebukes Job's Three Friends as well for their narrow-minded piety—since they did not speak what was so, as did His servant Job (42:8). The story ends in reconciliation: Job prays for his Friends who have recognized that their pious platitudes were inadequate. Job's relationship with them is therefore reestablished, as is his relationship with God. Indeed, God forgives Job's interlude of impatience and rewards him with great wealth and a new set of children to replace the ones that were previously killed. The book of Job ends on this positive note.

Job can be said to make sense in this manner—although we should point out that the interpretation above still leaves us with the problem of explaining why the

25

Epistle of James insists that Job is the most patient of men. However, this line of exegesis ignores crucial evidence on the relative dating of the Prologue/Epilogue and the Poem, which makes this linear reading of the book of Job difficult.

Consider, in this respect, the work done by Avi Hurvitz on the language of the prose sections of Job.[32] Hurvitz undertook an analysis of the Prologue/Epilogue that sought "to identify linguistic elements, the very existence and unusual concentration of which" might reveal the chronological origin of this part of the text.[33] As a basis of comparison, he set the language of the prose sections of Job against books of certain postexilic date—for example, Esther, Chronicles and Ezra "which provide. . .us with reliable data for determining just exactly what late Biblical Hebrew. . .is."[34] His analysis of various linguistic elements in the Prologue/Epilogue led to a decisive conclusion:

> These deviations from standard B[iblical]H[ebrew] are duplicated in late Hebrew phraseology, both in biblical and non-biblical sources. Their wide usage in the late sources—as well as their complete absence, in similar contexts, from early biblical writings—is undeniable. . . .As far as can be judged from the linguistic data at our disposal, these *non*-classical idioms ought to be explained as *post*-classical— namely, as imprints of late Hebrew—thus making the final shaping of the extant Prose Tale incompatible with a date prior to the Exile.[35]

In contrast, no such linguistic elements, identifiable with late Biblical Hebrew, have ever been isolated by Hurvitz or any other scholar in the Poem of Job; and, in fact, its language seems quite distinct from that in the prose portions—indeed, quite distinct from other biblical Hebrew as well. The fact that the language of the Poem has so many dialectical idiosyncrasies, makes it difficult to date; still, the linguistic evidence tends to support the conclusion that the Poem is chronologically earlier than the Prologue/Epilogue. Thus, it seems altogether likely that these prose brackets were added to the Poem by a later writer or editor quite distinct from the Poem's author.[36]

Beyond the linguistic data noted above, there is an even more decisive piece of evidence that supports the view that the Poem is to be dated earlier than the Prologue/Epilogue: the presence of the Satan figure[37] in the latter in contrast to his complete absence in the former. As Hurvitz has pointed out,

> The clear emergence of *a definite image of "The Satan"*. . .is late. It is not until Zachariah (III 1,2) and 1 Chr. (XXI 1) that the Satan as such is first mentioned in the Bible (with or without the definite article). . . .In sum: the discussion of heavenly affairs and assemblies of celestial beings is by no means restricted to the late literature. However, the emergence of the figure of The Satan in the Bible. . .is an exclusive feature of post-exilic literature.[38]

The role the Satan plays in the Prologue of Job is of crucial importance: he is the instigator of the action against Job—or at least the catalyst of such action. Thus, one would expect that the author of the Poem of Job would in some manner refer to the role of the Satan in the story.

The fact that not a single verse in the poetic section of Job can be seen as constituting even an oblique reference to the Satan has broad implications.[39] Not only does this reinforce the linguistic argument made above in favor of the extant Frame Story postdating the Poem, but there also necessarily follows a corollary conclusion: that the story of Job, known to the author of the Poem, was in some form *different* from the authorized version we now find reflected in the Prologue/Epilogue. The Job story we read is not necessarily identical to the Job legend that was heard in the tradition. Thus the linear reading of Job presented above cannot be accepted—at least, from an historical-critical perspective. If we sense that there is a decisive break between the prose and poetic portions of Job, we have good reason to do so, since, text-critically speaking, such a break does indeed exist.

There is, in fact, some indication in the Prologue/Epilogue itself that there existed more than one level to the Job story. Certainly, if the language of the prose tale in the Bible shows various late linguistic elements and thus a late age, the whole tenor of the story—its patriarchal setting, the folkloric elements in its structure— also suggests that we are dealing with a story of great venerability. Note, in particular, that alongside the late linguistic features in the prose portions of Job there are also other words and phrases that seem quite archaic.[40] Of course, the sense of age one feels in the Prologue/Epilogue may be illusory—that is, the story may not be archaic but rather written in an intentionally archaizing style, a point noted, for example, by Hurvitz. But Hurvitz's alternate interpretation of the archaisms in the prose tale seems to me closer to the mark: "Another possible explanation of the existence of old linguistic elements could be, of course, that (some of) the material in the Prose Tale is indeed old, its final form being shaped, however, in a late period."[41]

Beyond this, it is interesting to note the curious circumstance of the Satan in the prose sections of Job. For not only is the Satan absent from the Poem, but he leaves no trace in the Epilogue as well. We have already noted that it is odd to find the Satan missing from the poetic section of Job, but his omission in the Epilogue is much more extraordinary. Since it was the Satan's challenge to God that set in motion all the action of the Job story, one expects him to play at least some role in the story's conclusion. The story almost demands that God direct some comment towards the Satan, and the fact that no such remark is forthcoming therefore constitutes a rather glaring loose end.

Again we find ourselves asking a question like those we posed before, when we considered Isaac's unexpected absence at the end of the biblical *Akedah*: How can the story—at its conclusion—pretend that the Satan is not there when at the beginning of the story he was such a major presence? How can the story ignore, indeed implicitly contradict, what previously it had plainly said? But if the question sounds familiar, perhaps the explanation should as well: the Epilogue probably presents the story as though the Satan never played a role in the action because in the more ancient tradition—in the story of Job that plays beneath the authorized prose version—the Satan did not exist. In the ancient story of Job, it was God *alone* who tested Job—just as it was God *alone* who tested the Abraham who dwelt *alone* in Beer Sheva in the more ancient *Akedah*.[42]

But if this is true, what accounts for the presence of the Satan in the authorized version? The answer to this is not hard to find: This is not the only occasion where the Bible, not to mention Jewish legend, has seen fit to interpose the Satanic presence between God and man. The parade example is 2 Sam. 24:1 versus its later rendering in 1 Chr. 21:1. In the former case we read, *wysp 'p-yhwh lḥrwt byśr'l wyst 't-dwd bhm*, "Once more the LORD became furious at Israel, so He incited David against them." Obviously, this is a rather bald statement in which God is clearly depicted as initiating adverse action against His Chosen People. Furthermore, no apparent reason is given in the biblical narrative why God is so angry with Israel *in this specific instance*. In the larger biblical context this may seem a minor point; after all, there is always ample cause for God's anger to rise against His continually erring people. Perhaps the statement in 2 Sam. 24:1 begins with *wysp* just to point this out—that God is angry *once more*.[43] In any case, if such a statement did not disturb the sensibilities of the writers/editors of 2 Samuel, the statement was not so easily tolerated in the later version in Chronicles. When the writers/editors of Chronicles reworked this tradition, they took steps to distance God from His anger. Thus, 1 Chr. 21:1 reports *wy'md śtn 'l yśr'l wyst 't-dwyd*, "Then Satan stood up against Israel and incited David. . . ." The Satan had to be injected into the story as a buffer to God, lest anyone impute to God even the hint of an unjust action.[44]

Note, by the way, how easily the *Akedah* can be reformed into a Joban image for much the same reason. A rabbinic story in Sepher Yashar Wa-Yera 42b, adds this prologue to the story in Genesis 22:

> Now there was a day when the sons of God came to present themselves before the Lord, and Satan came along among them. And the Lord said unto Satan, "From where have you come?" and Satan answered the Lord, and said, "From going to and fro on the earth and from walking up and down in it.". . .And the Lord said to Satan: "Have you considered my servant Abraham? For there is none like him in the earth, a perfect and an upright man before Me. . .and that fears God and eschews evil. As I live, were I to say unto him, Bring up Isaac, your son, before Me, he would not withhold him from Me, much less if I told him to bring up a burnt offering before me from his flocks and herds." And Satan answered the Lord, and said, "Speak now unto Abraham as You have said, and You will see whether he will not transgress and cast aside your words this day.[45]

Once again, it is significant to see that, in discussing the Joban tradition, we find ourselves making connections with the *Akedah*. But these connections are both natural and obvious since underlying the two traditions is very much the same kind of story: both traditions deal with patriarchal figures who are subjected to a severe testing by God—indeed, they are the two preeminent such stories in the Bible. Furthermore, they both require one to look hard at God's intentions towards mankind, especially when God decides to try an individual with undeserved hardship. Thus, it should not surprise us to see one version of the *Akedah* recreated in the image of Job. If God needed a Satan-buffer in the Job story, He certainly could use one as well in the *Akedah*.

Perhaps, though, we should look at things the other way around. If a later version of the *Akedah* can be remade to look like Job, then we should also not be surprised to discover that the earlier version of Job was much more in line with the story we find in the *Akedah*: if there was no Satan to propose the test of Abraham, so, too, there was originally no Satan to propose the test of Job. And the connections between the *Akedah* and the legend of Job may not end there. As we delve into the Joban tradition beneath the authorized Job of the Prose Frame Story, we may discover that the contrapuntal theme it plays beneath the extant prose tale comes closer to that lower melody found in the *Akedah* than we might first expect.

Actually, the key biblical passages that indicate that this may be so are not to be found in the book of Job at all. Rather, they are in the book of Ezekiel, the only other place in the Hebrew Bible where the Joban figure is mentioned outside of Job itself. In Ezek. 14:13–14 we read:

> *bn-'dm 'rṣ ky tḥṭ'-ly lm'l-m'l wntyty ydy 'lyh wšbrty lh mṭh-lḥm whšlḥty-bh r'b whkrty mmnh 'dm wbhmh whyw šlšt h'nšym h'lh btwkh nḥ dn'l w'ywb hmh bṣdqtm ynṣlw npšm n'm 'dny yhwh*
>
> Son of man, a land, when it sins against me most treacherously—should I then stretch out my hand against it and shatter its staff of bread and send famine against it and cut it off from man and beast—then were these three men in its midst, Noah, Danel[46] and Job, they could save only themselves by their righteousness. Word of the Lord GOD.

In verses 15–18 the prophet envisions a divinely inspired devastation of the land, first by marauding beasts (*ḥyh r'h*; 14:15), then by the sword (*ḥrb*; 14:16). Each time he reaffirms that "these three men" (*šlšt h'nšym h'lh*) could not save the land from God's wrath. More specifically he states that they could save neither sons or daughters (*'m-bnym w'm-bnwt yṣylw*, 14:16; *l' yṣylw bnym wbnwt*, 14:18) from the destruction that the LORD would bring. Finally, Ezekiel ends the oracle with a vision of plague (*dbr*) on the land, concluding with the now familiar refrain:

> *wnḥ dn'l w'ywb btwkh ḥy-'ny n'm 'dny yhwh 'm-bn 'm-bt yṣylw hmh bṣdqtm yṣylw npšm*
>
> As I live—word of the Lord GOD—were Noah, Danel and Job in its midst, neither son nor daughter could they save by their righteousness; they could only save themselves. (14:20)

As many have observed, Ezekiel refers here to the Job of legend and equates him with two other well-known legendary figures. But the crucial issue is why; what is the connection between the three? Fortunately, once again, we have Shalom Spiegel to guide us. His famous article "Noah, Danel and Job" considers precisely this issue; and thereby he reveals to us as much about the more ancient Job story as he did about the more ancient *Akedah*.[47]

Regarding Noah and Job (we will consider the special situation of Danel shortly), there is obviously one characteristic that they share and to which Ezekiel explicitly refers: righteousness. Gen. 6:9 tells us that Noah was *'yš ṣdyq tmym hyh bdrtyw*, "a righteous man, he was blameless among his contemporaries." So, too, we know that Job is described as a man *tm wyšr*, "blameless and upright" (cf. Job 1:1). But Spiegel further notes that Ezekiel has something special in mind when he refers to their exemplary righteousness. The prophet is himself playing a contrapuntal theme that precisely inverts what the legends must have told him. Ezekiel states that should God decide irrevocably to act against a land, even Noah, Danel and Job could not convince Him *through their righteousness* to turn aside. This obviously suggests that the three figures were known in legend to have achieved precisely the end which the prophet denies for them in Ezekiel 14; that is, their legendary righteousness was so great that, when adverse circumstances arose, it not only proved effective in saving their own lives but also the lives of others.

And who are these others? Ezekiel's oracle already suggests the answer. Since the prophet goes out of his way to declare that Noah, Danel and Job could save "neither son nor daughter"—it likely follows that it was precisely son and daughter that they *did* save, according to the traditions. Spiegel comments, "It must be admitted that Ezekiel's choice of three exemplars of piety would be particularly appropriate, if the mere mention of their names were to bring to mind a parallel feat or fortune, in short, if in common all three were known to have ransomed their children by their righteousness."[48] The appropriateness of Noah, in this respect, is clear. The biblical story not only praises his righteousness, but tells us that through that righteousness, he saved not only himself but his family as well. Thus, Gen. 7:13 states that on the day the Flood commenced, "Noah—and Shem, Ham and Japeth, the sons of Noah, and Noah's wife and the three wives of his sons with them—entered the Ark." Moreover, it is not the merit of the children and wives that has caused them to be saved; we certainly see that Ham, at least, is not viewed as a paragon of virtue (cf. Gen. 9:22 ff.). Rather, the whole tenor of the story makes it apparent that Noah's family is saved only through the merit of Noah.[49]

But what about the second figure on Ezekiel's list—spelled in Hebrew *dn'l*? Until relatively recently, this figure appeared to be a problem, since it was assumed that Ezekiel could only be referring to the biblical Daniel. Still, the chronology seemed odd; at best, Daniel would be Ezekiel's near contemporary and thus a less-than-appropriate figure to equate with the far more venerable Noah and Job. Furthermore, although Daniel could certainly be classified as righteous, no story about him mentions anything about saving others through his own merit. As for sons and daughters, if Daniel had any children, the Bible does not mention it. Besides, the spelling of the name in Ezekiel also is a bit strange—*dn'l* instead of the proper full writing *dny'l*.[50]

Fortunately, with the discovery of the Canaanite myths from ancient Ugarit (c. 1300 B.C.E.), it became clear that Ezekiel had quite another figure in mind. For among the Ugaritic mythological texts was the story of *dn'l*, spelled precisely as we find it in Ezekiel, and his son *'qht*, or, as we conventionally pronounce their names, Danel and Aqhat.

Unfortunately, as is so often the case with documents recovered from antiquity, the extant text is incomplete; most particularly, it is missing the conclusion. Spiegel spent a considerable amount of time in his article trying to reconstruct the complete myth from the remains left to us, as have many scholars both before and after him.[51] I shall not endeavor to do likewise here but rather simply point out several salient aspects of the preserved story relevant to our inquiry. In fact, we should be somewhat wary of relying too much on the specific details of the Ugaritic myth, since we can hardly be certain that the story of Danel and Aqhat found at Ugarit is precisely the version known centuries later to Ezekiel.[52] Indeed, considering that Canaanite deities—especially the hated Baal and his consort Anat—play an important role in the Ugaritic version, this seems rather unlikely. Still, the form of the story has aspects that should look familiar and, more importantly, should suggest why the prophet invoked Danel along with Noah and Job.

To begin with, Danel, like Abraham, is presented to us as a patriarchal figure—one upon whom people rely to keep order in the land. He also shares with the biblical patriarch another significant characteristic: initially, he lacks a son to carry on his line after him. However, his appeals to his patron god Baal are just as successful as Abraham's appeals were to his God (cf. Gen. 15:1–7); and he is finally rewarded with the birth of a son, Aqhat. But of course matters are not allowed to rest here. The son incurs the jealousy and then the wrath of a goddess, Anat; and she subsequently arranges the assassination of Danel's only son. The death of the only son has a predictably devastating effect on the father, indeed, on Danel's land as well; as the father bewails and curses, the land succumbs to famine and drought. A good deal of what follows in the Ugaritic tale involves Danel's search for the remains of his son, a search that ultimately proves successful. Having recovered the remains, Danel buries and bewails them for seven years. The extant story leaves the bereaved father as he begins sacrificing to the gods on behalf of his son.

Since we know no more about Danel than the Ugaritic story and Ezekiel 14 tell us, we can only speculate how things ultimately turn out. But our speculation can be guided by the Ezekiel passages, and Spiegel did not miss their implication. As he notes, "There is reason to expect that in the end Danel is not left uncomforted, and his son Aqhat is given back to him."[53] Certainly, if this is so, the story fits well with that of Noah—and especially with the legend of Abraham and Isaac. Perhaps the Danel that Ezekiel knows was tested by God by the loss of his son. Perhaps, too, Danel prayed for his dead son and, because of his great righteousness, the son was restored to him: just as the Abraham of legend regained the once dead Isaac, so did Danel regain the slain Aqhat.[54]

Finally, when we turn to the third figure invoked by Ezekiel, Job, Spiegel poses for us the obvious question: ". . .Job, of course, was a man 'perfect and upright' (Job 1:1, 8; 2:3), and can also be said to have regained his children even though new children. Or does the passage in Ezekiel suggest that in the old tale, Job actually saved his selfsame children, just as Danel saved Aqhat or Noah his own family?" One can hardly avoid answering this query in the affirmative. The pattern would seem to be clear: once more we find that the more ancient story tells of a man tested by God through the loss of his child(ren). Still, because he held fast to his integrity and did not waver in his steadfast faith, like Abraham he could achieve victory over death when a merciful God restores his children to him once more. Job, too, could save the life of his son and daughter through his own righteousness.[55]

So the ancient Job story and the ancient *Akedah* have much in common and are actually shown to be variations on a theme. Moreover, like the ancient *Akedah*, the original Job story is a more complete rendition than the one we now find in the authorized version. Consider, in this respect, that the restoration of Job's children, as depicted in the Epilogue, sits rather uncomfortably in that account. We are told (Job 42:13) that *wyhy-lw šbʿnh bnyn wšlwš bnwt*, "he had seven sons and three daughters"; but this is not a point that the story wishes to emphasize. Indeed, Job's children are mentioned only after we have first been duly impressed by the total of the property (cf. 42:10,12) that his newly doubled fortune has gained for him.

One can feel a certain reticence in the narrative here, as if the account is slightly embarrassed about this business of Job's children. And rightly so. For when we think of the new children of Job we inevitably also must think about the old children whom God has allowed to die without apparent cause simply so that He could test Job. This is certainly a point best left unemphasized; indeed, maybe we will not take too much notice if the new offspring are crowded in together with the other livestock and if we are then immediately launched on a discussion of the daughters' names—not to mention their beauty.

In contrast, how much more satisfying the story becomes when it is the children lost who are also the children regained. Then everything fits—the story leaves us no uncomfortable flaws to be concerned about.[56] Perhaps, then, it would have been better for the authorized version to say nothing about children at all. Yet the newer version dare not do this. Whoever put together the story found in the Prologue/Epilogue cannot ignore the most dramatic moment in the ancient tradition— the restoration of the children. If, from a theological standpoint, one cannot bring children back from the dead,[57] one must bring back children from *somewhere*.[58] The story may be changed, but it still must pay homage to the contrapuntal tradition that plays beneath it. The polyphonic relationship between what is ancient and what is authorized cannot be ignored or broken. Otherwise, it would not be the story of Job at all.[59]

Thus we see that the ancient story of Job and the authorized version found in the Prose Frame Story have the same sort of contrapuntal relationship as do the ancient and authorized stories of the *Akedah*. Once again, there is a dominant theme: but this time it tells us of a Satanic challenge accepted by God and of children killed rather than saved just in time. Once more, as well, we can hear an older theme playing an harmonic variation beneath the dominant melody—one where the Satan has no role to play, which instead depicts God alone testing Job to the limit—then rewarding him with the resurrection of his murdered children.[60] Though the authorized version is the one that holds our attention, when we listen more carefully, we hear the bass theme playing and even occasionally taking over the lead.

The author of the Epistle of James also listened to this Joban counterpoint and, in doing so, tuned his ear to the more ancient of its traditions: the Job of legend who not only saved himself but, through his righteousness, could even prevail on God to bring back son and daughter from the dead. Moreover, James may well have felt that he had a legitimate right to single out this more ancient theme, just as Rabbi Ephraim did in regard to the death and resurrection of Isaac in the *Akedah*: For the *real* Job is certainly the Job who suffered and yet held fast to his integrity. Whether tempted by his wife to curse God and die, or perhaps challenged by his Friends to give in to his anger, he endured and triumphed miraculously because he did not sin with his lips.

Such a tradition has great power, especially in a Christian context; for the ancient story of Job is a story that looks forward: it tells those who hear it that if they can patiently endure their current suffering, they will prevail in the future. What is lost now can be regained later, and he who is persecuted and dies innocently and patiently may well in the end be restored by a merciful God to life.

James may have seen in the test of Job the image of the test of all Christians who must endure the loss of the son, the *yaḥīd*, the only one, Jesus Christ—and who must suffer as he suffered as a result of that loss. Note that James speaks in 5:11 of *to telos kuriou*, "the purpose of the Lord," in connection with *tēn hupomonēn Iōb*, "the patience of Job." What the writer of the Epistle suggests here is that one must see a purpose to Job's—and indeed all Job-like Christians'—suffering. Such suffering is not gratuitous; it is instead God's necessary test of one's steadfastness, of one's faith. This may well be the reason that what "you have heard" (*ēkousate*) about Job and what "you have seen" (*eidete*) are immediately juxtaposed in James' statement. One must hear the legend of Job in the context of what one has seen and witnessed as a Christian. Then the import of James' comments becomes clear: a genuine Christian must go the full distance like Abraham[61] and Job. Only then can his faith be truly tried and thus tempered as steel is tempered. Then the reward can follow—the victory of life over death.

The term *telos*, "purpose," which all true Christians must see in God's action in both the Job legend and in their own lives, can be understood in two senses, "outcome, completion"[62] and "end, conclusion."[63] In the context of James 5:11, both nuances are to be understood. One comprehends the outcome, the completion of Job's and every Christian's suffering, in the end of the story, where that lonely suffering receives its miraculous reward. Moreover, this fulfilling conclusion also reveals that in God's purpose, one sees His true nature: that He is compassionate and merciful—*polusplagkhnos. . .kai oiktirmōn*. Thus, for the author of the Epistle of James, Job can be the paradigm, the perfect example of how to endure persecution and suffering.[64] Can one then be surprised that he invokes the patience of Job as the standard by which all Christians must measure themselves?

4

Super-Job

Yet we cannot tie things up quite so easily—there still remains a loose end of rather major proportions: the Poem itself and its impatient Job. The author of the Poem also heard the ancient theme of Job, but he chose to score quite a different melody over it than the one that the author of James seems to hear: his hero is Job the Impatient, not Job the Patient. So where does the Poem fit within the contrapuntal, Joban harmony?

In order to understand this better, we need a different sort of guide; for the Poem, by and large, is a work of imagination that draws from the Joban tradition but is itself individual, for the most part the work of a single creative intellect. Thus, another creative intellect might show us things in the Poem we would otherwise miss. With this in mind, then, let us for the moment, take leave of the world of biblical scholarship and turn to a story from the Yiddish literature that also plays a contrapuntal theme off the tradition of Job, a theme not unlike the one the poet of Job composed over the Job legend. It is a short story about another figure created in the image of Job—one who suffered in silence and received his just reward: Y. L. Perets' "Bontsye Shvayg"[65]—Bontsye the Silent.

To my knowledge, no study in the limited critical literature on "Bontsye Shvayg"[66] has made note of its use of the book of Job as a thematic point of reference, even though Perets explicitly compares his protagonist with Job, "Job did not endure; he [Bontsye] is far less fortunate" (*Iev hot nisht oysgehaltn, er iz umgliklikher gevesn*), the declaration of the angel charged with defending Bontsye (*meylets-yosher/malekh-meylets*) before the Supreme Assembly. Besides this, other aspects of Perets' story are reminiscent of the Job story, especially as we see it depicted in the Prologue of the biblical book. Like the Prologue, "Bontsye Shvayg" has two locales—Heaven and Earth. Note, too, that the action in the Yiddish story alternates between these two very different settings. Again, this is very much the manner in which the story progresses in the Prologue of Job. There is a Heavenly Assembly in Perets' story, which recalls the gathering of the "sons of God" (*bny h'lhym*; cf. Job 1:6, 2:1) in the prose tale of Job, and finally there is certainly a Satan-like presence in the guise of the Prosecuting Angel (*der kateyger*) charged with attacking Bontsye's integrity. While it would be overarguing the case to see too exact a parallel between the action of the Bontsye story and that of the Job story, still, Perets wishes to place Joban themes in the background of his tale so that his

34

readers will make an implicit connection: when they think of poor Bontsye, to some extent they will also recall the unfortunate Job.[67]

Yet Bontsye is not merely a Job. In fact, one could say that Perets takes the suffering Joban figure to its logical extreme. After all, Job was at one time a rich man, with family, friends and honor in his homeland—"the greatest of all the sons of the East" (Job 1:3). Granted, he did indeed suffer; but, at least at a point previous to his suffering, he was a fortunate and happy man. But Bontsye—from the time he is born to the day that he dies—suffers continually with virtually no respite. As the Presiding Judge of the Supreme Assembly (*ov-bezdn/bezdn shel mayleh*) tells Bontsye, ". . .you have always suffered. . .! There is not a single member, not a single bone in your body without a wound, without a bloody bruise, there is absolutely no secret place in your soul where it shouldn't be bleeding. . . ."[68] Nonetheless, as the Presiding Judge also declares at the end of this statement, "You always kept silent" (*du host alts geshvign*); and this is the other characteristic that makes Bontsye a purer sufferer than Job was. For the biblical Job did cry out—he lost his patience in chapter 3. But Bontsye keeps silent—"Not a word against God; not a word against Man!" (*Keyn vort kegn Got, keyn vort kegn layt!*), as his angelic Defender tells us—even though he is far more unfortunate than Job. In this respect one might say that Bontsye is a "Super-Job."

However, if Perets presents us with a story with unmistakable Joban overtones, he also takes some care to demarcate one sharp distinction between his story and its biblical point of reference. Both the ancient and authorized story of Job are about trial and judgment: God, amid the divine assembly (with or without the Satan's encouragement), tests Job to see if he will hold fast to his integrity. On the surface, one might think that "Bontsye Shvayg" is about trial and judgment as well; for there is a trial and the object of the trial would appear to be Bontsye. Indeed, ostensibly, as is the case with Job, the Heavenly Court would seem to be intent upon assaying our protagonist's integrity. But a closer look at the story suggests that just the opposite is the case.

The suffering brought upon Bontsye, unlike the suffering brought upon Job, has no motivation, or at least no motivation that is explained to the reader. There is no hint of a test here, no implication that Bontsye is initially singled out by God, as were Abraham and Job, to be judged in regard to the steadfastness of his faith. Rather, his misfortune is presented as a "given"—the very essence of his life from the moment he first takes breath. In fact, Bontsye's suffering is depicted as nothing particularly special; his deprivation seems more to reflect the normal human condition. Perets tells us that many suffer and die; that is why no one takes very much notice of Bontsye's death in *this* world, the world below Heaven:

> *Here*, in *this* world, Bontsye the Silent's death made scarcely an impression! Just ask anyone who Bontsye was, how he lived, what caused his death! Did his heart give out, did his strength give way, or were his very bones crushed under a heavy load. . .who knows? Maybe he simply died of hunger!
>
> Had a trolley-car horse collapsed, there would have been more notice, newspapers would have written about it, hundreds of people would have gathered from all the streets to gawk at the carcass, even to look over the place where the collapse had happened. . .

> Still, the trolley-car horse would never get so much attention if there were a thousand million horses just as there are men![69]

Perets wants his reader to understand that Bontsye is merely one of these "thousand million" in regard to his suffering; in this respect he is quite ordinary—not extraordinary like Job.

Note, too, that the trial of Bontsye is presented as being quite different from the test of Job—or, for that matter, of Abraham. Perets establishes that his protagonist's trial is, as the angels declare, "no more than a mere formality. Even the Prosecutor will not be able to find an argument against Bontsye the Silent! The 'case' will last but five minutes." Note that Perets even qualifies "case" (*dyele*) with quotation marks in order to emphasize how open-and-shut Bontsye's trial is seen to be. In contrast, a Job or an Abraham needed to be tried; without a trial of their integrity, their steadfastness could not have been established *for sure*. But Bontsye seems really to need no trial: the rightfulness of his entry into Heaven is ostensibly shown to be self-evident to even the littlest of child angels. Thus, when the Presiding Officer (*der prezes*) initiates this mock trial with the words "Read, but keep it short!", he does so because he recognizes the mere formality of the proceedings. The Defender and Prosecutor are to move with all deliberate speed so that Bontsye can take his rightful place among the most saintly of saints as quickly as possible.[70]

And what makes Bontsye so special that he requires only the most cursory of judgments from the Heavenly Council? Certainly not the fact that he has suffered greatly; as noted above, Perets wants his reader to understand that suffering is an ordinary phenomenon. Rather, what makes Bontsye so very exceptional is that he has always suffered *in silence*. Indeed, this not only makes him special, but also downright dangerous.

Because Bontsye never complains even once in his life, calling his deplorable condition into question, that condition is never relieved in even the slightest way: He never cries out, so humanity never really notices that he is in truly grave distress. Thus, no one takes steps to relieve his pain. As a result, his suffering necessarily becomes increasingly worse and more desperate. Of course, this has few or no repercussions in *this* world, but in the *other* world the repercussions are profound.

For as Bontsye's suffering increases, so does the moral injustice that tolerates this suffering. Since, as Perets implies, the existence of such injustice on earth must be viewed ultimately as the responsibility of Heaven, one might say that Bontsye builds up a moral debit against that "other world" because Heaven has allowed his unjust treatment to persist without any redress. To be sure, every other member of the human race might be said to hold a similar debit of some quantity. But, because all other human beings cry out when stricken, in consequence, their suffering tends to be proportionately relieved and their respective moral debits against Heaven are lessened. As the saying goes, "the squeaky wheel gets the grease." The quantity of injustice may in some specific cases become quite large—in Job's case, for example—however, it is never so large that Heaven cannot, as it were, "cover" the debt it owes without going morally bankrupt. In fact, as the biblical account shows, steps were taken by Heaven to relieve Job of his suffering long before he died, steps taken as a direct result of Job's vocal complaint to Heaven.

But Perets makes it clear that the moral debit that Bontsye holds against Heaven, because of the enormous injustice of his situation, constitutes the greatest of all liens in the universe. Ultimately, the moral debt owed by Heaven to Bontsye becomes so great that should Bontsye finally demand payment, that is, should he cry out, demanding redress of his grievances, Heaven could not hope to compensate him as it had so effectively compensated Job: the injustice done to Silent Bontsye is simply too great.

Thus, Perets presents us with a Bontsye who, for all intents and purposes, holds the mortgage on Heaven. Moreover, with one distressed cry for payment, Bontsye can effectively rend the moral fabric of that "other world" beyond all hope of repair. The situation we find in "Bontsye Shvayg", therefore begins to look like an ironic inversion of Job's or Abraham's dilemma as depicted in the ancient traditions. In those cases, God pressed the integrity of His chosen subjects to the limit, and one word from them against God would have sealed their tragic fate. But in Perets' story a "nobody" named Bontsye presses the integrity of Heaven to the limit, and one cry for justice from him would be more than Heaven could tolerate and survive. This is the import of the Presiding Judge's words when he declares at the end of Bontsye's trial: "There [on earth] no one understood all this. Indeed, you, yourself, perhaps did not realize that you can cry out; and, due to your cry, Jericho's wall can quake and tumble down! You, yourself, did not comprehend the extent of your sleeping power. . . ." Little wonder then that all of Heaven breathes a sigh of relief when Bontsye finally dies without uttering the words that would bring the universe, quite literally, tumbling down.[71]

In light of this circumstance, the angels can only consider it close to absurd to judge Bontsye's soul. Rather they wish to coronate him:

Young little angels with little sparkling eyes, dainty, golden, filigree wings and tiny silver slippers rushed out to meet Bontsye with joy! The whir of the wings, the tapping of the little slippers, the jubilant laughing from the young, fresh, rosy little mouths pervaded all the Heavens and, even God Himself knew that Bontsye the Silent was coming!

Father Abraham sat waiting at the gate of Heaven, his right hand outstretched in a warmhearted "Peace be with you!" and a sweet smile lit up his old face!

What are they rolling across Heaven?

Why, it's two angels wheeling into Paradise an easy chair of pure gold on little wheels for Bontsye's journey.

What just flashed by?

Why, they've just taken in a golden crown set with the most precious jewels! All for Bontsye!

Still, the "mere formality" of the trial must be attended to, and the Defending Angel—rhetorician that he is—determines to make the most of the situation, despite all urging to the contrary from the Presiding Officer.[72] If the Silence of Bontsye, is what distinguishes him from all other men who suffer—what has given him the power to bring Heaven to its knees—then the Defender will vocally celebrate this Silence for all that it is worth. He therefore begins his speech by declaring that Bontsye's name (or perhaps we should say his title) "suited him like a garment made by the finest tailor's hand for a delicate body." As the Defending Angel warms to his subject, chronicling the life of Bontsye, tragedy-after-tragedy, the fact of the Great Silence progressively becomes his constant refrain. The repeated phrase "he always kept silent" (*er hot alts geshvign*) begins to fall like hammer blows, drumming into everyone's consciousness how Bontsye endured such an horrific life without a word of complaint—even at the point of death:

"He kept silent even in the hospital, where you have the right to *cry out!*
"He kept silent even when the doctor would not attend him without a charge of fifteen cents or the attendant change his linen without a charge of five cents!
"He was silent at the last gasp—he was silent at the final instant of death. . .."

When the turn of the Prosecuting Angel comes at last, for the first time the Satanic accuser finds that he does not have a word to say, that the silence of Bontsye is an impenetrable defense that can only be reluctantly matched by a similarly unprecedented, diabolic silence:

"My lords!" a cutting, stingingly caustic voice starts up, but then he stops short.
"My lords!" he starts up again, but more softly, and again stops short.
Finally there can be heard, coming out from that very same throat, a soft voice, just like butter:
"My lords! *He* was silent! I will be silent, too!"

Of course, the trial concludes exactly as predicted: no sentence can be passed on Bontsye. Who in Heaven would dare even judge our hero? The Presiding Judge acknowledges as much and then grants to Bontsye what, for all intents and purposes, he already owns: "On you, the Supreme Assembly shall pass no judgment; on you, it will make no ruling; for you, it will neither divide nor apportion a share! Take whatever you want! *Everything* is yours!" Finally, the moment comes for Bontsye to break his silence. For the entire trial, for his entire life, he has been silently passive, accepting all his misfortune without response. Indeed, to this point in his story, Perets has not allowed his protagonist to utter even a single word. But now Bontsye for the first time prepares to speak:

Bontsye, for the first time, raises his eyes! He is just about blinded by the light on all sides; everything sparkles, everything flashes, beams shoot out from everywhere: from the walls, from the vessels, from the angels, from the judges! A kaleidoscope of suns!
He drops his eyes wearily!
"Are you sure?" he asks, doubtful and shamefaced.
"Absolutely!" the Supreme Judge affirms! "Absolutely, I tell you; for everything is yours; everything in Heaven belongs to you! Choose and take what you wish. You only take what belongs to *you*, alone!"
"Are you sure?" asks Bontsye once more with growing confidence in his voice.
"Definitely! Absolutely! Positively!" they affirm to him from every side.
"Gee, if you mean it," smiles Bontsye, "what I'd really like is, each and every morning, a hot roll with fresh butter!"
Judges and angels lowered their heads in shame. . . .

If Perets had ended "Bontsye Shvayg" just here, one could only look at his hero's simple request as the very essence of humbleness and therefore of piety.

Offered the entire universe, Bontsye simply asks for the smallest of comforts—a hot, buttered roll for breakfast each morning. What clearer confirmation of the goodness and piety of Bontsye Shvayg?

But Perets does not end the story on this note; rather, he appends one final phrase, which, like a dissonant cord at the end of a musical coda, alters the entire coloring of the piece. For the last part of the story actually goes this way:

> Judges and angels lowered their heads in shame; the Prosecutor burst out laughing.[73]

The Prosecuting Angel, who only moments before had been completely stymied, utterly silenced, suddenly disturbs the serenity of the scene with a burst of laughter. The reader is thus left with a question at the story's conclusion: Why does this Satan-figure now laugh?

One might be tempted to argue that this is a laugh of "sour grapes"; that is, the Satanic angel, faced with the majestic simplicity of Bontsye's humble piety, laughs in order to take the edge off of his own defeat—he "laughs to keep from crying." Yet if this were so, one could only wonder what the Satanic laughter would add to the message of the story. If Perets' intent was primarily to show the extent of Bontsye's piety, then the most dramatic ending would also be the most simple and direct: Bontsye makes his humble request for a hot, buttered roll, and the last picture we see is the angels' awed silence: the denouement of the whole account.

Elsewhere, Perets is more than capable of keeping the ending simple yet awe-inspiring. Compare, in this respect, the conclusion of his story "If Not Still Higher." The hero of this tale is the Rebbe of Nemirov, a traditional figure of piety in hasidic legend. This Rebbe has the curious habit of disappearing during the period of the Slichos, that is, between the Jewish New Year and the Day of Atonement, when Jews offer penitential prayers. Rumors begin to spread that he must be in Heaven, where he can appeal directly to God to forgive the sins of his people. The disappearing Rebbe arouses the skeptical interest of a Litvak (Lithuanian Jew), who finally determines to conceal himself in order to follow the Rebbe and thus find out where he really goes during Slichos. What the Litvak discovers is that the Rebbe of Nemirov, dressed *incognito* as a common peasant, brings wood to a sick and helpless Jewish woman as a simple act of charity and recites his penitential prayers while offering her this one small comfort. This so impresses the Litvak that he abandons his earlier skepticism and becomes one of the most dedicated disciples of the Rebbe of Nemirov. Finally, Perets concludes the story:

> And after that when any disciple would relate that the Rebbe of Nemirov at Slichos time arose every morning and flew up to Heaven, the Litvak would not laugh, but would add quietly:
> "If not still higher!"[74]

In this instance the last phrase brings everything to a tight conclusion: it serves as a "punch line" that not only conveys a sense of the true piety of the Rebbe of Nemirov but also explains why the short story was given its title, a point that had not been clarified before. Had Perets intended a similar effect in "Bontsye Shvayg," the "right" conclusion would have been the awed silence of the shamed angels—a silence that would reflect back on the title and meaning of the story in just the same manner the conclusion of "If Not Still Higher" does. The addition of the phrase "the Prosecutor laughed out loud" can only detract from this effect.[75]

Perhaps, then, one should take the Prosecutor's laugh in another way, as bitterly ironic. The laugh could then be seen as almost a cry of despair (if not rage), expressing, as M. Waxman suggests, "a strong protest against the devastating effects of poverty upon the human soul." Bontsye is so desperately poor that the best thing he can think of when offered the entire world is merely a hot, buttered roll. Again we might follow Waxman:

> And of all the riches and treasures offered him, Bontsye asked, to the great confusion of the court, for a hot roll with fresh butter every morning. This was the *summum bonum*, the height of delight for Bontsye who during his lifetime hungered and only occasionally munched a dry crust of bread. Perets does not write tirades against social injustice and against the scourge of poverty, but the answer of Bontsye speaks volumes.[76]

The Prosecutor's bitter laugh would be the exclamation point at the story's conclusion, an extra fillip that emphasizes the author's revulsion to the desperate poverty portrayed in "Bontsye Shvayg." One might say that the Prosecutor's laugh mocks the reader or anyone who would stand by and silently accept so desperate a want as Bontsye's.

Still, if Perets simply wished to use his short story as a means of indicting society's tolerance of poverty, he might have chosen a different symbol than Bontsye Shvayg. For his desperate poverty is really too much of a bad thing. As we have already noted, he certainly is one of the millions who suffer and die. But one of the major thematic points in the story is that his suffering goes beyond what any other human has ever endured—even Job. If it is the *reality* of poverty that Perets desired to take on, he might have portrayed Bontsye in a more human rather than a super human light.

Elsewhere, Perets has certainly shown that he can portray the scourges of poverty in a more realistic fashion. Consider, for example, the character Shemayah in "The Messenger."[77] He too is a desperate figure who dies tragically after a difficult, poverty-stricken life. But his tragedy is always kept within realistic proportions. Because Shemayah is a person who could very well have lived the life that Perets gave him, his desperation also seems real. Thus, it effectively drives home a hard message about, as Waxman notes, the "state of society which warps natural desires of men and reduces them to a minimum."[78]

But the extreme view of poverty one sees in "Bontsye Shvayg" goes beyond reality. Moreover, if this view is taken at face value, Perets is vulnerable to the criticism that he has overdone his story, making it far too sentimental, if not bombastic. Note, in this respect, the criticism of S. Pinsker, who apparently sees the story in precisely this light: "The story of Bontsye is a heavy dose of Yiddish sentimentality, the sort of unadulterated play to the emotions that has led more than a few critics to feel that Yiddish literature is a decidedly second-rate product."[79] However, there is more to this short story than simply a overdone condemnation of poverty, and Perets has placed the Prosecutor's laugh at its conclusion in order to compel the reader to recognize this.

In fact, one cannot escape the feeling that the Prosecutor's laugh is not simply mocking but, rather, intrusive. It does not seem intended so much to underscore an apparent theme (be it the piety of Bontsye or the horrors of poverty) as to act to "break the spell" of the story. It catches the reader off guard and disturbs him. In this respect it seems to be yet another loose end that cannot be so easily explained away. But that is just the point: Perets is much too good a writer to have left a glaring loose end like this at the end of his story if this were not for a particular purpose. The loose end is intentional. Like the singular verbs applied to Abraham at the end of the *Akedah*, the Prosecutor's laugh is meant to draw attention to itself. And, as its implication starts to sink in, we begin to realize that this is not a laugh of sour grapes nor one merely of ironic bitterness. It is rather a laugh of triumph; for the Prosecutor has won the day.

The assumption on the part of all Heaven had been that Bontsye kept silent because his goodness made him too pious and righteous to complain against God and man. But when he finally opens his mouth for the first time, his *true* nature and the true meaning of his silence are suddenly revealed. The logic of the situation begins to be all too clear: when offered the universe, Bontsye only wishes for a hot, buttered roll. Why a hot, buttered roll? Because this is the grandest thing he can think of. Why is this the grandest thing he can think of? Because he is a fool—or perhaps we should better use the Yiddish term that conveys more precisely what Bontsye is: he is the ultimate schlemiel.[80]

The Prosecutor laughs because he realizes that Bontsye is not the most virtuous but merely the most stupid of men. And the angels realize this, too. They lower their heads in shame, not because they are in awe of Bontsye but rather because they are embarrassed at their own, previous misinterpretation of Bontsye's silence. Bontsye the fool has made them all look foolish.

Previously, the Presiding Judge had stated, "In the other world your silence was not compensated, but that is the *Realm of Lies*, here in the *Realm of Truth* you will receive your compensation!" But, as it turns out, the inhabitants of Heaven do not understand Bontsye any better than do those of Earth. The angels, the Defender, even the Presiding Judge, have all been deluded.[81] They expected a pious hero who would come almost like a Messiah to possess the universe and discover, instead, an ignorant fool content with a roll for breakfast—certainly a most appropriate "compensation" for Bontsye Shvayg.[82]

Moreover, it is not only the inhabitants of Heaven that have been tricked. Of much more significance is the trap that Perets has artfully laid for the reader, a trap that is only "sprung" when the last phrase of the story is revealed.[83] "Bontsye Shvayg" is a superbly subtle literary exercise in misdirection and reader manipulation. Up until the last phrase, Perets has given his reader every signal that his story is focused on celebrating a common figure in Yiddish, if not all Jewish, literature: the pious, usually long-suffering, poverty-stricken Jew. But his intentions for Bontsye are quite different: The aim is not celebration but rather satire (a genre of writing in which Perets is certainly at home); and, as is always the case in great examples of the form, the purpose here is to relay a very serious message by making his targeted "sacred cow" look absurd. In the final analysis, it is not only Bontsye who is this target. Bontsye, after all, is a schlemiel—at best to be pitied, at worst to be laughed at. Rather, Perets takes aim at those who would praise any man who would passively endure great suffering and deprivation without complaint. Such a silence, Perets tells us, is not the stuff of piety and innocence, but rather the very essence of foolishness and ignorance and should be recognized as such. Indeed, Jews who would argue that a silent acceptance of pain and suffering is worthy of praise are, like the inhabitants of Bontsye's Heaven, greater fools than that silent protagonist.

But Perets is not content only to underscore this point. The author also wishes the reader to confront his own unconscious attitudes toward suffering and those who would endure its pain without complaint. This is why he structures "Bontsye Shvayg" as he does. It is necessary for the reader to be "led down the garden path." Perets wants the reader ultimately to discover that he, like Bontsye, has also been silent and passive, accepting uncritically the attitude of Heaven that Bontsye is the greatest of all saints. Only after the Prosecutor's laugh has awakened him to the true circumstance does the reader begin to grasp that what previously had looked like a story of pietistic praise is in fact heavily tinged with irony.

Thus, for example, only in retrospect does one really begin to grasp the true sense of how Bontsye viewed his life: "He, himself, had never given a thought about his whole life. In the other world he had forgotten each moment the previous. . . ." This is not the view of a pious man but rather that of the simpleton, a figure so dense that he is not able to achieve even the barest perspective on his life. Little wonder that such a figure can look at the succession of horrendous experiences that Bontsye endures and draw the simplistic conclusion, "That's just my lot" (*Mayn mazl. . .iz shoyn azoy*).

Even the Defending Angel's speech, which heretofore had seemed so eloquent, must be reevaluated after the Prosecutor's laugh. In fact, it has been subtly but intentionally overdone by Perets until it is just a bit too sentimentalized and heavy-handed.[84] The reader ultimately realizes that he has been manipulated by an expert speaker (or should we say preacher?) with a voice as sweet as a saccharine violin. The Defending Angel knows how to play for every sentiment, touch every nerve. He even knows how to wait for just the right dramatic moment to sip a bit of water.

The impatient chiding of the Presiding Officer: "Come now, cut out the similes. . . .Cut out the rhetoric. . . .Facts, dry facts. . . .Keep to the point. . . ." should warn the reader that this schmaltzy celebration of Bontsye's silence is not all that it seems to be. But Perets knows that the reader will brush these objections aside, just as the Defending Angel does.[85] At one point the Presiding Officer even declares: "Come now, cut out the *realism!*" (*Nor on* realizm!)[86] To be sure, in the immediate context the Presiding Officer voices this objection to restrain the Defender from getting too graphic in his description of Bontsye's botched circumcision. But on a more subtle level Perets is making a telling comment about not only the attitude of all Heaven but also of us the readers of the story:[87] We, too, would like Bontsye's story without realism; we do not want to know the truth about Bontsye Shvayg. Rather, we wish to be seduced by the Defending Angel and accept his aggrandizement of the silence of our "hero." Only after the Prosecutor has mocked our sentimental seduction with his triumphant laugh do we truly understand what fools we have been. We then realize that the primary target of Perets' satire is not the angels in the "other" world, nor any "other people" whom they might represent: his target is ourselves.[88] But this is not all. There is yet one other target that Perets wishes to take aim at: the famous writer of traditional Yiddish stories, Y. L. Perets, himself.

There are really two sides to Perets' writing. As Waxman notes, "He. . .learned to differentiate between the essence of religion and tradition and their form. The first he glorified while he attacked the second more subtly but nonetheless vigorously."[89] The glorification of true religion and piety and of those who exemplify these ideals is an important theme in many Perets stories. Certainly Perets' depiction of the Rebbe of Nemirov in "If Not Still Higher" represents quite well this aspect of his writing. Many other similar examples could be cited. But it would be a mistake to assume that all Perets' stories are celebrations of piety and that all his protagonists are paragons of Jewish virtues. A story such as "Bontsye Shvayg" reflects the other side of Perets' literary output, the side that steps back from the traditional world of Eastern European Jews and Jewish themes and examines both with a critical, subtly satirical eye. Many other Perets stories do likewise, "The Pious Cat," "The Golem," and "The Diamond,"[90] for example, but none do so more brilliantly than "Bontsye Shvayg."

Perhaps we can best see what Perets has done in "Bontsye Shvayg" if we juxtapose it to another of his stories that seems especially close to it in subject and theme, "Joy within Joy."[91]

The focus of attention in this case is Reb Levi Yitskhok of Berdichev, a well-known figure of piety in hasidic legend and story, who, like Bontsye, is seen in the context of the Heavenly Court. Reb Levi Yitskhok, already among the heavenly saints, jeopardizes his position there when he attempts to destroy the adverse records held by the Devil against sinful mankind. He succeeds in tossing most of these into the flames of Hell but is caught in the act by the Satanic Prosecuting Attorney, who labels him a thief. Invoking the biblical precept, "The thief shall be sold for his theft" (Exod. 22:2), the Devil insists that Reb Levi Yitskhok be auctioned off to the highest bidder.

In the ensuing auction, the angels and saints offer all they have to buy Reb Levi Yitskhok for Heaven, but the Devil always manages to top their bid. Finally, with all of Heaven's stores exhausted, it seems as though Satan has won the day: "A crooked and vindictive grin spreads over the Devil's lips and triumph flickers in his eyes. Oh, what a catch, what a haul, what a victory for hell! . . .the Devil places a hand on Reb Levi Yitskhok's shoulders and points significantly to the door on the left, the door opening on hell. 'This way, please.' " But just at this dark juncture Perets adds a stunning climax:

> Horror runs through the ranks of the blessed. What! Reb Levi Yitskhok lost? It cannot be! And yet—what is to be done?
> The horror and confusion increase until they are suddenly stilled by a Voice. It is the Voice from the Throne of Glory.
> "*I* buy him!"

And again through the deathly silence: "I raise the bid! 'For Mine is the earth and fullness thereof'—and I give the whole world for Reb Levi Yitskhok."[92]

Once again we find a case of a human whose soul, like that of Bontsye, is prized in heaven, indeed, whose righteousness is deemed worth the price of the universe. Once more we have a Voice from on high speaking in favor of that soul, and afterwards we are even presented a "deathly silence" of awe and wonder reminiscent of the silence that greeted Bontsye Shvayg. Yet in this case there is no hint of irony or of any subtle double meaning. Reb Levi Yitskhok is a pious man, and Perets spares no effort to present his piety in the most positive manner.

"Joy within Joy," then, is a completely straightforward pietistic Yiddish story and well illustrates Perets' mastery of the genre of the folk or hasidic tale.[93] What is so cleverly devastating about "Bontsye Shvayg" is that it masquerades as an example of this same genre only to reveal, at the last possible moment, that it is just the opposite of what it seems: in actuality, not a pious story at all but rather a parody of piety. In this respect we might well say that Perets is ultimately mocking himself: one catches a sense that Perets the satirist does not always entirely approve of Perets the "traditional" Yiddish writer.

I have already suggested that "Bontsye Shvayg" must be seen as a satire; however, we can now be more specific than this. As I have already hinted above by calling the story a "parody of piety," it may be better classified as a particular sort of satire—the *parody*. And it is here that we begin to harmonize our excursus on Perets' "Bontsye Shvayg" back into our larger subject—the contrapuntal structure of Job; for parody is itself a kind of counterpoint—in the musical sense—much in the spirit of the biblical examples we considered above. As in those cases, there is a traditional theme and another theme that plays against it while nonetheless always maintaining a relationship to the underlying theme. After all, a parody cannot exist in a literary vacuum: it must have a subject matter that the reader knows quite well, like an often-heard melody or lyric. Only then can a parody act on the reader as it plays its countervailing theme over the traditional one. While the reader hears this dominant satirical theme, it can mean nothing to him if the older traditional theme which it parodies is not also present in contrapuntal harmony, playing, as it were, in the background.

But parody is not simply to be understood as counterpoint in musical sense: it has far too biting an edge for this to be a sufficient characterization. Parody must be seen as counterpoint in the forensic sense as well. Its intent is not merely to play its theme against the more traditional one but also to oppose that original theme, to deny its validity. Parody takes the common values and normal conventions of the tradition that are its object and twists them, usually turning them inside out— thereby making them look ridiculous and absurd. The surprise, even shock, of this effect compels readers to take a closer look at these traditional values that previously they had unquestioningly accepted as normal. Because the parody displays these values from a completely different perspective, readers see them with fresh eyes and begin to grasp what is abnormal in the "normal," what is unconventional about the conventional. Usually this counterpoint is amusing because the effect of seeing traditional values in an untraditional manner is almost inevitably comic. Yet beneath the comedy there can also be something a good deal darker: at the base of parody one commonly encounters anger playing a bass harmony against the comic melody.

This is certainly true of "Bontsye Shvayg." The story is always kept light and amusing, even when the most grim horrors are being shown to us. The ending is a comic tour de force, a stunning reversal keyed to a laugh that makes all the conventions of the pietistic Yiddish tale look ridiculous. But beneath all this there is a deep and abiding anger. Perets is angry at those elements in his Jewish society who may think that a noble silence is the only pious response to the afflictions the community endures. He is angry at any who say, "It is God's will" and mean by this much the same as Bontsye does when he says, "It is my lot." He is even angry at that part of himself that accepts "God's will" if that means the silent acceptance of a divine injustice. Indeed, he is angry at that aspect of every man that clearly sees the presence of evil in the world but blindly hopes for the providence of Heaven. Perets' anger is a visionary anger, a prophetic anger that seems not only to rebuke the suffering silence of Jews in his nineteenth century world[94] but also to encompass the even deadlier silences to come in the twentieth century. Undoubtedly, "Bontsye Shvayg" was written under the shadow of the palpable anti-Semitism of Perets' time and the violent pogroms that were its clearest manifestation. But his story transcends its own time: it seems today a much more modern story than any other that he wrote, with a moral even more relevant now than it was then.

5

Anti-Job

We can now turn back to the question that led us into this excursus on "Bontsye Shvayg": the loose end of the Poem of Job. In light of what we now know about Perets' story, let us pose again the essential question: How does the Poem of Job fit within the contrapuntal harmony that constitutes the Joban tradition?

We can begin by recalling that Perets' intends Bontsye to imitate the biblical Job but further takes that character to its logical extreme: Super-Job, the pure sufferer who *never* cries out against God or man, as opposed to the biblical Job, who begins patiently like Bontsye but who has lost his patience by the time we reach chapter 3 of the biblical book. Perets only knows of this biblical Job, who is composed of the amalgam of the Jobs we find respectively in the Prologue/Epilogue and Poem of Job. But in light of our earlier discussion on the underlying Joban tradition, we should recognize that there is yet another Job that should be considered in this discussion, the *traditional* Job, the patient Job of legend whose story was heard, for example, by the author of the Epistle of James.

What is important to realize is that this traditional Job is not so different from Bontsye Shvayg. He, too, is Super-Job who holds fast to his integrity—not a word against God, not a word against Man—Job the Silent.[95]

Consider, in this connection, the words Job uses in the Prologue of the biblical book to rebuke his wife: *gm 't-ḥṭwb nqbl m't h'lhym w't-hrʿ l' nqbl*, "Indeed, shall we accept Good from God and not accept Evil?" (Job 2:10). This passage comes at a climactic moment in the biblical version of the story, constituting the last words Job speaks before his great curse in chapter 3. Note, too, that the passage is forthright in its attribution of both Good and Evil to God with no Satan-buffer factored in. Thus, it seems quite likely that this remark reflects the older legendary stratum of the story; in fact, it might even be deemed the credo of the traditional Job: whatever God chooses to give him, be it Good or Evil, the only proper thing for Job to do is to accept this without question, without complaint—with the same sort of pious silence with which Abraham received God's demand for the sacrifice of Isaac.

It is perhaps not without significance that the operative verb in this passage is plural rather than singular. Job does not say "shall *I* accept. . ." but rather "shall *we* accept. . . ." This encompassing plural has broad implications: Job is depicted here as speaking not merely for himself but, rather, for all humanity. If men would be "perfect and upright," they must follow Job's example and not open their lips to sin

46

(2:10c) by questioning God's intentions. Instead, they must accept whatever God gives them in silence. Only then is there the possibility of a divine reward so miraculous that it can even transcend death. As the author of the Epistle of James has already shown us, this patient silence is a sustaining foundation of faith in the face of suffering and affliction. It is strengthened by an unwavering hope that no matter how dark the current circumstance, if men can hold fast to their integrity, they can receive God's grace, just as Abraham and Job did. Even when things look hopeless—as they did for Reb Levi Yitskhok of Berdichev—ultimately God will step in on behalf of the pious and redeem the situation.

But what was the attitude of the writer of the Poem of Job when he faced this optimistic tradition of the pious and silent Job? I believe that his reaction was essentially much the same as that which motivated Perets to write "Bontsye Shvayg": anger. This poet looked at the traditional Job and saw him essentially as Perets did his Bontsye—not as the ultimate figure of piety worthy of our praise but, rather, as the ultimate fool. He angrily rejected the Joban message that a passive acceptance of God's will is the only proper recourse for mankind, his only hope for future reward. Moreover, like Perets, the Job poet's anger led him to take a critical, indeed, satirical view of the Job story. And the particular literary form that critical view took was also the form that Perets chose: the parody. The Job poet determined to write his own particular counterpoint, one that both played off the tradition and opposed it, denying its validity.

Accordingly, our author structured his poem in such a manner that the traditional conventions of the story were turned inside out. Thus, if the Job of legend was celebrated for his silence and patience in the face of adversity, then the poet's Job would be vocal and impatient, challenging the divine authority that would sanction—even initiate—the evil that befell Job without cause. If the traditional moral perspective embodied in Ancient Near Eastern Wisdom—that the righteous ultimately receive their reward and that the wicked are ultimately punished—was what the legend of Job promoted, then the poet's Job would challenge these values, attacking them with all the eloquence that his writer's art could muster. The poetic Job would become Anti-Job, the counterpoint to the traditional Job.

The role of Job's Three "Friends," Eliphaz, Bildad and Zophar, must be seen from a similar perspective. On the basis of the evidence currently available, we cannot be certain whether there were Friends in the traditional Job story or not. It is certainly possible that they were the literary invention of the Job poet himself. Still, if there was a Friends-role in the traditional Job story, then the Friends probably played a foil to Job's pious and silent refusal to question God; that is, they urged Job, much as his wife did, to abandon his integrity and curse God—advice that Job the Silent would reject at all costs.[96]

In the final analysis, it may not be of decisive importance whether or not such Friends actually existed in some form of the traditional Job legend. If they were not there in fact, they were at least there by implication. For Job's pious trust in God must be seen as an act of blind faith that is therefore open to rational challenge. The remarkable point of the Job legend is that its hero held fast even though his tragic circumstance gave him every logical incentive to do otherwise. Whether the challenge mounted against his patience was given concrete embodiment in the Friends-role or not is really beside the point: the challenge was no less palpable, whether the Friends originally existed in the legend or not.

What the poet of Job has done with the Friends-role falls in line with his intention to parody the Joban tradition. For if Job in his new contrapuntal role as challenger has taken the critical line of attack, there must then be a "defender of the faith" role that advocates the traditional pietistic viewpoint of conservative Wisdom that the Job of legend had always epitomized. The Friends have been employed by the poet for precisely this purpose. If they were actually present in the ancient tradition, then, once again, this is a specific counterpoint to that tradition. The original detractors have been turned into pious advocates: the Friends have become, as it were, Anti-Friends who oppose the Anti-Job. But even if the Friends were invented by the poet to serve this purpose, the force of the parody is scarcely lessened.[97]

If this view of the Poem is correct, we can see that its author has done with Job what Perets does with Bontsye: he has transformed the tradition into a devastating satirical tool, utilized to surprise the reader, in fact, to shock him into seeing the Joban conventions in an unconventional fashion. Moreover, as in "Bontsye Shvayg,"—indeed, as in all great examples of the genre—the parody has not been created merely for the sake of the shock and surprise it engenders. Rather, there is a particular point to the parody: The poet wishes to compel the reader to redirect his attention in order to see the fundamental issues inherent in the story of Job from a new perspective. Thus, if we wish to understand the essential meaning of the Poem of Job, we must, therefore, consider this question: What is it that the poet of Job wants his reader to see? If the poet's intent is to redirect the reader's attention, in what direction does he wish the reader to look?

In order to answer this question, we must first consider where the traditional story of Job places its focus. To this there can only be one answer: the traditional focus is on Job, himself. As in the case of Abraham when told to sacrifice Isaac, the fate of Job is the issue of all-consuming importance: what he does, how much he can endure, the extent of his faith, the depth of his piety. He becomes the stand-in for every man, and we are implicitly urged by the traditional story to compare ourselves with him. Each person who encounters the Job legend is challenged: Could he (or she) measure up to Job? Moreover, this issue is not taken as being merely hypothetical. The Job story as much as says that each human must at one time or another encounter unjust deprivation approaching that of Job's; for life seems inevitably unfair if for no other reason than that it ends in that ultimate deprivation, death. The traditional story therefore urges the reader to face life's inescapable tragedies without complaint in pious silence; for only then is there hope for divine reward—even if, like Bontsye, one must wait until after death to receive it.

But if the role of Job in the traditional story is always in the spotlight, it is not so in the Poem of Job. A primary reason why the poet wishes to turn the story inside out is in order to break the reader's fixation on Job, his fate and (by implication) the fate of all humanity. The poet does not wish the reader to concentrate on Job but rather to look instead closely at the One who placed Job in his dreadful predicament: The poet wants the reader to look closely at the nature of God.

It is therefore essentially incorrect to argue that the main theme of the Poem of Job is the plight of mankind: Why do the innocent suffer? Why do the wicked prosper? Can there be justice for humanity in a world that seems ostensibly unjust?[98] Certainly, all of these points are important to the Poem, but they are best seen as subordinate to what is in fact its central focus: What is the nature of God? More specifically, what is the nature of a God who would test in so dreadful a fashion a Job, an Abraham—or anyone, for that matter, who endures tragedies of similar dimensions? The poet of Job is intent on exploring this issue to the fullest extent, and as one sees the debate progress between Job and his Three Friends, one also sees that the nature of God is the overriding subject of their argument. The Poem is committed to question unremittingly what the traditional Job story urges all never to question. And the crux of the Poem, the proposition its author most wishes to explore without quarter, is what the traditional Job legend avoids considering at all costs: Can God, from whom humanity receives both Good and Evil, be seen as a moral deity?

So we see that the relationship of the Poem of Job to the legend of Job is a contrapuntal relationship between a parody and its conventional tradition. Turning back to the question we posed about the loose end of the Poem and how it fits within the larger harmonic framework of the Joban tradition, we might now answer this query by stating that it "fits" by intentionally not fitting. Still, if this solves the problem of the origin of and rationale for Job the Impatient, it does little to address a far more difficult issue; namely, how does the Poem fit within the canonical[99] framework of the book of Job, as opposed to the broader framework of the legendary tradition? On the contrary, if our view of the Poem is correct, this question would seem more difficult to answer.

Thus, we must finally face the last and most demanding problem we set forth for ourselves at the outset of this study: how to understand the structure of the book of Job as we now find it in the Bible.[100]

Up to this point, we have side-stepped this problem by focusing our attention first on the Prose Frame Story and then on the Poem of Job, more or less in isolation from one another. We have seen that each has played its own particular melody in counterpoint to the underlying harmony of the ancient tradition. However, these respective melodic themes would seem hopelessly at odds. For the patient Job of the prose brackets is categorically opposed by the impatient Anti-Job of the Poem's parody. How then can these themes be canonically joined together when the dissonance between them would seem impossible to reconcile?

To begin with, perhaps we should not so much ask how as why. More specifically, why would anyone want to include the parody of Job the Impatient in the Bible when the view it presents so clearly challenges the very essence of what elsewhere the Bible takes to be most sacred? Of course, we know next to nothing about the undoubtedly complicated process by which the legendary and literary strands of Job evolved into the textual patchwork of its biblical form. Nor do we know how the final product (or products) subsequently entered the canon. Still, we must wonder why the redactor(s) of the book of Job, as well as the arbiters of the biblical canon (whoever they were),[101] did not simply choose to ignore or (if need be) suppress the Poem of Job. It would seem that the easier, more obvious and certainly most comfortable course for them would have been to promote and hold sacred a more "traditional" depiction of Job the Patient, Job the Silent.

There were definitely other, more traditional literary versions of the Job story available that could have been selected for inclusion in the biblical canon *in lieu* of the Poem of Job. Consider, in this respect, a parade example: the pseudepigraphal[102] *Testament of Job*.[103] This rendition of the Job story depicts its protagonist very much in the manner of the ancient legend—as a paragon of both virtue and patience. Indeed the *Testament*'s Joban hero can declare to his children at the outset of this work, *egō gar eimi ho patēr humōn Iōb ho en pasēi hupomonēi genomenos*, "I am your father Job, who exhibits complete endurance" (1:5). Note that once again *hupomonē*, the same term employed by the Epistle of James, is utilized here to epitomize the forbearance of Job. The Job of this work is so righteous that he can even put the Devil to shame. Faced with so great a Joban faith and steadfastness, Satan, like Perets' Prosecuting Angel, declares himself utterly defeated:

> Look, Job, I am weary and I withdraw from you, even though you are flesh and I a spirit. You suffer a plague, but I am in deep distress. I became like one athlete wrestling another, and one pinned the other. The upper one silenced the lower one by filling his mouth with sand and bruising his limbs. But because he showed endurance [*tēn karterian*] and did not grow weary, at the end the upper one cried out in defeat. So you also, Job were the one below and in plague, but you conquered my wrestling tactics which I brought on you.[104]

Job, who relates this encounter with Satan to his children in the *Testament*, cannot resist adding a moral for their benefit: "Now then my children, you also must be patient [*makrōthmēsate*] in everything that happens to you. For patience [*makrōthumia*] is better than anything."[105] This positive depiction of Job further emphasizes that such patience as he commands can only lead to triumph, no matter how pitiful his present circumstances: Job in the *Testament* has no doubt that he will gain a great reward in the future if he can only maintain his righteousness now. Our protagonist makes this point, for example, in what might be called the parable of the beleaguered mariner: "And I became as one who wishes to enter a certain city to see its wealth and obtain a portion of it splendor, and when he embarks with cargo in a sea-going ship and at mid-ocean sees the surging water and the opposition of the winds, he throws the cargo into the sea, saying: I am willing for everything to be lost solely to enter this city so that I might obtain things more valuable than the discarded objects and the ship."[106] This Job therefore willingly parts with his material possessions—property, flocks, children and, in this version, even his wife—for they are valued as nothing compared with the benefit that his patience must bring to him in the end. In fact, God informs this Job (in advance of his suffering!) that if he can just maintain his integrity in the face of Satan's scourging, he will not only find material reward in this world but also spiritual reward in the world to come:

> . . .he [Satan] will rise up against you with wrath for battle. But he will be unable to bring death upon you. He will bring on you many plagues, he will take away for himself your goods, he will carry off your children. But if you are patient [*hupomeinēis*], I will make your name renowned in all generations of the earth till the consummation of the age. And I will return you again to your goods. It will be

repaid to you doubly, so you may know that the Lord is impartial—rendering good things to each one who obeys. And you shall be raised up in the resurrection. For you will be like a sparring athlete, both enduring pains and winning the crown. Then will you know that the Lord is just, true, and strong, giving strength to his elect ones.[107]

We therefore can only concur with Judith R. Baskin's evaluation of the Job we find in the *Testament*: "The hero of the *Testament*, the 'man of God,' is a Job both more humble and more accepting than his biblical namesake; he is the innocent Job of the biblical book's prologue and epilogue."[108]

The depiction of Job we find here is hardly surprising. In light of the tradition and the ancient precedent it has established for seeing Job as the most patient of men, this is exactly what we would expect to discover in the *Testament of Job*. However, we would expect to find this portrayal of Job not only in this and other pseudepigraphal literature[109] but even more so in the authorized canon. The fact that instead, Job the Impatient is the centerpiece of the biblical Job story would thus appear to be a remarkable anomaly.

Still, if we look more closely at the *Testament of Job*, we may begin to see why it could never achieve canonical status. Moreover, in doing so, we may also be able to find some clues that will help explain why the Poem of Job did.

For one thing, the *Testament* is a very late work. The consensus of scholarly opinion views it as a Hellenistic Jewish document of around the first century B.C.E. to the first century C.E., originally written in Greek.[110] Thus, even if it had been the most brilliant literary depiction of Job, it probably would have been considered far too late to be seriously considered for the biblical canon by any Jewish or Christian group.

The fact is, though, that it is hardly a great piece of literature. R. P. Spittler's critical evaluation of the *Testament of Job* is quite cogent: "It is not equal to the literary and philosophic grandeur of the canonical book of Job but is prosaic and at times humorous."[111] Indeed, a sense of earnest mediocrity permeates its story, its style of writing and even its manner of casting the inherent drama of Job's patient suffering. Nothing in the *Testament* lifts it up to the level of great literary art: it has neither the elegant simplicity one finds in the biblical Prologue/Epilogue nor the scope and rhetorical flourish of the Poem. Again, the uninspired manner in which the Job theme is handled in the *Testament* could only help guarantee its exclusion from the canon.

Finally—and this is the key point—the *Testament of Job* could not achieve canonical status because it stands much too far in the shadow of the book of Job itself. Moreover, the writer of the *Testament*[112] seems self-consciously aware of this circumstance; and there can be no question of his awed respect for the earlier work. After all, the biblical Job is everything that the *Testament* is not: it is (at least by 100 B.C.E.–100 C.E.) a venerable work also universally recognized to be a consummate work of literature. There is simply no way the *Testament* could compete with, and prevail over, such a great and famous masterpiece of literature for a place in the canon.

It is interesting to consider more closely how, then, we should characterize the relationship of the *Testament of Job* to the book of Job; especially since, in doing so, we will come upon a familiar theme. We have already noted the awed admiration the author of the *Testament* has for the biblical Job. Note, for example, that there are over 60 references and allusions to specific passages from the book of Job to be found in the later pseudepigraphal work.[113] But there is more involved here than simply admiration: the book of Job holds too central a position in the *Testament* author's consciousness to be characterized as merely an object of admiration. Rather, the book of Job is best seen as constituting his *authority*: regardless whether the author of the *Testament* considered the book of Job officially canonical or not, it is the foundation on which his *Testament* rests, and its contents—including the Poem—are the standard of reference by which he measures his own literary output. While the author of the *Testament* may go to considerable effort to reformulate or even blunt the message of the book of Job, especially in respect to the picture of the impatient Job found in the Poem—he will not and cannot ignore the overall contents of the book itself, nor does he dare pretend that the depiction of Job found in the Poem does not exist. Job has, by his time, become too well known and too well established to be discounted in even the slightest fashion.

The correspondences we have just outlined above are quite well known to us, and they point to an obvious way to characterize the relationship between the book of Job and the *Testament of Job*: it is a contrapuntal relationship. Even as the author of the *Testament* strives to conform his theme to the ancient tradition of the patient and silent Job, there is another, later—but still underlying—theme that interposes itself, one which he also hears and to which he must likewise pay heed: that of the book of Job and its predominant picture of Job the Impatient. He can (and indeed does) deny the validity of the impatient Job; but this picture of Anti-Job portrayed in the Poem nonetheless inevitably marks his later composition.

There is a struggle manifest in the writing of the *Testament of Job* that illuminates the broader issue with which we began this discussion on the structure of the canonical Job. We can see that the author of the *Testament* is trying to uphold the conservative tradition, but even as he does so, he must also respect the greatness of the book of Job and its Poem. At an earlier time—but in a similar fashion—the redactors of the book of Job, and then subsequently the arbiters of the biblical canon also had to struggle with a great dilemma: how to reckon with the reality of the Poem and the picture of Job it presented. For the Poem, simply because it was recognized as a magnificent work of literature, was famous, so famous that it indelibly marked the tradition of Job. Furthermore, in doing so, it inevitably became tied to the legend that it had originally opposed. The problem this presented to the guardians of the traditions that ultimately formulated the biblical canon is manifest; for they could not pretend that the Poem and its picture of Job the Impatient did not exist. It was a problem that had to be dealt with, just like the tradition of the death of Isaac in the ancient legend of the *Akedah*.

Of course, as we have already noted, the arbiters of the biblical canon could have decided to exclude the Poem of Job. Indeed, they could have gone further than this. They could have excluded any version of the legend of Job entirely from the Bible because of its inevitable association with the poetic parody that had become irrevocably tied to it. Thus, once more we come back to our question: Why did they not choose this apparently easier and more obvious course?

Since there is no record of any early debate or discussion about the book of Job in regard to its canonicity,[114] let alone about how its redactors put it together, no concrete evidence allows us specific insight into this issue. Still, there are preserved among the early rabbinical records other debates in reference to other biblical books about which various Jewish teachers felt some discomfort. Perhaps if we look for a moment at these disputes and how they were handled, this can help us understand better the rationale that allowed the Poem of Job to become the dominant work in the book of Job and what then led to the book's entry into the canon.

Particularly useful in this regard is the debate that swirled around the Song of Songs. However one may wish to characterize this biblical work in more specific terms,[115] the Song of Songs is most obviously a collection of poems or lyrics celebrating human love in a frankly erotic manner. As R. Gordis notes, there is good reason to question why such a work should be in the biblical canon:

> The Song of Songs is unique among the books of the Bible in spirit, content and form. It is the only book in the canon lacking a religious or national theme, the Divine name occurring only once and then only as an epithet (8:6). To be sure, Esther also makes no direct mention of God, but its national emphasis is unmistakable. Even that is lacking in the Song of Songs. The reason for the doubts as to its canonicity is not hard to discover. Fragments of secular poetry are imbedded in the Bible, but this is the only complete work which is entirely secular, indeed, sensuous in character.[116]

Such a nonreligious and erotic collection of songs as one finds here would seem more at home in a tavern or similar secular environment than in the Bible. Actually, there can be no question that the Song of Songs was sung in just such places. We know this is so because the rabbis made specific mention of the fact, although they obviously disapproved. Thus, the renowned Rabbi Aqiba (second century C.E.) felt constrained to opine, "He who trills his voice in chanting the Song of Songs in the banquet house and treats it as a sort of song has no part in the world to come."[117] An anonymous comment in the Babylonian Talmud made the same point: "He who pronounces a verse of the Song of Songs and makes it a sort of song and pronounces a verse in a banquet house not in its time brings evil to the world."[118]

We should therefore not be surprised to discover that the early rabbis[119] raised the question among themselves regarding whether the Song of Songs was sacred— to use the expression they employed, whether it "defiled the hands"—and thus was appropriate for inclusion in the canon.[120] This in itself should not occasion great surprise, but what *is* surprising and therefore also insightful is the rather extraordinary lengths to which Rabbi Aqiba went in order to defend the presence of the Song of Songs in the Canon. Not only did he state that Canticles defiles the hands, he went much further: "R. Aqiba said: God forbid. No man in Israel ever disputed the status of the Song of Songs saying that it does not defile the hands; for the whole world is not worth the day on which the Song of Songs was given to Israel; for all the Scriptures are holy, but the Song of Songs is the holy of holies."[121]

There are really two things about Aqiba's statement that immediately draw one's attention. First of all, he declared that no Jew ever disputed the status of (*l' nḥlq. . .'l*) the Song of Songs. Obviously, this was not so since the very discussion in which Aqiba's statement is to be found records the traces of just this sort of dispute. Besides, it is doubtful that Aqiba was ignorant of such differences of opinion over Canticles. We have already noted how he disapproved of the Song of Songs being sung in the banquet houses as though it were an ordinary song rather than a sacred hymn. But such a purely secular employment of this love lyric is, in and of itself, evidence that some Jews took its status to be more profane than sacred—evidence of which Aqiba was quite obviously well aware. Besides, the very zeal with which he defended the Song of Songs indicates how sensitive he was to these very disputes.

Of course, it is precisely Aqiba's zeal for the Sublime Song that is the other aspect of his statement that one can hardly miss. He did not declare the Song of Songs to be merely a laudatory piece of literature or simply a work that is quite properly to be found in the Bible or a work that should be viewed as sacred; rather, he stated that it belongs in the Bible because it is the *most* sacred of all the biblical writings (*qdš qdšym*, lit. "the holy of holies") of greater value than the entire world. Again, Aqiba would seem to be affirming what was obviously not so. Granted, we might expect this learned rabbi to defend the Song of Songs' place within the Holy Scriptures—despite its rather erotic flavor. But he would seem to have protested a bit too much, to have overargued his case in claiming that this song of love is more holy than anything else in the Bible. Why then has he taken such an extreme position? Why has he made a claim that seems clearly not so?

One might simply assume the obvious, that Aqiba has gotten carried away with himself in the heat of the moment, and, in doing so, has made a claim that is at best a bit impetuous, at worst a little foolish. However, to see things so superficially would be to do an injustice to this great teacher; for the arbiters of the biblical writings (of which Aqiba undoubtedly was one[122]) faced a dilemma in respect to the Song of Songs that was not dissimilar to the dilemma posed for them by the Poem of Job. Like the Poem, Canticles was also universally recognized by the time of Aqiba (second century, C.E.) to be a venerable and consummate work of literature. On the other hand, like the Poem of Job, it could also have easily been seen as running counter to the predominant biblical message. After all, the Song of Songs celebrates human love virtually to the exclusion of everything else. One might therefore say that this single-minded fixation upon passion in the profane sense constitutes a direct challenge to the Bible's demand that God's Chosen People's love Him with total devotion: "You shall love the LORD your God with all your heart and with all your soul and with all your might" (Deut. 6:5). In consideration of this, one might well imagine the rabbis' viewing Canticles suspiciously. They could have seen in this celebration of the joys of the flesh yet another attempt to seduce Israel from God, a seduction not unlike that proffered by the infamous idols after which Israel had always loved to "play the harlot."

The most obvious manner in which the rabbis might have decided to deal with the Song of Songs would have been to reject it—to exclude it completely from consideration within the framework of their religious worldview. Just as God is jealous, so could they have been jealous for God and have urged their students in particular, as well as the larger religious community in general, to avoid Canticles' corrupting influence. Yet, we should consider: If they had done so, would they have accomplished very much or, on the contrary, would their efforts at suppression have been counterproductive? We know that the Song of Songs was famous and quite popular—clearly a perennial favorite in the taverns and banquet houses. The Sublime Song would not have ceased to exist, nor would its influence have been noticeably lessened had the rabbis chosen a course of suppression. More likely, just the opposite would have happened; simply by attempting to squelch this collection of love songs, the rabbis would have given them more notoriety. The Song of Songs would thus have been labeled as "forbidden fruit," all the more tempting to the taste.

Beyond this, there is another point to consider. The sort of physical love that Song of Song celebrates also cannot easily be suppressed. The Bible may tell the pious to love God to the exclusion of all else, but such a purely sacred love is beyond the capacity of most humans to maintain for very long. The pleasures of the flesh are also the *necessities* of the flesh: the rabbis could not have convinced very many (including themselves) to take their love of God to its logical extreme and thereby to give up the profane love that Canticles espouses in favor of a celibate devotion to God.

Rabbi Aqiba understood this circumstance very well, as did his forerunners who decided to bring the Song of Songs into the canon. Their solution to the dilemma posed by Canticles was both simple and effective: they determined not to reject this love song but rather to embrace it; they decided not to suppress its celebration of human love but rather to redirect its energies toward a more passionate commitment to God. If the pleasures and necessities of the flesh could not be denied, then they were to be utilized for the greater good and the Song of Songs was to be just the right "teaching" to lead the way. Thereby, the Chosen People could come to understand that profane love should not be seen as necessarily in opposition to sacred love. Instead, it should be seen as merely a preliminary step towards love of the divine. For in embracing one's partner in physical love, one begins to know the sense of ecstasy that can only come from an unreserved devotion to God.

When the Song of Songs is seen from this perspective, Aqiba's statement that it is the most holy of all biblical writings begins to make eminent sense. Canticles is, according to his view, not to be taken literally—or, rather, we should say that a literal interpretation is far too limiting because it does not encompass the more profoundly passionate commitment to God of which the Song's imagery is merely a representation. The Sublime Song could be "the holy of holies" simply because the unrestrained love that it celebrates is to be understood as figuring forth in allegorical terms the love the Jewish people owe to God and, no less, the love God has shown for the people He has singled out among all the nations of the earth. Indeed, the more profanely sensual the description of love found here, the more one must be compelled to recognize Canticle's sacred underpinnings. It is therefore hardly surprising that due to the efforts of Aqiba and many others, the Song of Songs became, according to early rabbinic interpretation, a revelation of God's love affair with Israel. As Pope notes, "The period between the destruction of the Temple, A.D. 70 and the revolt of Bar Kochba, A.D. 132, apparently saw the development of the normative Jewish interpretation of Canticles as an allegorical account of the history of the relationship between the Divine Presence of God, the Shekinah, and the Community of Israel from the Exodus from Egypt onward."[123]

It is also understandable why Aqiba insisted that no Jew ever disputed the status of the Song of Songs. If Canticles is so very sacred, how *could* anyone who is a true Israelite question its sacredness or its position in the canon? To hold the view that Canticles is not a sacred celebration of love is to label it instead as merely a paean to carnal proclivities. But according to Aqiba, such an opinion would be no less than blasphemous. It therefore follows that anyone who has so argued is, by definition, excluded from the holy community of God's Chosen.

We therefore can see that the strategy by which Aqiba and his fellow rabbis dealt with the dilemma posed by the Song of Songs was a strategy of inversion. They took the obvious correspondences of this love poem and turned them inside out. If on the surface the Song of Songs purports to be an overtly secular, humanistic and erotic presentation of profane love, then they claimed that just the opposite is its true, underlying meaning: in reality, Canticles was a religiously devoted, divinely oriented, Platonic representation of sacred love. If one would think, on cursory consideration, that this book could only be at home in a tavern or banquet house and is completely out of place in the Holy Scriptures, then, upon deeper contemplation, one had to realize that not only is it appropriately found in the Bible but also that it is the *most* appropriate book in the entire Canon. In contrast, the tavern and banquet house are the last place where the Song of Songs should be sung. If learned voices were raised to challenge whether Canticles could "defile the hands," then the voice of the greatest teacher of his generation would silence them by stating that no true believer would *dare* even to question the sanctity of this holy book.

A brilliant logic guides the interpretation of the Song of Songs espoused by Aqiba; moreover, it must have been just this sort of logic that supplied his forebears, the arbiters of the biblical canon, with both the motivation and justification for bringing Canticles into the Bible. But what is particularly striking is the *nature* of this logic; for, on consideration, we discover that once again we have come upon an exercise in historical counterpoint. In fact, the approach we find here is reminiscent of that we have found in Perets' "Bontsye Shvayg" and in the poet of Job's parody of the Job tradition. Just as in those instances, the conventional correspondences have been turned inside out so that interpreters will view the conventional in an unconventional fashion, so that they will see a work of literature, having one ostensible meaning, with fresh eyes that will lead them to see it in quite another. The intent is once more to refocus the readers' attention, as they contemplate Canticles, to make them rethink what aspect of the theme should *really* hold their interest. And, just as in the Poem of Job, the new center of focus has been shifted in the same direction: away from man and towards God. Obviously, however, it would be wrong to call this Aqiban interpretation of the Song of Songs parodistic. If anything, it is just the opposite of this; for Aqiba's intention—and the intention of those who brought the Sublime Song into the canon, was not to challenge their religious audience in order to make them see the traditional values in a more critical fashion. Rather, their intent was to reaffirm these values, to take a carnal love song that could seriously undermine the ideals of biblical piety and reform it into a bulwark in defense of these very same ideals.

When we turn from the Song of Songs back to Job, we can begin to see how an understanding of the approach to Scriptures exemplified here by Aqiba can aid us in explaining the presence of the Poem in the center of the book of Job and its ultimate elevation to canonical status. For, as was the case with Canticles, it would have been counterproductive for the early Jewish religious leaders to have tried to suppress the Poem. If the rabbis (or anyone else) had tried to brand so famous a work of literature as infamous, they would have only contributed to its notoriety and in doing so would have dramatically enhanced its usefulness to those who—like the author of the Poem—wished to attack the pietistic ideals at the very heart of early Judaism.

Moreover, the basic issues emphasized in the Poem of Job are as irrepressible as those fundamental urges that are the vital force in the Song of Songs. For just as it is inevitable that profane love will tend to dominate the emotions of humanity, so too will the basic questions about the nature of God that are the subject of the Poem of Job always be at the forefront of humanity's intellectual speculation. Thus, even if it had been decided to banish the Poem of Job from study within the confines of pietistic Jewish religion, the issues raised in this great debate about God and His intentions toward man would not have ceased to exist. This being so, the wiser course was not to reject the Poem of Job and thereby make it an intellectual renegade in opposition to the biblical religion but rather to follow the Aqiban strategy and embrace it. By doing so, the guardians of the tradition could more effectively bend their efforts towards transforming it into a vital part of the tradition. This is why the Joban poetic parody is in the canon: Granted, within the canon it still poses grave danger because of the way in which it probes unremittingly the issue of whether God is a moral deity; but it would present an even greater danger to the ideals of the biblical religion if it were outside the canon. At least within the embrace of the tradition it could be rethought and recast, just as was done with the Song of Songs. If Job superficially seems to be impatient and questioning, then perhaps, encapsulated within the framework of the traditional Joban legend, Anti-Job could once more be converted into Job the Silent.

Still, the guardians of the biblical traditions set for themselves no easy task when they determined to accept rather than reject the Poem of Job and thus try to assimilate Anti-Job back into patient Job. In this respect, the Song of Songs was an easier work to reformulate along the lines suggested by Aqiba. In this latter instance one really did not have to transform the message of profane love; rather, one could simply superimpose over it an allegorical level of interpretation, the hidden meaning of which could complement and extend the simple meaning without significant conflict. But such was not the case with the Poem of Job; for there is no easy way to superimpose patient Job over impatient Job—the conflict between them is too dramatic for the one to serve simply as the complement or the extension of the other. Thus, although we can understand the rationale for accepting the Poem of Job—*why* the Poem had to be brought into the biblical tradition—we still have to consider *how* this was done.

Once again, we may be better able to come to grips with this issue if we consider a parallel model, that is, another literary work composed as a critical parody of a well-known tradition, but which has not been rejected by its traditional, conservative audience. Like Song of Songs and the Poem of Job, this tale has been embraced and has been seen in a manner Rabbi Aqiba would endorse: as the *most* traditional of stories, whose hero is the most pious of men. Moreover, in making our comparison, we need not search out a new parallel model but need only extend a parallel already closely considered: For the tale I have in mind is Perets' "Bontsye Shvayg."

6

Super-Reality

Anyone who knows Yiddish literature, especially the work of Perets, also knows that the view we have presented above of "Bontsye Shvayg" is not the popular view of the story.[124] While we have argued that Perets' narrative is designed as a parody of the pietistic Yiddish tale, the more common perception is that this is no parody at all, but rather the very epitome of what a pietistic Yiddish story should be. Leo Wiener, for example, writing only a few years after "Bontsye Shvayg" was first published in Perets' anthology *Literatur un lebn*, offers a typical interpretation of this type. He contends that Perets' story "presents, probably better than any other, the author's conception of the character of the virtues of the long suffering masses. Who can read it without being moved to the depth of his heart? There is no exaggeration in it, no melodrama, nothing but the bitter reality. It expresses in a more direct way than anything else he has written, his faith that the Kingdom of Heaven belongs to the lowly."[125] I need hardly add that Wiener's view could not be at further variance from that presented above. Where I have seen intentional, ironic exaggeration and melodrama and a character whose suffering silence goes beyond reality—all for the purpose of satire—he has seen just the opposite. In a much more recent discussion of Yiddish stories, Maurice Samuel shows us that the reading of "Bontsye Shvayg" as a straightforward pietistic tale still holds popular sway. In a chapter entitled "The Simple in Heart" he writes this short introduction to a translation of "Bontsye Shvayg": "Not all of Perets' folk tales are scrutinies of human motivations and lessons in the subtle temptations. Some are merely wondrous lessons woven round humble and lovable figures. They do not contain specific analyses of egotisms. They are so to speak songs to the virtues of modesty, forbearance, patience, gentleness, incorporated in people of no worldly importance."[126] Of course, what may seem a "wondrous lesson" to one interpreter can be seen as bombast by another. This accounts for Pinsker's scathing criticism, already mentioned above, that tales like "Bontsye Shvayg" give Yiddish literature the reputation of being second-rate.[127] But such a view could only be espoused by Pinsker because he, too, has accepted the popular interpretation of our story without recognizing its ironic undercurrent.[128]

Thus, we see a curious circumstance not dissimilar to others we have considered above: a story interpreted in a particular manner even though the evidence clearly leads to a conclusion that just the opposite is the proper, indeed, the most obvious interpretation. As Ruth Wisse puts it, we have a story that is "actually a socialist's exposure of the grotesquerie of suffering silence" that is nonetheless "now widely misread as a study of sainthood."[129] Why is this so?

One essential factor involved in this popular misreading of "Bontsye Shvayg" is the operation of what we might call the "Ozymandias effect," after the well-known sonnet, "Ozymandias," by Percy Shelley. This sonnet reads:

> I met a traveler from an antique land
> Who said: Two vast and trunkless legs of stone
> Stand in the desert. . .Near them, on the sand
> Half sunk, a shattered visage lies, whose frown
> And wrinkled lip, and sneer of cold command,
> Tell that its sculptor well those passions read
> Which yet survive, stamped on these lifeless things,
> The hand that mocked them, and the heart that fed:
> And on the pedestal these words appear:
> 'My name is Ozymandias, king of kings:
> Look on my works, ye Mighty, and despair!'
> Nothing beside remains. Round the decay
> Of that colossal wreck, boundless and bare
> The lone and level sands stretch far away.

In this poem, especially in the line, "The hand that mocked them and the heart that fed," Shelley tellingly depicts the complex relationship between sculptor and king, that is, between an artist and his audience. What he shows is a sculptor intent on subtly creating through his work an artistic monument that delivers one sort of message and a king equally determined to see in it quite another.

The sculptor's intent here is not to present in his artistic work a mirror of reality; that is, an objective depiction of Ozymandias as he looked "in the flesh." Rather, he wishes to portray the king in a manner that goes well beyond reality, to show the king's features in colossal and therefore superhuman terms, much like Perets has done in portraying Bontsye as Super-Job. Moreover, also like Perets, Shelley's sculptor distorts the characteristics of his subject's face—the "frown and wrinkled lip and sneer of cold command"—not for the purposes of aggrandizement but rather for purposes of satire. He wishes to mock his benefactor, to take the conventions of monumental sculpture and distort them just enough so that the king's face becomes a parody of reality, a parody that reveals the vanity and pretension of this self-styled "king of kings."

Yet it is these very distortions that Ozymandias reads as being the very epitome of his true nature. The vain king sees no irony in the haughty, sneering visage that the sculptor gives his likeness; rather, this is more real for him than the reality itself. The hand of the artist may satirize, but the king draws sustenance all the more from the parody while being totally blind to the irony that lurks beneath it: the hand that mocks and the heart that feeds.

This "Ozymandias effect" is a common by-product of parody, especially great parody; for the best parody tends to be both subtle and sophisticated. As I have said above, parody masquerades in the forms of the convention that it wishes to mock. It should therefore not be all that surprising that this parodistic disguise can often be misconstrued by its audience: the sham taken for the real thing. After all, a given audience (or some part thereof) may not be quite as sophisticated as the writer or as quick in catching the ironic import of the distortions the writer has so deftly woven into the fabric of his satire. For them these very touches can become the essential focus of attention, and like an Ozymandias, they too can grasp these same distortions—shorn of their ironic subtleties—and embrace them as a reality better than reality. Indeed, this is often intentionally part of the "joke" in parodistic writing; that is, the satirical writer often hopes that he can dupe the unsophisticated into taking the masquerade world of his parody as genuine. In a sense, this acts as a validation of his artistry by showing how close to the convention he can come while still undermining the very assumptions upon which the convention depends. Certainly, this was the attitude Shelley portrays in his sculptor, who read quite well the passions of his patron. There really is a double sense to this: the sculptor both read the passions which made Ozymandias such an appropriate subject for satire; and, at the same time, he also understood that these very same passions would blind the vain king to the mockery inherent in the artist's work.[130]

That such a misunderstanding of "Bontsye Shvayg" by its audience might occur is almost to be expected. For if this story is read as a straightforward pietistic tale like so many others of the genre—indeed, like others that Perets himself wrote— then the super-reality it portrays could very well speak directly to the heart of its Yiddish-speaking audience. In fact, this is precisely what did happen. As Pinsker comments:

> As a kind of Yiddish Everyman, Bontsye crystallized the experiences and aspirations of a people who saw themselves reflected, all too clearly, in the mirror of his life. This is not to suggest, however, that all of Bontsye's readers were as badly off as he was; rather, it was Bontsye—orphaned and alone, silent and long-suffering— who became a convenient index for the *tsoriss* [distress] of a people, if not of individual persons.[131]

As C. A. Madison further notes, this attitude "symbolized the pious Jew's complete credence in life after death, his belief that suffering on earth would be compensated by the pleasures of Paradise."[132] Of course, as I have argued, Perets wrote "Bontsye Shvayg" to attack precisely this attitude; yet if his audience chose (and continues to choose) to be blind to the subtle irony of his story, then the "Ozymandias effect" could work with full force to transform the story into an exemplary tale of piety closely akin in form and message to what the original legend of Job was—the very legend whose promise of life beyond death made it so effective a symbol for the author of the Epistle of James. Therefore, we can attribute the popular reinterpretation of "Bontsye Shvayg" in part to this fairly typical misapprehension of parody— but only in part. So far, we have only considered the process by which the popular misreading of Perets' story *could* occur. Still, beyond this, we must also consider what compelling motivation would lead Perets' audience to misread so willfully the intent of the author, to let their hearts feed upon the story while entirely ignoring the hand that mocked them. Such a motivation is not hard to find: it manifests itself in the historical circumstance of Perets' time and, all the more, the times that have followed.

We have already alluded to the events contemporary to Perets' time—the end of the nineteenth century and the beginning of the twentieth—that inevitably dominated life and refocused Jewish thought in Eastern Europe: the series of pogroms beginning in the 1880s, and the anti-Semitic policies of the various governments that fostered the environment in which such attacks against the Jews could so easily occur.[133] We need not dwell on the historical details extensively, but a few points may be mentioned.[134]

The immediate catalyst that prompted these violent outbursts against East European Jewry was the assassination of Tsar Alexander II in 1881. During this tsar's reign, which had been marked by some reform in the laws that had so long suppressed both the Jews and the Russian lower classes, there had emerged some small hope that Jews might be able to assimilate into normative society. Moreover, in the context of this freer political atmosphere, many Jews gravitated towards liberal and socialist groups bent on reforming East European governments from top to bottom—if not through orderly means, then through revolution.

But whatever hopes Jews had held for the future were dashed after Alexander II was succeeded by his reactionary son, Alexander III, whose government helped instigate and then nurture the violence against the Jews. As L. S. Dawidowicz recounts:

> . . .[news]papers close to [Russian] officialdom began hinting the Jews were to blame for the assassination [of Alexander II] and for the revolutionary movement as well. . . .emissaries from Petersburg appeared in South Russia with secret talk that the "people's wrath would be vented on the Jews." On April 15, [1881,] just six weeks after the Tsar's assassination, a pogrom broke out in Yelisavetgrad, a South Russian city of about 30,000. That started a wave of pogroms that continued into 1882, affecting some 225 communities. . . .Men women and children were attacked, raped and killed.

Other pogroms followed outside of Russia, including in Warsaw on Christmas day, 1881.[135]

Perhaps just as hard as the physical blows the Jews had to bear at this time was the psychic blow that came with recognition that liberal, East European groups were not about to rally to the aid of their Jewish "brothers." Instead, the leaders of those movements mostly offered no protest against the pogroms, preferring rather to remain silent. The year of 1881 therefore became, as Dawidowicz notes, a watershed for Jewish self-consciousness and identity: "The year 1881 radically affected the course of Jewish history. It marked the first major rupture among modernist Jews with the philosophy of enlightenment and emancipation. Like a prism, 1881 refracted the Jewish experiences of the past and bent them in another direction. Not since 1648 had the consciousness of being Jewish in an alien and hostile world been so vivid. First the paralyzing shock, then the visceral reaction: flight."[136]

Of course, in the decades that followed 1881—and with the further pogroms and anti-Jewish regulations that came in their wake—this flight was often a literal one: Many Jews either emigrated or accommodated by accepting religious conversion.[137] But by the same token, the shock of the pogroms also caused a psychological flight, as Jews—particularly the mass of traditional Jews—turned inward, seeing in this modern pattern of isolation and persecution the reverberation of more ancient patterns of suffering and deprivation by which the Jewish people had identified themselves since biblical times. For if traditional Jews saw themselves as the Chosen People, to many it seemed equally true that—as the Bible made abundantly clear—they had been chosen to suffer. In fact, some pious Jews certainly felt that such suffering was a kind of validation of their chosenness, a proof that God still held them to a standard to which no other people were held and to which none other could aspire. Thus, even as the pogroms caused great changes in Jewish self-identity for some, at the same time they served to reaffirm to others the more ancient identity to which traditional Jews had always clung. Within such a worldview, there could only be an ancient interpretation of modern events: "Masses of Jews remained in that world of traditional piety, accepting pogroms, economic hardships, and deprivations as God's will."[138] To such as these, Bontsye Shvayg could well be seen as a natural, even an inevitable, hero.

This was particularly so because the flowering of Yiddish literature also occurred just at this time. This, too, must largely be seen as a direct reaction to the hard political realities that Jews were compelled to confront at the end of the nineteenth century. And Perets, as a leader of this movement, can be singled out as one whose work especially shows the marks of his times.[139] There can be little question that the pietistic strain in much of his literary output chronicles his own attempt to turn inward, to draw on Jewish themes and traditions that could give meaning to a Jewish identity that in any case, neither he nor his community would be allowed to forget.[140] One might say that Perets' "Bontsye Shvayg" and his other satirical writings represent his caution lest this turn toward a renewed Jewish identity go to absurd extremes in which a silent, pious trust in God was taken to be the Jews' sole help in time of crisis.[141] Perets wished to emphasize that one had to temper faith with practicality, with the recognition that God helps those who help themselves.[142] Still, we should not be too surprised that so many chose to ignore this caution and rather more were inclined to follow an attitude like that of Wiener who saw in "Bontsye Shvayg" "no exaggeration. . .no melodrama. . .nothing but bitter reality." To be sure, the reality was bad enough; but there were not a "thousand million" suffering, Super-Joban Jews in Eastern Europe at the turn of the century. Still, by filtering reality through the super-reality of "Bontsye Shvayg," Jews could allow themselves to see themselves as more than what they were—as a people singled out to suffer silently and piously in the model of Father Abraham. They could create themselves in the image of Bontsye, who would only ask for a hot roll with fresh butter in return for his suffering. At the same time they could harbor a secret hope in their heart of hearts that God would return a far greater reward for such forbearance, if not in this world, then certainly in the next.[143]

The pietistic interpretation of "Bontsye Shvayg" that emerged around the turn of the century must therefore be seen to involve a certain element of self-delusion—a willingness by many East European Jews (and others) to take the super-reality of Bontsye's world as a legitimate picture of their true circumstance even though their true circumstance had not yet reached so grave an extreme. But this overdrawn picture of Jewish suffering at the end of the last century could hardly be seen in the same light by the middle of the current century, in a post-Holocaust world. For just as the Holocaust swept away the world of East European Jewry, it ushered in a world of surrealistic dimensions: a world where what had seemed absurd became actual, where the extremes of deprivation and suffering became commonplace, and thus where the super-reality of the world of "Bontsye Shvayg" could be seen as a *genuine* reality that one could document as meticulously as the Defending Angel had documented Bontsye's life.

The trauma of the Holocaust naturally caused Jews to reevaluate and rethink everything, from great to small; and within the context of this dramatically altered historical environment, an equally dramatic reevaluation of the meaning and message of "Bontsye Shvayg" was also a predictable byproduct; for no longer could the manifest absurdities, that Perets had placed in his story to indicate it was a parody be so easily taken as absurd. Note, in particular, that what might be deemed the two central, absurd elements in "Bontsye Shvayg" had to be rethought after the Holocaust.

The first absurdity was that someone could endure the extremes of suffering and want that Bontsye endured without *ever* crying out in pain and protest. In the reality of Perets' world such a suffering silence was completely without precedence. In fact, Jews did not endure the pogroms and the draconian, anti-Semitic policies at the turn of the century in pious silence. The historical record clearly shows that Jews took action: they protested and in many cases actively resisted the attacks against their communities. When such actions made little impact upon officialdom, they sought other recourses. The intensification of emigration, Zionism, hasidism and the Yiddish revival, among other things, was a clear manifestation of this Jewish action and reaction and well documents just how unsilent Jews were. As I have said, Perets wrote "Bontsye Shvayg" in order to endorse and emphasize the necessity of such action. Bontsye was thus presented as a manifest absurdity, a fool beyond all fools whose inaction no one should emulate.[144]

The second absurdity Perets placed in his story involves Bontsye's request, upon being offered the entire world, for only a hot roll with fresh butter (*a heyse bulke mit frisher puter*). The naiveté of this "humble" request was meant by Perets to appear to go beyond belief. More importantly, our author wanted to emphasize that Bontsye's wish was not motivated by his virtue. Perets indicated this in the way he had his protagonist make his request. Bontsye does not simply ask for a crust of bread but for a bit more, a roll—and not just any roll but a *hot* roll—and not merely a hot roll but a hot roll with butter—*and* the butter had better be fresh! Perets intentionally piled on these qualifiers (just as earlier in the story he had piled on the sentimentalized descriptions of Bontsye's suffering) in order to indicate that there is something not quite right in Bontsye's request.[145]

Note that when Bontsye finally makes his desires known, he asks *only* for something for himself. He never asks, for example, that Heaven intervene to relieve the suffering of all the "thousand million" others who have been victimized by the cruel injustices of Life. He never seeks redress of their grievances or forgiveness of their sins. In this respect, Perets marks a telling distinction between Bontsye and his truly pious characters (for example, the Rebbe of Nemirov or Reb Levi Yitshok of Berdichev) who think only of the welfare of others and ask nothing for themselves. In fact, Perets wanted his readers to recognize that there is not even a hint of piety in Bontsye or in Bontsye's wish; rather, Bontsye's request is motivated by a baser instinct: greed. If his wish is limited, it is not because Bontsye is humble, but merely because he is too dense to know he could have asked for more.[146]

Consider, in this connection, the observation of Esther Hautzig who relates Bontsye's desire to that of her own child: "Since he was nine and first heard the story of Bontsye Shvayg, my son says each time he has a warm roll with butter, 'You know, Bontsye had the right idea.'"[147] In saying this, she apparently means to imply that Bontsye's wish manifests a childlike innocence. But there is an unintentional irony to her remark; for one can hardly see a hungry nine-year-old as truly innocent. If such a child has not yet been initiated into all the seven deadly sins, he is at least well acquainted with some of them, including avarice and gluttony. Such a child might well ask for the world if he were smart enough and were given half the chance.

Of course, this is just the point that Perets wished to convey: that not only is one a fool who endures suffering without complaint but he is equally a fool who would not ask for a good deal more than just a hot roll with fresh butter when offered the entire universe. And there is a serious message that Perets offered here to his community: not only must Jews protest their deprivations loudly, but they should also demand a great deal. Furthermore, they should neither demand what they require out of simple greed nor should they look only to their own individual needs to the exclusion of others as Bontsye does. Instead, the Jewish community should speak with one voice for the benefit of all because they have this minimal right as human beings. Perets thus wished to make clear in "Bontsye Shvayg" the absurdity of one who does not insist forthrightly on basic human dignity and, as well, the foolishness of one who would settle instead merely for a morsel of compensation.

As stated here, these points seem obvious and unquestionably correct: one should not endure punishment without protest; one should not greedily seize the smallest favor offered by ruling authority but, rather, insist on the essentials that are the birthright of all humanity. Yet such grand principles tend to blur in the eyes of those whose suffering approaches that of a Bontsye Shvayg—and the suffering of those who endured the Holocaust did just that. From our vantage point in a post-Holocaust world we can hardly chide such as these for being both as silent and as greedy as Bontsye. Rather, the enormity of their silence, the pitifulness of their greed, are so awesome as to strike us dumb.

That there is a sense of profound silence intimately involved with the experience of the Holocaust is a point that hardly needs emphasizing: there is the silence of those who knew of the atrocities even as they were happening but did not actively protest and the silent testimony of the millions who died, who seemed to go quietly to their deaths like so many Isaacs.[148] But even beyond this there is a deeper level of silence that is emblematic of the Holocaust because, in essence, the experience it embodies is incapable of being communicated. This is a point that the most eloquent spokesperson for the generation of the Holocaust, Elie Wiesel, has returned to again and again: "In 1945 I felt we cannot really communicate the experience, that all we can do is show the impossibility of communicating the experience—if you take these two facts together, you have a certain need for silence. But the silence is not against language; it is a remedy to language. It tries to purify it, tries to redeem it, to give it back its innocence, its weight."[149] Such a silence is, as Wiesel has also emphasized, not merely the manifestation of a despairing futility but rather "a very eloquent silence, a screaming silence, a shouting silence"[150] that therefore can communicate more about the Holocaust than mere words can ever convey:

> What happened 25 years ago cannot and will not—and perhaps should not—be recorded. For what happened goes beyond words, beyond imagination. To make words of it would be blasphemous. Rebbe Mendel of Kotzk said that truth can sometimes be communicated by words, though there is a level of truth so deep it can be conveyed only by silence. And then, lastly, there is somewhere in man a truth so profound and so disturbing that it cannot be transmitted at all. The Holocaust must then be placed in this last category.[151]

The silences manifest in "Bontsye Shvayg," when seen from this perspective, can hardly be deemed absurd. Rather, both the silence of Bontsye's fellow men who never offered him the slightest respite and the silence of heaven, that allowed his suffering to continue without redress seem manifestations of the silence one finds at the heart of the Holocaust experience. Especially, the silence of Bontsye himself can be easily equated with that deepest level of silence that Wiesel characterizes as the most profound truth of the Holocaust. Seen in this light, Bontsye's silence is not that of the simpleton but rather of one whose suffering has driven him to a point beyond words.

Wiesel himself has made it clear that he interprets the sense of silence in Perets' "Bontsye Shvayg" in just such a manner. Indeed, he sees the suffering silence of Bontsye as representative of that of the entire Holocaust generation. In this respect Bontsye's final request represents to Wiesel the most profound manner of breaking silence and conveying to the world the impossibility of communicating the Holocaust experience—simply because it says the most by saying the least: "This timeless story also reflects the Jewish condition of today: the generation that is mine could have shouted so loud that it would have shaken the world. Instead it whispered, content with its 'buttered roll.' "[152]

Likewise, we can hardly blame those who were driven to the edge of sanity and beyond if they seemed overwhelmed by a greed of the pathetic proportions of a Bontsye. Rather, we can only remember what extremes had reduced them to such an end. Once again it is Wiesel, in describing his own Holocaust experience, who has succinctly delineated what that end truly was: "Bread, soup—these were my whole life. I was a body. Perhaps less than that even: a starved stomach."[153] To sufferers who were no longer humans but simply stomachs, greed had to become an essential element, the minimum requirement in order to survive. Bontsye's request for a hot roll with fresh butter would hardly seem absurd to those in the Nazi concentration camps. Rather, it might well have been the ultimate thing imaginable. Consider, in this respect, a scene described by Wiesel, which merits quoting at length:

> One day when we had stopped, a workman took a piece of bread out of his bag and threw it into a wagon. There was a stampede. Dozens of starving men fought each other to the death for a few crumbs. . . .

. . .I noticed an old man dragging himself along on all fours. He was trying to disengage himself from the struggle. He held one hand to his heart. I thought at first he had received a blow in the chest. Then I understood; he had a bit of bread under his shirt. With remarkable speed he drew it out and put it to his mouth. His eyes gleamed; a smile like a grimace, lit up his dead face. And was immediately extinguished. A shadow had just loomed up near him. The shadow threw itself upon him. Felled to the ground, stunned with blows, the old man cried:

"Meir, Meir, my boy! Don't you recognize me? I'm your father. . .you're hurting me. . .you're killing your father! I've got some bread. . .for you too. . .for you too. . ."

He collapsed. His fist was still clenched around the small piece. He tried to carry it to his mouth. But the other one threw himself upon him and snatched it. The old man again whispered something, let out a rattle and died amid the general indifference. His son searched him, took the bread, and began to devour it. He was not able to get very far. Two men had seen and hurled themselves upon him. Others joined in. When they withdrew, next to me were two corpses, side by side, the father and the son.[154]

This scene of parent and child seems far removed from that of Abraham and Isaac or that of mother Hannah and her seven sons. But then neither Abraham and Isaac nor Hannah and her children were ever driven to the extremes of those who endured the atrocities of the Holocaust. Ironically, it is in a story like "Bontsye Shvayg," where extremes have been piled on by the author for parodistic effect, that one finds a figure whose suffering silence seems directly comparable to that of the Holocaust victims or whose basic, animalistic greed is akin to their desperation. When Wiesel describes the gleaming eyes of the father, his grimace of a smile—motivated by his all-compelling greed—one can hardly fail to be reminded of Bontsye's smile on being reassured that he can have anything his heart desires.

Because the events of the Holocaust serve to legitimize the account of "Bontsye Shvayg," the story can no longer be what it had been, what its author had intended it to be. For events have robbed Perets' story of its absurdities by turning them into realities and, in doing so, has changed what was originally meant as a parody into a history before its time.

Thus, the world of "Bontsye Shvayg" and the world of the Holocaust may be said to transform each other as they play an historical counterpoint against one another. For the Holocaust inevitably must give a new depth of meaning to Perets' story, validating the reality of its world in a manner its author could never have imagined.[155] Likewise, Perets' story can be seen to give the ostensibly hopeless world of the Holocaust a sense of meaningfulness, especially for those who suffered in the Nazi concentration camps. In Bontsye they can find a "Super-Job" with whom they can identify, someone whose suffering seems as real as their own. Moreover, in Bontsye's perceived vindication in heaven, their suffering may be given a sense of purpose that the hard reality of the events alone could never give. Beyond this, the Holocaust survivor can perhaps receive some comfort in identifying with someone who suffered as they did but somehow seemed to endure, someone whose silence seemed much the same as their own silence. Hautzig speaks of just this sort of comfort in describing her own harrowing journey into Soviet Russia: "Perets' people 'traveled' with me to Siberia when I was ten years old, although I did not have a single Yiddish book in the five years we spent in that desolate part of the world. In Siberia my dream of Paradise often centered on having all the bread and all the sugar I could eat. My wish was not far removed from Bontsye's simple request of the Heavenly Court. Sometimes remembering Bontsye eased my own misery."[156]

In a post-Holocaust world "Bontsye Shvayg" and the Nazi atrocities against the Jews are not separate entities. Rather, their contrapuntal relationship impels a reciprocal reevaluation: if the Holocaust is to be seen as having some sense of purpose, it is through a story like "Bontsye Shvayg" that an insight into that purpose may be gained. But this can only happen if "Bontsye Shvayg" is taken seriously rather than satirically. In fact, to take Perets' story otherwise becomes nearly intolerable. For "Bontsye Shvayg" is now a legacy to the contemporary Jewish community, inherited from the destroyed world of East European Jewry in which its author lived and wrote. In particular, the force of history must act on the figure of Bontsye in a decisive manner to change him from what he was to what he must become in a post-Holocaust world: no longer the ultimate fool, the ultimate schlemiel, but, rather, the ultimate victim.[157] In fact, to call him a fool would have the concomitant effect of labeling as fools the remnant of those "thousand million" who reenacted his story in the Nazi camps and survived to bear quiet witness—and to do this would be no less than obscene. As D. G. Roskies observes, the tradition of Yiddish parody could hardly survive without reinterpretation in such an environment: "What has happened to the [Yiddish] parodic tradition after the Holocaust is that no one seems able to get the joke anymore. That is because everything Yiddish has automatically been shrouded in an aura of holiness. After the Great Destruction we can no longer view the Yiddish world except as a paradise lost. All the archetypes are now protected by the Holocaust, so that parody of any kind becomes sacrilege."[158]

If, as Pinsker notes, it was less than accurate for Jews at the turn of the century to find in Bontsye "a convenient index for the *tsoriss*" in their lives,[159] this is no longer true. Today he can be a most appropriate symbol for the Ultimate Victim of the Holocaust—and in this manner he is largely taken by his contemporary audience. If this requires that his original purpose be subverted, so be it. The forces of history all but demand this change of interpretation.[160] Indeed, it is altogether likely that, if Perets had lived until the Holocaust and by some miracle had survived its atrocities, then, in a post-Holocaust world, he would have insisted upon this reinterpretation himself.[161]

Still, if Perets is no longer present to rethink "Bontsye Shvayg" in the light of the Holocaust, there are others more than willing to do so on his behalf. Note, for example, the Yiddish poet and critic Eliezer Greenberg who, in his poem "Y. L. Perets and Bontsye Shvayg in the Warsaw Ghetto,"[162] well articulates this demand of history in a post-Holocaust world to give Silent Bontsye a voice. Greenberg published this work in 1946, obviously reacting to the impact of the initial graphic revelations of the Nazi concentration camps as well as to the story of the Warsaw Ghetto. His poem depicts the smoldering ruins of Warsaw as seen through the eyes of Perets, who is envisioned as touring the desolate scene of his home city. Finally, Perets comes upon a picture that appears to be intentionally cast in Joban imagery: his creation, Bontsye Shvayg, sitting on a pile of ash (see Job 2:8), muttering psalms to himself.[163] But Greenberg's Bontsye will not remain so subdued for long; rather, he is made to cry out, not only to his creator, Perets but also to the divine Creator Himself. At the climax of this speech, Bontsye declares,

I want, now, to cry out all the years of silence,
I want you to give me a tongue, to give me now a voice!
. . . .
To be a witness to how the world kept silent, to how silent the Creator kept
When our race was mowed down—kith and kind—the poor just as the rich!
—O my creator,[164] call once more the whole world to a Tribunal,
But let me—the eternally silent one—now be their Defender!. . .

Let me open these eternally sealed lips,
Which for a lifetime have been locked with silence!
Let me throw open my heart, which has sobbed for a lifetime
In silence—locked with a thousand locks!. . .[165]

Greenberg then continues his poem with a picture of these two ghosts, Bontsye and Perets, whom he has resurrected from the world before the Holocaust—united in bewailing the immeasurable loss of the entire Jewish civilization of which they themselves had become so much a part:

His [Bontsye's] lamentation rises and turns into a wild howling,
His voice now pounds like wolf-and-dove roaring.
Until the morning starts to burn with feverish madness—
And Perets wails and Bontsye wails—and all around is frozen still.

How deserted lies the city, once so full of people, she is like a widow. . .
Is this the city that they call the perfection of beauty, the joy of all the earth?. . .
Two Jews sway in the shine of a disappearing moon,
Of the entire city there remains only Bontsye and Y. L. Perets.[166]

It is striking to see how Greenberg has self-consciously decided to alter the correspondences that Perets had established in his story. The key lines in this respect come at the end of the twentieth stanza where Bontsye demands a new Tribunal (*din-toyre*, cf. the *bezdin/bezdin shel mayleh* in Perets' original story), one in which the previously silent protagonist can take on a new role.[167] Bontsye now insists on taking the place of the original Defending Angel (the same term that Perets used, *meylets yoysher*, is also employed by Greenberg) and would personally argue a case before both God and Mankind. Moreover, Greenberg endows the suddenly articulate Bontsye with more than enough rhetorical flourish to be equal to this task.

The case Greenberg would have Bontsye the Defender argue is no longer his own. Instead, Bontsye demands to speak on behalf of the entire generation of Jews who were victimized in the Holocaust since they—kith and kind, rich and poor— are no longer present to speak for themselves: just as Bontsye has taken on the role of a now-vocal Defending Angel, so has the generation of those murdered in the

Holocaust been cast into the silent role to which Bontsye had been previously consigned by Perets. And, Greenberg clearly implies, there should be no hesitation now for Bontsye to speak out, even though to speak forthrightly of so grave an injustice as that engendered by the Holocaust must shake the moral structure of Heaven to its foundations. After all, the poet seems to suggest, the walls of Jericho have already fallen; their ruins may be seen among the ravages of the Warsaw Ghetto. Indeed, these modern ruins are figuratively joined by Greenberg to those ancient ruins, which Jews have always seen as their basic point of reference for tragedy: the ruins of Jerusalem and its Holy Temple. Perets and Bontsye therefore speak for the lost generation of the Holocaust in the traditional manner, quoting the words of the biblical book of Lamentations.[168]

Greenberg's poem is, of course, a creative work and thus one in which the author can certainly allow himself wide latitude in manipulating the Bontsye story. But one can also see historical forces working in what should be the more circumscribed area of Perets criticism, affecting how critics have read into "Bontsye Shvayg" interpretations not intended by its author. This point may be well demonstrated through a resurvey of the critical views of some of the interpreters of "Bontsye Shvayg" whom we have mentioned above.

We may best begin by considering what Greenberg himself has to say about "Bontsye Shvayg" in an article he wrote with his long-time collaborator I. Howe in 1974. In this study Howe and Greenberg declare that Perets' story "touches. . .on one of the major themes of modern literature: the radical, hopeless incommensurability between morality and existence, the sense of a deep injustice at the heart of the universe which even the heavens cannot remedy."[169]

This nihilistic viewpoint, which Howe and Greenberg specifically characterize as somewhat Kafkaesque,[170] quite naturally maintains a continuity with the outlook found in Greenberg's poem. But I believe that it is not very much in line with what Perets himself intended to emphasize when he wrote "Bontsye Shvayg." Perets is not Kafka, nor did he endeavor to cast Bontsye into a Kafkaesque role. The whole point of "Bontsye Shvayg," as I have tried to emphasize, was to spur people to action: Perets set the absurdity of the story's protagonist before the mass of East European Jews in order to educate them through his example, to present to them a clear-cut case of how *not* to act in the face of strife and suffering. He had no intention of primarily projecting through Bontsye the sense of the "radical, hopeless, incommensurability between morality and existence" that Howe and Greenberg read as the main thrust of the story. To be sure, a deep, abiding sense of the unfairness of Life does act as an important background theme in "Bontsye Shvayg"; still, Perets does not counsel an existential despair in the face of this injustice. Rather, he wishes to stimulate action to redress the grievances that Life has imposed upon humanity in general and on the Jews of Eastern Europe in particular.

Howe and Greenberg have thus taken what was at best a secondary theme in "Bontsye Shvayg" and brought it forward as the central point of Perets' story. Because they have done so, we learn more about them than we do about Perets. The fact is that—as Greenberg's poem makes explicitly clear—they cannot really separate their interpretation of Bontsye and his suffering from their picture of the victims of the Holocaust.[171] Furthermore, because they read the picture of the Holocaust into "Bontsye Shvayg," they are also constrained to view the Bontsye figure seriously without putting any emphasis on the fundamental absurdity that Perets placed at the heart of his depiction. Thus, they have converted Bontsye from a didactic example for nineteenth century Jewry into a nihilistic symbol for mid-twentieth century humanity. In doing so, they have focused on precisely the kind of despair for the human condition that contemplation of the Holocaust can so naturally give rise to in a post-Holocaust world.

Of course, Howe and Greenberg's view also has strong points in common with the interpretation of "Bontsye Shvayg" expressed by Wiesel.[172] As noted above, Wiesel has equated the figure of Bontsye with "the generation that is mine"[173]—the generation of the Holocaust—much in the manner Greenberg's poem. It is therefore hardly surprising that like Howe and Greenberg, Wiesel also chooses to ignore any sense of Bontsye's absurdity. Rather, he takes Perets' protagonist absolutely seriously, rather than satirically.

Wiesel therefore depicts Bontsye as "the meekest among the meek, the eternally offended, the condemned. . .who has never known a moment of respite, of serenity; who has received nothing but blows and insults all his life"[174] without even hinting that he recognizes that Perets has portrayed his protagonist in this manner for parodistic effect. When Wiesel considers the "shame" of the "celestial tribunal" he gives no indication that this shame is really the result of the angels' embarrassment before a fool whom they have mistakenly taken as a figure of ultimate piety.[175] Bontsye's simple request and what follows from it are too profound to Wiesel to be so ironically discounted in even the slightest manner. Most tellingly, Wiesel finds no blame in Bontsye; for he must be seen as a victim rather than a schlemiel. Wiesel instead affixes the blame for Bontsye's suffering on "all the others"—both God and Mankind.[176]

Overall, Wiesel thus sees "Bontsye Shvayg" as a "timeless story"[177] that vividly portrays all the basic issues of the human dilemma that have been so sharply demarcated for him by the Holocaust experience. Like Howe and Greenberg, he has failed to recognize that Perets had really intended his story to be timely rather than timeless—a story tailored to speak to Perets' generation rather than to Wiesel's and to provoke vocal action rather than invoke what Wiesel has called the "weight" of silence.[178]

Other critical approaches to "Bontsye Shvayg," in which Perets' protagonist is seen as the blameless, innocent victim, also conform to a concept of the idealized East European Jew martyred by the Holocaust. Note, in this regard, the interpretation of Bontsye presented by Samuel in his book on Perets and Perets' writing, *Prince of the Ghetto*. As I have mentioned previously, "Bontsye Shvayg" is for Samuel a "folk tale" of a type that celebrates "wondrous incidents woven round humble and lovable figures." Such tales, he declares, are essentially "songs to the virtues of modesty, forbearance, patience, gentleness" of the poorest Jews, "the most oppressed layer of human society, the lowest level of the pyramid."[179]

In his specific discussion of "Bontsye Shvayg," Samuel makes no mention of his grounds for seeing Perets' protagonist as such a pious symbol of the East European, Jewish lower class. However, in his more general discussion of Perets, he makes quite clear the forces that have decisively shaped his view of the writer's work. On the basis of these more general remarks, it is therefore not particularly difficult to extrapolate why Samuel views the story as he does.

This viewpoint is perhaps best shown in Samuel's characterizing Perets as "Prince of the Ghetto." Samuel explains that Perets is best entitled a "prince" because he was able "to distill in Chassidic and folk tales the spirit of east-European Jewry."[180] He further elaborates, "He, who on the surface was apparently a modern 'public worker,' was secretly a legendary prince, entrusted with the timeless treasures of his people, the accumulated inheritance of many generations. Incognito during his life time, even to himself, he was to become the eternal representative of Polish Jewry by the grace of God."[181] In delineating this viewpoint of Perets, Samuel has essentially marked a distinction between Perets the man and Perets the Legend. According to Samuel, Perets the man was "in the highest and humblest sense a teacher" who "preached a Jewish national awakening."[182] Such a teacher is certainly to be admired, but for Samuel the "princely" aspect of Perets the Legend is of far more importance; indeed, Perets the Legend must take precedence over Perets the man:

> . . .there was a kind of misunderstanding about him at the [i.e., in his own] time; and Perets himself shared it. Such a man as I have described above could not be called "Prince of the Ghetto." Teacher, perhaps, or leader—but not prince. But the truth is that thirty years ago the mortal Perets still overshadowed the immortal Perets; his conscious programmatic work obscured his true character. His great creations, the folk tales and the Chassidic tales. . .were regarded as almost incidental to his educational purpose. It was a hopelessly false perspective.[183]

What Samuel says here about Perets reminds one of the Presiding Judge's remarks to Bontsye at the conclusion of Bontsye's trial: "There they did not understand such things! It may be that you yourself did not know. . . ." He insists that neither Perets himself nor his contemporaries of the now-vanished world of "thirty years ago" could hope to understand the true significance of the Yiddish writer. Only from the vantage point of the time in which Samuel lives can Perets' contribution to the Jewish heritage be truly appreciated. In more specific terms, this means from the vantage point of 1948, when *Prince of the Ghetto* was published, a chronological moment when the shadow of the Holocaust naturally dominated the intellectual milieu in which Samuel was writing. Of course, Samuel could hardly avoid being acutely sensitive to the Holocaust, and there can be no question that its impact played a decisive role in shaping his view of Perets the Prince and of his "princely" writings. Samuel forcefully says as much himself:

> The Polish Jews who were the objects of Perets' passionate and scrupulous concern have been wiped out by the modern world. Of the three and a quarter million, three million were done to death—gassed, machine-gunned, bombed, burned or buried alive. . . .A whirlwind of human evil, altogether beyond their control and not to be evaded by any stratagem, came upon them. And if human wisdom and goodness do ultimately triumph, there will be no Polish Jewry to take part in the universal rejoicing. Perhaps it is this reflection that throws back upon my contact of thirty years ago a quivering sensitive light.[184]

Thus, Samuel touches on a theme we have also found in the interpretations of Howe, Greenberg and Wiesel. Perets, he declares, must speak for those who are no longer present to speak; his writings must be seen in terms of their traditional world—destroyed but not forgotten. Perets cannot be allowed to be a teacher for his own time; instead, he must be magnified into a legendary "Prince" for all time, "the eternal representative of Polish Jewry by the grace of God." We can see, too, that Samuel does not hesitate to celebrate this lost world of East European Jewry, even to the point of a conscious emphasis on sentimentality. In fact, he declares, the intervening devastation between then and now virtually compels him to do so: "It is possible again that the years between have colored the memories which filter through them. I may be persuading myself that I remember more vividly than I do. And on the other hand the intervening horror, the destruction of Polish Jewry, may in fact bring to the surface recollections that in a normal way would remain buried forever."[185]

If Samuel would thus coronate Perets as Prince, it is only logical that he would do likewise to Bontsye—much as the angels did for him on his entry into heaven. Moreover, it is equally clear that for Samuel any hint of didactic purpose in "Bontsye Shvayg" must be shorn away from the story—indeed, from all of Perets' stories. For to Samuel it is only Perets' ability "to distill. . .the spirit of east-European Jewry" that really counts. Any overt attempts at teaching can only detract from Perets' true purpose. Samuel will even go so far as to chide Perets for straying from this "princely" path. Thus, the critic declares that Perets "was on solid ground when he sought to improve his people simply because he loved it; not so when he exhorted it to 'merit' partnership in the modern world."[186]

It is therefore hardly surprising that Samuel turns a blind eye to the ironic exhortation that Perets had so carefully imbedded into his satirical parody. Samuel believes that Bontsye must be viewed as someone simply to be loved because, he— who suffered and who is now dead—must stand in for his generation, the generation of those wiped out by the Holocaust.

Of course, the process of raising up Bontsye to the status of legendary sainthood was well under way even before the Holocaust period. The Holocaust simply gave this process a greater intensity, a stronger impetus. We can see this process at work when we consider the observations of Madison who first formulated his published views of "Bontsye Shvayg" in the period just at the start of the Nazi era, but who restated his case even more forcefully in post-Holocaust times. What makes Madison's remarks particularly interesting is that they reveal a critic who seems caught between his own critical judgments of Bontsye and the counterforce of the popular conception of this "sainted" figure. As a result, while Madison acknowledges the satirical and didactic intentions of "Bontsye Shvayg," he then hesitates to press this satirical line of interpretation to its logical conclusion.[187]

That Madison recognizes the satirical thrust of Perets' story is shown in the way he characterizes the Yiddish writer as one who was "irritated" by the attitude represented in Silent Bontsye: "Perets knew only too well that the resulting meekness and self-abnegation were suicidal in an unconscionable world, especially as the faith that had kept the Jews alive for centuries was losing its hold upon them."[188]

Thus, he further notes, "Bontsye Shvayg" was utilized by Perets as a "springboard for social satire and religious irony."[189] But having said this, Madison then proceeds to make the following remark in the course of comparing Bontsye to the figure of Shemayah, the protagonist of Perets' story "The Messenger"[190]: "Yet he [Perets] loved [Bontsye] the poor porter and [Shemayah] the old messenger and sympathized with their naive piety, artless mind and simple wholesomeness, and his portrayal made them memorable additions to Yiddish literature."[191]

When one looks closely at this line of interpretation, one discovers an argument that seems largely at odds with itself. On the one hand, Madison grants the satirical force of "Bontsye Shvayg" but then, on the other hand, states that Perets, despite his satirical intentions, really saw Bontsye as a sympathetic character to be "loved" for his "naive piety, artless mind and simple wholesomeness."[192] Moreover, Madison further seems to suggest that it is essentially these pietistic attributes in Bontsye that make him a "memorable" addition to Yiddish literature. Indeed, the critic appears to conclude that it is those "lovable" aspects of Bontsye—in particular, those characteristics which he shares with Shemayah—that must be given precedence over the ironic undertones Perets wrote into his portrayal.

This view of "Bontsye Shvayg" has more in common with Samuel's interpretation than first might appear to be so. For Madison, like Samuel, recognizes in this instance the teaching function in Perets' writing but then, by and large, discounts it. He concludes instead that what Samuel would call the "folk" or "hasidic" elements in the story, those elements that celebrate Bontsye's "simple wholesomeness" are what *really* make the story a significant contribution to Yiddish literature. In fact, if we follow the logic of Madison's remarks, he would seem essentially to be arguing that "Bontsye Shvayg," is an important story not because it is so fine an example of parodistic satire but *despite* this being so.

What is particularly difficult to accept about Madison's argument is the way in which he has read Perets' intentions for Bontsye; for if Perets had created Bontsye as a truly lovable, pietistic hero, as Madison contends, then the entire force of the satirical parody would have been seriously subverted. Rather, as we have seen, Perets intended his protagonist to masquerade as such an "hasidic" hero only to be unmasked in the end as a wholly unsympathetic fool. At best, the Yiddish writer therefore saw his protagonist as someone to be pitied, but not loved.[193] Likewise, Bontsye cannot be portrayed as someone motivated by any hint of genuine piety. Instead, it is just as important to Perets to show that Bontsye is not only the greatest of all fools but that he also is motivated in his "humble" request by an all-compelling greed. As I have emphasized above, these two factors—Bontsye's stupidity and his greed—are the central elements that make him absurd and thus the factors on which Perets' satire necessarily depends. Madison's approach to Perets' story is fundamentally misguided because it would rob the protagonist of this stupidity and greed. But without this central focus on Bontsye as greedy fool, Perets's satire would lose its "bite," leaving only the semblance of a satire without the substance.

Why then must Madison insist on seeing Bontsye as both lovable and pious, indeed, virtually a stoic with a "fatalistic attitude towards life"[194] even though, in doing so, he undercuts his own argument that "Bontsye Shvayg" is a satire? The likely answer is that Madison's reaction to the Bontsye figure is more psychological than logical: the critic simply cannot escape (at least not entirely) being influenced by the increasingly sacrosanct status of Perets' protagonist, a status that becomes more firmly entrenched as events progressively shape Bontsye's misfortunes into the reflections of reality. Madison's comments simply acknowledge how untouchable Bontsye has become.

In this respect, it may well be significant that only in Madison's 1968 comments does one find this emphasis on the lovableness of Bontsye being the essential factor in his portrayal, the primary factor that makes him an important figure in Yiddish literature. This statement goes a good deal further in underscoring the importance of the hasidic aspects of "Bontsye Shvayg," at the expense of its satirical aspects, than Madison's earlier remarks. But then Madison is self-consciously aware that "the tragic events of the 1940's—Nazi crematoria and the suppression of Yiddish under Stalin—have extirpated or stifled the main body of Yiddish readers as well as many writers"[195] and that these historical forces have thus threatened the viability of Yiddish culture and literature. Within this context, Madison may well feel that a more forceful apology for Bontsye is necessary.[196] Thus, even though Madison does not hesitate to present Bontsye as a satirical figure, he draws back from pressing this interpretation too vigorously. Because in the popular conception Perets' protagonist is beloved, so, Madison feels constrained to argue, Perets intended to make him lovable. To look at Bontsye differently would be, as Samuel would say, a "hopelessly false perspective" Madison refuses to challenge.

Finally, even when a critic decides to attack the "lovable" image of Bontsye without quarter, it is the saintly Bontsye of popular conception who is attacked rather than the satirical figure that Perets created. This is, I think, the only way to account for Pinsker's spectacular misinterpretation of "Bontsye Shvayg," referred to above.[197]

The irony in Pinsker's viewpoint of Silent Bontsye is that by and large, it is in accordance with Perets' own negative view. For, unlike Madison, Pinsker has no intention of softening his stern criticisms of what he sees as the archetypal, sentimental, Yiddish hero; instead, like Perets himself, this critic is determined to unmask the dark side of Bontsye without even a hint of sympathy, let alone love. Thus, Pinsker rightly sees and clearly condemns Bontsye for being "the saint-as-mentsch, an extension of the shtetl's belief in the transitory nature of this life and the eternal justice of *Gan Eyden* [Paradise]." He also shows no patience for the "relatively easy solution of 'silence'" that he sees being served up as the sure means to sainthood.[198]

But while Pinsker can see clearly the issues that lie at the heart of "Bontsye Shvayg," by the same token, he is completely blinded—or perhaps we should say dazzled—by the "legendary" stature of its hero. As a result, he completely confuses the popular reading of the story with its author's intentions and proceeds roundly to condemn Perets for his "unadulterated play to the emotions."[199]

Behind Pinsker's consequent dismissal of "Bontsye Shvayg" as "second-rate," one senses the same sort of anger that motivated Perets to write the story in the first place. The critic shares with the Yiddish author the same sense of contempt for anyone who would celebrate silent forbearance and acquiescence as the only appropriate response to undeserved affliction. And one cannot avoid a further suspicion that Pinsker's anger is particularly sharpened by his perception that Bontsye is an especially poor model to praise in a post-Holocaust world or, perhaps better, the wrong sort of figure to see as emblematic of the Holocaust generation. Pinsker makes no explicit statement to this effect, but perhaps he deemed the point altogether too self-evident to require a clarifying comment. In any case, we do know that he self-consciously writes against the background of the Holocaust experience, for his dedication reads "For the six million," which also requires no further clarification.[200]

Regardless of how one may wish to speculate on what agenda stands behinds Pinsker's remarks, at least one thing cannot be gainsaid. For him Bontsye is the *sainted* Bontsye; the popular view is the *only* view he seems to know or, at least, is willing to acknowledge. Nothing could more effectively demonstrate that by the time Pinsker is writing (1971), this view of Perets' protagonist had become such a given that even a serious critic of Yiddish literature can accept it without a second thought.

7

The "Sincerely Wrong" Approach

Thus far, we have looked at the popular conception of "Bontsye Shvayg" as a stimulus for creative response and critical evaluation in a post-Holocaust world. Perhaps though, in consideration of the discussion above, we should not be surprised to discover that the sort of reinterpretation of "Bontsye Shvayg" we have outlined goes beyond even these literary boundaries. In fact, yet a further reshaping of Perets' work can be documented, one that goes beyond opinion and proceeds to affect the text directly; for not only do we find that Perets' original intentions have been altered in the popular conception, but we can find instances where the story itself has been changed as well.[201]

These changes do not occur, to my knowledge, in any Yiddish editions of the story but rather in translations. For our purposes, two such examples are especially significant: the translation of the story done by Hilde Abel,[202] since it is probably the most widely read edition of the text in English; and the dramatic rendition in Arnold Perl's play, *The World of Sholom Aleichem*, since this stage production has probably done more to bring Perets' story before contemporary audiences than anything else.[203]

In both these recastings of the Bontsye story into English, one can note numerous paraphrastic departures from the original Yiddish. In the specific case of Abel's version, these free translations can often be less than felicitous.[204] Still, all in all, the liberties that Abel and Perl take in their respective recountings of "Bontsye Shvayg" do not appreciably alter the basic theme of Perets' story—that is, until one comes to their individual treatments of the story's conclusion. For in each instance they have altered the crucial last line and, in doing so, have given it a particular interpretive twist. Because Perets has placed so much thematic weight on this last line, these respective alterations have a predictably dramatic impact upon the story, its meaning and its message.

As may be recalled,[205] the last line of "Bontsye Shvayg" reads:

Dayonim un malokhim hobn aropgelozt di kop farshemt; der kateyger hot zikh tselakht.

Judges and angels lowered their heads in shame; the Prosecutor burst out laughing.

Abel's paraphrastic rendering reads as follows:

77

A silence falls upon the great hall, and it is more terrible than Bontsye's has ever been, and slowly the judge and the angels bend their heads in shame at this unending meekness they have created on earth.

Then the silence is shattered. The prosecutor laughs aloud, a bitter laugh.[206]

One might be tempted to label Abel's version of the conclusion as more commentary (or perhaps even targum) than translation. That is, she is clearly trying to do more here than just convey what Perets wrote; rather, she very much wants to explain in her text exactly how she feels the conclusion of "Bontsye Shvayg" should be understood.

Abel's view of Bontsye is one we know quite well; he is Bontsye, the silent saint, whose piety can only strike the angels with awe. In her depiction of the final scene, the angelic "shame" has nothing to do with embarrassment before a fool. Rather, it is a *genuine* shame; the angels are simply abashed that they have been responsible for so grave an injustice as that evidenced in the life of Silent Bontsye. Abel underscores this interpretive point by labeling Bontsye's "unending meekness" as that which "they [all Heaven] have created on earth." And in Abel's view, this cosmic, moral inequity, for which Bontsye bears silent witness, is a truly monstrous thing; and the unanswerable silence of their shame is "more terrible than Bontsye's has ever been."

But if one cannot find words to answer the Silence of Bontsye, Abel finds in Perets' story a response that for her goes beyond words: the Prosecutor's "shattering" laugh. From her perspective this laugh is no longer the laugh of triumph that Perets intended it to be; instead it is "a bitter laugh" that drives home a sense of despair in the face of unimaginable suffering that has become all too real, a "Kafkaesque" hopelessness reflecting "the incommensurability between morality and existence." These last sentiments, it may be recalled, come from what I have called the "nihilistic" interpretation of "Bontsye Shvayg" that emerges out of Howe and Greenberg's response to the Holocaust.[207] There can be little question that Abel aligns herself with their interpretive view. Indeed, this is entirely to be expected, since her translation/commentary of Perets' story appears in a collection that Howe and Greenberg have themselves edited.[208] One might say it is simply their interpretation of the story "made flesh."

When we turn from Abel's version of "Bontsye Shvayg" to Perl's dramatic depiction, we should perhaps be mindful of the dramatist's own admonition. In his introduction to Perets' story (delivered in the play by a grandfatherly "Mendele the Book Peddler"[209]) he notes, "The story runs in English, it runs nine pages, nine and a half. In Yiddish it runs twelve. In Yiddish a story is always 25 per cent better, 25 per cent longer anyhow."[210] In point of fact, Perl may be said to demonstrate the truth in these remarks in the way he depicts the conclusion to Perets' story. As we would expect, the playwright presents to his audience the familiar Bontsye who comes to the climactic moment when he is offered anything in the universe he desires. But in this version of the story, the ending is shorter than that found in the Yiddish, and, from the standpoint of Perets' original intentions, certainly not better. It simply goes (including stage directions):

BONTSYE. (*Smiles for the first time.*) Well, in that case—if it's true—could I perhaps have, every day, please—a hot roll with fresh butter? (*All lights except Bontsye's fade out. The Angels turn away ashamed. Even God is ashamed. Bontsye smiles. Then the light on him goes out.*)[211]

Just as we have previously seen critics like Wiesel, Samuel and Pinsker reacting to the figure of Silent Bontsye as though the Prosecutor's laugh had never disturbed the serenity of his final scene, so here again we see this interpretation become tangible in the text of the story itself. If one should feel the "weight of silence" at the conclusion of Bontsye's drama, then Perl will fulfill this desire in his play. Thus, the Prosecutor's laugh ceases to exist; rather the spotlight is quite literally placed upon the smiling face of Bontsye to the exclusion of all else.

We might be tempted at this juncture to draw a parallel between Perl's play and the sort of "Victorian *Hamlet*" or the "happy ending" version of the story of Jephthah and his daughter that we considered early in this study.[212] To some extent, such a parallel is certainly valid. If tragedy has not exactly been transformed into comedy, at least, a foolish protagonist has been reformed into an all-too-heroic hero, an idealized Super-Job, who has not only kept his lips from sin but who has never opened them at all. Indeed, we might rightfully go further still and join with Pinsker in seeing such a purely pietistic version of "Bontsye Shvayg" as both bombastic and second-rate.

But in the final analysis, if we couch our judgments within the framework of these terms alone, if we survey the Bontsye-as-saint-tradition—as we have above—and simply conclude that it is "wrong," we will lose more than we will gain. Or, to return to the metaphor that is the leitmotif of this study, we will not be listening carefully enough to all the melodies that make up this complex of historical counterpoint.

For Perl's version of "Bontsye Shvayg"—or, for that matter Abel's version—cannot be properly viewed in isolation, without the underlying history that plays a bass theme against their respective reworkings of this Yiddish melody. Just as the critical opinions noted above are a response—a reaction to the historical context in which the Bontsye tradition has developed—so, too, these "versions" of the story are best seen as refractions from out of the same historical prism: the Holocaust experience. Perl himself makes this quite explicit. When his Mendele introduces "Bontsye Shvayg" to the audience, he places the story within this specific historical context and thus virtually dictates the way the story's ending must be portrayed:

This story, and others, he [Perets] used to read—in the language of the working people—in Yiddish—to working people. And because, in those days, this was not very popular with the Czar (reading in Yiddish to working people)—Isaac Loeb Perets spent a little time in jail. It's a fact, what can I do? And later, nearly fifty years later, in another terrible time for the Jews—in the Hitler-time—in Warsaw, in the Ghetto itself, this story was read—at the risk of your life. And still people read it.[213]

Note how the last part of this statement—"and still people read it"—is self-consciously placed by Perl against the background of the Warsaw Ghetto and its martyrs. The playwright as much as says that now one can only see Silent Bontsye essentially as Greenberg depicts him—as someone from out of the "Hitler-time." His story can only be read against the shadow of those who risked and lost their lives lost in that ghetto (and the other Nazi-created hells), who saw in the story of this innocent sufferer the image of their own lives and deaths. In fact, Perl further declares—much after the manner of Samuel—even when we look backwards to Perets' own time, we must see the Yiddish writer from this same point of reference, from the standpoint of the Holocaust. The dramatist implies that Perets must be viewed as a kind of precursory Martyr-of-the-Ghetto, who suffered the indignity of jail as punishment for speaking out in praise of Bontsye the Silent. Needless to say, Perets would hardly recognize himself in this distorted, aggrandized depiction by Perl. Nonetheless, even though what the playwright says is hardly true from an historical standpoint, it has nonetheless become within the tradition—as Mendele assures us—"a fact, what can I do?"

How dominant a "fact" the Perl version of "Bontsye Shvayg" actually is cannot be really appreciated unless we expand the scope of our inquiry beyond what one finds in the written texts. For it is clear that Perl did not invent the "Bontsye Shvayg" tradition that concludes the story without the Prosecutor's laugh. Rather, like the author of the Epistle of James, he is simply reflecting a long-standing oral tradition and also chooses, as did the epistle's author, to give precedence to what was heard over what was read. Oral traditions are always difficult to pin down since, by their very nature, they tend not to be recorded as the authorized texts are recorded. But we can note, for example, D. N. Miller's comment that his grand-father knew of this oral tradition as early as 1903, only nine years after the initial publication of "Bontsye Shvayg."[214]

Beyond this peripheral sort of testimony, one can only appeal to personal experience. In this respect, my own experience is remarkably consistent: whenever I speak to Jews or other lovers of Yiddish about "Bontsye Shvayg," the oral tradition we find reflected in Perl's account always comes up; it is always the one people know about, the one they identify as the "popular" version of the story even if they know about the authorized version as well.

Recently, the other tradition, the one that concludes with a "bitter" laugh and which Abel's translation of "Bontsye Shvayg" reflects, has also come up as an oral tradition of sorts in a circumstance that impressed on me the power such traditions can exert. In this particular case, a lover of Perets' stories came up to me after a lecture and insisted that "Bontsye Shvayg," as Perets wrote it, ends with the Pros-ecutor laughing a bitter laugh. In order to prove his point, the Perets-lover de-manded to see the Yiddish text of the story; and I, of course, complied by showing him the text—the authorized text in Yiddish with the authorized ending—the sim-ple, final phrase that Perets wrote and never changed. Despite this, the Perets-lover pointed to this ending and declared, "There, you see! The story *does* end with a bitter laugh!"

Once again, we might say that we have encountered an interpretation that is "wrong," a view of "Bontsye Shvayg" that without question, is in error because it goes against what the text plainly reads. However, we should also recognize some-thing else: that an interpretation of this nature is not merely wrong, it is also quite *sincerely* wrong; that is, the interpretation of the Perets-lover or those of Abel, Perl, Samuel, Wiesel, Howe and Greenberg and so on are not intended by their respective authors to be willfully perverse. They are not to be viewed as self-consciously twisted perspectives instituted with malice aforethought by a given critic in order to remake Perets into his own image. In each instance the interpretation is sincere; in each case there can be little question that the critic believes he is doing justice to Perets' message, that he is reflecting the author's original intentions. If the interpretation is "wrong," from our perspective[215] this is only because we can perceive historical forces—whether made manifest in the pogroms or in the consummate disaster of the Holocaust—which have become so dominant that they act upon and transform the "wrong" interpretation into what *has to be right.*

By the same token, if we return to a consideration of the Aqiban viewpoint of Song of Songs as *qdš qdšym*, the "Holy of Holies" in light of our discussion above, we can see that this view must also be understood to be "sincerely wrong." Previously, we spoke of the rabbinical approach to Song of Songs—the rationale that allowed it to become a part of the biblical canon—as a "strategy of inversion."[216] But this characterization should now be further qualified; for this Aqiban approach to Canticles really is better seen as involving a "*sincere* strategy of inversion."

To be sure, in what can only have been the most calculating of fashions, the early rabbis built a complex allegorical framework over the bare text of Canticles. But this was not done in a cynical manner merely to achieve some sort of Machiavellian end through whatever interpretive means possible. Just as Perl sincerely believes in Bontsye's piety that no prosecutorial laugh could ever challenge, just as Abel sincerely believes that a bitter laugh is the only possible climax to Perets' story, so too did Aqiba and his forerunners, the arbiters of the biblical canon, sincerely believe in the sanctity of Song of Songs—regardless of what the text plainly says. After all, just as our modern Yiddish critics are constrained by historical forces that shape the counterpoint they score over Perets' original melody, likewise the early rabbis were constrained by the forces of their own history and traditions to fashion a contrapuntal interpretation that both draws from, and stands against, the Song of Songs.

It is through an understanding of this "sincerely wrong" interpretive approach to an authorized text that we may find our way back from this discussion of "Bontsye Shvayg" to the larger issue that was our point of departure: how to explain the contrapuntal structure of the book of Job. We previously noted that the task faced by the rabbis when they reshaped the interpretation of Song of Songs was not as difficult as the task involved in rethinking Job the Impatient into Job the Patient.[217] But what our discussion of "Bontsye Shvayg" has shown is that—given the right historical circumstances—even so extreme a transformation as that we find in Job is not out of the question. If a Yiddish parody that unremittingly attacks the pietistic norms of its time can be rethought into a paragon of piety, perhaps a similar process can act upon an ancient parody and turn its antihero back into a symbol of patience par excellence.

We can, in fact, look elsewhere in the Bible and find precisely this sort of process in action. Consider, in this connection, the book of Ecclesiastes, especially in terms of its conclusion.[218] Here we find a work that like the poem of Job cannot be so easily reformed in the manner of Canticles into a "holy of holies." R. B. Y. Scott makes precisely this point:

> Ecclesiastes is the strangest book in the Bible, or at any rate the book whose presence in the sacred canons of Judaism and of Christianity is most inexplicable. The Song of Songs with its frankly erotic tone may seem equally out of place. . . .The Song, however, can be interpreted as an allegory of the love of Yahweh for Israel or Christ for his Church. . . .In the case of Ecclesiastes there is no such possibility of allegorization to bring it into line with the tone and teaching of the rest of the Bible. It diverges too radically.[219]

Despite this, an editor writing what amounts to an "afterward" to Qoheleth's[220] work, declares: *bqš qhlt lmṣ' dbry-ḥpṣ wktwb yšr dbry 'mt*, "Qoheleth sought to find elegant language and to write[221] straightforward, truthful words" (Eccles. 12:10). Perhaps we should expect this sort of defense of the message of Ecclesiastes by a sympathetic editor; still, what is much more extraordinary (very much like Aqiba's comments on Song of Songs) is how this editor continues his apology for Qoheleth's message.[222] After several cautionary remarks about the demands and burdens inherent in the study of Wisdom (Eccles. 12:11–12), the editor concludes,

> *swp dbr hkl nšmʿ 't-h'lhym yrʾ wʾt-mṣwtyw šmwr ky-zh kl-h'dm ky 't-kl mʿśh h'lhym ybʾ bmšpṭ ʿl kl-nʿlm 'm-ṭwb wʾm-rʿ*
>
> The conclusion of the matter—all having been heard: Revere God and keep His commandments. For this applies to all mankind.[223] For every deed will God bring to justice; indeed, every hidden thing, whether good or evil. (Eccles. 12:13–14).

As Scott, for example, notes, these remarks are undoubtedly "intended to fix a line of orthodox interpretation which would help to safeguard the faith of the uncritical reader."[224] This is done in the only manner possible—by appending to the book's conclusion universal statements about God's relationship to mankind that reflect the traditional viewpoint of Hebrew Wisdom, the view found, for example, in the book of Proverbs. But here we encounter an interpretive dilemma because, in making these pronouncements, our editor must contradict the essential message found in Ecclesiastes. In particular, the editor's certainty of a divine justice, the judgment of an active Deity who will sort out and appropriately requite both good and evil deeds, even when hidden, directly challenges Qoheleth's view of a God disengaged from mankind. After all, it is clear to anyone who reads Ecclesiastes that Qoheleth sees no possibility of justice in a world that blindly grinds through the cycles of life and death without concern for the particular ends of the wise or foolish, the good or evil.

We might therefore be tempted to conclude that this editor wishes to state that while Qoheleth attempted to cast his worldview in straightforward, truthful terms, Ecclesiastes is, nonetheless, "sincerely wrong." But if our editor's intention was merely to point out how much Qoheleth is in error from the perspective of long-standing, conservative Wisdom tradition, we would have to wonder why he has also taken such great pains to preserve Qoheleth's writings in the first place. Further-more, we would also have to wonder why he has characterized Qoheleth's message as *dbry-'mt* (lit. "words of truth"). Instead, we might have expected him to suppress (or at least not promulgate) so radical a work as Ecclesiastes—despite its sincerity—simply because it so eloquently endeavors to tear down every traditional assumption that our editor, as his final comments reveal, must hold sacred.

In fact, though, these editorial remarks should not be seen as intended simply to challenge or contradict what Qoheleth declares to be true; rather, they must be viewed as explanatory. Like the lover of Perets who knows that "Bontsye Shvayg" has to contain a bitter laugh, our editor has looked at Ecclesiastes and concluded that beyond what it plainly says, it also *has to mean* something else. Of course, from a strictly "logical" point of view, the final, overall meaning—"the end of the matter, all being heard"—that Qoheleth's editor wants to elicit from the text is simply not there. It is "wrong" in the same sense that the pietistic interpretations of "Bontsye Shvayg" are "wrong." But one should not deal with the epilogue of Ecclesiastes in such a logical manner. A better approach is in terms of historical counterpoint.

Once more, we must listen to the polyphonic themes that play between the verses and the traditions. In this respect, the dominant theme is that which Qoheleth himself plays against the long-standing tradition espoused in conservative Wisdom circles. In particular, he wishes to oppose the traditional depiction of God the Involved, with a contrary depiction of what amounts to Anti-God, the Uninvolved. He further wishes to counter the assumption that *hokmah* (Wisdom) is a wise man's means of coming closer to God, of gaining divine favor. Rather, he wishes to portray Wisdom as Anti-Wisdom, that which God has and man does not, a deprivation that inevitably isolates man from the Deity.

But this is not the only theme to be heard in Ecclesiastes. There is a second theme that plays behind the primary melody, that of the conservative tradition itself: the tradition that affirms the righteous action of God and the possibility that man may come closer to God through the diligent acquisition of Wisdom. To be sure, it is Qoheleth's theme that dominates throughout his book; nonetheless, the more traditional theme is always there in contrapuntal harmony, providing the point of reference for every departure—however radical—to be found in Ecclesiastes.

Qoheleth's editor, the author of the verses that conclude Ecclesiastes, responds to both of these themes. On the one hand, he is moved by the eloquence of Qoheleth's language and can see in his message genuine elements of truth. Qoheleth's depiction of the divine plan as a series of natural cycles incapable of being altered by human design or invention is, after all, very much at home in the Ancient Near Eastern milieu where that which is fixed and traditional tends to take precedence over the innovative and new. The cyclic view of Ecclesiastes would therefore be easily accepted by his editor as the basic observation of What Life Is. Moreover, considering that the book of Ecclesiastes comes late in the biblical period, one is tempted to speculate whether the biblically attested cycles of tragedy after tragedy could not have but sharpened the editor's sensitivity and receptivity to Qoheleth's picture of a God who hides Himself from a mankind lacking the Wisdom to find Him. Thus, when this editor declares that Qoheleth "sought to find eloquent language and to write straightforward, truthful words," he also is affirming the worthiness of Qoheleth's message, a worthiness that makes the book well worth both celebration and preservation.

But on the other hand, our editor cannot allow Qoheleth's *dbry-'mt*, "words of truth," to reign supreme. If within the immediate context of Ecclesiastes a radical theme dominates, the editor must also remind his readers (particularly those unused to the rigors and subtleties inherent in Wisdom books) that within the broader context of Jewish tradition, the authorized view must take precedence. It is the final arbiter of Qoheleth's message and therefore the means by which even so contrary a view can be elevated into a traditional context. Thus the editor of Ecclesiastes portrays a Wisdom of contraries, in which Qoheleth's radical "truth" is encapsulated by the larger, conservative "Truth." Both views are thus joined in a biblical counterpoint that must mean more than would the choosing of one to the exclusion of the other.

Beyond this, we must assume that the process through which Ecclesiastes entered the canon also involved a rationale very much like that which guided Qoheleth's editor to preserve this teacher's writings in the first place. As elsewhere, we have little specific knowledge of the steps involved in this process of canonization, although we do know about rabbinical debates over the sanctity of Ecclesiastes similar to those we have noted above in reference to the Song of Songs.[225] Still, the arbiters of the canon must have found the same sense of eloquent truth in Qoheleth's work that his editor found—indeed, that anyone must find who reads this great literary work of art. They might have chosen not to recognize this book or even to suppress it simply because of its author's ability to write so brilliant an attack against the authorized view of God, mankind and the nature of Wisdom. But instead, they determined—much after the manner suggested above for Song of Songs—that such a contrary a view could not be allowed to exist in overt opposition to the pietistic norms. Consequently, Ecclesiastes was embraced in the Aqiban manner so that its radical viewpoints, although still dangerous, would at least be engaged within a sacred context. For once Ecclesiastes was deemed to be sacred, even its most contrary views might be properly rethought in pietistic terms—much as Bontsye Shvayg could be remade within popular Yiddish tradition, once his figure had become sacrosanct. Certainly, Ecclesiastes' editor had already suggested a means by which just this end could be achieved; and it probably did not hurt that at some point in the development of the Qoheleth-tradition, Solomon was enlisted to be the "official" author of this work. Still, the primary motivation for canonizing Ecclesiastes must be seen to involve the legitimization of a process by which even this most challenging attack on the norms of Judaism could be turned in upon itself. In this way Qoheleth could be said in essence to mean more than what the text itself clearly says. One must simply tune one's ear—in the manner of the author of James—to what is heard within the tradition as one reads the text before one's eyes.

Finally, as we turn back to a consideration of the book of Job, we can see that the same process we exemplified in our discussion of "Bontsye Shvayg" and that molded both Song of Songs and Ecclesiastes also worked to mold the canonical shape of the book of Job. What remains for us now is to turn to the aggregate of Job's polyphonic melodies and delineate how its contrapuntal themes are played out.

PART II

8

Barriers to Interpretation and the "Bontsye-Model"

But it is precisely here where we must face our most daunting task; for no longer do we have the luxury of being able to rely confidently on clear-cut historical evidence, as has largely been the case in our discussions above of Y. L. Perets and the nineteenth and twentieth century context in which his "Bontsye Shvayg" was written and subsequently interpreted.

The primary premise on which our contrapuntal interpretations have been based is that traditional literary works cannot be viewed in isolation from their historical and cultural environments if we are properly to understand the dynamics of their development. Rather, we must consider how the forces of history actively work on such texts, shaping and altering them as well as their interpretations. For example, if we are to understand the motivation for Perets' writing of "Bontsye Shvayg," we must recognize that it is a response—indeed, a reaction—to a specific historical event: the pogroms against the Jews in the 1880s. If we are to appreciate why Perets chose the parodistic genre as the form for his story, it helps to know about the more traditional hasidic-type story and the pietistic, "put-your-faith-in-God" attitude that he wished to attack. It is also useful to know that satire and parody were typically the weapons of choice for the Yiddish writers who emerged out of the *Haskala*, the Jewish Enlightenment, and who were intent on educating the masses of East European Jews. If we are to comprehend why the audience for "Bontsye Shvayg" refused to read the story as a parody but rather embraced it as the epitome of the pietistic story it meant to subvert, we need to know about the historical forces that shaped their viewpoint: the rising cycles of violence perpetrated against the Jews, which culminated in the Holocaust.

The trouble is that when we turn from the relatively modern history that shaped "Bontsye Shvayg" back to the ancient history that shaped the canonical form of the book of Job and its earliest interpretations, we are seriously handicapped by the paucity of evidence. To be sure, we can speak generally of certain historical events that *may* have played a role in shaping the book of Job and how it was understood: for example, the downfall of the northern kingdom of Israel at the hand of the Assyrians (eighth century B.C.E.), the destruction of the Temple in Jerusalem by the Babylonians and the Exile (sixth century B.C.E.), the persecutions involved in the attempt to Hellenize the Jews in Seleucid Palestine (second century B.C.E.), the Christian persecutions by the Romans and the First and Second Jewish Revolts and their disastrous aftermaths (first and second centuries C.E.). Still, we cannot connect these or any other historical events *specifically* to the development of the Joban counterpoint.

There are significant reasons why this is so. First and foremost, we have no firm criteria by which to associate any part of the poetic sections of the book of Job with even a rough sense of date. Only when we come to the Prose Frame Story do we begin to gain a somewhat more certain historical fix. As noted above, this is particularly due to Hurvitz, whose linguistic arguments have convincingly placed the Prologue/Epilogue sometime within the post-Exilic period (although just how early or late in the post-Exile is anybody's guess).[226] If the arguments presented in this study are correct, the Poem of Job must predate these prose brackets; still, there is no certain means of determining just how far back we should push the dating of the Poem. Is it post-Exilic, Exilic, or pre-Exilic? Scholars can muster problematical hypotheses to back any of these competing date-scenarios,[227] but the lack of definitive evidence precludes any conclusive judgments. Thus we are left without a means of anchoring the Poem of Job to any chronology.

Moreover, there is a second problem: Just what do we mean by the "Poem of Job" in the first place? Or, to put this more precisely, what should we consider the "original" Poem of Job and what (if anything) should we consider later additions and interpolations? Once again, there is a wide range of scholarly opinion.

Some scholars are prepared to argue that Job is a complete unit with a single author from start to finish—even including the Prose Frame Story. In fact, lately there has been a notable resurgence of arguments in favor of the literary unity of the book of Job.[228] However, the prevailing opinion, which I also endorse, is that the Poem of Job, like many Ancient Near Eastern literary works, has attracted a number of interpolated compositions.[229] The most obvious candidate for such an addition is the Elihu cycle of speeches (Job 32–37). As D. N. Freedman notes, the reasons for viewing the Elihu speeches as an addition to the Poem of Job are fairly obvious:

> It is generally agreed by scholars that the Elihu speeches in the book of Job. . .did not belong to the original draft of the work but constitute an addition to it. As evidence in support of this view, it is pointed out that Elihu appears nowhere else in the book, not even in the Epilogue where he ought to have been noticed along with the other participants. Further his speeches interrupt the continuity of the Dialogue (between Job's final challenge to God in chap. 31 and the divine response in chap. 38). Finally the speeches contribute little if anything to the content or movement of the book.[230]

Another section of Job that has long been singled out by scholars as a likely interpolation is chapter 28, the "Hymn to Wisdom." Unlike every other discourse in the book, this has no introductory formula (e.g., "Then ——— answered. . ."). Moreover, it is not obviously related to the immediate context; that is, it does not naturally follow upon Job's declarations in chapter 27, nor, for that matter, is it consistent with the viewpoint expounded by Job throughout the previous poetic Dialogue. Rather, it has all the earmarks of a separate composition that has been placed in its particular position (just at the conclusion of the Dialogues between Job and his Three Friends but before Job's Final Speech) to give a broader perspective on the themes of the debate. Thus, scholars have tended to view the Hymn to Wisdom as essentially an editorial gloss that, as Pope notes, is "almost universally recognized as extraneous."[231]

Beyond these two proposed interpolations, there is a good deal less consensus among scholars as to whether any other section of the Poem is best viewed as a later addition. Still, a good many exegetes have argued that the Theophany—God's confrontation with Job from the whirlwind (Job 38–42:6)—has been added to a debate whose closure was already signalled by the statement, "The words of Job are ended" (*tmw dbry 'ywb*) in 32:40. Still others are willing to accept the authenticity of the initial speech of God (Job 38–39) but query whether the second speech, focusing on Behemoth and Leviathan (40–41), is not best viewed as both redundant and secondary.[232] And, of course, scholars have also pinpointed various other passages scattered throughout the Poem as potential interpolations.[233]

There is also the question whether the original Poem has suffered any deletions.[234] This issue is especially relevant to the Third Cycle of debate between Job and his Three Friends (Job 22–27). While this exchange begins in exactly the same manner as the previous cycles of debate with a speech by Eliphaz (chapter 22) and a response by Job (chapter 23), the text beginning at 24:18 shows every indication of having been altered and/or disturbed during the course of its transmission in antiquity.

Here we suddenly find Job taking a line of argument in verses 18–25 that God is a deity of strict justice who always requites to the wicked the punishment they richly deserve. At the end of this speech Job would seem to declare (24:24–25) that the wicked "may lead the high life just a moment; then they are nothing. . . .and if it is not just so, who would prove me false and deem my point worth nothing?" (*rwmw m't w'ynnw. . .w'm-l' 'pw my ykzybny wyśm l'l mlty*). The answer to this rhetorical question might easily be lifted from the earlier speeches of Job himself. Indeed, the argument expressed here is diametrically opposed to the Joban worldview we find elsewhere in the Poem (see, e.g., Job 9:22–24) and seems, rather, to fall in line with the opinion typically advocated by Job's Three Friends (see, e.g., 8:13–22). Consequently, scholars have generally viewed Job 24:18–25 as a misplaced speech of one of Job's Friends that now fills out the conclusion of an apparently truncated pronouncement of Job.[235]

Directly after this, there are indications of further textual confusion. Bildad's response to Job (Job 25:1–6) seems to have lost its beginning;[236] furthermore, the speech is uncharacteristically brief, consisting in its entirety of only five verses. Both points taken together suggest the obvious likelihood that we now have only a fragment of what was once a much longer text. When we turn to chapter 26, now labeled as Job's response to Bildad, it is hard to determine just who was originally speaking to whom. The text of verses 2–4 might be viewed as an ironic diatribe by Job against Bildad. On the other hand, it would not be hard to imagine the same speech being used by one of the Friends to upbraid Job.[237] The rest of the speech (Job 26:5–14) consists of an extended praise of the power of God. Yet, once again, it shows indications of having lost (or having been detached from) its beginning.[238] Then, just when we would expect a response from Zophar, the third of Job's

Friends, in chapter 27, we find instead that this speech is entirely lacking. Rather, chapter 27 is labeled as yet another speech of Job's (presumably, the one we would expect as a response to Zophar, which would then conclude this third round of the debate). Whoever placed the editorial introductions at the beginning of each of the speeches in the Poem of Job seems sensitive to the obvious problem that an expected response is now absent. Instead of beginning Job's speech in chapter 27 with the standard introductory formula always employed previously (lit. "Then so-and-so answered and said. . . ." [*wy'n* PN *wy'mr*]), a different formula is introduced: *wysp 'ywb ś't mšlw wy'mr*, "Then Job once more took up his discourse and said. . . ." Thus, the editor essentially acknowledges that there is something missing here, that Job, quite literally, has to "add" (*ysp*) to his response in order to compensate for this unexpected loss. In sum: the current state of the Third Cycle in the Joban debate seems to be quite a mess from a text-critical standpoint, and there is little hope that we can now properly reshuffle what remains into its original order,[239] let alone reclaim what has been lost. As the discussion above indicates, we are therefore confronted with quite an array of potential additions and subtractions to the original Poem of Job. Even if we may feel that we can sort these out with reasonable confidence, nonetheless, there is little likelihood that we can develop certain criteria by which to judge the order in which changes occurred nor can we even make a serious guess as to when various changes might have taken place or under what particular circumstances. Obviously, these problems also place a severe handicap upon our ability to consider in any subtle manner just how the interplay of editorial and historical forces shaped the canonical form of the book of Job.

But the problems do not end even here; for there is yet one other difficulty that tends to inhibit our ability to analyze the structure of Job: Specifically, what are we to make of the unusual dialect of Hebrew in which most of the Poem is written; and how are we to assess its implications? We have already alluded briefly to the fact that the Hebrew of the Job Poem is a good deal different from that found in any other portion of the Bible.[240] An indication of just how distinctive this Hebrew is can be judged by the variety of theories scholars have brought forward to explain its eccentricities.

One of the most prominent of such proposals is the so-called "Edomite" theory first suggested by the eminent biblical historian, R. H. Pfeiffer.[241] He has suggested that the Poem of Job was a literary product of the school of Wisdom that, as the Bible mentions in various places, centered in Edom, especially in the Edomite city of Teman.[242] Thus, its peculiar language would be more properly designated as Edomite rather than Hebrew. N. H. Tur-Sinai, one of the most formidable philologists to devote sustained attention to the book of Job, has endeavored to explain the oddities of the Poem's Hebrew in a different, though somewhat similar, manner. He believes that Job was originally written in Aramaic and was subsequently translated (often, he frequently argues, incorrectly!) into Hebrew.[243] Yet another proposal has been brought forward that the original language of Job was essentially more Arabic than Hebrew.[244]

None of these or other similar theories has achieved broad scholarly backing, nor is it my intention to endorse any of them as correct.[245] In fact, as our knowledge of the Northwest Semitic[246] languages has continued to grow, scholars have come to realize that there was a broad spectrum of related but distinct dialects within the linguistic sphere of ancient Syria-Palestine.[247] In such a circumstance, a unique although essentially "Hebrew" dialect of the sort we find in the book of Job is hardly to be considered all that extraordinary.[248]

Still, the fact that the Hebrew of the Job Poem cannot be easily equated with more "standard" biblical Hebrew (poetic or otherwise) highlights a potentially serious problem: Namely, we cannot be sure that the Poem of Job was written within a specifically Israelite/Jewish cultural milieu; that is, we cannot take it as a matter of course that the writer of the Poem was a Jew or an Israelite and thus someone intimately familiar with other literary works found in the rest of the Bible.

Granted, it does seem clear that the view of the deity found in the Poem is not dramatically different from the depiction of God we find elsewhere in the Scriptures. In particular, the fact that throughout the book of Job we are essentially in a world dominated by a single, omnipotent God rather than in a world populated by numerous, powerful deities,[249] reinforces the likelihood that the religious worldview of the Poem of Job has much in common with that found predominantly in the rest of the Bible. However, we really cannot go further than this. After all, our knowledge of religious beliefs and practices within the broader environs of ancient Israel and Judah are dramatically limited. It may well be that Israelites were the only group within these environs to develop a religion centered exclusively on a single "God-like" deity, but this need not necessarily be so.[250] Indeed, it might well be argued on methodological grounds that such a *sui generis* religion is most unlikely.[251] Rather, just as the Job Poem's dialect shows a clear connection with the rest of biblical Hebrew but is nonetheless capable of being linguistically separated from it,[252] so it may be that the religious-cultural environment of the Poem of Job shows a relationship to Israelite/Jewish religion but is still a thing unto itself.

But if this is so, or at least possibly so, we must take care not to assume a direct and facile relationship between the Poem of Job and the rest of the Bible. For example, while it may be fair to say that the author of the Poem is certainly familiar with the worldview found in the book of Proverbs, it does not necessarily follow that he knew of the book of Proverbs *itself* (or some part thereof preserved within Israelite/Jewish circles) or that he was reacting specifically to the book of Proverbs. While his language and poetic style may show some affinities with the writings of Jeremiah[253] or Second Isaiah,[254] we cannot further grant that the poet had actually read or known about either of these Jewish prophets (or, conversely, that either one of them knew about the Poem, or poet, of Job). While the text of the Poem may apparently quote or show familiarity with poetic passages also known, for example, from the Psalms,[255] it does not necessarily follow that the poet had read (or heard) these passages in a specifically Israelite/Jewish environment or even that he recognized them as specifically Psalmic passages.

Obviously, the fact that the Poem of Job is in the Bible is proof positive that it ultimately entered into normative Jewish circles. But simply because it ended up in this religious-cultural environment, we cannot be certain that it began there as well.[256] And if the Job Poem originally had an existence outside a specifically Israelite/Jewish sphere, we then have no clear criteria by which to determine just how close to that sphere it was initially nor when it entered that sphere nor what circumstances prompted this entry. This, therefore, is also a serious barrier to our properly interpreting the development of the historical counterpoint that ultimately resulted in the book of Job as we find it in the biblical canon.

As the above survey makes abundantly clear, however we choose to proceed in interpreting the development of the book of Job, we will be launched on what can only be a highly speculative exercise. The fact that there are already such a large and disparate array of scholarly interpretations is ample demonstration that the limited nature of the hard evidence allows for a wide latitude of choices and conclusions. In consideration of this, our best course will be to consider the overall structure of the book of Job only in the broadest of terms. This is not to say that minutely detailed reconstructions of the formation of the book of Job are inherently wrong or wrongheaded. It is simply that any overly complex and precise reconstruction, postulating, for example, redaction-after-redaction and attempting to place even the smallest editorial element in its proper place, becomes too esoteric an exercise to be all that useful, let alone convincing. Rather, we must respect the limitations of the evidence and try, at best, to catch just a sense of the dynamics that shaped what ultimately became the book of Job without becoming enmeshed in too microscopic an exposition.

In doing so, perhaps we can open up a fruitful avenue of scholarly interpretation by doing what we have done before: playing Job against Bontsye. After all, we have already developed a sustained argument that there is a useful analogy between "Bontsye Shvayg" and the book of Job, especially when they are seen against their respective cultural environments. If this analogy has genuine validity, it may have facility as well; that is, since we cannot really track the historical counterpoint to be heard among the various strands of Job in specific terms, perhaps we can utilize the process we have traced for the development of "Bontsye Shvayg" within Yiddish tradition as a framework for contrapuntal interpretation.

Using this "Bontsye-model," we may better be able to "read the score" of the ancient biblical composition by hearing in the polyphony of its various editorial levels much the same series of actions and reactions, interpretations and reinterpretations that we found in the more modern Yiddish composition and its subsequent interpretations. To be sure, other factors, which we have discussed above also must contribute to our criteria for judgment; especially, the manifest discontinuities and dislocations in the book as well as its stylistic and linguistic disparities. Still, a close analysis of these factors alone cannot aid us very much in understanding the motivations that lie behind the decisions that resulted in the book of Job. However, by seeing Job in terms of the Bontsye-model, we may perhaps be able to gain a better insight: not only a consideration of the editorial mechanics that led to the canonical book of Job but also a better sense of their relationship to one another and their rationale.

9

The Art of Parody:
The Dialogue/Appeal

We can begin by considering the "original" Poem, or, more precisely, by defining the dimensions of the original Poem in terms of the Bontsye-model. As I have already argued, the poet who wrote this literary masterpiece was motivated by much the same aims, and functioned within a cultural context analogous to that, which motivated Perets to write "Bontsye Shvayg." Like Perets, the Job poet was intent upon "slaying the sacred cow"—a pietistic worldview in which righteous suffering always receives an inevitable, even a miraculous, reward. Moreover, the poet achieved this end in the same way Perets did, by subverting tradition: converting a famous symbol of this pietistic attitude into its opposite—Job the Patient into Job the Impatient.

Granting this analogy between Job and Bontsye, there are certain collateral assumptions that follow. First and foremost, the Poem of Job is best defined as the portion of the biblical book that, like "Bontsye Shvayg," maintains a sharply critical line against the pietistic worldview that the poet, like Perets, wished to attack. In specific terms, this would essentially mean that the debate between Job and his Three Friends, as well as Job's final speech (chapters 29–31)[257] would be taken to be part of the original Poem, whereas the "Hymn to Wisdom" and the Elihu speeches, both of which function to mitigate the critical line, would be taken to be secondary. Also, the entire Theophany, since it maintains essentially the same sharp attack against the pietistic viewpoint, especially in terms of its depiction of the nature of God, is also taken to be a part of the original Poem. Indeed, it is best considered as its thematic denouement.

None of this is particularly surprising—especially as regards the Wisdom Hymn and Elihu. As the discussion above has already indicated, scholars have long had ample grounds for considering these parts of Job as secondary. My inclusion of the Theophany as part of the original Job Poem is also scarcely a controversial view-point. The speeches of God from the storm maintain a logical continuity with what precedes them in the Dialogue and serve to reinforce the Poem's basic themes. Even if we were to assume that the Theophany was penned by a second poet, we would have to grant that he was a brilliant disciple intent on bringing the original master's work to a climactic conclusion.[258] If the fairly conventional view of the Poem presented here were the only product of considering Job in terms of the Bontsye-

93

model, there would be little point in drawing the comparison. However, there are other more subtle characteristics in the Poem, which become clearer when we probe our analogy more deeply. Specifically, our analysis of Perets' short story as a parody of a tradition, has shown certain factors coming into play that are also useful when considering what the Job poet was trying to achieve.

These factors are those inherent in parody, and which I have discussed in some detail above. I have noted that in order for a parody to work, it must have an underlying traditional theme (or a series of such themes) as a point of reference against which it can play its counterpoint. There can be no question that Perets wrote "Bontsye Shvayg" with precisely such thematic ideas in mind. It is for this reason that his short story is best understood when contrasted to more traditional Yiddish stories, for example, stories like his own "If Not Still Higher," "The Messenger" and "Joy within Joy."

Similarly, if we are truly to understand the Poem of Job, we must consider what its poet wished to turn inside out for purposes of parody. Of course, we have already done this in the most general of terms by arguing that the poet focused on the legend of Job (as reconstructed above) and proceeded to reverse its thematic correspondences—Job into Anti-Job, Friends into Anti-Friends and so on. However, if the Poem works as a parody in these broad terms, it should do so on a smaller scale as well; that is, just as Perets drew on a whole array of Yiddish themes and types for purposes of his satire (e.g., the trial in heaven, the poor but pious hero, just recompense for righteous suffering, the humble wish greatly rewarded, etc.), so, too, should we expect to find that the poet of Job drew on a repertoire of themes and types from his own cultural milieu as the points against which to play his parodistic counterpoint.

Unfortunately, isolating such themes and types in Job is not as easy as is it is in "Bontsye Shvayg." In the latter instance, we have a relative wealth of contemporaneous information, both historical and literary, from which to draw. In the former case, we cannot even be sure what *is* contemporary to the writing of the Poem and, in any case, examples of potential literary comparisons are pitifully small. On the other hand, two factors weigh in our favor.

First, Job as a literary work clearly stands within the "Wisdom" tradition; and the literature identified with this tradition,[259] more than any other type in the Ancient Near East, seems impervious to parochialism. Rather, there is a marked sense of a shared worldview within all Ancient Near Eastern Wisdom writings, whether they be found in Egypt, Mesopotamia or Israel and its environs. Thus, it is reasonable to assume that the poet of Job essentially drew on basically the same Wisdom repertoire as that we find reflected elsewhere.

Second, literature within the Ancient Near East is remarkably conservative. Texts and types of texts typically have a longevity that stretches from centuries even to millennia. So we need not be overly concerned whether a given theme or type manifest in Ancient Near Eastern literature was closely contemporary with the Poem of Job or not. Rather, we can allow ourselves broad diachronic latitude when considering other literary texts or genres from which to draw potential comparisons.

I believe that we should make the same assumptions about the writer of the Poem of Job as we have shown to be true about Perets, namely, that he was acutely aware of the literary context of his art and that he drew on numerous motifs from within this milieu that his audience would easily and quickly recognize. To some degree, a certain amount of his parodistic art is inevitably lost on the modern reader; for in many cases—perhaps even in the majority—we are ignorant of the traditions that serve as the butt of parody. Still, when we *can* isolate a given theme or genre, drawing upon our broader knowledge of Ancient Near Eastern literature, then we can see how the poet manipulates it to serve his larger end.

No attempt will be made here to be comprehensive in considering such themes; indeed, our ignorance of many of the traditions utilized by the poet of Job precludes any possibility of our doing so.[260] Still, we can note sufficient examples of the poet of Job playing off tradition to make the point.

We can start with a consideration of the genres that inform the basic structure of the Poem itself, first as a dialogue between Job and his Friends and then as an appeal by Job to his God. In this instance we have a fair amount of material from out of the Mesopotamian Wisdom tradition to draw on for purposes of comparison. The most obvious such parallel is a text usually called the *Theodicy* or *Babylonian Theodicy*.[261] It dates from approximately 1000 B.C.E. but seems to have been known in editions as late as the Seleucid period.[262]

We will not attempt a detailed analysis of the Theodicy here, but even a cursory examination shows clear affinities to the Poem of Job. In both cases the focus is on a "Righteous Sufferer," that is, one who has been abandoned to severe affliction and misfortune by his patron deity (or deities) despite the fact that the Sufferer has done no wrong. Indeed, on the contrary, a point is made in both the *Theodicy* and the Poem of Job that the afflicted protagonist has been especially righteous and most solicitous to honor and worship his patron god. The *Theodicy* also parallels the form of the Job Poem in that it depicts the Sufferer engaged in a Dialogue with a Friend, who essentially tries to justify the deity's ways to man. Of particular note are the many points highlighted in the Dialogue of the *Theodicy* that are also to be found in Job's Dialogue with his Three Friends.[263] For example, just as Job cries out that God subverts the good and upholds the wicked, so, too, does the Sufferer in the *Theodicy*.[264] Just as Eliphaz affirms that on the contrary, the good are always rewarded and the wicked punished, so, too, does the Friend in the *Theodicy*.[265] Just as Job chronicles the drastic nature of his afflictions, so can the Sufferer in the *Theodicy* match him with a similar litany of adversities.[266] Indeed, it would be quite possible to lift whole sections from the *Theodicy* and place them in Job (or vice versa) without noticeable effect.

It is hardly to be viewed as a coincidence that both the author of Job and the author of the *Theodicy* chose the Dialogue-form as a major organizing structure to express their similar themes.[267] Rather, it is much more probable that both these writers were drawing on a common genre from out of the Wisdom tradition that would be well known to their respective, ancient audiences.[268] Still, in one respect the Poem of Job is more expansive than the *Theodicy*. The latter text stays within the confines of a Dialogue between Sufferer and Friend, but the former goes further in having Job address God directly and even receive a response from the Deity. But this is almost certainly not to be viewed as an innovation on the part of the Job poet. Rather, once again, he is playing off a particular literary genre also manifest in texts from both Mesopotamia and Syria. This is a type of text we might characterize as the "Righteous Sufferer's appeal to the deity."[269]

The most famous such text comes from Mesopotamia and is usually called after its ancient name, "*Ludlul bēl nēmeqi*,"—often abbreviated to *Ludlul*—(lit., "I will praise the Lord of Wisdom," the first line of the text).[270] Once more, the similarities of *Ludlul* to the Poem of Job are unmistakable, indeed, sometimes this Mesopotamian work is simply called the "Babylonian Job."[271] The focus of attention is upon a Job-like Sufferer, that is, a figure burdened with afflictions and misfortunes despite his righteousness and his devotion to his deity (Marduk, the patron deity of Babylon). In this case the entire work is a long appeal by the Sufferer (whose name apparently is Shubshi-meshre-Shakkan; cf. tablet 3, line 43) addressed to Marduk, who has apparently abandoned him to unmerited evil (see, e.g., tablet 1, lines 43–44). The Sufferer chronicles his distresses in great detail, and, not surprisingly, they are much the same as those that befell Job.[272] Also like Job, the Sufferer wonders about the ways of a god who would abandon such a devoted servant (tablet 2, lls. 29–36):

> I instructed my land to keep the god's rites,
> I taught my people to value the goddess' name.
> I made praise of the king like a god's,
> And taught the populace reverence for the palace.
> I wish I knew that these things were pleasing to one's god!
> What is good to oneself is an offense to god;
> What in one's mind seems despicable, is proper to one's god,
> Who knows the will of the gods in heaven?[273]

Finally, the Sufferer's appeal gets a response from his god. In fact, several divine emissaries from Marduk come to him in a dream, heralding his complete recovery from all setbacks and afflictions. The last of these declares (tablet 3, lls. 42–44):

> Marduk has sent me.
> To Shubshi-meshre-Shakkan I have brought prosperity,
> From Marduk's pure hands I have brought prosperity.

There are several other texts that exhibit much the same features we find in *Ludlul*. For example, one such text comes out of the Sumerian Wisdom tradition (c. 1700 B.C.E.). Just as *Ludlul* is sometimes called the "Babylonian Job," so this text has been typically deemed the "Sumerian Job."[274] It also is essentially a chronicle of the sufferings a god has inflicted on an innocent man coupled with an appeal from this Righteous Sufferer for relief from all his divinely inspired woes. And just as is the case in *Ludlul*, the appeal of the victim is granted: "[His prayers and petitions] his god heard. . .the righteous words, the artless words uttered by him, his god accepted" (lines 118, 120). Thereafter, the Sufferer's cries of distress are turned into songs of praise and joy.

The two other examples that appear to be of the same literary genre come respectively from Babylon (19th century B.C.E.)[275] and Ugarit on the coast of Syria (14th century B.C.E.).[276] Both show the expected pattern, an appeal by a Righteous Sufferer to a patron god, which is ultimately answered by the god sending relief from strife. Thus, we see that this sort of text was well established in the Wisdom traditions of the Ancient Near East, and we can assume with fair confidence that the author of Job was familiar with this genre of writing and decided to incorporate this motif into his Poem. In fact, it would appear that the poet of Job determined to amalgamate two genres together, coupling Dialogue with Appeal—the common denominator in both types being the focus upon a Righteous Sufferer—a figure that is certainly quite appropriate as a model for Job.[277]

However, there is more involved here than just the incorporation of what probably were well-known literary stereotypes into organizing structures of the Poem of Job. Just like Perets, the author of Job has much sharper intentions than simply this. More important than merely identifying the literary genres the poet of Job utilized is recognizing how he has manipulated them to serve his ends.

Several points can be made. First, I suspect that the poet chose to utilize the Dialogue/Appeal forms because they contrast dramatically with the tenor of the original Job legend in one major respect: their verbosity. Of course, the only definitive source we have for the Job legend is its late reworking in the Prose Frame Story. Still, even here we can catch a strong sense of the laconic style, the sort of "bare bones," direct narrative that probably was the hallmark of the original folk tale and that is often cited as being characteristic of the best biblical prose.

In particular, the Job depicted in the Prose Frame Story is a man of few words. When confronted with messenger after messenger bringing news of disaster after disaster, he meets them all in stoic silence. Only after they have finally concluded relaying their dreadful news does he piously respond in a short, pithy, proverbial fashion, declaring forthrightly that he accepts all misfortune and still blesses God (see Job 1:21). When plague overtakes Job himself, again he does not cry out. Only when his wife begins to speak of blasphemy, does he feel constrained to silence her with the simple statement that one must accept whatever God sends, whether good or evil (2:10).

In many respects, the Job we find in the prose narrative is therefore very similar to the Abraham of the *Akedah*. And, just as with Abraham, it is as important to listen to Job's silences as it is to hear what he says. While, certainly, neither Job nor Abraham is as close-mouthed as Bontsye, they do share that same sense of restraint and resignation that is looked upon in folk stories of this nature as epitomizing the pietistic ideal—the sort of silence that Wiesel saw as the very essence of Bontsye Shvayg.[278]

This Job the Silent was therefore a natural target for the author of the Poem to turn inside out. Hence, when he decided to convert Job into Anti-Job, he looked for a literary form that would allow him to transform a figure previously known for his taciturn piety into an articulate speechmaker who could opine over his woeful situation at length. The Dialogue/Appeal form was an excellent choice through which to accomplish this goal. I suspect that the shock of this "playing against type" had considerable impact on an ancient audience familiar with the Job folk story: indeed, this impact seems reminiscent of the sense of disjunction one feels in Greenberg's "Bontsye Shvayg and Y. L. Perets in the Warsaw Ghetto," where the previously inarticulate Bontsye suddenly finds such a rhetorically eloquent voice.[279]

Moreover, this transformation of Job the Silent into Job the Verbose serves the poet's parodistic end on a thematic level as well. By substituting the Dialogue/Appeal form for the original, laconic folk form, the poet deftly counters what likely was one of the original points of the story: that piety is best exemplified by brevity, that a faithful "patience" in the face of unmerited disaster requires little explanation or elaboration.[280] One is reminded of Perets' similar intent to undercut the view that silent suffering is to be praised rather than condemned, his desire to educate his people so that they will not only speak out but also demand a great deal.

Beyond this, the choice of the Dialogue/Appeal form by the poet of Job has further facility because of the opportunities it opens for parodistic manipulation. As I have noted above, in many respects the Job poet closely follows the stereotypical formulas characteristic of such texts; but at the same time he subtly and ironically twists them around so they are not quite what they should be: Just as Perets does with "Bontsye Shvayg" the poet of Job substitutes a masquerade for the real thing.

Note, in particular, how the poet depicts Job—especially in terms of his relationship to God—as opposed to how the Righteous Sufferer is normally portrayed in conventional Dialogue/Appeal texts. S. N. Kramer succinctly describes the role a typical Righteous Sufferer must play: ". . .in cases of suffering and adversity, no matter how seemingly unjustified, the victim has but one valid and effective recourse, and that is to continually glorify his god and keep wailing and lamenting before him until he turns a favorable ear to his prayers."[281] This is an essential point in the Dialogue/Appeal genre: that the innocent victim must always keep his complaints within the bounds of propriety. He can wail about his desperate condition at length and in detail, but he must do so humbly while always maintaining a respect for his patron god at all costs. After all, the point of the complaint is to get the patron god first to listen and then to act in the Sufferer's favor. Therefore, a Righteous Sufferer pleads, cajoles, begs, perhaps even nags his god. But he dare not speak too sharply lest he provoke the deity to anger and thereby completely undermine any likelihood of gaining the god's sympathy. Indeed, he should give every indication that he is ready to substitute praise for despair at even the first hint of a divine pity for his abject condition.

As scholars have often pointed out,[282] in essence, the discourses found in stereotypical Dialogue/Appeal texts therefore have much in common with the sort of personal lament one often encounters among the Psalms. One can compare Psalm 73, for example,[283] where a Righteous Sufferer cries out: "Alas, for nothing have I maintained my mind's purity and have washed my hands in innocence!" (73:13) or Psalm 22 which begins with the famous lament: "My God, my God, why have You forsaken me?" (22:2). Yet in each case (as in many similar examples) the apparent hopelessness is not absolute. The author of Psalm 73 finds his despair giving way to hopeful praise on entering God's sanctuary (73:17). He recognizes that there is nowhere else for him to turn but to God: "Who else for me in heaven?. . .My body and mind may fail but God is my mind's strength and portion forever!" (73:25, 26). Likewise, out of the depths of despair in Psalm 22 comes the call, "But You, God, do not stay distant!" (22:20), which becomes a preamble to deliverance and praise.

By its very nature, this lament-form directs attention toward the Sufferer. The victim says to his god and fellow human beings alike, "Look at me, pity me!" This, of course is precisely the intent in the Dialogue/Appeal texts we have considered above. Note, for example the concluding plea of the Sufferer in the *Theodicy*: "You are kind my Friend; behold my grief. Help me; look on my distress; know it" (lines 287–288). But it is precisely this fixed attention on the Righteous Sufferer that the poet of Job is determined to break. As I have suggested above,[284] the intent of this Joban author is to redirect our attention. So his Sufferer does not so much say, "Look at me," but just the opposite: "Look at Him; look at God." In doing this, the writer of Job initiates a dramatic departure from convention.

The poet achieves this end by having Job raise the one issue that is always delicately avoided in the Dialogue/Appeal genre as well as in the personal laments they so closely resemble: the issue of the righteousness of (a) god. It is the question that is, as I have proposed earlier, at the heart of the Poem of Job: If a god can allow or even instigate adverse action against a righteous and worshipful human being, can he be viewed as a moral deity?[285] The poet of Job transforms the role of the stereotypical Righteous Sufferer in order to dramatize this question. To be sure, his protagonist takes on all the expected trappings of the Righteous Sufferer when Job chronicles his abject condition—all the indignities and plagues that have befallen him. But while a "proper" Righteous Sufferer would never question the righteousness of God, the Job of the Poem goes on the attack, stating forthrightly that a Deity who would afflict the innocent and leave the wicked unpunished cannot be just:

> When the scourge suddenly strikes down
> The ordeal of the guiltless He mocks.
> Earth is given into the hand of the wicked;
> The faces of His judges He covers:
> If not He, then who?   (Job 9:23–24)

While the "correct" role of a Righteous Sufferer is to plead for help from an inscrutable god, Job instead demands justice or, more properly, he demands that God be just:

> Though He may kill me, I will not wait,
> I will still argue my rights before Him.
> Indeed, this is my salvation;
> For he who is impious dare not come before Him.
> Look now: I have prepared my case.
> I know I will be acquitted.
> Who will litigate with me?   (Job 13:15–19a)

This Sufferer is not going to lie down and beg; instead, Job forthrightly calls on God to redress his grievances for a simple and obvious reason—because it is the only right thing for God to do.

Of course, issues of justice and righteousness do play a role in the standard Dialogue/Appeal. But in all cases, questions of innocence and guilt are kept within the human sphere. The issue is never, Is God just? but rather, Is a particular man (i.e., the Sufferer) just? or, more broadly, Can *any* man be just? The Friend in the *Theodicy* makes these kinds of queries and draws his "just" conclusions; so, too, do the Three Friends in the Poem of Job. In this respect, the poet seems to have adopted the traditional Friend-role of the Dialogue-form into his work with little modification.[286] Yet even here, we can note some distinction between the way a

Friend approaches a Sufferer in the *Theodicy* and how the Job poet plays off this tradition.

In the *Theodicy*, I think it is fair to say, the Friend endeavors to be a genuine comforter to the victim-in-distress. He may chide the Righteous Sufferer; he may remind him of what has long been taught to be so—that no innocent has ever been punished in vain and that, in fact, it is quite impossible for a man to claim complete innocence. But this is done without rancor and with all due sympathy for the Sufferer. The Friend always tries to soothe his distressed colleague, as if to say: "I know that it is your pain that makes you cry out in distress. I share your pain, I wish to help you endure it in the only way possible, by submitting to our god and pleading for mercy."

One can especially see that the bond of sympathy between Friend and Sufferer is never broken in that they continually maintain an air of mutual respect and courtesy. With hardly an exception, they both are sure to compliment one another at the beginning of their respective discourses. For example, the Friend will call the Sufferer, "O palm, tree of wealth, my precious brother, endowed with all Wisdom";· and the Sufferer will then respond, "Your mind is a north wind, a pleasant breeze for the peoples. Choice Friend, your advice is fine."[287] This continues throughout their debate, even as they proceed to deny the validity of each other's points.

This sort of courtly behavior might be taken to be pro forma, or simply exaggerated and insincere; but it seems more likely that it connotes a genuine sense of identity between Friend and Sufferer. The former desires to be a genuine aid, and, even more significantly, his words do indeed seem to bring some measure of comfort to the latter. Perhaps the clearest indication of how genuine is the relationship between Sufferer and Friend is how they each express themselves in their last exchange. Here, the identity of the Friend with the victim is so strong that he appears almost to go over to the Sufferer's side. He declares that the gods have given mankind "distorted speech; they endowed mankind with lies and not truth, forever" (lines 279–280). Moreover, his final words (lines 283–286) seem to match the level of despair previously found only in the Sufferer's speeches:

> Like a thief they [the gods] treat a poor man
> They lavish slander upon him and plot his murder,
> They cause all evil to seize him, like a criminal, because he has no *protection*;
> Terrifyingly they break him down and extinguish him like a flame!

Yet it is precisely at this point that the Sufferer seems to be able to achieve the reconciliation and peace that the Friend had previously urged him to strive for. Thus, the victim finally pleads, "May the god, who has thrown me away, give help! May the goddess, who has [abandoned me] show mercy!" (lines 295–296).

At the end, it may be the Friend's willingness to identify with the Sufferer, to take on his very arguments, that allows the victim finally to come to his own revelation. Because the Friend is ultimately willing to grant that much of what the Sufferer has said is true, so this seems to stimulate the victim into a recognition of a greater truth: that however inexplicable the gods may be, man's only recourse is to accept them and seek their aid. This is a key point in the *Theodicy*: in the final analysis, the Friend is deemed to be right; the arguments of the Sufferer are taken to be wrong—or perhaps we should say "sincerely wrong." The conclusion of the *Theodicy* must be seen much in the same way we saw the conclusion of Ecclesiastes: as a case where a radical truth is finally encompassed (but not replaced) by a traditional truth.[288] Moreover, in the final analysis the *Theodicy* must also be seen as a hopeful document that looks forward to the divine aid, sure to come, which will rescue the Sufferer from all his distress.[289]

When we compare the *Theodicy* to the Poem of Job, it becomes clear that the author of the latter has developed a very different class of Friend for his protagonist. Indeed, he has cast the relationship between his Sufferer and colleagues in a manner that seems especially designed to subvert the conventions of the Dialogue-form, as sketched above.

For one thing, the poet goes to great lengths to emphasize that there is little love lost between Job and his Friends. To be sure, when Eliphaz initiates the first of the Friends' retorts to Job's speeches, he does begin in a delicate, sympathetic fashion, reminiscent of the *Theodicy*: "Should one try a word with you, would you be weary?" (Job 4:2)[290] But very soon after this, sympathy gives way to sarcasm on the part of the Friends, a ridicule that Job returns in kind. Thus, Bildad is moved to chastise Job in blunt fashion: "How long will you speak thus: A great wind are the utterances of your mouth!" (8:2). And Job has his own blast at the Friends: "I have heard too much of this! Hapless comforters are you all. Is there an end to words of wind? What possesses you to speak so?" (16:2–3). These cutting remarks about one's wisdom being a "great wind" or "words of wind" are certainly quite another thing from the "pleasant breeze" by which the wisdom of the Friend was characterized in the *Theodicy*, and most unfriendly diatribes of a similar nature continue throughout the Dialogue.

This sort of blow and counterblow is indicative of a much deeper conflict between Job and his Friends—a point the poet obviously desires to underscore. This conflict can be summed up, to a large extent, in the way Job characterizes the Friends in the quotation above: as *mnḥmy 'ml*, "hapless comforters" (lit. "comforters of trouble/strife"[291], virtually an oxymoron). I think that this is precisely the point the author of the Poem wishes to make: Comforters—at least, comforters in the traditional mold—are of absolutely no use to a Sufferer who seeks justice rather than a humble reconciliation with his God. Job's Friends rehearse the same arguments that the Friend in the *Theodicy* has espoused—what we should probably assume are the "classic" arguments of comfort for a victim-in-distress. But the poet of Job wants to make it clear that in his version of the Dialogue-genre, such arguments are pointless. As Job says to the Friends, "Your maxims are ashen aphorisms, defenses of clay your defenses" (13:12).[292] In the *Theodicy*, ultimate resolution comes with the Sufferer's recognition that when all is said and done, the Friend is right. But in Job, the poet subverts this conventional view by characterizing Sufferer and Friends as implacable antagonists: Job will never give in to their view; hence, although the Dialogue concludes, there remains a good deal to be said.

Once more, by transforming the traditional relationship of victim and comforter in this fashion, the poet of Job has made a telling thematic point—that one can justify righteous suffering only by avoiding all consideration of the righteousness of God. In Dialogues like the *Theodicy*, the Friend counsels that it is the very obscurity of the gods' intentions that must inevitably lead one to submit without question to a divine authority that offers no answers. By having his Job vehemently reject this archetypical "Friend's view," the Job poet has reinforced his primary aim: he has redirected his ancient audience's attention away from suffering man and back towards the inscrutable God, and even more to the point, he has made a dramatic issue precisely of this divine inscrutability.

Finally, there is one other aspect of the Dialogue/Appeal form that the poet of Job utilizes in his own characteristic manner: the divine response to the Righteous Sufferer's plea. As we have noted above, this response is the climactic moment in the Appeal-texts we have considered above. According to the convention, the Sufferer's patron deity, apparently moved by the eloquence of his servant's humble plea for mercy, restores him to his former state of health and prosperity. This denouement plays an essential role in texts of this nature because it serves to reinforce the pietistic norms that are at the heart of the Wisdom tradition.

The restoration of the Righteous Sufferer demonstrates that no matter how hopeless the circumstances of the innocent, no matter how obscure the action of the gods, *ultimately* things do turn around right. If unmerited punishment can be quick and devastating, so can restoration be swift and dazzling. Furthermore, the righteous victim of divine wrath is doubly blessed. Not only does he ultimately receive miraculous reward, but the divine trial of his innocence has also proven—and, in fact was the only way really to prove—that his piety is truly of heroic proportions. In a sense, the extent of his suffering is therefore a kind of verification of his own merit as well as a sign of his god's special favor—a favor that finally can only lead the deity to respond positively to the Righteous Sufferer's distress in the most dramatic of fashions. In this respect, the Appeal-form shows a thematic continuity with stories like the *Akedah* and the traditional legend of Job, because it also looks forward to the reward that must inevitably follow on unmerited suffering, the joy that must come out of the distress of those have plumbed the depths of despair but who have, nonetheless, somehow managed to preserve their faith.[293]

However, as we have already noted, Job in the Poem does not come to praise God but to provoke him. And when God does appear, He does not do so because He has been moved to pity by an abject supplicant, as would be expected according to convention, but rather because He has been greatly angered by the unflinching demands of an antagonist who is anything but abject. One can catch this sense of anger from the outset of the divine speech (Job 38:2):

> Who is this who darkens counsel,
> With words without knowledge?

One catches not only the unmistakable edge of sarcasm in this remark,[294] but also a sense of surprise or even shock—as if God were saying, "Who *is* this, who refuses to play his proper role, who does not plead as a proper Righteous Sufferer should plead?"

The departure from the expected correspondences here could not be more dramatic. As we noted above, the Righteous Sufferer always is careful not to become so strident as to provoke his god, lest that god turn a deaf ear as a result. But in Job precisely the opposite happens: Job has broken this taboo, and conversely (if not perversely) God's response may be characterized as direct reaction to this flouting of convention.

Needless to say, the manner in which God responds to Job is also a good deal different from the manner in which a deity normally responds to a Righteous Sufferer. In the Appeal texts we have considered above, the god acts decisively and dramatically to restore the victim. No divine explanation is offered, either for the initial punishment of the Sufferer or for his redemption—in all such instances, godly actions are deemed to speak louder than words. But in Job, the poet achieves precisely the contrary effect: divine words are deemed to speak louder than actions. Instead of a god who offers swift and inexplicable restoration, the book of Job portrays God as a deity who offers no reward and who is inclined instead to talk with Job at length.[295]

This then is the final bold maneuver that the poet has made through his manipulation of the Dialogue/Appeal genre. He has achieved in the climactic Theophany precisely the focus that his entire Poem has striven for from its outset: he has brought an angry God directly before Job and hence before his ancient audience. No other means could do more to focus attention on the essential theme in the Poem of Job: the nature of God, the question of the morality of God.

Thus, by playing his counterpoint against the Dialogue/Appeal genre, the poet of Job has advanced his parodistic purpose in brilliant fashion. Still, it would be a mistake to view the poet's design only, or even primarily, in the terms of the Dialogue/Appeal form. This is only one line in the complex of Joban harmonies. In particular, there is another dominant theme that must be attended to, if we are to appreciate the polyphonic relationships established in the Poem of Job; for the poet casts his Poem not only as a Wisdom Dialogue between Job and his Friends but also as a litigious debate between judicial adversaries; Job's complaint is to be viewed not only in terms of a Righteous Sufferer's Appeal to his god, but also in terms of a judicial appeal to higher authority that legally compels a response. Indeed, if the fundamental question in the Job Poem involves deciding whether God is righteous, then, the poet requires that his readers judge this issue by juridical standards. As these points suggest, the relationship between Job, his Friends and God must not only be seen in terms of the Dialogue/Appeal but also in terms of jurisprudence. Hence, if we are to gain further insight into how the poet has developed his Joban counterpoint, we must also consider how he has developed this legal metaphor as a means of defining relationships within the Poem and how he has then manipulated this metaphor in his own characteristic way.

10

The Art of Parody: The Legal Metaphor

From a legalistic standpoint, the Poem of Job can be seen as something considerably different from an example of Dialogue/Appeal. Note, in this connection, the observation of B. Gemser:

> The book not only abounds in judicial phraseology, but formally cannot be better understood than as the record of the proceedings of a *rīb* ["lawsuit"; pron. "reev"; see below] between Job and God Almighty in which Job is the plaintiff and prosecutor, the friends of Job are witnesses as well as co-defendants and judges, while God is the accused and defendant, but in the background and finally the ultimate judge of both Job and his friends. [296]

It is interesting that nowhere in conventional Dialogue/Appeal texts known from antiquity does any legal metaphor play even the slightest role. [297] To be sure, as we have already discussed, the issue of the righteousness of the Sufferer is definitely a major consideration in this genre. However, this is never really couched in terms of legal "guilt" or "innocence," nor is there ever any talk of hauling one party or another into court to decide the issues in contention. The legalisms that abound in the Poem of Job reflect the poet's own innovation and must be seen as part of his general modus operandi. Just as he has apparently amalgamated Dialogue with Appeal, so, too, it would seem that he has engrafted a legal metaphor on to his design, thereby making a hybrid form even more of a hybrid.

This is a point little emphasized in the modern exegesis of Job. Scholars will, on the one hand, dwell at length on the relationship of Job to Ancient Near Eastern Wisdom prototypes such as the *Theodicy* or *Ludlul*, or, on the other hand, they will consider Job in terms of the extensive use of the legal metaphor throughout the Poem. But such discussions are most typically compartmentalized; that is, if one deals with the Dialogue/Appeal aspect of Job, little or no mention will be made of the legal metaphor in that context. If the legal metaphor is the subject at hand, then this will be considered largely without reference to the Dialogue/Appeal texts in the Wisdom-tradition that so closely inform the basic structure of the Poem. [298] Perhaps one advantage of seeing the Job Poem in terms of counterpoint is that this leads one to be sensitive to the play of one theme against another. In any case, it is essential that the relationship of Dialogue/Appeal to the legal metaphor in the Poem of Job be carefully considered, if we are properly to appreciate the poet's intentions.

I have already begun to indicate how I think this relationship is best understood in the discussion above on the poet's use of the Dialogue/Appeal form. There, it was suggested that the author of Job broke out of the confines of this genre and proceeded to subvert its conventions by raising the one issue that is usually avoided at all costs: the question of the righteousness of God. It is through the extensive use of a legal metaphor that this "break out" is specifically achieved; that is, when the poet has his Job question the righteousness of God, he does so in the role of an offended party in a court case. Moreover, this appears to be done "according to the rules"; that is, Job's speeches are often structured as though they were wholly conventional testimonies, employing the stereotypical language expected in adjudicated proceedings. Yet, at the same time, when one probes the use of this legal metaphor more deeply, it becomes clear that all is not quite as conventional as appearances would first suggest. Once more, we discover that the poet of Job has actually twisted around the normal correspondences in a judicial proceeding in order to prosecute his parodistic ends to the maximum extent.

Perhaps the best way to consider how the legal metaphor is utilized in Job is to focus upon the Hebrew term that, as Gemser declares in the quotation above, seems to be the very essence of the Poem of Job from a legalistic standpoint: *rīb*.[299] This term, to judge from its use in various biblical contexts, has a wide range of meanings. In the broadest sense it can be understood as "strife, quarrel," that is, any sort of conflict expressed between hostile parties. But the term is also employed in a number of contexts where it clearly has a far more narrow, specifically juridical, definition. Indeed, *rib* seems so closely identified with courtroom proceedings in such contexts that it might be fair to call it the legal term par excellence in the Bible.[300] J. Limburg, in his careful studies of *rīb* both as a noun and verb in the Hebrew Bible, comes to the definition which seems especially applicable to this legalistic nuance of the term: "To *rīb* is to engage in hostile unilateral speech activity against an aggrieving party. To *rīb* is to make a complaint, make an accusation. The verb denotes the carrying out of this speech activity and the noun denotes its content. A *rīb* is a complaint or accusation which an aggrieved party makes against the one held responsible for the grievance."[301]

A point of particular note in Limburg's characterization of *rīb* is that the term connotes a "speech activity." As S. Scholnick declares, in further clarifying the term, it is utilized to refer "almost exclusively to a verbal confrontation between adversaries."[302] When this accusation becomes a public record, then a trial of the *rīb* must be conducted. This is indicated, for example, in the description of the conduct of a *rīb* in Deut. 25:1. The passage states, *ky yhyh ryb byn 'nšym*, "When there is a *rīb* between men," *ngšw 'l mšpṭ wšpṭwm whṣdyqw 't-hṣdyq whršy'w 't-hršʿ*, "they go to judgment and they are judged: the innocent is deemed innocent and the guilty charged as guilty." Elsewhere, we learn that in a properly conducted, public *rīb*, judgment is to be rendered impartially, testimony is to be given honestly, bribes are to be eschewed and the rights of an individual are not to be subverted simply because he or she is the weaker party in a dispute (cf. Exod. 23: 2–3, 6–8).[303]

We might say that a *rīb*—requiring adjudication—connotes a civilized proceeding in which disputants are enjoined from trying to win their point through the exercise of power (whether physical, fiscal or whatever). Rather, they are juridical opponents who must argue their respective cases before a judicial authority who will determine the outcome fairly, based upon legal precedent and the merits of the issues.[304] A $r\bar{\imath}b$, as we find it in the Bible, then would seem to be an early affirmation of the rule of law-and-order over the law-of-the-jungle. The fact that the term also shows up in an early Aramaic treaty document with much the same force of meaning also gives one confidence that this characterization of $r\bar{\imath}b$ may have had broad, international standing.[305]

This concept of $r\bar{\imath}b$ is of particular serviceability for the poet of Job. By casting Job's response to misfortune in terms of precisely this sort of legal grievance, the poet gives his protagonist a classic recourse against the arbitrary exercise of power: impartial judicial procedure. Job's chronicle of misfortune thus becomes more than simply a Righteous Sufferer's lament, but also a public statement of complaint. Thereby Job can legitimately proceed to call for the sort of "fair play" that the conventions of a legal proceeding require.

The fact that Job feels that God has resisted this equitable and appropriate legal recourse is a point that the poet emphasizes from the first time that he brings the legal metaphor into play (chap. 9). Job declares at the beginning of his response to Bildad (9:2–3): *'mnm yd'ty ky-kn wmh-yṣdq 'nwš 'm-'l: 'm yhpṣ lryb 'mw l'-y'nnw 'ḥt mny-'lp*. It is important to note how the use of legal terminology transforms these remarks of Job. His first statement (9:2: *'mnm yd'ty ky-kn wmh-yṣdq 'nwš 'm-'l*) might be literally translated, "Truly I know this is so. But how could man be righteous with God?"[306] This would seem to be a pious statement very much at home within the archetypical Dialogue/Appeal. Moreover, Job's statement that he "knows this is so" would appear to confirm a traditional, pietistic viewpoint and, in fact, specifically echoes the climactic statement in Eliphaz's first speech (4:17): *h'nwš m'lwh yṣdq 'm-m'šhw yṭhr-gbr*, "Can man be righteous before God, or a mortal be pure before his Maker?"

But Job's next statement (9:3: *'m yhpṣ lryb 'mw l'-y'nnw 'ḥt mny-'lp*) employs specifically legal terminology, especially $r\bar{\imath}b$, and thus requires that the statement in the preceding verse be reinterpreted in light of this. The entire passage in 9:2b–3 must therefore be rendered, "But how could a man win against God if he desired to file a complaint against Him? He would not answer him[307] one in a thousand!" Hence, what might at first have easily been taken as a pious maxim, "Who can be righteous before God?" is transformed into a far sharper and more challenging legalistic statement: "Who could win against God?"[308] Moreover, Job's problem is thrown into even sharper relief because he further forthrightly affirms that, after all, despite all appearances to the contrary, *tm 'ny*, "I am blameless" (9:21).[309] Job believes without question, were his conduct objectively measured against any reasonable legal standard of justice, he could establish his innocence to the satisfaction of any fair-minded judge.

Of course, the reason no one can win a case against God is because God has the monopoly of power, a power the poet proceeds to describe in 9:5–13 in considerable detail. Job then summarizes his and therefore mankind's predicament when confronted by a hostile God in 9:19: *'m-lkh 'myṣ hnh w'm-lmšpṭ my yw'ydny*, "If it's power, look how mighty He is![310] But if it's legality,[311] who will set me a time?"[312] Ideally, what is needed is a judicial entity to serve as an adjudicator of the complaint

Job would like to file against his Deity. If such could be found, Job declares, he could proceed to testify about his grievance, certain of the protection of a judicial system in which both the weak and strong are treated alike. The fact that this is not the case allows the poet to establish that the way Job has been handled is not only unfair but is also essentially illegal:

> There is no[313] arbiter between us
> Who could lay his hand upon the two of us.
> Let Him [God] remove his rod from me,
> And let Him not unhinge me with His terror:
> I would speak and not be afraid!
> But it is not so for me.[314] (Job 9:33–35)

As the debate between Job and his friends continues, the poet frequently returns to this legal metaphor, reemphasizing the points in Job's *rīb* as outlined here: Job reaffirms his innocence; demands, yet despairs of, legal recourse; and longs for someone to adjudicate the grievance he desires to bring against God.[315]

Finally, the legal metaphor reaches its climax at the conclusion of Job's final, long speech in chapter 31. M. B. Dick, in his studies of the function of chapter 31 within the book of Job,[316] may come closest to classifying its legal import. He suggests that this statement is best understood as a declaration of innocence made by an aggrieved party, petitioning for a judicial appeal. It is Job's final demand for a hearing, to be conducted before an impartial judge, against his *'îš rīb*, his "opponent-at-law"; and it concludes with what appears, for all intents and purposes, to be Job's filing of a legal petition that should compel a response: *my ytn-ly šm'-ly hn-twy šdy y'nny wspr ktb 'yš ryby*, "If only I had someone to give me a hearing! Here is my signature; let the Almighty respond against me—(with) a cross-complaint[317] my opponent-at-law has written." (31:35).[318]

The way the poet leads up to this climactic statement in 31:35 is significant. Job first recalls, as if it were a dream, what his life as a great and wise man was like before God had afflicted him (chap. 29). Then he proceeds to chronicle how his life has been so cruelly changed; how debilitating and humiliating has been his lot since God cast him away (chap. 30). A number of scholars have noted how the sentiments expressed in these chapters reflect standard lament forms found, for example, in the Psalms.[319] However, as Dick notes, "instead of completing this lamentation with the customary plea for help, the author of Job has altered the pattern so that it culminates in the trial request before a judge."[320] Of course, as our discussion above has indicated, this is characteristic of the poet's method of operation. Once more, the legal metaphor undercuts the reader's conventional expectations by transforming Job's declaration from a Righteous Sufferer's Appeal into a judicial appeal.

The oath, which comprises most of chapter 31, must be considered the key element in this culminating long speech. Here Job swears that he is innocent of all potential offenses that would give God grounds for punishing him. This is done in most emphatic terms as Job proceeds to affirm that he has never committed all manner of specific crimes[321] and further dares his Deity to strike him down if what he has sworn is not true. M. Tsevat has appropriately labeled this "the most terrible oath in the Bible," not merely due to its dramatic length but also because, unlike most oaths encountered in the Bible, it is couched in such shockingly explicit terms.[322] This defines the terms for a legal "showdown" between Job and God. Thus, Dick observes, "The expansion [by Job's oath] of the customary sworn statement/document of innocence usually accompanying appeals of this type has considerable force: in no more emphatic way could Eloah [God] be made to justify himself.[323]

But what is most remarkable is that Job's legal strategy, as portrayed by the poet, ultimately seems to yield definitive juridical results. Job has filed his grievance, as it were, against God; and his Deity, like any conventional *'iš rîb*, opponent-at-law, appears in order to defend Himself.[324] Moreover, when God proceeds to make His defense against Job, He also drops into the terminology of Job's legal metaphor and thereby seems both to endorse and legitimize it.

This is already indicated by the fact that God responds with a speech instead of with a simple exercise of brute force. As we have indicated above, this is the most characteristic aspect of a public *rîb*—it is a battle of words-against-words rather than force-against-force—and God is portrayed by the author of Job as being more than willing to abide by this overriding rule of adjudication.[325] Besides this, the mode of God's speech is also characteristically legal. He challenges Job at the outset: *'š'lk whwdy'ny*, "I will interrogate you and you make disclosure to me" (38:3b), just as if He were intent on taking a deposition from a colitigant in a typical court case. Further, when God continues with his list of interrogatories in chapter 40, He once more renews this same juridical challenge (40:7b), as if to make sure that Job understands that he is still, as it were, "under oath."

God's acceptance of the judicial terms of His encounter with Job is finally made most explicit in His colloquy with Job at the conclusion of His first long speech. There, the poet portrays God as functioning completely within the conventions of the *rîb*. First the Deity declares: *hrb 'm-šdy yswr mwkyḥ 'lwh y'nnh*, "Will a plaintiff file a grievance against the Almighty? Let he who calls God to court give testimony against Him!" (40:2). Then, a few verses later (40:8), God even seems to go so far as to grant that the basic issues at stake in this adjudication are best framed in terms of legal guilt or innocence. This assumption underlies His greatest juridical challenge to Job: *h'p tpr mšpṭy tršy'ny lm'n tṣdq*, "Would you even throw out a ruling in My favor? Would you declare Me guilty so that you may be deemed innocent?" Indeed, we have here the crux of the case the poet has established through the use of his legal metaphor. If there is going to be a decision-at-law in the case of Job versus God, someone has to be declared innocent and someone guilty. Who, then, is it going to be?

Altogether, we therefore have a remarkable, yet wholly conventional, set of circumstances established through the poet's utilization of the legal metaphor in the Poem of Job, the sum constituting what Scholnick has quite properly characterized as a "Lawsuit Drama."[326] By superimposing the conventions of an adjudicated proceeding over the structure of a Dialogue/Appeal, the author has required his audience to rethink the relationship between Job and God in legalistic terms. In fact, it might be fairly said that the poet has given mankind a "day in court" against a divine adversary not usually inclined to accept the service of a subpoena.

But it is just here that the legal metaphor begins to break down—or, more properly, we should say that it is just at this point that the poet of Job begins to subvert his own metaphor. We have noted above that a similar subversion was effected when the poet added an extra factor to the standard conventions of the Dialogue/Appeal genre by portraying Job as one who demands what a Righteous Sufferer dare not demand: that God be just. But in this instance he has accomplished the same thing by doing just the opposite. For up to the very end, the poet has essentially endeavored to withhold from consideration the most crucial element in any judicial system: what might be deemed its legal authority—specifically, its authority of enforcement.

This authority is essential for an obvious reason: a legal decision without authority is essentially worthless. After all, if two parties enter into litigation and a decision is rendered in favor of one and against the other, there has to be some entity empowered to enforce the decision—as the saying goes, to give the decision "teeth." Without this power to make the party-at-fault accept guilt, pay the penalty and/or make restitution to the party-in-the-right, the entire legal system would break down. It would be back to the sort of uncivilized tug-of-war that the legal system was designed to counteract in the first place.

In a Western democracy, the authority for enforcement is carefully insulated from the judiciary and is instead invested in the executive branch of government. But in the Ancient Near East, no such separation of powers existed. Rather, the authority to enforce was coupled with judgeship and invested in the ruler, usually a king.[327] In ancient Israel and Judah and, for that matter, in the surrounding environs of Canaan this was certainly true. In fact, it is hardly accidental that, in common usage among the Northwest Semitic languages, the term *špṭ*, means both "to judge" and "to rule."[328]

Of course, in the final analysis the king or ruler, although invested with authority, was not perceived to be the ultimate source of power. Rather, he acted on behalf of (and/or was seen as a manifestation of) divine power on earth; for in Ancient Near Eastern eyes all authority came from the gods, or, in the particular case of the biblical world (including the world of the poet of Job), from God.

This is indicated, for example, in the way legal authority is characterized in the great Mesopotamian law codes. Thus, in the prologue of the Code of Lipit-Ishtar, the king declares, "I, Lipit-Ishtar. . .[estab]lished [jus]tice in [Su]mer and Akkad in accordance with the word of (the god) Enlil."[329] Similarly, the beginning of the famous Code of Hammurapi reads, ". . .(the gods) Anum and Enlil named me to promote the welfare of the people, me Hammurapi, the devout, god-fearing prince, to cause justice to prevail in the land, to destroy the wicked and the evil, that the strong might not oppress the weak, to rise like the sun over the black-headed (people) and to light up the land."[330] Each of these kings lays claim to the power of enforcement, the authority that makes their respective laws worth more than the stones or tablets they are written on, a power that is legitimized because it comes directly from the gods. Note, too, that when a man-in-distress makes an appeal: "O Sungod, you are judge, judge my cause, make decisions, decide for me!"[331] this is not only because the Sungod, Shapash, is traditionally associated with justice, but also because he is deemed to have the power to make his judicial decisions stick. Authority, as manifest in biblical contexts, is essentially analogous to this. The series of laws Moses hands down from Sinai in Exodus and Deuteronomy are taken to be God's laws; and when a Moses, a Joshua, a Samuel or a David functions as both ruler and judge, it is clear that they are seen as deriving their power of enforcement from their divine Lord.

Most often, the authority—whether of god or king—was called on to judge between two parties, to render a verdict and to guarantee its enforcement. But there could also arise a circumstance in which the wrong committed was perceived to be against the source of authority itself. For example, a great monarch might make a treaty with his vassal, the obligations of which the vassal proceeded to violate. Or alternatively, a god might make a covenant with his people which the people then openly and continually violated. At such a juncture—from a legal standpoint—the source or agent of authority also had a grievance and thus took on an all-encompassing legal role: not only as judge and enforcer but also as prosecutor/plaintiff as well.

This can be demonstrated from the annals of Ancient Near Eastern international law. Note this angry accusation of the Assyrian suzerain Tukulti-Ninurta I against his wayward Kassite vassal, Kashtiliash:

> . . .Why did you retreat and [find] your way (where there was) no exit and extricate yourself without fighting. . .? You have ravaged the people of Ashur. . .by an untimely death they perish continually. . . .I will lift up (my voice) and will read (aloud) the tablet of the covenant between us to the Lord of Heaven. . .and I will publish abroad the outrage. . . . Wait for me until I lift up [my voice?]. . .and in our encounter by battle may the Ruler of. . .decide the cause between us. Today, we are wrath (?). . .peace cannot be made without war. . . .[332]

In this instance the royal authority has been challenged and the king responds not only with the accusation of a plaintiff but then proceeds to judge and condemn the defendant and to institute dire steps to enforce his verdict through war. Note, too, that he also makes his case before his deity (once again, Shapash); thus, the god also is identified with the process of prosecution-judgment-enforcement instituted by the king. One might say that the king not only prosecutes and judges his own grievance but also simultaneously makes an appeal, quite literally, to a higher court to sanction his actions. Indeed, the defendant in this suit is well aware that he has violated not only royal law but divine law as well. In response to his suzerain, the vassal thus declares, "Now do I feel the terror for my land; grave is the punishment of misdeeds! The oath of Shapash oppresses me. . . .I have delivered my people into a ruthless hand, a bondage [unyielding]. . . .Punished are my sins before Shapash. . . .Who is the god who will rescue my people from [this danger?]"[333]

In the Bible, the most famous examples of authority, in particular, divine authority, acting as plaintiff, judge and enforcer come from the "prophetic lawsuit" pericopes. A parade example is Hos. 4:1–3:[334]

> Hear the word of the LORD, you Israelites. For the LORD has a grievance against [rîb 'im] the inhabitants of the land: There is neither honesty nor loyalty nor is there recognition of God in the land! False testimony,[335] murder, theft and adultery have run rife! Bloodshed leads to bloodshed! Therefore, the land will wither[336] and all that dwells on it will be sucked dry. The beasts of the field, the birds of the air, even the fish in the sea will perish!

God has a grievance because his people have committed one sin after another, thereby breaking the tenets of the law that were an essential part of Israel's covenant obligations. Thus, God proceeds with his complaint: prosecuting it, judging it and finally imposing a dire sentence. As K. Nielsen notes, "The Yahweh who pronounces judgement over His people is the same Yahweh who prosecutes accusations against them. . . .The fact that He has both roles derives from the theology of the Covenant; only Yahweh can be a guarantor of the Covenant, even if He is a participant in it."[337]

Without question, it is precisely this sort of divine authority, emanating from a power which no mere mortal could match, that was taken to be the driving force in Ancient Near Eastern jurisprudence. But it is also precisely this most fundamental juridical assumption—that all law derives its authority from God—which the author of Job has targeted for special attention in his Poem. For within the framework of his legal metaphor, the poet endeavors to do an unprecedented thing: to divorce God from his role as this Ultimate Legal Authority. And in so doing, he turns the conventions of Ancient Near Eastern law on their head.[338]

This attempt to alter so fundamentally the divine role in law is implicit in Job's legal demand in 10:2: *'mr 'l-'lwh 'l-tršy'ny hwdy'ny 'l mh-trybny*, "I would say to God: Do not declare me guilty. Tell me the grounds for your case against me." What Job essentially says here is that God should step down on this occasion from His conventional role as judge and instead take on the role of a colitigant—in fact, a defendant in a court case. Even more to the point, Job really wants God to give up His power of enforcement, so that they, together, can then proceed to argue in court fair and square. Job states as much in 13:21–22: *kpk m'ly hrḥq w'mtk 'l-tb'tny: wqr' w'nky "nh 'w-'dbr whšybny*, "Remove your hand from me, and stop intimidating me with your terror. Then call and I will respond. Or I will testify and you answer me." No departure from the conventions of Ancient Near Eastern law could be more dramatic; for it is simply without precedent to demand that God step down from the bench and enter the dock. After all, how could God be designated as Job's *'iš rib* (lit., "man of [his] *rib*") when, in fact, God is not an *'iš* (a "man")?[339]

A similar altering of roles can be seen in the way the poet handles the Three Friends in terms of his legal metaphor. When Eliphaz, Bildad and Zophar come upon the scene, they seem desirous of fulfilling their conventional roles after the manner of the Friend in the *Theodicy*. But as we have already seen, Job's arguments goad them into an adversarial position, transforming them into the opposite of what they should be: not genuine comforters but, rather, "comforters of strife."

In terms of the legal metaphor, the poet goes even further; for Job would enlist them into his court case whether they like it or not. He even goes so far as to depict them almost as "shyster lawyers" who speak falsely for God (13:7). Job then queries (13:8): *hpnyw tš'wn 'm-l'l trybwn*, "Would you be His advocate, even lodge God's complaint?" The answer I think the Friends would give to this query is most emphatically negative. They want no part of Job's court case. To them, it would be the height of impiety and impropriety to imagine speaking for God in a court of law; and in fact, they largely avoid the use of legalistic terminology in their speeches,[340] as if to emphasize that this is Job's metaphor, not theirs.[341] The Friends would prefer to speak about *ṣdqh*, "righteousness," *rš'*, "wickedness," and *mšpṭ* "justice" as moral concepts; it is only Job who would give these concepts a legal twist, reinterpreting them, respectively, as "innocence," "guilt" and "legal proceeding." But Job refuses to allow the Friends to be conventional Friends, or even simply "anti-comforters"; rather he keeps insisting on redefining their roles in legalistic terms, making them reluctant parties to his court case—sometimes depicting them as legal advocates, at other times treating them as witnesses to the proceedings.

But a more dramatic reversal of legal roles is reserved by the poet for Job himself: If God is placed in the unprecedented role as a defendant in a court case, then Job must take on an even more extraordinary position as the plaintiff who prosecutes God. This is a role Job embraces without reservation. And just as a good prosecutor should do, he boldly hurls one accusation after another at God, listing in detail all the wrongful actions of the Deity, which have led to Job's prosecuting of his suit. Note, for example, this list of accusations, which constitute just one of a series indictments brought by Job against God (19:6–12):

> Know, certainly, that God has ruined me.
> His siege works He has thrown around me.[342]
> Look, I cry, "Violence!" but I get no answer,
> I scream, but there is no justice.[343]
> He has walled off my way, so I cannot pass,
> And put darkness in all my paths.
> He has stripped away my worth from me,
> And removed the crown from my head.
> From all sides He breaks me down—I'm done in!
> And He uproots my hope like a tree.
> His rage consumes me,
> He marks me as his enemy.
> His troops mass together,
> Lay a siege against me,
> Their camp encircles my tent.

There is undeniably an impression left here that Job has a valid complaint. The passion that underlies his accusations takes the reader up and carries him along, rather like the speech of the Defending Angel in "Bontsye Shvayg." And because we are moved by the sincerity and forthrightness of Job's complaint, and perhaps especially because it comes out of the depths of his despair, we may at first be less sensitive to how thoroughly the poet has endeavored to subvert the legal system in this and other Joban speeches. Only when we consider the implications of Job's prosecution of God do we begin to recognize that this can only be seen as a sham legal process. Once more, we are being treated to a masquerade rather than the real thing. For, from the standpoint of the conventions of legality in the Ancient Near East, Job's position as prosecutor is not only untenable, it is simply outrageous.

One is reminded, in this connection, of the proverb quoted by Second Isaiah (45:9): *hwy rb 't yṣrw ḥrś 't-ḥrśy-* [read *ḥrś*] *'dmh hy'mr ḥmr lyṣrw mh t'śh wp'lk 'yn ydym lw*, "Woe to him who would lodge a complaint against his Maker: a pot with the potter! Does the clay say to its maker, 'What are you doing? This work of yours has no handles?'"[344] Note that the prophet defines the relationship between someone who would contend (once again, the term employed is *rīb*) with God strictly in terms of power and authority. The authority to question has legitimacy only if it has the power to back it up: Second Isaiah demonstrates this with his analogy to the potter and the clay. The potter controls his medium; hence, he alone can be the final arbiter as to how that clay is to be shaped into a vessel. It is manifestly absurd for the pottery vessel to second-guess the potter—to say, "What are you doing?" or "Don't you think this would work better with handles?"—because the pot has no power over its own destiny. Perhaps, it might be argued, a given pot would *seem* to serve better with handles—but this is irrelevant: only the one who does the shaping has the authority to make the rules, not the object that is being shaped.[345]

What makes Job's prosecution of God so outrageous from a legal standpoint is that it endeavors to bypass the power that makes the legal system work. Job would ask God, "What are you doing?" (9:13) even though he is no more than clay in the hands of the Cosmic Fabricator. In this respect, the poet's parody of the legal system could not be better fashioned; for everything has been turned inside out: indeed, Job is depicted as one who—armed only with his innocence—would desire to approach God on an equal legal footing. Moreover, as we noted above, the poet has his protagonist affirm that if God refuses to respond to Job's legal accusation, or intimidates Job with His divine power, then God has broken the rules of adjudication and thus must be seen as a lawless Deity. But this ignores the most fundamental rule of law in the Ancient Near East: that God *is* the Law; for without divine authority the law ceases to exist. Job claims that God has violated juridical procedure, but in fact, as Second Isaiah could tell Job, this is impossible: God cannot violate Himself, nor can mankind claim the protection of any system of law separate from God's authority.[346] Still, Job's bold declaration at the conclusion of chapter 31 completely ignores this reality. Rather, he presses his prosecution, certain that no countersuit from God could harm him. In fact, if God would dare to make a cross-complaint, it could only prove to be Job's trophy. Job declares that such a legal document would become the prize for him to carry off after gaining the inevitable victory in his legal battle (31:36–37):

> Yes, I would wear it on my shoulder,
> I would bind it on like a crown.
> I would tell Him the number of my steps,
> Like a Prince I would approach Him!

But even this is not the final twist given by the poet of Job to his legal metaphor. If God is to be the defendant and Job the prosecutor in this topsy-turvy legal world, then, there is still one issue that remains unresolved: Who is to judge? Or more broadly, who has the power and authority to judge the case of Job versus God? The way the author of Job has his protagonist answer this question is perhaps the most extraordinary thing of all.

This answer is contained in four related passages interspersed through Job's speeches. Two of these have already been cited above—9:33–35 where Job speaks of a *mwkyḥ*, an "arbiter," who could mediate the dispute between Job and God; and 31:35 where Job wishes for a *šmʿ*, literally, an "auditor," to hear his case. Two other texts are also relevant to the issue, especially because they seem to go beyond hoping for such an arbiter and appear to affirm that such an agent does indeed exist.

In the first of these (16:19–21) Job speaks of this arbiter as a "witness/advocate" ('d/śhd) who will intercede on his behalf:

> Even now—look: my witness is in Heaven.
> He who vouches for me is on high:
> My advocate, my representative to God.
> ⟨Unto him⟩ my eye weeps!
> He can arbitrate between a man and God—
> As a man might do for his companion.[347]

The other text, 19:23–25 is one of the best-known passages in the book of Job. There Job invokes his "Redeemer" (gō'ēl) who finally will come forward to save him:

> Ah! If only my words were written down!
> If only they were carved on a stela!
> With an iron chisel and lead—
> Forever cut into the rock:
> I know my redeemer lives!
> Finally, upon the dust he will arise. . .[348]

Many have seen these passages, especially the last one, as making reference to God Himself. However, the assumption that the Deity is Job's intercessor is difficult to maintain in light of the broader context of the Poem. Note, in this connection, the argument mustered by N. Habel in opposition to identifying God as the gō'ēl, the Redeemer, referred to in Job 19:25 and following:

> A major argument against viewing God as the gō'ēl is that it would mean a complete reversal in the pattern of Job's thought to date, a pattern which also persists after this famous cry of hope. Job has portrayed God consistently as his attacker not his defender, his enemy not his friend, his adversary at law not his advocate, his hunter not his healer, his spy not his savior, an intimidating terror not an impartial judge. In subsequent speeches Job continues to be overwhelmed at the anticipated appearance of God's terrifying "face" (23:14–17); he identifies God as his accuser and adversary at law to the very end.[349]

The points made in Habel's argument cannot be seriously disputed. Nonetheless, there are characteristics of this intercessor that certainly seem Godlike. For one thing, he certainly must be some sort of divine figure, since he is characterized in 16:19 as a witness "in Heaven." Besides, if this being is going to summon God to court, he had better be able to match God's divine power, if not exceed it. But the only being who has that much power is God Himself. Hence, the dilemma that exegetes have struggled with as long as there have been interpretations of Job: How can one have a godlike Redeemer/Arbiter who is not himself God? It has even been suggested that the only way to resolve this conundrum is to assume that another deity, namely the Canaanite Baal, has been called in (presumably from the neighboring jurisdiction) to preside over this special trial of his fellow divine jurist.[350]

While this last approach is difficult to accept, it does, perhaps, hint at a possible solution to this long-standing debate as to whether Job's Redeemer/Arbiter is God or some other agent. In fact, he seems to be a bit of both; that is, the poet has had his

Job envision a god-figure: not so much a specific deity like Baal as what amounts to an undefined divine entity with both the power and the authority to defend Job and at the same time to oppose God and bring Him to justice. In a sense, this divine agent is seen by Job as the one means of solving his legal dilemma. Job's problem, as we have seen, is that he requires an Ultimate Legal Authority who can serve in place of God as the power behind the law. Job's Redeemer/Arbiter would seem to have suddenly come on the scene to fulfill just this end.

Yet there is more here than meets the eye, or—more to the point—there is less: Certainly, the poet's descriptions of Job's Redeemer/Arbiter/Witness are moving; he endows this divine agent with all the trappings that such a god-figure should have, thereby making him all the more believable. And, as many have noted, Job's appeal to him seems at first to be a ray of hope, lighting, if ever so briefly, the darkness of a Sufferer's despair. But when we begin to consider the poet's intentions more closely, we discover what we have discovered before, a sham substituting for the real thing; for this Redeemer of Job's is quite literally conjured up out of nothing. He is the product of Job's desperate hope against hope that *somehow, somewhere* there must be a divine *Someone* who can act on his behalf. The Redeemer/Arbiter becomes the focus of this hope; but—as is the case throughout the legal metaphor in Job—this expectation is misplaced: just as it is absurd to try to make God a juridical defendant and impossible for a mortal to try to prosecute God, so too is it finally unimaginable that a divine agent might exist who could enforce a legal decision against God. Rather, this pseudodivine being has been created by the poet of Job for quite another purpose: to serve as the agent of his sharpest parodistic thrust, his ultimate reversal of roles: a "counter-deity," invoked out of thin air by Job, to oppose the *real* Deity.

What makes the poet's portrayal of Job's intercessor particularly cutting, from the standpoint of parody, is that the it draws upon traditional images of God as champion of the beleaguered and downtrodden and makes them instead the attributes of Job's "counter-god." Indeed, Job's phantom vindicator is the mirror image of God, the offended suzerain; for, if the latter typically takes on the role of Judge-Prosecutor, then the former is portrayed by the poet as Judge-Advocate.

Such images of God-as-defender are prominent in Ancient Near Eastern Appeals and often appear to have specifically legal connotations. I have already mentioned in passing that pleadings of the sort, "judge my judgment, decide my decision," occur in Mesopotamian incantations and prayers.[351] Obviously, the appeal being made in such contexts is not so much for an impartial judge but for the same sort of Judge-Advocate that Job envisions. Similar sentiments are also found among the Psalms and other biblical prayers. Note, as a representative case, Ps. 119:154a, where appeal is made to God, *rybh ryby wg'lny*, "Plead my case and redeem me!" It is particularly noteworthy that once more, the archetypical legal term *rīb* is used in this context, this time in close association with the verb *g'l*, "redeem," which is obviously reminiscent of the *gō'ēl*, "Redeemer" of 19:25.[352]

But the most striking imagery of this sort in the Bible appears among the prophetic lawsuit speeches to which we have alluded before. We have already seen how the Lord could act as prosecutor and judge of His people, but in other contexts He could be portrayed as their advocate and defender as well. Not surprisingly, we find such a sentiment among the oracles of Second Isaiah, the prophet of consolation. In Isa. 49:25b the Lord tells his people, *'t-yrybk 'nky 'ryb*, "Against your adversary will I make accusation" with *rīb* once more acting as the operative verb and God, the people's Advocate, once more designated as their Redeemer (*g'lk*; see 49:26). Similarly, Jeremiah uses this terminology to declare that God will rise to the defense of the people of Israel and Judah: *g'lm ḥzq yhwh ṣb'wt šmw ryb yryb 't-rybm*, "Their Redeemer is strong; the LORD of hosts is His name! Truly, He will make their accusation for them" (Jer. 50:34; cf. 50:33). In such contexts, God serves not only as His people's defender but also as a prosecutor/judge who tries, condemns and punishes their adversaries (cf. Isa. 49:25a, 26a; Jer. 50:34b, also 50:35 ff.).[353] It is this type of statement that the poet of Job enlists in order to instill the semblance of substance into his Redeemer/Arbiter. Indeed, if we could be certain that the author of Job was familiar with the writings of the biblical prophets cited above, we might be led to conclude that he intended to play his counterpoint specifically against these and similar biblical texts, themselves.[354]

It is really only in the Theophany that Job's carefully constructed legal edifice is finally exploded. In this respect we might say that Job's encounter with God serves the same role in the Poem that the Prosecutor's laugh does in "Bontsye Shvayg": it shocks the reader into a recognition of the way things *really* are as opposed to the way the reader (or, at least, Job) would like them to be. For when God appears at last to confront Job, there is no Redeemer, Advocate or Witness to come forward to protect this mere mortal. Job must make do for himself.

Moreover, while the poet gives the Theophany the semblance of a judicial proceeding, in actuality it is nothing of the sort. None of the conventions of a public *rīb* are really observed: There is no give-and-take with each of the colitigants having his proper say, nor is the case impartially adjudicated on its legal merits, nor is the guilt and innocence of the respective parties duly accessed and judged. Rather, the encounter is totally dominated by God. It is He who does all the talking while Job can only lay his hands upon his mouth and admit that there is no possible counterargument for him to present against his adversary (40:4–5). The substance of God's speech also has nothing to do with the legal merits of Job's case. Rather, God declares that none dare judge Him unless they, too, can match both His wisdom and His power. It is only this all-encompassing, all-controlling force that decides who wins or loses, not an impartial court proceeding. Finally, any thought of measuring guilt or innocence in a case against God is summarily brushed aside. God simply declares that the issue is not relevant, not applicable to Him. Once more, it is power that defines the roles of God and man: God dominates, man submits. Whether this is right or wrong has nothing to do with the case.

It is due to the emphasis he has placed on these points that the poet is able to give the most ironic turn to his legal metaphor. For when God throws Job's case out of court in the Theophany, in a real sense He is reestablishing the conventional correspondences of Ancient Near Eastern law: Job is back in his proper role— indeed, the only role a mortal can have before his offended, divine suzerain—as defendant; and God is back where He should be, not only as Prosecutor and Judge but also as the Ultimate Authority who defines the law and gives it meaning. We might say that when God acts in a "lawless" fashion in his confrontation with Job, he paradoxically reaffirms the rule of law.

The denouement of the legal metaphor in the Theophany is finally achieved in 40:8–14. Here the true legal situation of Job and God is defined by the poet in its starkest terms. God essentially challenges Job, stating that if he really wants to contend with God, he had better be prepared for a test of strength, not of law. In 40:9–14 God throws down a gauntlet that Job cannot hope to pick up:

> So, have you an arm like God,
> Or can you thunder with a voice like His?
> Come, array yourself with grandeur and majesty,
> In splendor and glory enwrap yourself.
> Loose your limitless wrath:
> Stare down every proud one and humiliate him.
> Stare down every proud one and abase him.
> Mow down[355] the wicked where they stand.
> Hide them in the Dust, together,
> Bind up their faces in the Hidden Place!
> Then I too will grant
> That your own right hand can rescue you.

The verse immediately preceding this challenge is one we have looked at before; but in that instance I translated it so as to emphasize the encounter between Job and God as a conventional legal battle between colitigants: "Would you even throw out a ruling in My favor? Would you declare Me guilty so that you may be deemed innocent?"[356] But this verse could also just as easily be rendered so as to emphasize a more traditional viewpoint in which God's $m\check{s}p\underline{t}$ connotes His "justice" rather than a "ruling" for Him[357] and where $\underline{s}dq$ and $r\check{s}^c$ are seen in terms of "righteousness" versus "wickedness" rather than legal "innocence" versus "guilt." In that case God statement in 40:8 would be understood, "Would you annul My justice? Would you hold Me to be wicked so that you could be righteous?" The beauty of the Hebrew phrase is that both meanings are present rather than either one. The meaning and the counter-meaning in this verse fuse together even as they define the contrasting views of legality that the poet has so deftly instilled into his legal metaphor in the Poem of Job. And like Job, we must confront God's question on both its levels before we decide how to formulate our answer.

11

The Art of Parody: The Death Theme

Finally, there is one other theme in the Poem of Job on which I would like to focus particular attention: the theme of death and the netherworld. The allusions to death in the book of Job have received somewhat less attention in the scholarly literature than the Righteous Sufferer motif and the legal metaphor which we have considered above. Still, the emphasis on mortality in the Poem of Job is just as extensive as is the case for these other themes, perhaps even more so. In fact, it could be fairly stated that, verse-for-verse, no book in the Bible is more death-oriented than Job. Because of this, exegetes commonly depend upon Job as one of their most basic resources for illuminating the concept of death within the biblical milieu and, more generally, within the broader religious and cultural environs of the Ancient Near East.[358]

In many respects the way in which the poet of Job utilizes the theme of death appears to be entirely conventional. It seems only natural that Job should speak at length about death and the netherworld. Death thoughts are, after all, just what we would expect to be on the mind of one who has suffered what Job has suffered. But the Joban author has a further purpose as well. Once more, he desires not only to take a theme and give it the highest artistic expression but also to shape and manipulate the motif in order to serve his parodistic ends.

Before we can consider how the poet of Job has manipulated the death motif, we first have to consider exactly what aspect of of death interests him.[359] As is now well known, there was a highly developed mythology in the ancient Near East, centering upon various divine, chthonic figures who reigned over the underworld and who could even wreak havoc upon their fellow deities. For example, in the famous account of *Inanna/Ishtar's Descent into the Netherworld* from the Sumerian and Akkadian literature of Mesopotamia, Ereshkigal, queen of the netherworld, is depicted as just this sort of pernicious goddess. When her sister-goddess, Inanna/Ishtar dares to enter the realm of the dead, Ereshkigal strips her of all defenses and proceeds, quite literally, to hang Inanna/Ishtar out to dry.[360]

Much closer, both geographically and culturally, to the milieu in which the Poem of Job was written, are the accounts of the Canaanite God of Death, Mot, which are attested among the alphabetic cuneiform writings of ancient Ugarit.[361]

Once more, the texts speak of a fierce deity who, in this case, is seen to be the most deadly foe of the god who is usually taken to be the "hero" in the Ugaritic myths, the "rider of the clouds," Baal. On one occasion, Mot is described in quite graphic terms as the very embodiment of the "jaws of death" that would swallow up his divine adversary:

> [A lip to ear]th, a lip to the heavens,
> [A ton]gue to the stars:
> [Ba]al will enter his [Mot's] innards,
> Into his mouth he will descend . . .[362]

There are strong indications that the poet of Job was well aware of myths of this sort, and it is even possible that he placed in Job's mouth a direct reference to the Death-God Mot, himself.[363] However, it is not so much Death as manifest in the form of a malevolent deity that is the essential focus in the Poem of Job. Rather, the Joban author depicts death more as a realm, a netherworld to which all mortals must eventually go.[364] This realm of the dead is the place of no return, usually called *Sheol*,[365] sometimes simply referred to as "There"[366]—the ultimate end for all humans once the breath of life has left them and they pass from a state of being to this inevitable and final state of unbeing. The poet of Job describes this passage from life to death using a simple but effective metaphor in 7:9–10:

> A cloud fades and disintegrates;
> So he who goes down to *Sheol* never comes up.
> He will never return to his abode,
> Nor will his place regard him again.[367]

Of course, this sort of characterization of death is hardly original to Job but is instead normative in Ancient Near Eastern literature. We might say that death in the Ancient Near East is that which most emphatically separates man from god. Furthermore, it is the ability of the gods (or, in the Bible, God) to impose death on humanity that most decisively brings about this separation and ensures the subservience of mortals to their divine master(s).

Even the greatest hero of Mesopotamian legend, Gilgamesh, ultimately cannot overmatch the gods when it comes to control of life and death. Although in his final quest he strives mightily to gain immortality, it ultimately eludes him. His search for a means to forestall death is revealed to be no more than a fool's errand. In the long run, he might have proven to be wiser (although not nearly as heroic) if he had heeded earlier the advice of the innkeeper Siduri, who counseled him:

> Gilgamesh, where are you wandering?
> Life, for which you are searching everywhere, you will never find.
> When the gods created mankind,
> They fixed Death for mankind
> And held back life in their own hands.[368]

A similar sentiment is voiced by the Ugaritic hero Aqhat, who, when offered eternal life by the goddess Anat, forthrightly rejects immortality on the grounds that this is something no mortal can gain, even as a gift from the gods:

> Then Maiden Anat declared:
> Ask for Life, O Hero Aqhat.
> Ask for Life and I will give it to you,
> Immortality, and I will bestow it on you:
> I will let you count the years with Baal,
> And you shall count the months with the children of El!
> . . . .
> But Hero Aqhat replied:
> Do not lie, O Maiden!
> To a Hero your falsehoods are traps.
> As for Man—what shall he get at the end?
> What final place will Man get?
> Glaze will be poured on my head;
> Plaster upon the top of my skull.
> [Just as] everyone dies, so shall I die;
> Yes, I must surely die.[369]

In the Bible itself, the idea that God separates Himself from man by keeping immortality as his exclusive domain probably lies in the background of the story of Adam and Eve (see Gen. 2:15, 3:3–5).[370] In the biblical conception of things, even the spark of life itself is but a temporary gift of God to mankind—a loan that always ends up being withdrawn. So Qoheleth observes: When a mortal dies, "the dust returns to the earth as it was, and the spirit returns to God who gave it" (Eccles. 12:7).[371]

Since death thus constitutes mankind's ultimate deprivation, not surprisingly, it is a natural subject matter, perhaps even *the* natural subject matter, for a man as greatly deprived as Job. As we have seen, the author of the Poem often has his protagonist lament about his woeful condition in the best tradition of a Righteous Sufferer; and, in doing so, Job's preoccupation with death is an ever present theme. Note, for example, Job's lament in chapter 17. This speech is an extended complaint chronicling a variety of sufferings and humiliations that Job has had to endure. But the lament finds its anchor in the figures of death which both begin and end this litany of sorrows. First, Job declares, "My spirit is broken; my days are done; it is the grave for me!" (17:1)[372] and concludes with much the same sentiments in vv. 11–16:

> My time is past;
> My plans have crumbled;
> Even my cherished dreams.
> Night is turned into Day,
> Light gives way before Darkness.[373]
> If I must expect *Sheol* as my home,
> In darkness spread my bed,
> Call to the Pit: "You are my father,
> "My mother, my sister," to the worm,
> Where, then is my hope?
> My hope, who will regard it?
> Will it go down to the gates[374] of *Sheol*?
> Will we descend[375] together to the Dust?

Similar figures can be found in *Ludlul*, where the Righteous Sufferer declares that he is on the brink of death:

> (My) god has not come to the rescue; he has not taken my hand.
> My goddess has not shown me pity; she has not gone at my side.
> My grave stood open, my funerary paraphernalia were ready;
> Before my death, lamentation for me was finished.[376]

Even closer parallels come in the lament Psalms where figures of death are commonplace. A parade example is Psalm 88, perhaps the most "lamentable" psalm in the Bible. This death-oriented complaint could be interpolated into one of Job's speeches, and we would hardly notice the difference:

> . . . my soul is filled up with troubles;
> My life draws near *Sheol*.
> I have been reckoned with those who go down to the Pit;
> I have become a man sapped of strength.
> Among the dead I am released,
> Like corpses lying in the grave
> Whom You [God] no longer remember—
> They who are cut off from Your care. (88:3–6)[377]

In this respect, the poet's use of the death-motif in Job falls in line with the way this theme is usually employed in Ancient Near Eastern literary texts. It is depicted as the ultimate figure for a sufferer to invoke when he is *in extremis*, as if to say, nothing more drastic can befall him save death itself. Yet, on closer consideration, the poet's use of the death-motif reveals a slight variation from the norm. Once more, the poet seems to have added an extra factor that consequently stretches the convention beyond the standard expectations. In fact, in portraying Job's death laments, the poet has his protagonist go a bit too far. Not only does Job opine that he is at death's door, but he further affirms that, this being so, he might as well be dead.

This death-wish of Job's proves to be slightly troublesome; for it does not quite mesh with either the Righteous Sufferer motif or, for that matter, with the legal metaphor we have considered above. "Why," Job laments, "did I not die at birth; emerge from the womb and perish?" (Job 3:11). This might seem just the right sort of sentiment for someone as deeply despairing as Job. But it is not the sort of statement one usually finds a Righteous Sufferer making, nor is it the sort of statement expected from an aggrieved party in a court case.

Note, in this connection, that none of the Righteous Sufferers in the *Theodicy*, *Ludlul* or any of the other texts of this type considered above ever cry out that they would like to die. And this is also true in the various biblical laments we find in the Psalms. This is scarcely surprising; indeed, there is a very good reason for it: such a wish would run directly contrary to what a Righteous Sufferer wants to bring about. He may be afflicted to the point of death, but what he truly desires is relief—cure from his affliction and restoration to health—not to be put out of his misery.

A similar point can be made about an aggrieved party in a court case. No legal plaintiff ever glosses his testimony with a statement that he has been so horrifically wronged that he would just as soon be dead. Such cannot be found in any biblical *rib*, or, for that matter, in any legal complaint among other Ancient Near Eastern juridical documents. Once more, the reason is apparent: It would simply be counterproductive to voice such a sentiment. A litigant may wish to see a sentence of death imposed on his adversary—but certainly not upon himself.

Because Job voices a desire to die when we might expect him to demand a renewal of his former happy life, his speeches sometimes seem to take an unexpected turn and even seem on occasion to border on the illogical. For example, in chapter 6 Job initiates a discourse in the best tradition of a Righteous Sufferer.[378] He declares:

> Ah, could my anguish truly be weighed,
> And all my distress[379] be heaped upon the scales,
> For now it would outweigh the sands of the seas.
> No wonder my words rage![380]
> For the Almighty's arrows are embedded in me,
> So that my spirit drinks their venom.
> God's terrors line up against me!   (6:2–4)

This speech builds to a climax in verse 8, where Job finally makes an appeal to God: "Oh, that my wish might be granted, and God might fulfill my hope!" But the "hope" Job desires is not the one we might expect; for instead of asking for deliverance from all his afflictions, as a Righteous Sufferer should, Job instead requests (6:9–10),

> Might God be so kind as to crush me,
> Might he loose his hand against me and cut me down.
> This would be such a comfort to me!
> I would jump for joy,[381] though he spare me no pain . . .[382]

The line of argument presented here by Job does not quite make sense. If Job is suffering, why should he want more suffering? Moreover, if he wants to be put out of his misery, why wait for God to act? It would seem to make more sense under the circumstances if Job simply were to take his own life. That would end his troubles for good, and he could at last be at rest with all the shades in *Sheol* (cf. Job 3:17–19). Actually, there is really only one *logical* reason why Job does not kill himself but rather continues complaining—because he wants his afflictions lifted. Hence, when he finally asks for "help" in this passage, we can only wonder: Why should it be in these peculiarly masochistic terms?

The same problem also crops up in Job's legal testimony. Chapter 13, for example, is full of legalisms, as Job demands a court date with God (13:3) and accuses his friends of being poor lawyers for the Deity (13:6–11). Finally, in 13:17–19, Job makes this legal declaration:

> Listen closely to my testimony,
> Let my statement be well heeded:
> Look now, I have prepared my case.
> I know I will be acquitted.
> Who would dare litigate with me?
> For I would then keep silent and die.

Job's statement makes sense in terms of the legal metaphor until we get to the last line in this passage (13:19b). But there, one almost feels the need for a double take. For everything Job says up to verse 19b would seem to focus on his demand for a trial. But, assuming Job were to get this wish, we would hardly expect him then to be satisfied, fall silent and expire.[383] Such a "trial," which not only would convert a legal action into inaction but also would end with the plaintiff content to die would be both patently absurd and utterly pointless. In fact, Job picks up his legal metaphor in verses 20 and following as though the statement in verse 19b had never been made, once more vigorously prosecuting his suit and demanding legal fair play from God.

How, then, are we to deal with passages like these? We might try to explain them psychologically; that is, we might argue that Job, overwhelmed by his despair, simply gives in, on occasion, to his darkest moods. Just as his mood sometimes seems full of hope when he declares his witness or redeemer will certainly rescue him, so at other times he is certain that his situation is hopeless and there is no alternative but death. Almost certainly, there is a definite element of truth in such a line of reasoning. But I suspect that the poet has more in mind here than simply portraying the mood swings of his protagonist. Just as we have seen that the passages focusing on Job's hope for a hypothetical Judge-Advocate serve a more subtle and ironic end, so may these death-wish passages have a similar function.

The passage which may show this most clearly is, not surprisingly, the one that gives Job's death-wish its fullest figuration. I refer to the opening speech in the Poem—chapter three, where Job not only affirms that he wants to die but also takes this desire to its logical extreme by wishing that he had never been born. Job begins the curse:

> Strike off the day on which I was born,
> And the night that declared, "It's a boy!"
> That day—let it be darkness.
> May God not recognize it from on high,
> Nor may light ever shine on it.   (3:3–4)

Variations of these darkly shaded sentiments continue until verse 10, where the curse is restated in terms of its rationale. There Job declares that the day of his birth should be damned "because it did not shut up the womb's doors, and hide trouble from my eyes." There follows a series of rhetorical questions that develop the theme further:

> Why did I not die fresh from the womb?
> Perish upon coming forth at birth?
> Why did the knees receive me?
> What reason for breasts, that I should suck?   (3:11–12)

The curse continues with a final focus on the netherworld, where Job longs to be (3:13–19), where the afflictions he most feared (3:25) could no longer overtake him and he could be at last in peace.[384]

What makes this passage so illuminating is that it has a close parallel in the writings of the prophet Jeremiah. If there is little evidence of a Righteous Sufferer stating his desire to die, then Jeremiah's curse of the day of his birth in 20:14–18 would appear to be the most magnificent exception. But it is the exception that proves the rule.

Jeremiah declares, using nearly the same cursing form we find in Job 3:

> Cursed be the day I was born,
> The day my mother bore me, let it be unblessed.
> Cursed be the man who brought the news to my father, saying:
> "Your baby is born; it's a boy!"—making him so happy.
> Let that man be like cities the LORD has overturned without remorse.
> May he hear cries in the morning and alarms at noontime,
> Since he slew me not in the womb, so my mother could have been my grave,
> And her womb forever great with child.
> Why is it that I issued from the womb?
> To see strife and sorrow—
> And spend my time in disgrace?

No passage could be structurally closer than this to Job 3. It could even be said that Job 3 and Jeremiah 20:14–18 are two of the most structurally parallel passages in the Bible.[385] However, especially in consideration of the lack of a clear textual relationship between the two texts, I must agree with C. Westermann's conclusion that a direct dependence of one on the other is hardly a necessary assumption.[386] More likely, we are dealing once again with a particular genre (in this case a lament genre) that both Jeremiah and the poet of Job draw on for their own particular purposes.

In broadest terms these purposes seems to be the same—to depict a sufferer so driven to despair that he feels moved to repudiate his very existence. In Jeremiah's case, his despair can be tracked especially well through reference to his socalled personal laments, which reveal how deeply the burden of prophesying in God's name affects him (Jer. 11:18–12:6; 15:10–21; 17:14–18; 20:7–12; and the present passage).

As these texts poignantly reveal, Jeremiah regrets that he was ever born because he views his situation as truly desperate. As a prophet of God, he finds himself to be completely helpless, utterly subservient to a divine demand that requires him to relay a message of doom to his own people. As Jeremiah tells us, this doom-saying makes him the object of derision and rebuke; indeed, plots have been hatched against him, even conspiracies to murder him (see, e.g., Jer. 11:19). He is thus in a wretched predicament, forced to deliver a dreadful message that he abhors having to deliver even though he is certain it is true. In the passage immediately preceding the cursing of the day of his birth, Jeremiah laments this circumstance eloquently:

> . . . every time I speak, I must cry in alarm,
> "Lawlessness, violence," I must proclaim.
> For the word of the LORD has made me a constant disgrace and laughingstock.
> I have thought, I'll try to ignore Him, I'll speak no more in His name.
> But it has become like a raging fire in my brain, a suppression of my very self.
> I've tried to hold it in, but I can't!   (20:8–9)

We might characterize Jeremiah's lament as portraying the despair of the prophet-as-slave in the thrall of a divine master intent on making him do the worst of all possible tasks. The prophet-slave feels cut off, without recourse, and finally must cry out in order to make sure that his master recognizes how intolerable the circumstances have become. He as much as says, "Look, you're killing me, and, if you keep this up, not only might I just as well be dead, it would be better if I had never been born!"

Still, such an outcry is not to be seen as an act of rebellion or, worse, a signal of the prophet's desire to abandon his God. Rather, it is just the opposite. Implicit in so drastic a lament as we find in Jer. 20:14–18 is a restatement of the most basic prophetic obligation: Jeremiah, for all intents and purposes, reaffirms here that he must do his master's bidding, no matter the personal cost. But there is more involved here than just this; for, by casting his lament in such extreme terms, Jeremiah also tacitly reminds his Deity that the obligation established between God and his prophet is *mutual*. A prophet owes his God complete allegiance, but God also owes his prophet the due consideration that a good master must have for so obedient a servant. Jeremiah is sustained by his unshakable belief that God will ultimately prove to be just such a good master. The prophet may be at the end of his rope, but the one thing that keeps him going, the one thing that keeps him from totally giving in to his despair, is that he knows, deep down, that God will never abandon him.

This is indicated in general terms in all of Jeremiah's writings, but it is particularly manifest in the personal laments. Jeremiah may feel that he has been led like a lamb to slaughter by God (11:19), but he also firmly believes that God will ultimately punish the prophet's enemies (11:21 ff.). Jeremiah may imagine making a legal complaint against God because the Deity allows the wicked to prosper (12:1–2), but he ends up abandoning this idea as patently absurd and instead appeals for God's help (12:3).[387] Perhaps most significantly, Jeremiah can begin a lament almost in the exact terms we find in the curse of the day of his birth—"Alas for me, my mother, that you bore me, a man of conflict and strife to all the land" (15:10)—but then proceed to plead for help (15:15–18); and, significantly, God does respond with assurances, "I am with you to save and rescue you" (vs. 15:20, cf. also the preceding verse).

Jeremiah's curse of his birthday must be seen in this light, as on the surface, a statement of utter despair but beneath, a tacit appeal to which God will certainly respond. In this respect Jeremiah's lament is reminiscent of the ending of the *Babylonian Theodicy*, considered above. While no explicit divine response comes to the Righteous Sufferer's cry at the *Theodicy*'s conclusion, I have argued that such a response has to be assumed. Only in this way can the entire work come together as a profound statement of faith rather than as an ode merely to despair.[388] So, too, Jeremiah's curse must be seen as his own darkest night of the soul; but it would be a serious misinterpretation of everything Jeremiah says and believes to assume that in the curse of 20:14–18 the prophet has lost all hope of a coming dawn.

We cannot be certain whether the poet of Job knew of the "curse-of-the-day-of-birth" lament in the specific terms of a prophetic statement, such as we find in Jeremiah.[389] But he certainly must have known of it in more general terms as an extreme type of implicit appeal, a lament-of-final-resort. The function of such a lament must have been well known and well recognized by his ancient audience: to portray a sufferer's distress in the most nihilistic terms possible for the purpose of attracting God's attention and thus leading to the rescue of the sufferer from affliction.

This would seem exactly what the author of Job has in mind when he has his protagonist initiate the Poem with this lament-*in-extremis* in chapter 3. Job would seem to be following convention, displaying, by means of an archetypical death-wish, the sort of abject humiliation that should elicit anyone's pity, especially God's. Note, in this respect, that Eliphaz certainly reacts to Job's initial cry of despair with appropriate sympathy, responding to Job's speech with the gentle query, "If one were to try to speak to you, would you be weary?" (4:2).[390] Eliphaz simply reacts as a stereotypical comforter ought to react to the despair of a Righteous Sufferer; and he proceeds further in chapter 4 in the traditional manner judiciously to remind Job to put his trust in God.

But just as Eliphaz and the other friends soon discover that they have completely misunderstood what Job is trying to say when he curses his birthday, likewise, the reader of the Poem begins to recognize that he, too, has misapprehended Job's intentions in chapter 3. One is reminded of Perets' strategy of leading his reader "down the garden path" when he has his Defending Angel present the story of Bontsye's life as the stereotypical story of the downtrodden Jew. In a similar fashion the author of Job misdirects his ancient audience by starting his work with what appears to be an archetypical lament. Then the ancient author, like the more modern Yiddish author, reverses his field, as he does so often in the Poem of Job. Job's continued demand for justice in the Poem once more has the same effect as the Prosecutor's laugh in the Yiddish short story: The reader is shocked to discover that this plaint of a Righteous Sufferer is actually just the opposite of what it seems—yet again, a sham substituting for the real thing.

For Job's lament in chapter 3 is not meant to connote his complete subservience to his divine master, no matter what the personal cost, as is the case in Jeremiah 20:14–18. Rather, it is Job's opening battle cry. It is his means of serving notice on God that *this* Righteous Sufferer has had enough. To be sure, Job may have been pushed to such a desperate circumstance that he wishes he had never been born. But, unlike Jeremiah, he has no intention of abjectly humiliating himself before his divine master in the hope that this will elicit the requisite divine pity that might save him. Instead, Job is determined to stand his ground against his Deity, even if he must first retreat to *Sheol* in order to do so. Job's position is one of radical disjunction in which he would rather be a shade in the netherworld with his sense of justice intact than alive in this world groveling before God, despite his innocence. In this respect, Job's death-wish almost reminds one of the famous cry of Satan in the Hell of Milton's *Paradise Lost*:

> . . . . Here at least
> We shall be free; th'Almighty hath not built
> Here for his envy, will not drive us hence:
> Here we may reign secure, and in my choice,
> To reign is worth ambition though in Hell:
> Better to reign in Hell, than serve in Heav'n.[391]

While Job, like Milton's Satan, has no particular love for the netherworld per se, he is more than willing to go there if, in doing so, he might find the one and only retreat where God would at last leave him alone with his integrity intact.[392]

It is this last point, in particular, that makes Job's version of the birthday curse such an effective counterpoint to the conventional form of this lament as we see it exemplified in Jer. 20:14–18. As we have seen, in the final analysis Jeremiah does not really wish he were dead or that he had never been born; most important, he certainly does not wish to be cut off from God. But when Job declares that he wishes to be dead or that he had never been born, he is entirely sincere; he really *would* prefer the shadow existence of the netherworld if it would afford him protection from his divine adversary. Thus, by couching Job's initial lament in these terms, the poet of Job once more has turned a convention on its head: turning a covert appeal for help into an overt demand to be left alone.

The death-wish passages we find scattered elsewhere throughout the Poem of Job should be seen similarly. Ostensibly, they look like standard statements of despair designed to elicit divine pity and help. But they are nothing of the sort. If they seem not quite to fit within the broader context of a Righteous Sufferer's Appeal or a plaintiff's legal brief, this is, I suspect, intentional. The poet wants his reader ultimately to recognize that things are not meshing together in the conventional fashion. Job's despair truly is nihilistic and disjunctive, perhaps even intentionally illogical. For only then can it undercut the stereotypical lament on death and thus have the appropriate parodistic value that the poet intends it to have. Only then can the reader be made to realize that the Job of the Poem wants no forgiveness, no reprieve, no pity, no pardon.[393] Instead, his intentions are to affirm his innocence, make no apologies and demand justice.

Thus, the poet of Job, by playing his counterpoint against conventional expectations, again brings the issues at the heart of the story of Job into sharp relief. We might say that by using the death-motif as he does, the Joban author serves notice: There will be no retreat from a full consideration of the central issue of the Poem—whether God is a moral deity—nor will Job compromise his pursuit of this issue with a "plea bargain." If the reader expects to find an implicit appeal for mercy lurking beneath Job's wish to die, the reader is wrong: this Job is in deadly earnest.

Finally, before we proceed further, one other aspect of the death theme needs to be explored, and it may be the most crucial of all: how the author of the Poem uses this motif specifically to play against the themes of the folktale of Job itself. The fact that the author of the Poem may be using the theme of death as a means to counter the message of the original legend has not been recognized in the scholarly literature, perhaps because scholars tend to think of the legend of Job and its existing rendition, the Prose Frame Story, as much the same thing. But, granting this, the death theme becomes valueless as a potential target for contrapuntal manipulation. In fact, we might best characterize the way the theme of death functions in the Frame Story versus the Poem in terms of cause and effect; that is, in the Prologue death makes its presence felt in Job's life and the lives of his family, and this naturally leads him to focus his laments frequently upon its baleful touch in the Poem. The Epilogue then focuses upon Job's narrow escape from death and his figurative rebirth through the reestablishment of his new progeny. In this respect, there would seem to be no opposition set up between legend and Poem but, rather, a marked continuity.

However, if the arguments presented earlier in this study are correct, the original legend should not be assumed to be identical to the version of Job we now find in the Prose Frame Story. In particular, I have argued above that there is one crucial theme present in the original legend that is lacking in its later refiguring in the Prologue/Epilogue. Moreover, this theme is of special importance because it serves to bring about the original climax of the folktale: I refer, of course, to the resurrection of Job's original children from the dead. Assuming that the poet knew of a Joban legend in which the selfsame children who die are brought back to life, his concentration of so much of his creative energies on depicting death and the netherworld as he does begins to make eminent sense, especially in terms of parodistic counterpoint.

In connection with this, it is important to note that along side the death-wish motif we have been discussing above, there is really only one other theme that seems to dominate the poet's depiction of mortality: the concept of death as permanent nonexistence, from which there is no further recourse. Job frequently reemphasizes the fact that when you die, you are dead for good and that there is no return from the netherworld. We have already noted this theme in 7:9–10 (see also 7:7), where Job characterizes life as something that ultimately vanishes like a cloud, never to return again. A number of similar statements could also be cited. Compare, for example, Job 10:18–22, where Job addresses God, virtually restating his sentiments of chapter 3, and then concludes with reflections upon the transitory nature of life and the permanency of death:

> So why did You bring me out of the womb?
> Would I had perished, sight unseen.
> Just like someone who never was, would I have been—
> Carried from womb to tomb.
> Are not my days but a few? Leave me be!
> Let me alone, so I can gain a little happiness,
> Before I go—never to return—
> To the Land of Darkness and Death's Shadow,
> The Land as Dark as Darkness itself,
> Death's Shadow where there is no more meaning
> Where Darkness is all there is of light.

As we have already demonstrated with examples cited at the outset of this discussion of death, such sentiments are stereotypical. Even one of Job's friends, Bildad, can voice similar sentiments when he declares, "Our days are but a shadow on the earth" (8:9), as if to say that at least on this one point, he and Job are in agreement. But it is important to realize that there is a particular sharpness to the expression of such archetypical sentiments in the Poem of Job when they are seen against the backdrop of the original folktale. For they serve to belie and hence to subvert the most miraculous message of the original Joban legend. The poet understands that the power of the legend of Job to transform profound despair into equally profound hope comes from its message that God's merciful power knows no boundaries, not even the boundaries of death. The original tradition offers those who suffer, especially those whose grief comes from bereavement, a hope against hope: Perhaps, the legend hints, if a sufferer can be as righteous, as patient and as uncomplaining as Job, God may do for him as he did for this legendary righteous man—restore all health, all wealth and even bring those who have died back to life again.

If there is one aspect of the legend of Job that the author of the Poem wished to attack without quarter, I think it is what he perceived to be this false hope of resurrection. And in doing so, he characteristically uses established, stereotypical sentiments about the permanence of death in order to drive his point home. In a real sense, the poet uses tradition to counter tradition—indeed, what better weapon could he utilize in order to strike at the very core of the Joban legend? I think one might fairly argue that no counterpoint in the entire Poem is more clearly set against the original message of the folktale than this.

But the poet's attack upon the hope for resurrection in the legend of Job is not limited to the use of stereotypical figures that emphasize death's permanence and life's fragility. He also plays his counterpoint against other figures, which must have also coexisted within the traditions[394] and which focused on the idea of rebirth from the grave.[395] There are, in particular, two passages in the Poem where the Joban author plays off of this resurrection theme. The first of these occurs in Job's speech of chapter 14, and it illustrates especially well how effectively the poet can manipulate this motif.

The poet begins Job's discourse in chapter 14 with what was certainly an often invoked observation on the transitory nature of a mortal's life:

> Man, born of woman,
> Short of days, but long on trouble,
> Like a flower he blooms and then withers,
> Vanishes like a shadow and cannot stay. (14:1–2)

This stereotypical meditation[396] continues on to verse 5,[397] and then concludes with a familiar Joban plea that God might leave mortals alone and not add to the already tasking duties of their lives (14:6).

It is in verses 7–9 that the poet begins specifically to touch on the resurrection theme. He starts by having Job observe,

> For a tree there may be hope:
> If cut down, still, it may recover;
> And its shoots not give out.
> Though its root be long gone in the earth,
> And its stock dead in the dust,
> At the scent of water, it buds,
> Puts out shoots like a sprout.

The Joban author depicts a figure for agricultural renewal in this passage. He may even be making indirect allusion to cyclic rebirth as celebrated, for example, in the Canaanite legends such as those found in the texts of ancient Ugarit. In these accounts, as mentioned above, the god Baal, lord of the rains, engages in conflict with the death god Mot. Baal's subsequent dying and rising from the netherworld seems in some manner connected with the withering and renewal of vegetation in the agricultural cycle of Syro-Palestine. This is clearly manifest, for example, in this account of a vision by the patriarchal God El of the resurrection of Baal:

> In a dream of Beneficent El, benign,
> In a vision of the Creator of all things:
> The heavens rain down oil,

> The wadis flow with honey.
> Thus, I know that Mighty Baal lives,
> That revived is the Prince, Lord of the earth.[398]

But if a tree like a god can be resurrected from the dust, then the poet sharply notes the contrast to mortal men, who can harbor no such hope (vv. 10–12):

> But a man dies, and is laid low,
> A mortal perishes, and where is he?
> Water drains from a sea,
> Or a river evaporates and dries up—
> So a man lies down and does not rise
> Not to wake until the heavens are no more.

Thus, the poet reaffirms the permanence of death for mankind, over against the possibility of agricultural rebirth. He seems especially anxious to deny any potential association between the life cycle of mortals and vegetation. Note, in contrast, that just such a connection between the fate of vegetation and mankind is evidenced in the Danel/Aqhat story, if only in reverse. When Aqhat is struck dead, as a result of his conflict with Anat, then, in a manner that seems analogous to the death of Baal, there is a direct effect on agriculture in his father Danel's kingdom. When Aqhat dies, the vegetation immediately withers and fades as the result of the sudden onset of drought; and, almost certainly, this is viewed in the story as cause and effect. This may give us a reasonable expectation that were Aqhat to be resurrected from the dead like Baal, again the crops would renew themselves in Danel's land.[399]

Presumably, it is just this sort of story—which, as we have noted, shares such close affinities with the original Joban legend—that the author of the Poem endeavors to discredit in the first part of Job's speech of chapter 14. Indeed, it may not be unreasonable to assume that when he has Job declare, "A man lies down and does not rise," he is not only giving the lie to stories of human resurrection but is, at the same time, making it quite clear that a mere mortal can never be equated with a legendary god who might somehow manage to defeat Mot. There will be no human redemption from death, the poet of Job declares, this side of paradise.

But the poet is not content with just making this point. In 14:13 and following he goes a step further by having his Job take an imaginary leap: Suppose a mortal really *could* go down to *Sheol* and then be rescued like an Aqhat or an Isaac by a merciful god from the jaws of death? This idea becomes focused in 14:13–17 in terms of a wish Job directs to God:

> If only You might hide me in *Sheol*,
> Conceal me until Your anger relents,
> Set for me a time limit, then remember me:
> If he die, might a mortal live again?
> All my burdensome days I would wait,
> Until my relief would come:
> Then You would summon and I would answer You,
> You would be mindful of that which Your hand has made.
> For then you would number my steps
> Without taking note of my sin,

My transgression would be sealed up in a pouch,
And You would cover up my iniquity.

This wish of Job's begins with yet one more statement that borders on the illogical. Job appeals to God to hide him away in *Sheol* and protect him from that wrathful Deity who is out to destroy him. Of course, the problem here is that God, the Protector, is also this same wrathful Deity. This makes for a circumstance bordering on the impossible; for how can God possibly hide Job from God?[400] In fact, in order for Job's wish to be fulfilled, the poet almost has to imagine that God is two separate entities: both Attacker and Defender. In this respect, we find once more that the poet is developing the image that plays such an important role in his legal metaphor: the imagined "counter-Deity" who defends Job against the real God.[401]

It is to this God-as-Defender that Job turns in his hope, not only to escape from his divine persecutor, but even from death itself. He asks this Deity to hide him in *Sheol*, the one place where God-as-Attacker might leave him alone. But this interment in the netherworld is not portrayed as being for eternity, as is typically the case in Job's other depictions of death. Rather, Job envisions a resurrection. Like the God who brings back Job's children from the dead to give the folktale its "happy ending," our protagonist hopes for a time to come, when his Redeemer will bring him back from *Sheol* to the world of the living. But this would be no ordinary world; on the contrary, it would be a world dramatically transformed, where everything has become as Job would wish it to be. God in this new world is no longer the wrathful Deity; and when He calls to Job, it is no longer in anger. Instead, this transformed God shows nothing except His solicitous concern for what His own hands have made. As for Job, whatever paltry sins he may have incurred are completely forgiven; his iniquities pardoned. Most importantly, God-as-Defender has now become the master of the universe and no longer needs to protect Job against God-as-Attacker. We might say that when Job comes back to life in his dream-vision, the wrathful God dies, never to rise again.

This is Job's grand dream and he equates it with mankind's age old dream of escape from death. Job wonders, could it be? Could God do such miracles— bringing the dead back to a world that has become a veritable Joban utopia? If so, Job declares, then he would gladly abandon his impatience. Like the Job of legend he would wait, quite literally, until Hell freezes over.

But just as Job's dream reaches this climax, the poet shatters it with a strong dose of reality in 14:18–22. Job is made to wake once more from his reverie and confront the hard facts of the real world, in which he remains sated with pain but starved of justice. In such a world time is relentless, death is certain, and a return of the dead to the living is absolutely impossible. Job looks to the destructive forces of nature themselves and sees in them sufficient proof that his dream is false: there can never be a resurrection to a perfect world in which God and man have a utopian relationship. Just as the hardest rocks give way before the onslaught of nature, so, too, do we see Job's imagined hope crumble as he turns once more to face the reality of his merciless God, the Master of Time, who guides all mortals to their inevitable end:

> But, alas, a mountain collapses and crumbles
> And the rock wastes away from its place.
> Water wears down stone,
> And its torrents sweep down the dust of the earth:
> Thus, You destroy the hope of Man.
> You always prevail over him and he passes away,
> You alter his looks, then dispatch him.
> His sons may gain honor, but he never knows;
> Or are humiliated, but he remains in the dark—
> Only his flesh feels pain,
> And his soul is all that mourns for him.

Job's hope, which tries so desperately to raise itself out of the depths of his despair, is made here to die before it hardly has had an opportunity to live. The poet thus emphasizes that this stillborn expectation has no more chance of success than a mortal has of coming back from *Sheol*. Moreover, besides making this point, the author of Job uses this passage in chapter 14 deftly to undercut the brightest theme in the original Joban legend, the miracle of resurrection, revealing it instead to be no more than a miraculous mirage.

The second passage the poet uses to play against the resurrection theme in the original folktale is not quite as extensive as chapter 14, but it has become far more prominent. It is the famous Redeemer passage in chapter 19, which we have already considered, in part, above.[402] In my previous discussion, I focused only on the way this text functions within the context of the poet's legal metaphor; but its relevance to the theme of rebirth from the dead is equally important. This motif begins to be introduced into Job's speech in 19:23–24, which is couched, like chapter 14, in terms of a wish:

> Ah! If only my words were written down!
> If only they were carved on a stela!
> With an iron chisel and lead—
> Forever cut into the rock.

Putting up a stone inscription, of course, was a popular endeavor for rulers in the Ancient Near East, and there was good reason for this to be so. After all, outside of engendering progeny, the making of a stela was a man's one sure means of living beyond the grave and his only way to speak directly to those who follow. Not surprisingly, kings therefore used such memorials to make their most important statements, words that were intended to endure all the tests of time. This is the concept that lies behind Job's wish expressed in 19:23–24. He, too, would like to leave a memorial, something that might endure long after he is gone, a stone to preserve his most important pronouncement, the one message that he would leave to posterity.

This message, presumably, is what follows in verses 25 and following. It begins with the famous passage in verse 25, "I know that my Redeemer lives, finally upon the dust he will arise." We have already noted that this Redeemer might be best understood as an imagined 'counter-Deity' who serves as Job's Judge-Advocate. What interests us here is the imagery associated with his sudden emergence, seemingly out of nowhere. As has often been noted, the literary figure utilized by the poet is immediately reminiscent of the passage in the Ugaritic myth, quoted above, where El affirms in his vision of Baal's resurrection from the netherworld, 'I know that mighty Baal lives!'[403] Moreover, the second part of verse 25 further reinforces this imagery by describing Job's Redeemer as a figure that arises from the dust. This would seem, once more, likely to be an allusion to the rising of a god from out of *Sheol*, especially in consideration that "dust" (*'pr*) is a common term for the netherworld in the Bible as well as in the Ugaritic myths.[404]

It would therefore seem that the Redeemer is not really envisioned by Job as coming out of nowhere; rather, he is portrayed as arising out of the netherworld, where, presumably, he has long been buried.[405] This in itself is a rather startling image, especially if, as appears to be so, the poet is intending to play off divine conflict stories like that exemplified in the story of Baal's struggle with Mot. Such stories are widespread in the Ancient Near East and also show their impact on biblical texts. A number of references, especially in the prophetic books and the Psalms, depict God as fighting an implacable divine enemy. God's defeat of this foe is often invoked as his greatest triumph in the ages long past.[406] But in all such stories, both in and outside the Bible, the hero-deity is always, as it were, on the side of the angels; that is, he fights on behalf of order, fertility and rebirth and against chaos, decay and death. But the poet of Job, once more inverts the conventional correspondences. For it is the Redeemer, newly reborn out of the chthonic Dust, who takes on the 'hero' role; even more strikingly, it is God, the expected hero in such a story, who is placed in the role of divine enemy, as the one who must be vanquished if the Redeemer is to save Job.

The passage that follows, 19:26–27, is commonly considered the most controversial and difficult to interpret in the entire book of Job, and there is no scholarly consensus as to how the text should be translated, let alone understood. As a consequence, any judgment as to the import of the passage must be viewed as tentative. Still, we may try to assay the meaning of this text in light of our discussion above of the resurrection motif in chapter 14. In this passage, I think that the poet endeavors to extend the apparent analogy between Job's Redeemer and the god rising out of the netherworld. Just as a reborn deity brings with him the power to restore life to the land, so Job's rescuer seems to be endowed with a similar ability to bring a Righteous Sufferer back to life, much after the manner in which God restores the children in the old folktale.[407]

Job seems to envision an ultimate moment in time (cf. *'ḥrwn*, "finally" in 19:25b[408]) when all that remains of him and what he has suffered would seem to be preserved as a memory on the stela for which he wished in 19:23–24. But it is just at this final point that Job's Redeemer will act in the most dramatic fashion to effect a resurrection, much like the resurrection Job imagined in chapter 14. The divine rescuer will bring Job back from the grave; and, even though time has literally stripped the skin away from this Righteous Sufferer's body, nonetheless it will be Job, in the flesh, who will rise once more to see at long last a beneficent God:

> And, long after my very skin has been stripped away,
> Then from my flesh shall I see God—
> Whom I will see myself
> And my eyes will view—no other,
> Though my innards have been consumed within me.[409]

This is in essence Job's greatest dream. It goes beyond the reverie of chapter 14; for in that instance, Job finally rejects the vision. But here he seems to have cut himself loose from despair and to have affirmed once and for all that there *will* be a final vindication, even if it must take place beyond the grave. The stela with its Redeemer-inscription serves as a witness[410] for all humanity of this "second coming" of Job so that his hope will persist generation after generation, even when he is no longer alive to affirm it with his own lips. Yet as we have shown above, this dream ultimately proves to be false; for the Theophany effectively bursts this bubble of hope. Job's final reckoning with God is not going to wait for some Ultimate Moment but is coming very soon. Nor will it be accompanied by a miraculous scene of a rising Redeemer who not only defeats death for his own part but further rescues a Righteous Sufferer from its clutches. Instead, it will be a hard encounter offering a very mortal Job little recourse and nothing but his right hand to save him.

The poet of Job thus raises up this vision of renewal and resurrection so that he can then ultimately and utterly discredit it. This may be already indicated well before the Theophany by the way Job's resurrection in chapter 19 is specifically depicted in verses 26–27. Actually, if one reads this text literally, the poet portrays quite a ghoulish picture, and certainly not the conventional depiction of resurrection from the dead. After all, when figures like Isaac, Aqhat or the children of Job return from the dead in the ancient traditions, they come back completely restored, completely whole, just as they were before they died, if not better. As Paul declares in his First Letter to the Corinthians (and as Handel then set to music in his *Messiah*), "the trumpet will sound and the dead shall be raised incorruptible" (1 Cor. 16:52).

But when Job envisions himself risen out of the grave at the beckoning of his Redeemer in chapter 19, he is not a pretty sight. With his skin stripped off and only the bare, presumably rotting flesh left, he seems more a risen corpse than a reborn man. The image is no less than shocking because it is so dreadfully wrong—a perversion of bodily resurrection rather than its embodiment.[411] But this, I suspect, is precisely what the poet intended it to be. He shows here in the most graphic terms the impossibility of resurrection from the dead: like the grotesque lump of flesh conjured out of Job's vision, it is the opposite of what it appears, more dead than alive. The poet seems to say: though the hope of resurrection is something men desperately try to bring to life in stories like the legend of Job or of Abraham and Isaac, it is a forlorn hope. Mortals should not allow this hope to rise up in their consciousness; rather they should bury it with their dead, deep in the netherworld.[412]

Still, this may not be the complete message offered in the twisted vision of resurrection in chapter 19. Perhaps there is one image from this passage that is to be taken more positively than negatively: the picture of the stela, with its words cut in the rock forever. In one respect, this too can be seen as an ironic image—reminiscent of the broken statue of Ozymandias in Shelley's sonnet, which we considered earlier. The inscription carved on that monument—"My name is Ozymandias, king of kings: Look on my works, ye Mighty and despair"—shows an almost messianic pride in the certainty of its truth. But it, too, proves to be a hope as forlorn as Job's visionary "I know my Redeemer lives. . . ." In each case we imagine a "colossal wreck" preserving long dead, long discredited sentiments while "boundless and bare the lone and level sands stretch far away."

Yet there is also a counterpoint to this monumental scene of shattered mortal pride. One is reminded of the words that begin and end the story of Gilgamesh, perhaps the most celebrated account of man's striving with gods in the Ancient Near East. When this hero has finished all of his journeys and has finally come to terms with his defeated attempt to secure the gift of immortality, the story declares,

> He carved on a stone stela all of his toils,
> And built the wall of Uruk-Haven,
> The wall of the sacred Eanna Temple the holy sanctuary.
> Look at its wall which gleams like copper (?),
> Inspect its inner wall, the likes of which no one can equal!
> Take hold of the threshold stone—it dates from ancient times!
> . . . .
> Go up on the wall of Uruk and walk around,
> Examine its foundation, inspect its brickwork thoroughly.
> Is not (even the core of) the brick structure made of kiln fired brick,
> And did not the Seven Sages themselves lay out its plans?
> . . . .
> Find the copper tablet-box,
> Open the . . . of its lock of bronze,
> Undo the fastening of its secret opening.
> Take and read out from the lapis-lazuli tablet
> How Gilgamesh went through every hardship.[413]

Once more there is a description of a monument, which the story suggests might be inspected to this very day, long after the bodily remains of Gilgamesh have returned to the dust. The story affirms: one can *still* find the place where the sacred writings are kept and can read from the precious tablets, thus bringing the story to life once again. To be sure, one would now be hard pressed to find where among the ancient rubble the legendary lapis tablets might lay hidden. Still, the story endures, as does Shelley's sonnet and—no less—the Poem of Job. This, above all, is the continuing message that the author of Job conveys in his own literary monument; and perhaps lies behind the message of the stela in chapter 19. Hope of bodily resurrection, the poet declares, cannot stand before Death. But the very words that proclaim such a hope can endure; and all men, who would be immortal, can live through no other means than the great writings and monuments they leave behind to the mortals that follow in their paths toward oblivion.

12

Supplemental Themes

It would not be difficult to extend this discussion of the parodistic aspects of the Poem of Job; there are a number of studies in the scholarly literature, highlighting various satiric and ironic elements in this biblical book that have already led the way in this respect.[414] Where I really depart from these other interpretations is in my contention that this is all part of a grand design, that parody is not simply an aspect of the Poem but is instead the very essence of what the Poem actually is.

In this connection, it is insightful to note the difficulties scholars have perceived in attempting to characterize the genre of the book of Job. The Poem seems especially hard to classify because of its tendency to segue from one theme to another, leaving the reader with the impression that the Dialogue—especially Job's speeches—is composed of a medley of motifs, almost a hodge-podge of stereotypes and conventions, drawn from all aspects of religion, literature and culture in the Ancient Near East. While there is general agreement that Job stands within the biblical/ancient Near Eastern Wisdom tradition, beyond this, scholars tend to see the book as far too eclectic to be amenable to a definitive, literary labeling. The observation of J. L. Crenshaw is representative: "Perhaps the only area in which something resembling consensus has formed concerns the *sui generis* nature of the work."[415]

To some extent this is an appropriate judgment in that there is no other Ancient Near Eastern literary work that seems directly comparable to Job. Rather, it appears to emulate a wide range of materials at one point or another. Still, if this work is best classified as a parody, then the way the Poem turns from type to type, from genre to genre, begins to make better sense; for this is the typical method of operation in a parody, that is, the parodist is usually not content to aim his satirical barbs at only one target. Rather, more often he tries to slay as many sacred cows as possible; indeed, the more broadly based the satire, the more it tends to range across the entire cultural landscape in search of one target after another to mock.[416] In this respect, parody is a literary chameleon, taking on the coloration of first one thing, then another—but always, as I have noted, for purposes of masquerade.

This is certainly true for the Poem of Job. No other work in the Bible tries to take on the appearance of as many different themes and types as it does. But what is particularly important to realize is that parody serves as the common denominator in all cases; that is, the author never intends merely to portray parallel upon parallel. Rather, in every instance where the author of Job incorporates something from his religious/literary/cultural milieu—whether it be an allusion to Canaanite religion or saga, the incorporation of legalistic terminology, a lament form, the format of a dialogue, a Righteous Sufferer's Appeal or whatever, the intent is never simply to imitate but also to oppose: to depict not only the convention but also the counterpoint to the convention. Thus, each archetype is set up only to be knocked down; and this overall parodistic intent gives what might otherwise seem a chaotic jumble of disparate motifs its shape and logic.

It is not hard to understand why a parody on the scale of the Poem of Job tends to be eclectic, why the intent of the satirist is to take aim at as many targets as possible. We should recall what we learned from our close analysis of Perets' "Bontsye Shvayg"—that most often, a deep and abiding anger serves as the motivation for the best parodistic work.[417] Such an anger is expansive; a writer who is outraged at what he perceives to be the flaws in his society is usually not content to confine his attack to just one or two topics. Instead, his passionate concern more often leads him to "take on the world," to let fly at all aspects of his society and its cultural foibles.

We can see this in Perets' work, and it is equally manifest in the work of the poet of Job. He will not be content simply to discredit an ancient and beloved folktale; this serves merely as his point of departure for an all-encompassing onslaught against the most basic, conventional assumptions about the nature of God and his relation to mankind. In this respect, the Poem is not unique; for it is not difficult to find other examples of parody and satire in the Ancient Near Eastern world, both in and outside the Bible.[418]

For example, the biblical prophets often turn to parody in order to emphasize that the relationship between God and his chosen people is fundamentally different from what the people perceive it to be. In this respect, one almost has to assume that, when an Amos angrily declares that the "day of the LORD" "will be darkness and not light" (5:18), he is parodying a stereotypical statement of hope, known to all, that this day of reckoning will be "light and not darkness."[419]

But where the Poem of Job may be said to be exceptional is in the scope of its parodistic vision. There is simply no other work known to us from this ancient world that tries to attack so much with such relentless zeal. Perhaps what is truly unique about the Joban author is the extent of the passionate outrage that his work reflects. In fact, it might be fair to argue that we know of no other writer from the ancient world who was angrier than the poet of Job.

As was the case with Perets, the anger of the Joban author was inspiring and visionary, and it produced a work of such magnitude that it could not be ignored, let alone suppressed. Still, it could elicit a strong reaction; indeed, of necessity, those who would maintain the traditional worldview had to do something to counter so thorough an attack on their most basic assumptions about God and man. I have already suggested in the broadest terms the direction that this reaction took: the Aqiban strategy that motivated the reincorporation of Job the Impatient into Job the Patient.[420] But, in order to consider this in more specific terms, it will be helpful, once again, to turn to our Bontsye-model for guidance.

In the case of "Bontsye Shvayg," as we have seen, the forces of history went to work on the story. Because reality for Jews was so profoundly changed by events in the first half of the twentieth century that seemed of cataclysmic proportion, Perets' message also had to be rethought and reshaped to reflect this new world of Jewish consciousness, especially in a post-Holocaust age. Of course, as has already been emphasized, there is no way to track what succession of events led to the apparent rethinking and reshaping of the Poem of Job.[421] Still, there are two points which may be noted.

First, whatever the cultural context of the original Poem, the evidence suggests that all the additional material that ultimately coalesced around it to make the canonical book of Job was written within a specifically Israelite/Jewish environment. In the case of the Prose Frame Story, this is clearly indicated by the name used for the Deity who acts against Job, Yahweh, a theophoric title reserved only for the God of Israel (see 1:6, etc.). Likewise, the same title is used wherever possible in the rubrics introducing the speeches in the story (i.e., in the Theophany, see 38:1, etc.).

In the case of the Hymn to Wisdom (chap. 28), the phrase $yr't$ 'dny hy' ḥkmh, "awe of my Lord—that is Wisdom," occurs in vs. 28. This appears to be a specific allusion to the motto of the book of Proverbs (see Prov. 1:7) and more generally to a proverbial expression closely identified with the pursuit of Wisdom in a specifically Israelite/Jewish environment.[422] Moreover, the theophoric title 'dny, "my Lord," is a late circumlocution for God's name, known elsewhere only in Jewish contexts.[423]

Finally, there are the Elihu speeches. While nothing internal to these discourses can be shown to prove decisively that they were composed in an Israelite/Jewish cultural context, there is the fact that the name of the speaker to whom these speeches are credited, is identifiably Israelite/Jewish in origin. Note, in particular, that "Elihu" (i.e., 'lyhw') is a well-documented biblical name; moreover, if the variant spelling 'lyhw (i.e., "Eliyahu"; see 32:4, 35:1) is taken seriously, it contains the "Yahu" theophoric element and is therefore clearly to be associated with the Israelite/Jewish God, Yahweh.[424] Besides this, Elihu's identification with the "family of Ram" (32:2) gives him specifically Judahite connections and thus also tends to fix his origin within a Jewish context.[425]

In the case of "Bontsye Shvayg" we know that specific historical events served to fix the Yiddish story in Jewish consciousness and to make its "hero" an emblem for the suffering that the Jews endured. While it is true that in the case of Job we cannot be so precise about its historical context, in the final analysis, this may not make all that much difference. The fact is that the Israelites and the Jews endured such a succession of disasters throughout most of their history that any one of these setbacks (or any combination thereof) could have served as a catalyst for fixing the Poem of Job in their consciousness and for transforming its protagonist into an emblem of their own tragedies. After all, there is much in the Poem of Job with which God's special people could identify. Like Job, they had been singled out for unusual treatment: most notably, they were chosen by God to the exclusion of all others; and because of their chosenness, they had to suffer. Job's cries of despair directed toward God could, with a little imagination, be seen as representing the cry of the Israelites, carried off by the Assyrians and/or the despair of the Jews when the Temple was destroyed. Job's hope of a witness from on high, a Redeemer who finally would arise upon the dust, could be seen as prefiguring the Jewish hope for a return to the Promised Land, the rebuilding of the Temple and the coming of the Messiah. Hence, the circumstance we have traced in modern times may be not so different from the circumstance in ancient times: If a Bontsye might be seen as a convenient index for the *tsoriss* of his people in one instance, why not Job in another?

The second point to be considered is that when the Israelites and/or Jews chose to rethink the Poem of Job, they did not so much try to alter the text itself as to bend their efforts towards supplementing it. This is a process I have touched on before in reference to the book of Ecclesiastes.[426] When Qoheleth's editor set about collecting the writings of his mentor, he apparently did not alter them in any significant way, even though they were hardly compatible with his own traditional worldview. The reason for this should be clear: the editor deemed the writings in Ecclesiastes to constitute a work of genius. Thus, for him to change the texts would have seemed tantamount to violating that very genius which he so much admired and which had motivated him to preserve these writings in the first place. Still, as we have noted, the editor of Ecclesiastes also deemed it essential to explain Qoheleth, to set his radical "truth" within the context of a more conservative viewpoint of "Truth." If this could not be done by directly violating the text itself, there was only one viable alternative left—to explain through supplementation in lieu of alteration. Therefore, this is precisely what Qoheleth's editor proceeded to do when he appended his note to the end of Ecclesiastes.

A similar process—but on a grander scale—must be seen as taking place in the book of Job. The original Poem was also deemed to be a work of genius that later generations of writers and redactors held in awe and therefore hesitated to violate in any significant fashion. Still, much like the editor of Ecclesiastes, they felt the need to explain the Poem's radical version of truth in terms of a more traditional worldview. So they took the same approach, adding to the text instead of changing it.

Of course, such a process of supplementation is not unique to the books of Ecclesiastes and Job but is commonly seen in other traditional literary works with long redactional histories, both in and outside the Bible. M. Greenberg, in his consideration of this process of editorial supplementation in Exodus, has argued that there is a characteristic pattern to the way such additions occur. The model he proposes seems particularly applicable to the book of Job. He observes,

> A blatant contradiction, a break in progress, a marked change of style and tone—these are, as a rule, most plausibly accounted for by the assumption that heterogeneous elements, originally independent of one another, have been combined. The less integrated the disturbance is into its context, the later it may be assumed to have been combined. For plasticity and integrative capability are characteristic of early stages of transmission; rigidity and unassimilability, characteristic of the quasi-canonical status of the material in the time of redaction. The grossest disturbances are thus to be ascribed to the last redactional stage of combination, while lesser disturbances belong to earlier development of the tradition complexes.[427]

More recently, this theoretical overview of the process of redaction of ancient documents has been shown by J. Tigay to have empirical grounding. He has demonstrated that precisely this process shaped the complex of literary strands that ultimately became the "canonical" version of Gilgamesh.[428]

140   JOB THE SILENT

The supplements to the Poem of Job seem to be best understood in accordance with Greenberg's redactional model. Their very intrusiveness indicates that they are heterogeneous elements, and the relative degree of disjunction between each addition and the original Poem seems to show an increasing chronological distance from this original, creative work. Thus, while the Hymn to Wisdom and the Elihu speeches are more closely integrated into the fabric of the Poem itself, the Prose Frame Story shows a much more profound disjunction from the poetic body of Job, probably indicating a substantially later date (an assumption also confirmed by Hurvitz's analysis of the language of the Prologue/Epilogue).[429] Still, I think none of the later interpolators intended to hide their additions to the text of Job. Like the writer(s)/redactor(s) of the *Akedah* they meant for their additions to call attention to themselves so that the reader could distinguish the different levels that formed the complex of Joban counterpoint.

As we have seen, "Bontsye Shvayg" was treated similarly by its Yiddish audience. By and large, the original story remained untouched. Only Perets himself had the nerve to revise his work in any significant fashion—and then the satire was only intensified. But this does not mean that Perets' sharply critical message was allowed to hold sway without eliciting a strong response. Critics and creative artists, compelled by the need to see Bontsye in the harsh light of the twentieth century, responded to the story by encapsulating it in reinterpretations. Thus, they transformed the story and its hero from what Perets had originally intended them to be into what they had to be after the pogroms and the Holocaust. Perhaps, then, if we look at the supplements to Job in a similar manner, they, too, will be better understood as the counter to the counterpoint, aiming to reestablish the tradition that the Poem itself had challenged.

We can begin by considering the Hymn to Wisdom (chap. 28). We have already noted the apparent discontinuities between the Poem and the Hymn that have led most scholars to conclude that the latter is an originally independent, interpolated addition to the book of Job.[430] Even beyond this, the contemplative tone of this meditation on the inaccessibility of Wisdom should signal to the reader that the presence of a new voice that has drawn back from the rough-and-tumble of debate to see things from a more dispassionate perspective.

In doing so, the author of the Hymn seems particularly anxious to emphasize that mere mortals cannot hope to find resolution to the issues raised by Job and his Three Friends, especially the issues that are the primary concern of the Poem: What is the nature of God? Is He a moral deity? At best, mankind may have enough intelligence to pose these questions, but, it is incapable of gaining sufficient insight to frame a viable answer.

Still, if this is the main theme of the Hymn, its author begins his work by highlighting a contrasting figure—man's probing of the earth in search of its hidden treasure. The Hymn's poet suggests that there are virtually no physical boundaries that a determined miner cannot penetrate. If there is something precious to be gained, he will focus his energy and ingenuity on breaching any barrier. The Hymn to Wisdom even seems to suggest that men will probe right up to the borders of the netherworld in their quest for the wealth of the earth:

> He hems in the darkness,
> And every recess he probes—
> Rock in pitch dark and Death's Shadow. (28:3)

This image is particularly well suited for a poem about Wisdom because it plays off a cliché that seems to have been frequently associated with the pursuit of knowledge. In the book of Proverbs it is stated in this manner (3:13–15):

> How happy is the man who discovers Wisdom,
> And the man who extracts understanding.
> For its gain is superior to the gain of silver;
> Far more than gold is its profit.
> It is more precious than rubies,[431]
> And none of your goods can compare to it.[432]

This proverbial observation makes the point that no material wealth compares with Wisdom; it is simply the most valuable commodity that any person can acquire.

This much is obvious; but there is a second, slightly more subtle point implicitly made in this and similar comments about the value of Wisdom; namely, that Wisdom is not all that easy to acquire. Like money, it "doesn't grow on trees." Rather, one must work determinedly and devote all one's energies toward its acquisition. One must probe, dig and sift through mountains of extraneous material in order to extract just one or two nuggets of real value; and then one must also be sure that the treasure acquired is the genuine article rather than simply "fool's gold."

The trouble, the author of the Hymn to Wisdom declares, is that while man has all the skills needed to find the most precious material treasures, when it comes to the acquisition of Wisdom, he is completely stymied; for this is a treasure that cannot be located anywhere in humanity's universe:

> But Wisdom—where may it be found?
> And where is the place of understanding?
> No man knows its worth,[433]
> Nor is it found in the land of the living.
> The Deep says, "not in me."
> The Sea says, "not with me." (28:12–14)

The traditional view of Wisdom as the most precious thing recurs in the following verses,

> It cannot be traded for the finest gold,
> Nor weighed out like silver for a price.
> It cannot be valued for the bullion of Ophir,
> Nor for fine onyx or sapphire. (28:15–16; cf. vv. 17–19)

But in the Hymn this truism is given an ironic twist: Wisdom is celebrated in the conventional fashion for its unique value; but in this case its uniqueness is seen as a curse rather than a blessing. This poem dangles Wisdom, like the finest of jewels, before humanity's ignorant eyes, but then snatches it back well beyond its intellectual reach.

The author of the Hymn to Wisdom is thus playing his own particular counterpoint against convention in the first part of his poem by taking a stereotypical statement, celebrating the value of knowledge, and accentuating its negative implications rather than the usual positive aspects. The book of Proverbs forthrightly declares, "The beginning of Wisdom is: acquire Wisdom! No matter what else you gain, gain understanding!" (4:7). But *true* Wisdom is seen in chapter 28 of Job as coming with the recognition that this simply cannot be done, that this particular treasure cannot be had for love, money or anything else.

That such emphasis should be placed on humanity's incapacity to gain genuine Wisdom at the conclusion of the debate between Job and his Three Friends is altogether appropriate. After all, the primary reason that nothing is resolved at the debate's conclusion is simply because humanity does not have the inherent knowledge to decide such overwhelming questions. Both Job and his Three Friends would grant as much. The Hymn to Wisdom thus serves a valuable function by setting the Joban debate in perspective: If questions about the nature of God cannot be answered by mere mortals, then the Hymn, in most elegant fashion, explains why this is necessarily so.

Still, one could reasonably argue that when God appears in the Theophany, he makes much the same point and far more emphatically. Therefore, the addition of the poem in chapter 28 could be seen, by and large, as a redundancy. This is, to some extent, a fair evaluation; yet it is not hard to see what rationale might have led a later writer and/or editor to add this interpolation to the Poem of Job.

The Theophany offers no quarter. It hits hard at its theme and shows little gentleness in its depiction of God's overwhelming onslaught on Job's puny intelligence. It may well be that chapter 28 was placed in Job to soften this blow. Note, in this respect, that its placement is strategic, especially if one assumes it was inserted into the Poem of Job before the Elihu speeches were added. For then it would precede the final, climactic denouement initiated by Job's great curse and God's dramatic response. Thus, the very challenging words of Job and the even more challenging response of the Deity would be buffered by a Hymn that probes much the same issues but does so in a far more constrained manner, thereby preparing the reader for the confrontation to come.

Such a scenario makes even more sense when seen in light of the final part of the Hymn to Wisdom (28:23–28). Here the poem takes a dramatic turn as it reveals the true source of ultimate Wisdom:

> God understands how to find it,
> Indeed, He knows its location.
> For He surveys the ends of the earth;
> What is below all of heaven, He sees.
> When He set a weight for the wind,
> And measured out the water's portion;
> When He gave the rain its orders,
> And a direction for the thunderstorm—
> Then He saw it, evaluated it,
> Established it, yes, searched it out with care.
> And He said to Mankind:

Behold, awe of my Lord—this is Wisdom,
To shun evil is understanding.

The conclusion of the Hymn thus depicts the sweep of God's Wisdom as well as the magnitude of His cosmic powers. Once again, the placement of emphasis on these themes seems to anticipate the Theophany, but there is no hint of confrontation here. Rather, stress is placed upon the celebration of God's knowledge, by which He controls all the forces of the universe. In this respect, this passage shows a clear affinity with the introductory chapters of Proverbs, and especially to Proverbs' own hymn to Wisdom (Prov. 8, cf. esp. 8:22–31).

Most importantly, the Wisdom Poem sees God, the Wise Lord of all things, as a Deity whose essential beneficence is revealed in his attentiveness to everything beneath the heavens. The Hymn implicitly suggests that if God directs the wind, rain and storm with such finesse, He must direct the course of human events in an equally masterful, and therefore positive, fashion. In any case, He certainly is beyond questioning by humanity on this point.

The clearest indication that this is meant to be the import of the Wisdom Hymn is to be found in its last verse (28:28), which stresses the necessity of showing the proper, awed respect for God. Verse 28 declares that if a mortal is to grasp anything of Wisdom at all, it is through this recognition of God's decisive role in shaping the lives of all mankind. Moreover, the added, concluding affirmation that all men must shun evil not only aligns the Wisdom Hymn with the conservative, moralistic view exemplified in the book of Proverbs but also makes a conscious connection with the traditional, depiction of patient Job. For Job, too, is described as a man who "fears God and shuns evil" in the Prologue (see 1:1, etc.) with phrasing nearly identical to that found in 28:28.[434]

This last verse has been viewed by many scholars as suspect, possibly a late pietistic interpolation into the Hymn to Wisdom.[435] This may well be so, although in that case vs. 27 would seem a rather abrupt ending to the poem, depriving it of the strong climactic finish that vs. 28 now gives to the entire piece.[436] In the final analysis, there is really no decisive evidence by which to determine the redactional history of chapter 28 or to decide how vs. 28 should be seen in terms of this redaction. Even if the Wisdom Hymn, in a version without the final verse, was originally added to the Poem, it still has a significant mediating effect along the lines considered above, especially in reference to the Theophany. Nonetheless, there can be little question that the addition of vs. 28 causes the Hymn to have a far more profound impact on the development of the Joban counterpoint. Hence, it is this final form of chapter 28 that must be most carefully considered.

What is particularly important to notice is how the last verse, whether written by the original author or added by a later editor, really transforms the import of the entire Wisdom Hymn. For it seems to effect a major shift: the pessimistic emphasis on mankind's isolation from wisdom is altered toward a far more optimistic emphasis on a mortal's ability to begin to grasp intelligence through awe of the Lord and proper moral conduct. Without the last verse the Hymn to Wisdom would be a completely different poem requiring a substantially different interpretation.

In this respect, one again thinks of the contrapuntal forces that acted upon the book of Ecclesiastes. For it is striking to notice how reminiscent Job 28:28 is of the editorial addition to Qoheleth's work, both in terms of what it says and how it functions vis-à-vis the rest of the poem. Obviously, this is even more the case if we accept the view that it was a late, editorial addition to the text.

There can be little question that the depiction of Wisdom as a treasure beyond man's reach is a view shared by Ecclesiastes and the Hymn. But just as Qoheleth's editor searched for a more pietistic insight than that portrayed by his mentor's worldview, so the author of chapter 28 in Job (or at least the author/redactor who wrote the last verse) sought to set the pursuit of Wisdom within a similar context. To be sure, the final verse of chapter 28 might be said to contradict the rest of the Hymn to Wisdom as thoroughly as the view of Qoheleth's editor contradicts the overall message of Ecclesiastes. But the intent at the conclusion of the Wisdom Hymn, as in the conclusion to Qoheleth's work, is not simply to oppose but rather to play the optimistic counterpoint of tradition against the Wisdom Hymn's more dominant pessimistic message and to emphasize that when all is said and done, this traditional message must take precedence and be seen as the decisive guide for human conduct.

Moreover, in broader terms, this is also how the final author/redactor of the Hymn to Wisdom wants his ancient audience to see the Poem of Job. The Poem, he declares, also has to be set in a more traditional context. The clash of wills between Job and his Friends must be seen for what it is: an attempt by mere human beings to reach intellectually beyond their collective grasp. The final confrontation of Job and God serves to underscore this point: humanity is incapable of perceiving the nature of God, nor can a mortal set himself up in judgment of God's morality (or lack thereof). He must simply keep faith with tradition—respect God and shun evil; for (to use Qoheleth's words) "this is the conclusion of the matter—all having been heard."

It seems to me altogether likely that the author or redactor of the Hymn to Wisdom, in a manner similar to the editor of Ecclesiastes, well understands the critical emphasis in the larger work for which his poem serves as a commentary. He knows what issues are at stake, and he understands how sharply they have been drawn in the Poem of Job. He may even recognize the parodistic elements that are such an essential part of the earlier work. Certainly, the Ecclesiastes-like worldview found in most of Job 28 reflects such an understanding of the human predicament only too well. Yet at the final moment the author of the Wisdom Poem (or, a later glossator) turns dramatically away from this more critical emphasis and turns towards a more pietistic view of life and the relation of God to mankind.

Perhaps we can better understand this turn from pessimism to optimism if we refer back to the Bontsye-model for guidance; for among the critical reactions to the Yiddish story we can find a circumstance somewhat similar to the one we have been considering here. I am thinking, in this connection, of the comments made by Madison, whose interpretation of "Bontsye Shvayg" we have considered earlier in this study.[437] Madison is also a discerning critic who understood Perets' sharply critical, parodistic intent that was Perets' goal in writing his short story. Yet in Madison's discussions of the Yiddish story, he too draws back at the last moment and refrains from pressing the satirical interpretation of "Bontsye Shvayg" too vigorously, thereby implicitly contradicting and undercutting his preceding interpretation. Madison finally focuses instead on a portrayal of Perets' protagonist as the "lovable" Bontsye. Even more significantly, the critic suggests that this is the most important element in the story, the one thing that really makes it memorable. Hence, for all intents and purpose, he allows the "lovable" Bontsye to take precedence over Bontsye the schlemiel, the tool of Perets' satire.

It may be useful to try to understand the motivations of the author or redactor of the Hymn to Wisdom in light of how we understand the motivations of Madison. I have suggested that Madison's reaction to "Bontsye Shvayg" is best characterized as being more psychological than logical. Moreover, there are two closely related factors that shaped his reaction: the increasingly sacrosanct status of the Bontsye-figure, which was in turn shaped and legitimized by the genuine sufferings and deprivations that Perets seems almost to have prophetically forecast in his short story.

It may not be unreasonable to suggest that whoever added the Hymn to Wisdom, in its final configuration, to the book of Job was caught in the same sort of counterforces that gripped Madison and shaped his critical judgments. If Job, like Bontsye, had become a potent emblem of suffering to the Jewish culture of which the author of the Wisdom Hymn was a part, it would make sense that this poet would bend his efforts toward a deemphasis on the satire when he tried to explain the Poem of Job. For to accept the satire as it stands would mean to attack the image of God, who is the only one who has the power to save his chosen ones from their sufferings. But to attack the Deity would be tantamount to cutting oneself and one's people off from all hope of a future in which God may restore the fortunes of all, just as He restored the fortunes of Job. Rather, the story of Job, his Friends and his God must be rethought in the light of tragic events. Their encounters must be interpreted with the emphasis placed on the ignorance of humanity, which makes it impossible for a mere mortal to understand why God has done what He has done; on the wisdom and power of God itself, which cannot be seen as being inherently pernicious; and finally on the need to submit to God's intelligence, which offers mankind its only chance to survive and endure.

Madison felt compelled by the forces of history to seek *true* meaning by means of a reading of "Bontsye Shvayg" that departs from its author's parodistic intent. This may be the best way to grasp the purpose of the author of the Wisdom Hymn, too. Perhaps he felt, as he stood in the shadow of the tragedies of *his* time, that the "joke" of the Joban parody wasn't funny anymore—that the time for satire had passed. The Hymn to Wisdom was his response to this need, and if this poem does not characterize God as "lovable," it at least redefines God's role in Job in traditional terms as the inscrutable but ever-supportive Deity that He must remain if people in the grip of despair are to have any hope at all.

When we turn from the Hymn to Wisdom to a consideration of the Elihu speeches, we reach a far more prominent and clear-cut stage of Joban counterpoint. For if the Hymn's intent is not so much to oppose the Poem of Job as to derive a traditional insight from it, with Elihu the opposition is overt and well demarcated. Even if there were not the obvious disjunctions and discontinuities between the Elihu chapters and the rest of the book of Job (which we have noted above)[438] the dramatic difference in the mode of expression and method of approach found in Elihu's commentary would be sufficient grounds for seeing it as the work of a different writer. Everything about this section of Job suggests that the Elihu author has quite a different agenda from the author of the original Poem and, for that matter, from the author of the Wisdom Hymn.

Some exegetes who wish to take the Elihu speeches as part of a unified book of Job have sought to explain its discontinuities, vis-à-vis the Poem of Job in terms that might seem at first quite sympathetic to the parodistic approach I have presented above. In effect, the argument has been brought forward—especially in the more recent literature—that the Elihu chapters are satire and that Elihu himself is meant to serve as a foil to the rest of the speakers in the book.

Habel has given the most cogent argument in support of this position. He declares that when Elihu endeavors to arbitrate Job's cosmic dispute, he only underscores that this is, quite literally, a fool's errand: "It is my contention that in his portrait of Elihu's role as arbiter, the poet also suggests indirectly that Elihu is a fool, albeit a brilliant young fool, but nevertheless a fool. In so doing he renders an implicit verdict on what Elihu is doing and saying. The three Friends are judged publicly by Yahweh after the speeches are concluded (42:7). Elihu, however, is permitted to condemn himself from his own mouth."[439] The reason for this satiric interlude, Habel contends, is to provide a kind of sham conclusion which, conversely, dramatically sets up the final confrontation of God and Job. This then serves to underscore the Joban author's message that simple, pietistic pronouncements like Job's Three Friends' and Elihu's cannot begin to explain the intentions of the Deity:

> Elihu's speeches are designed to provide an orthodox ending and a plausible resolution of the earthly dispute. That ending, however, is overridden by an answer from Yahweh that lies beyond the canons of orthodoxy and the strictures of the heavenly court. . . . Elihu argues on traditional theological grounds that God is beyond immediate reach of mortals and that it is presumptuous to summon him to appear. Thus Elihu's role and message are a deliberate anti-climax which sets the stage for the surprise advent of Yahweh in the whirlwind.[440]

This and similar arguments seem to me largely unconvincing. For one thing, if the Elihu chapters are an extension of the satire we have already found in the body of the Poem, it would have to be seen as a satire of quite a different sort. For the artistry of the parody in the Poem of Job lies in its very subtlety—its use of themes, types and motifs that are so close to the genuine article that they *almost* pass muster, much as is the case in "Bontsye Shvayg." But Elihu's speeches show none of this finesse; the opposition they express is blatant opposition, no motifs or types are really imitated and then subtly subverted after the parodistic manner of the Poem. Indeed, if one follows the interpretations of some commentators, the Elihu speeches as ironic satire are best seen more in terms of slapstick than parody.[441].

But besides this, there is an even more basic reason why it is difficult to take the Elihu section as an integral part of the Poem or, more generally, the book of Job, at least from the standpoint of the arguments presented above. To put it simply: the Elihu speeches, taken as satire, do not fit very well within the parodistic design presented above, especially in terms of the legal metaphor and how it is used in the Poem of Job.

I have argued that the legal metaphor is almost exclusively confined by the author of the Poem to Job himself—that the Three Friends, by and large, neither accept, nor want to play, a part in any legal suit that Job would bring against God.[442] In fact, it is precisely through this ploy that the poet of Job so effectively subverts the Sufferer/Comforter stereotype.

A proper Righteous Sufferer cannot demand justice, nor can a proper Comforter countenance such a demand; the Comforter must instead counsel humility and submission which, conventionally, a Righteous Sufferer ultimately accepts as his only proper course. As we have seen, the poet of Job plays off this normative expectation by having his Job demand legal justice instead of pleading for mercy as a Righteous Sufferer is supposed to do. Further, it is precisely this Joban demand for justice that provokes the Three Friends and, more than anything else, goads them into being outraged opponents, rather than the sympathetic Comforters they are supposed to be.

Finally, by characterizing God as an opponent-at-law rather than the source and authority of Law, the poet also redefines the divine role and makes it into something entirely opposite to what it ought to be. It is only in the Theophany, where God rejects Job's legal gambit, that the correspondences are restored to what they should be, with God once more in his proper place as the Master of the Universe, beyond all questioning or comprehension by humanity.

Elihu, portrayed as a "brilliant fool," upsets this grand parodistic design. First, by accepting the legal role the Friends had earlier rejected, he effectively undercuts the tension the original poet has so carefully set up between them and Job. To be sure, he thus becomes a foil to the Friends' role, but this has the effect of neutralizing their arguments and thus their position in the story, thereby making them seem almost superfluous to the author's overall parodistic aims.

Even more serious is the way Elihu, by anticipating the arguments that God will bring in the Theophany, undercuts their dramatic effect. Habel is right when he states that the Elihu speeches are anticlimactic in that they set up a climax before the *real* climax of the Poem. But this can hardly be viewed as an effective literary device especially designed to set up the final denouement. On the contrary, such a strategy is better viewed as being altogether counterproductive, especially because it tends to make the Theophany redundant or, as Habel terms it, a "surprise."

I doubt the poet desired that the final, climactic encounter of Job and God be taken in such a manner, like an unexpected, "trick" ending in a detective novel. For one thing, a concluding encounter between a Righteous Sufferer and his deity is altogether a conventional, rather than an unexpected conclusion, as my earlier discussion of the convention has demonstrated. Consequently, the sharp, parodistic intentions of the poet are not effectively served by a "surprise" that is not really much of a surprise. Rather, the *genuine* surprise comes from the reversal of correspondences in the convention: one expects a merciful God to reward an abjectly pleading, but wholly righteous, man-in-distress. Instead, the poet of Job gives his ancient audience a determined, would-be prosecutor who will not plead for help, pitted against an equally determined God who will offer no mercy and certainly grant no reward.

When Elihu declares that no man should contend with God and that God has a perfect right to discipline even his most righteous followers without justification (see e.g., 32:12 ff.), he decisively blunts the force of the Theophany. Once more, there is no surprise at all when God says and does much the same thing to Job. To return to the detective novel figure just used above, Elihu is like an uninvited but all-too-knowing cub detective who comes on the scene of the crime a chapter too soon. He then proceeds to destroy all the dramatic tension by letting everyone know then and there that "the butler did it," thus making the final, climactic revelation scene hardly a revelation at all.

But if the Elihu section is an interpolation rather than an integral part of the original design, there is a good reason why this is so. After all, the author of Elihu has already read the book; so he knows, as it were, where all the bodies are buried. The question we must therefore ask ourselves is why he is so anxious to "spoil" things by subverting the carefully structured parody of the Poem of Job? Even if he must "fix" the text to his own satisfaction, why then in such an anticlimactic manner?

One thing that should be clear from the way the Elihu speeches begin is that this decision to tamper with the Poem of Job is not taken lightly. The author of Elihu section has his protagonist agonize over this issue at some length before proceeding; in fact, most of chapter 32 (32:6–22) is nothing more than a long preamble in which Elihu emphasizes how reticent he is to give voice to his own arguments. The principal reason for Elihu's hesitation is made clear from the outset. It is because, by speaking out, he must violate one of the most time-honored tenets of Ancient Near Eastern Wisdom, that youth should give way before age. Hence, at the beginning of his first speech, Elihu is moved to declare,

> I am but a youngster, while you are venerable,
> So I have recoiled from the very idea
> Of declaring my view to you.
> I considered: experience should speak,
> Advanced years should explicate Wisdom.   (32:6–7)

It is often suggested that the pose of youth given to Elihu is meant to explain the impetuous brashness that leads him to interrupt his elders, but I suspect there may be more involved. It may be that the writer of these speeches is trying to use Elihu as a mouthpiece through which to express his own concerns and trepidations as he confronts the awesome artistry of the Poem of Job.

If the Poem of Job was already a venerable work of literature by the time the Elihu-author encountered it, one could well understand his reluctance to tamper. He might well feel a little like a lover of Shakespeare's *Lear* who has long felt that the play would certainly benefit from a couple of added dramatic moments (maybe, for example, a scene that shows what became of Lear's fool). Such a desire by the aficionado to "fix things up" where he feels that Shakespeare has done a less-than-perfect job could be an immense temptation. Still, it would take a lot of nerve to tinker with the Venerable Bard; one might even be inclined to preface one's changes with a lengthy justification before proceeding to the dramatic work at hand.

Both this desire to fix, and reluctance to tamper with, the Poem of Job may be manifest in the Elihu-author's preliminary remarks. If so, then the strong emphasis he places on the figure of youth defying age should not simply be taken as representing the conflict between Elihu and his seniors. Instead, this conflict should be taken as a conceit through which the Elihu-author tacitly tries to explain his own approach to the Poem of Job. By having his protagonist justify his interruption of Job and his cohorts, the Elihu-writer also implicitly justifies the extraordinary step he has decided to take. It is his way of explaining why he must reluctantly defy the prevalent Ancient Near Eastern custom of literary conservatism, which would naturally tend to disapprove of a younger writer (probably generations younger) who refuses to show the proper "hands-off" attitude toward a literary work that has long stood the test of time.

It is for this reason that the writer goes to such lengths to have Elihu declare that there *are* compelling reasons why he must bend the rules of literary propriety in this particular instance. Elihu declares that there are occasions when, of necessity, one must not shrink from correcting one's elders and should rely instead on God-given inspiration by which to see the correct course of action:

> But surely it is the inspiration in Mankind,
> The very spirit of the Almighty that gives them understanding.
> The venerable may not be wise,
> Nor the aged discerning in judgment.
> Therefore I declare: Listen to me!
> I will declare my opinion—also myself!. (32:8–10)

Clearly, the author of Elihu strongly feels that the case presented in the Poem of Job has not been satisfactorily resolved by the graybeards who have preceded him. And if no one else will come forward to do what he deems necessary, he must boldly wade into the fray himself and restate the case against Job.

It is particularly notable that in the last part of the passage just quoted above, the Elihu-author employs the emphatic construction $ʾp$-$ʾny$, "also myself!"—a phrase that is again repeated twice in 32:17: "I, also myself, will say my piece; I will state my opinion, also myself!" Once more we seem to have a phrase trying to draw attention to itself. In this case I suspect that the writer uses this repeated, emphatic phrasing to focus on his own rationale for intervention into the Poem of Job, as if to say, I *too* have been provoked—by Job because he has challenged God and by his Friends, because they have not put up a good enough defense on God's behalf. If Job has a grievance, so also does the author of Elihu; moreover, if the poet of Job was driven by his anger to attack the tenets of ancient tradition, the Elihu-author is equally furious because this attack has been made. For this reason he is more than willing to match the poet of Job, outrage for outrage.[443]

However, it is just at this point, when Elihu actually launches his counterattack against Job, that many exegetes have found their greatest difficulty in explaining the rationale for his interruption. The majority (although not universal) opinion is that Elihu may be full of sound and fury but his arguments signify nothing or, at least, nothing very new. Elihu has a number of harsh things to say about the Friends' arguments. He declares,

> Look, I've waited for your words,
> I've attended to your reasonings

> While you groped for the right things to say.
> I've considered what you have done,
> But it's clear: you haven't gotten the best of Job;
> You haven't come up with a response to his arguments.   (32:10–12)

But as exegetes have often pointed out, when it is Elihu's turn to speak, he seems to do little more than restate the arguments of the Friends, the very arguments that he himself has labeled as inadequate. Pope's criticism of the Elihu speeches is representative of this view:

> Their style is diffuse and pretentious, a large part of the content of the four discourses being devoted to prolix and pompous prolegomena. For the most part Elihu's arguments merely echo what the friends have already said repeatedly, yet he has the effrontery to offer them as if they were novel and decisive. If Elihu has anything distinctive to contribute, it is the elaboration of the idea that suffering may be disciplinary (xxxiii 14–33), already suggested by Eliphaz in his first speech (v 17).[444]

It is because Elihu promises a good deal but seems to deliver so little that his speeches have attracted the heaviest criticism by interpreters of the book of Job. Even the satirical interpretation mentioned above works off a remarkably similar premise to that used to downgrade Elihu. In this case the reasoning goes, if Elihu seems unoriginal, repetitious and even bombastic, this must be the intentional design of the Joban author; that is, if Elihu looks like a fool, the author of Job must have meant for him to look foolish.

There may, however, be another way to approach Elihu distinct from either the sharply critical, or more recent satirical, interpretations that have generally carried the day. In this respect, the key question to pose is this: If Elihu essentially adopts the same pietistic positions as those of the Three Friends, is there any other factor that might allow us to distinguish his message from theirs? The answer to this is clearly yes, at least in one respect—the legal metaphor. For while the Friends decline to accept Job's legal metaphor and generally avoid the use of legal terminology at all costs, Elihu does quite the opposite. For him the legal metaphor seems to be just as important as it is for Job.[445]

Note that, when Elihu chastises the Friends for their inadequacies in responding to Job in his introductory speech, he really as much as says that they have failed to be good lawyers. This is first indicated in 32:9b and 12b, where Elihu utilizes specifically legal terms that Job has already prominently employed, in the first instance $m\check{s}p\underline{t}$, "justice, litigation," and in the second case $mwky\underline{h}$, "advocate-at-law." Hence, we can quite properly retranslate these passages (already cited above) to emphasize their legal nuance. In Job 32:9 Elihu warns that "the venerable may not be wise, nor the aged discerning in litigation";[446] and in 32:12bc he declares even more pointedly that "it's clear: none of you can be an adversary-at-law[447] against Job, capable of responding to his testimonies."

When Elihu turns from criticizing the Friends and proceeds to confront Job's arguments themselves, he frames his response in legalistic terms. In chapter 33:1,5 he launches his attack against Job with a challenge that clearly characterizes Job as an opponent-at-law:

So, Job, I want you to attend to my testimony;
Give ear to all my charges.[448]

. . . .

If you can, refute me,
Put your case in order, take the stand![449]

He then proceeds to argue his case in the forensic style of a lawyer, addressing Job by name as though he were a defendant in the dock, even quoting him (directly or indirectly) as though from a trial record and then refuting his arguments point by point.[450] Overall, it would be fair to say that the Elihu speeches therefore constitute the legal brief of their author against Job's legal position as set out in the original Poem.

In the final analysis, it should be clear that the Elihu-author is dissatisfied not so much with the substance of what the Friends have previously said as he is with how they have said it. He perceives what he takes to be a flaw in their presentation. Because they have refused to justify God in specifically legal terms, they have left what Elihu views as Job's most monstrous charge unrefuted. Specifically, the Friends have not countered Job's contention that, could he actually bring God into an impartial court, God could not win—that the Almighty would have to be ruled guilty while Job would be deemed innocent. This is why the Elihu-writer feels compelled to step in. Unlike the Friends, who are simply content to acknowledge the Lord's righteousness without defending his legal innocence, Elihu must muster a case by which to justify God's ways to man legally.[451]

In chapter 34, Elihu makes the argument that most clearly speaks to this issue. At the beginning of this discourse he calls together an audience of wise men to consider the merits of his legal brief (34:2-3). Then, in verses 4-9 he declares,

Let us consider the case for ourselves,[452]
Let us examine, among ourselves, what is best.[453]
For Job has stated, "I am innocent,
But God has thrown out my case.[454]
My case He has defrauded.[455]
I am wounded by his barbs,[456] though without guilt!"
Was there ever a man like Job?
He drinks up slander like water!
Goes in the company of evildoers!
And walks with wicked men.
For he has stated: There is no reason
For one to be reconciled with God.[457]

Elihu portrays quite accurately Job's view of his legal situation as we see it set out in the earlier dialogues. Job states that he is innocent and that God has perpetrated a miscarriage of justice against him; hence, it necessarily follows—God is guilty.

This view is completely unacceptable to Elihu. In his opinion, when Job makes such a statement, he has, quite literally, committed a crime. To put this more specifically, Job has slandered God because he has refused to be reconciled to the idea that the Almighty and justice are inseparable and coequal. As far as Elihu is concerned, this places Job beyond the pale; his flouting of divine justice puts him in the same camp with the worst evildoer, and his crime is not that much different from that of the most common criminal.

Moreover, strictly speaking, this guilty verdict that Job claims against God may not necessarily be mitigated in the Theophany, according to Elihu's legalistic view. To be sure, Job does recant before God (42:6); but when he makes this statement of submission, he never specifically abandons his judicial case. Instead, he only admits, "I spoke about, but did not comprehend, wonders beyond me which I could not understand" (42:3bc). Job thus acknowledges that the Deity cannot be confined by the legal strictures of men; but from a juridical standpoint this might be reinterpreted as meaning that God stands above the Law. Such a position could be viewed as less than perfectly satisfactory by someone like Elihu, who wishes to defend God's legality along with his majesty. It could even be argued that God evades a valid verdict by means of a technicality: because He is not really within the legal jurisdiction of the courts, the case of Job v. God is rendered moot and must be vacated, regardless of its intrinsic merits.

This is a legal loophole that the author of the Elihu speeches is most anxious to close. Because Job never explicitly admits that he is guilty and that God is innocent, this must be made perfectly clear. As we have seen, Elihu already condemns Job for his criminal acts in the first part of chapter 34; he then proceeds in verses 10–12 to state the converse of this legal point by also acquitting God of any and all guilt:

> Therefore, intelligent people, listen to me!
> How could anyone think that God might be guilty
> Or that the Almighty would act criminally?
> For he requites a man according to his actions,
> He rates a person according to his conduct.
> Really now, God will not deal wickedly,
> And the Almighty will never subvert justice![458]

According to Elihu, this simply has to be so: Even as God, by definition, is all-powerful and all-wise, so, too, is it only possible to see Him as all-just; for justice can no more be separated from the Deity than can His wisdom or power. As Elihu declares in verses 16–17, this point should be evident to anyone who has intelligence:

> So, if you have any comprehension, listen to this,
> Hearken to the logic of my argument:
> Could He who despises legality really govern?
> Would you deem guilty the Just-and-Mighty One?

As far as Elihu is concerned, the answer to this rhetorical question is and can only be most emphatically *no*! In verse 17b this is made especially apparent; for there Elihu calls God *ṣdyq kbyr* (lit., "Just-Mighty,"),[459] as if to say the power and justice of God are, in essence, one and the same. Even when God seems totally inaccessible to man and His purposes utterly obscure (see, e.g., 36:23), Elihu takes it as axiomatic that those obscure purposes must be compatible with justice. According to his worldview, there is no other alternative; and all arguments in defense of God's intentions must be restated and reframed from this standpoint and this standpoint alone.[460]

There can be little question that the author of Elihu wants to align his protagonist with the Three Friends when he states his case against Job; his close adherence to their line of reasoning makes this only too clear. I suspect that he also felt that by and large, the Friends' position is vindicated in the Theophany, where Job is rebuked, while they are not.[461] But their arguments do require his supplement so that the legal implications of their pietistic defense of God becomes explicit rather than implicit.

Whoever wrote the introduction to the Elihu speeches also understands this very well, since he distinguishes between Elihu's rationale and the Friends in precisely these same terms.[462] According to this introduction, Elihu feels compelled to speak because "Job represented himself to be innocent rather than God," and he is dissatisfied with the Friends because "they had not found a (legal) response and thereby had made God look guilty" (32:2,3).[463] This cannot be allowed; like that later apologist for God, Alexander Pope, the Elihu-writer wants to make sure that someone goes on the record to declare,

> All Nature is but Art unknown to thee;
> All Chance, Direction which thou canst not see;
> All Discord, Harmony not understood;
> All partial Evil, universal Good:
> And spite of Pride, in erring Reason's spite,
> One truth is clear, *Whatever is, is right.*[464]

Or, to put this in Elihu's terms, "whatever is, is just."

Finally, there is one other important point to make about the Elihu-writer in terms of his addition to the complex of Joban counterpoint. It is important to listen to whōm he is actually addressing his message. Ostensibly, he is speaking primarily to Job and secondarily to Job's Three Friends as he proceeds to correct their respective faults and inadequacies. But when we listen more closely, we begin to realize that his *real* audience are the people to whom he refers as *ḥkmym* or *gbr ḥkm* ("the wise"), *yd'ym* (the "knowledgeable"), *'nšy lbb*, ("intelligent people") or, more simply, "ourselves."[465]

I have already indicated that I think that the Elihu-author makes a prominent point of his protagonist's youth in order to emphasize that his literary work speaks for a later generation, before whom the original Poem of Job already looms as an awesome literary monument. The writer of Elihu feels that he must speak on behalf of his contemporaries and address them as intelligent men, the inheritors of ancient Wisdom tradition, who cannot let the "Wisdom" of the Poem stand unopposed. One catches a sense that when this writer formulates his answer to Job, he is not simply fulfilling a need but rather more a compulsion. This, then, leads one to consider, What lies behind this compulsion of the Elihu-author? Why did he simply *have* to violate the integrity of such a great work of literature and reconsider its issues both on his own terms and also as a self-styled spokesman for his contemporaries?

Once more, we are lacking in concrete evidence about the Elihu-author, his life and times; hence, any answer we might suggest must be highly speculative. Still, perhaps we can turn again to the Bontsye-model for a somewhat parallel circumstance that may at least point toward a way to understand the compulsion of the writer of Elihu better. In this instance it is Eliezer Greenberg's poem, "Y. L. Perets and Bontsye Shvayg in the Warsaw Ghetto,"[466] which seems to show certain affinities to the pronouncements of Job's Fourth Friend. Note that like the Elihu speeches, this Yiddish poem is a creative composition that is designed to supplement an already famous earlier work whose hero has come to symbolize all the suffering that his people have had to endure.

We have seen that Greenberg is not content to leave Bontsye alone in his silence. In his view, the experience of the Holocaust has made this silence no longer possible; indeed, to accept Bontsye's silence in a post-Holocaust world would be intolerable. One can feel the same sense of anger motivating the Yiddish poet as that which provoked the author of the Elihu speeches; moreover, as is also the case with the Elihu-author, this anger compels Greenberg to create a spokesman who will speak for *his* concerns, concerns that have been dramatically reshaped by the horrors of modern events. Note especially that Greenberg's Bontsye constantly emphasizes that he must speak "now" (Yid., *its*), much like Elihu who demands to be heard, "also myself."

Note, as well, that Greenberg also directs this anger toward a target; just as Elihu attacks Job, so, for all intents and purposes, Greenberg makes his transformed Bontsye attack Y. L. Perets. This is necessary because Perets' hero has come to represent the suffering-in-silence attitude that Greenberg finds he can no longer accept.[467] Since Perets is the creator of this emblem of suffering silence, it is he whom Greenberg must address and take to task much as Elihu upbraids Job. Greenberg as much as says: In the light of all *this*, your story must be rewritten; your silent hero must be given a voice; he must cry out for those who can no longer cry out—and if you are no longer here to do this, I must do it for you. Finally, we must recognize that, while Elihu ostensibly addresses Job and the Friends and Greenberg's Bontsye addresses Perets, this is really only a literary pose. In both cases the real audience is the generation of the writers, the inheritors of their respective traditions, who must now be made to see a well-known literary work from a new perspective.

If the analogy drawn here between Greenberg's poem and the Elihu section of Job is valid, this might help explain why the author of the latter could not let the Poem of Job alone. Once more, we would see the forces of history, especially as manifest in the succession of disasters that impinged on the Jews, casting their long, dark shadow over the Elihu-author and causing him to react so dramatically against the arguments voiced by Job in the Poem.

The impact of tragic events may have served to radicalize this ancient writer and sharpened his need to defend God's legal position. In his view, it may no longer have been sufficient to say that God's wisdom and power are beyond the comprehension of mankind, and that a mortal's only alternative is to submit before the divine majesty. In this respect, the message of the Theophany and the Hymn to Wisdom, while certainly "right," may not have seemed *right enough* for him.

The author of Elihu may have felt moved to declare that in the light of all *this*, in the face of the tragedies that he and his generation have inherited and known all too well, the Joban argument cannot simply conclude with a pious statement that God "moves in mysterious ways." God must be shown to be just in his actions; for, if his actions are not just, the disasters perpetrated upon the Jews become intolerable and God unacceptable. But such a circumstance is *itself* unacceptable. Just as the author of the Hymn to Wisdom felt compelled, in the face of tragedy, to preserve a supporting link between man and God, so, too, did the Elihu-writer. But the author of Elihu seems to have felt a need to go further. Perhaps he deemed it necessary to justify God, to acquit Him of all culpability because this served as well to justify his own generation of survivors and relieve them of the guilt they may have experienced just because they survived. Their survival had to have a reason and a rationale; hence, so, too, did God even though, in the final analysis, the Almighty's inherent justice and reasonableness might not be completely revealed to a suffering humanity.

There may be one part of the Elihu speeches, in particular, that gives circumstantial support to the argument presented above. While it is true that the substance of Elihu's justifications of God reflects the arguments of the Three Friends, in one respect he does seem to add something significant of his own, an argument that, like his adoption of the legal metaphor, goes well beyond what the Three Friends themselves have said. I refer to Elihu's argument that suffering is disciplinary. As mentioned above, M. Pope, among others, has pointed out that this line of argument is not completely original to Elihu, having been anticipated by Eliphaz.[468] Nonetheless, at best, this idea is just touched on in the speeches of the Three Friends; in Elihu, this justification is given a far more thorough treatment. It is for this reason that so many scholars, who would defend the importance of Elihu's contribution to the Joban debate, have focused upon this aspect of Elihu's message as being his most profound observation.

If the Elihu-author formulated his protagonist's argument against the backdrop of ancient tragedies, this emphasis upon suffering being a means by which man learns from God becomes an essential point in the legal defense of the Deity. For then the pain inflicted by God on humanity is not gratuitous; instead, divinely ordained suffering begins to make sense and becomes justifiable. More importantly, it supplies a rationale by which the survivors of disaster could come to grips with their losses and still maintain a relationship with God. Indeed, as we have seen, it is just this sort of rationalizing impulse that elevated Perets' story of silent suffering to such prominence and its hero to sacrosanct status in the eyes of the generations who endured first the pogroms and then the Holocaust.

It may not be happenstance that Elihu's argument in support of divinely ordained suffering is really the first sustained argument he makes on concluding his introductory remarks (33:14 ff.) This may be first because it *had to be* first, for suffering may well have been the primary thought in the mind of the author of Elihu and his generation, just as it was for Greenberg and his generation.

It also may not be coincidental that the turning point in Elihu's defense of suffering (33:23–24) focuses on intercession and mercy. Here, after describing a litany of distresses that lead a sufferer to death's door (see esp. 33:22) Elihu, like the poet of Job before him, looks for divine aid:

If he [a sufferer] has an angel to represent him,
A defender—one out of a thousand

To affirm a man's uprightness.
And he seeks mercy and says:
Spare him[469] from going down to the Pit—
I have found ransom.

There can be little question that Elihu is reacting to those passages in the Poem in which Job cries out for a Redeemer or Advocate to defend him.[470] More properly, this passage is trying to explain in Elihu's terms exactly how such a Redeemer/Defender should be characterized. The striking thing to note, of course, is how different Elihu's Defender is from Job's. As we have observed, the Redeemer of the Poem of Job is a Judge-Advocate who is imagined by Job to have enough power to match and even subdue God. Obviously, the author of Elihu cannot see such a saving entity in this light; yet he is drawn to Job's image of a savior. While the Elihu-writer implacably opposes almost everything that Job says, this seems to be one Joban concept he is anxious to preserve.

So Elihu transforms Job's Redeemer into a *ml'k*, an "angel" or, more properly, a messenger, someone to communicate humanity's desperation to God, just as the Defending Angel did Bontsye's.[471] The angel's task is to inform God of a sufferer's righteousness, presumably a righteousness proven to be legitimate through the discipline of suffering. The divine messenger then pleads that this proof, in and of itself, may be sufficient cause to save the righteous from certain destruction, to be quite literally a "ransom" (*kpr*), which, when offered as a gift to God (like the offerings the wandering soul gives to Heaven in another Perets story, "The Three Gifts"[472]), may cause the Deity at last to relent and grant relief.

The image of the Righteous Sufferer, tested by God to prove his righteousness and then finally rewarded is, of course, one we have seen exemplified before in stories like the accounts of the legendary Abraham and Job. And there is certainly every likelihood that the Elihu-author was consciously trying to present his view of divinely ordained suffering against the background of this stereotype. But he also has Elihu emphasize that the reward does not come swiftly. After all, an angelic advocate/defender is a rarity; he may not necessarily step forward today or tomorrow to plead a sufferer's case before God and ask for mercy from the heavenly Judge.

But here is a message of hope that could have special significance for Elihu's generation if they were the inheritors and successors of tragedy. It would not be difficult for a suffering people (or a people living in the aftermath of suffering) to find in Job's complaints the mirror of their own distress. The Elihu-writer understands this and perhaps it is the reason why Job is so important to him. However, the Joban mirror of suffering cannot be allowed to become distorted. If the people see themselves as innocent Job-like sufferers, they must not give in to impatience as Job does in the Poem. They must hope for a restoration to come: if the messenger is yet to arrive before the Throne of Glory to plead their case before God, at least Elihu's advice can be, for the time being, their consoling message: that ultimately a just God will act to bring them back from the brink of ruin, perhaps even to double their fortunes.

Before concluding this discussion of Elihu, we must focus on one further characteristic that these speeches share with Greenberg's poem: if my understanding of the Elihu-writer's intentions are correct, he, like Greenberg, has significantly misconstrued the original work that serves as his point of departure. We might say that each of these writers has taken his original in too "straight" a fashion without really considering or even recognizing the parodistic elements in play. In other words, both the Elihu-writer and Greenberg are victims of the "Ozymandias effect."[473]

We can implicitly see this in the way Greenberg portrays Bontsye in his poem, and, if there were any doubt remaining as to how he reads Perets' story, his critical writings make his opinions quite explicit. As we have seen, not once in any of his observations does Greenberg even hint that one should see the Yiddish story as a parody. Instead, he takes the silence of Bontsye in deadly earnest as emblematic of a despair that goes beyond words. This is the precisely the reason he reacts to Perets' story so strongly.

Likewise, the author of Elihu sees no hint of parody in the Poem of Job. For him, the speakers in the Poem make their positions known in a completely straightforward manner, which in turn prompts the Elihu-author to respond in a similarly sincere fashion. He sees in the conflict between Job, the Friends and God no literary poses, no ironic manipulation of stereotypes, no stretching of the limits of convention in which the arguments are intentionally overplayed for parodistic effect. In fact, it is the portrayal of extremes in the Poem—the extreme emphasis on God as a destructive power, Job as the ultimate Sufferer, the Friends as comforters of strife, a demand for legal justice that goes far beyond the conventional bounds of justice, the hope for an ultimate Redeemer who can do just about anything—it is these extremes that attract the Elihu-writer's attention and shape his reaction. The hand of the poet of Job mocks him; but, precisely for this reason, his heart feeds.

It may well be that he has been a witness, directly or indirectly, to events that have turned such extremes into realities, like events that turned the extremes portrayed in "Bontsye Shvayg" into documentable facts. And because the radical circumstances and issues found in the Poem may well have been realities to the author of Elihu, likewise he might have felt compelled to react extremely and present what amounts to a radical defense of God. He may have seen this as his single, possible alternative; for only then could he also defend his own generation and their continued existence in relation to God in such radical times.

The last great addition that essentially completes the canonical form of the book of Job is its prose supplements. We have already considered in the broadest terms how the most significant of these supplements, the Prologue and Epilogue, are used to encapsulate the Poem of Job and bring it in line with a more traditional viewpoint. It will therefore only be necessary at this stage to consider some more specific points concerning how the prose additions contribute to the Joban counterpoint.

We should start by noting that the Prose Frame Story really consists of more than just the Prologue and Epilogue. This frame really extends throughout the Poem in the guise of the phrases introducing the various speeches of Job, his Friends and God as well as the paragraph that introduces Elihu after the Three Friends and Job have concluded their debate (32:1–5). It is not at all clear whether all of these prose passages were added to Job at the same time or whether they reflect successive redactional editions of Job. The question is probably not resolvable on the basis of the evidence currently available. Nor will I try to enter into this debate here except to voice the opinion that all prose additions probably were inserted into Job at the latest stage of its editorial development after the Poem (probably including the Hymn to Wisdom and Elihu speeches) was essentially in the form we find today.

Whether all prose additions were added by the same hand or not, their ultimate intention and their overall effect was to draw the book together. And despite the obvious conflicts between the Prose Frame Story and the Poem of Job, this final editorial shaping of Job achieves this end to a remarkable degree. In particular, the insertion of the rubrics used to introduce the various speeches throughout the Joban debate give the book a consistent narrative framework and contribute to the impression that the Prose Frame and the Poem are all part of the same integrated whole.[474]

At every opportune moment the reader hears the voice of an omniscient narrator who breaks in like a master of ceremonies or, perhaps better, a referee, to declare who will be speaking next and under what circumstances. And because this narrative voice is also most easily identified with the storyteller who begins and ends the story of Job, the reader naturally tends to assume that the narrator is relating the same story that the storyteller is telling.

By leaving this impression, this final editorial layer of the book of Job has a decisive, indeed, probably *the* decisive effect upon the reader. The reader naturally tends to align himself with the storyteller/narrator and thus is inclined to see the biblical Job from his particular perspective. As a result, it is this perspective that tends to override all other views. In terms of the metaphor of counterpoint, we might say that the strategic placement of the prose supplements in the book of Job causes its melody to be amplified while the conflicting harmonies necessarily are forced to play in the background. They become the accompaniment.

Of course, of all the prose supplements to Job, the Prologue and Epilogue are naturally dominant, especially because they not only have the first say on Job but the last word as well. Much critical effort has been expended on this part of the Frame Story in order to delineate various editions and redactional layers of the narrative. In our earlier discussions of the Prologue/Epilogue, especially vis-à-vis its relation to the legend of Job, considerations of this nature have already played an important role. So we will not repeat here the arguments relevant to this issue. However, there is one point, not previously emphasized, that bears mentioning.

One might be inclined to assume that whatever editorial alterations and additions acted on the Prose Frame Story occurred at the time these brackets were engrafted onto the body of the Poem (or, if not then, shortly thereafter). For example, if Satan was needed to buffer God from adverse action against Job, one might assume that it was the writer/editor of the prose supplements[475] who inserted this diabolic figure into the story for this purpose. But this need not necessarily be so. Just as the Poem of Job underwent its own history of transmission involving alterations, additions and subtractions, so likewise is it quite possible that the folktale of Job continued along through its own separate and largely independent editorial tradition, acquiring its own alterations, additions and subtractions without reference to the Poem of Job at all.

At this point there is no certain means by which to decide just how much the Prologue/Epilogue was changed as a direct product of having been joined to the

Poem of Job and how much change it underwent within its own independent editorial environment. Obviously, some adjustment had to occur. After all, the shift from independent folktale to dependent Frame Story is, in itself, a significant adjustment. Still, I am inclined to believe that when the story of Job was joined to the Poem, it was essentially in its final form.

A point in favor of this last assumption is that the Prologue/Epilogue actually seems to take less cognizance of the Poem than we might expect. There are elements in the story (especially in the Epilogue) that seem completely extraneous, even in terms of the main story line of the folktale itself and that a ruthless editor might have been inclined to cut because of their lack of relevance to the major theological and moral issues raised in both the legend of Job and the Poem. The most obvious example is the discussion of Job's daughters in 42:14–15. One could excise these verses from the conclusion of Job's story without any adverse effect. One could even make a good case that this tightening of the narrative line would be a distinct benefit, since it would make the conclusion more direct and simple, thereby heightening its overall impact. Yet this could not be done. The discussion of Job's daughters had become a fixed part of the folk tradition by the time the story was joined to the Poem, and it simply could not be left out, however tangential it might seem to be.[476]

Note also the way the Epilogue deals with Job's Friends. Two of Job's three original Friends are barely acknowledged at all in the prose conclusion (42:7,9). Since Bildad and Zophar certainly play as prominent a role in the Joban debate as does Eliphaz, we might expect that they would get "equal billing" at the conclusion of the story. The fact that they are definitely placed in a secondary role to Eliphaz suggests that they may well have been of far less importance in the story than they were in the Poem, if they were part of the original story at all.[477]

The situation in regard to Elihu is even more dramatic. He is, quite simply, ignored in the Prologue/Epilogue. The most obvious reason why this is so is because he had no role in the folktale of Job itself but was a complete invention of the author of his speeches. Because the folktale was so fixed in its traditional form, he simply could not be added to the tale either at its beginning or at its conclusion. The only adjustment allowable was a short explanatory paragraph, preceding his speeches, which slips him into the narrative, as it were, "through the back door." But he could not be allowed directly to violate the integrity of the story itself, since he really was not a part of the *genuine* story.[478]

The fact that the story of Job, as manifest in the Prologue/Epilogue, had such authority in and of itself that its story line could not be easily adjusted, actually serves well the aim of the writer/editor who added this supplement to the book of Job. In his desire to amplify Job the Patient and make him override Job the Impatient, no strategy could serve his purpose better than to replay a rendition of the legend where this patient Job is the be-all and end-all.

I previously suggested that the Poem, because of its magnificent artistry, could not be easily violated by those who would endeavor to counter its message; the dominant tendency instead was to supplement rather than to change the Poem itself.[479] But with the Prologue/Epilogue added to the Joban counterpoint, it would not be difficult for an ancient audience to take things precisely the other way around. Because the Prose Frame actually is a manifestation of a tradition far older than the Poem, it might be easily taken by its ancient audience as the first and most basic line in the Joban counterpoint rather than the last and most superficial. From their perspective it would be the ancient folktale, as manifest in the Frame Story, that is the inviolate work that cannot now be adjusted, Conversely, the relatively more recent Poem becomes the supplement which must inevitably pale in the shadow of such an ancient authority and whose import must accordingly be adjusted to coordinate with the traditional pietistic view that the folktale has always represented.

That this is, in fact, what actually happened is demonstrated, for example, in the *Testament of Job*. While, as we have seen, the *Testament* reflects a detailed knowledge of the Poem of Job,[480] its essential subject matter concerns the issues taken up in the folktale of Job as portrayed in the Prologue/Epilogue. The actual Joban debate receives relatively minor treatment in this pseudepigraphal work.[481]

Besides this, there is another way by which the addition of the Prologue/Epilogue to the Poem tends to reinforce the view of Patient Job over Impatient Job. This involves the way the Prose Frame Story dramatically readjusts the reader's impression of the Dialogue/Appeal stereotype that, previously, the poet of Job had so effectively subverted—especially in the denouement of the Theophany. As noted above, the author of the Poem decisively undercuts the Dialogue/Appeal convention by presenting Job's confrontation with God in a manner opposite to the standard expectations. Where we would expect an abject Righteous Sufferer who, after pleading for mercy, is miraculously rewarded by his god, the poet portrays a Sufferer who demands rather than pleads and a Deity who upbraids rather than rewards.

But the addition of the Epilogue decisively changes all this; in fact, it has the overall effect of "reversing the reversal" and thereby restoring the Dialogue/Appeal to its conventional parameters. With the supplement of these prose brackets, we find all of the stereotypes of the Dialogue/Appeal reaffirmed: God appears and praises Job for his faithfulness and then proceeds to shower him with rewards. Undoubtedly, this "happy ending" largely follows the story line of the ancient folktale in substance. But it is equally important to notice that in form the ending shapes the entire book into a standard Dialogue/Appeal with an entirely normal outcome.

We should recall that there is a distinction between the original story type of the Job legend and the form of a Dialogue/Appeal. In the former the hero never cries out in complaint against his god because of the unwarranted, divine punishment brought down upon him. When one thinks of a Job or an Abraham, one sees them like Bontsye—silent in the face of their suffering. But this is not the case with the Righteous Sufferer of a Dialogue/Appeal. Such a sufferer complains to his god in scrupulous detail; indeed, the complaint is the essential means of attracting the god's attention, gaining his sympathy and, finally, his mercy.

The poet of Job, as we have seen, clearly patterns his protagonist much more in the image of such a Righteous Sufferer rather than in the form of a taciturn Abraham-like hero. As I have argued, we should even see this as a conscious attempt to play against type.[482] To some extent, this poses a problem for the writer/editor who added the prose supplements to the book of Job. He can no longer really portray his hero strictly as Job the Silent; far too much has been said by the Job of the Poem to make this credible. Instead, he has to accept Job in the form of a vocal Righteous Sufferer and proceed to reinforce this image in the most positive way possible. The way the Epilogue emphasizes reward and mercy (not to mention a Job who is once again piously seeking mercy) serves this aim rather well.[483]

Actually, in a way, the writer/editor of the prose supplements of Job can play things both ways in the conclusion. By showing his audience patient Job, he can reinforce the legendary image of the folk hero whose actions speak louder than words; but since the Poem has just shown how vocal (and even impatient) this Job can be, the Epilogue can also be seen as the conventional response to the pleadings of an innocent man in distress. Hence, Job can be silent folk hero and vocal Righteous Sufferer at one and the same time: the images superimpose upon one another—or to put this in terms of counterpoint, they form a contrapuntal duet.

Finally, in light of the discussion above, we must consider one further issue, to wit, just exactly how does the writer/editor of the Prose Frame Story hear the Poem, which he so clearly wishes to conform to the traditional folktale of Job? We have considered in some detail what he has done to achieve this end, but now we must also try to grasp his rationale.

In doing so, one thing seems clear: like the author of the Wisdom Hymn and the Elihu-writer before him, this writer/editor is also drawn to the artistry of the Poem and is moved by the passion of its suffering hero. On the other hand, if he hears the cry of anguish in Job's speeches and perhaps even identifies strongly with it, at the same time he seems totally deaf to the parodistic irony that plays against this anguish. Like the Elihu-author he is attracted by the extremes in the Joban debate, and the "Ozymandias effect" filters his perception of these extremes. As a result, he sees no exaggeration in Job, no melodrama; nothing but the bitter reality. This far, the writer/editor of the prose supplements and the Elihu writer approach the Poem of Job in virtually the same manner.

But only this far. Where the Elihu-writer and the author of the Prose Frame Story's writer dramatically part company is in how they choose to react. As we have seen, the Elihu writer reacts in protest. He sees Job's complaint as a direct challenge to God that must be refuted point by point. His intent is to rewrite Job or, barring this, at least he is determined to rewrite the role of the Friends. Not so the writer/editor of the Prose Frame Story. He takes precisely the opposite tack. He looks at the Job in the Poem and sees only the anguish without the protest; he hears Job's complaint, but all he comprehends is that Job does not, *cannot* sin with his lips. He feels the crushing power of a God who questions but does not answer, but for him this divine pressure is a profound burden that only the most righteous hero can bear. For the writer/editor of the Prose Frame Story, there can only be one way to see Job: as he has always been and always will be, the paragon of patience. This is the foundation of his interpretation, and everything must be seen in this manner or not at all.

Once more, if we are to understand why the writer/editor of the Frame Story must see Job the way he chooses to see him and in no other way, reference to the Bontsye-model can be of great aid. It is not difficult to find a parallel circumstance—interpretations of Perets' story where the view of its hero betrays the same sort of tunnel vision we see manifest here. I have actually already made an allusion to this type of viewpoint when I referred just above to Job as reflecting for the writer/editor of the Prose Frame Story neither exaggeration nor melodrama, only bitter reality. As may be recalled, this is exactly the way Wiener described his impression of Bontsye, word for word.[484]

It is also how Samuel and Wiesel saw Bontsye; in fact, it is the popular concept, really as much a cliché or stereotype today as is the proverbial patience of Job. Especially insightful is the manner in which Samuel wished to transform Perets from a teacher, writer and satirist for his own time into a "legendary hero" for all time, whose stories can be allowed only one interpretation—as beloved hasidic folktales with sentimental, lovable protagonists as their heroes. Quite naturally, Bontsye is a parade example; and in order to serve this end, no hint of irony or parody can be found in his story.[485]

Wiesel goes even further than this.[486] He turns Bontsye into the symbol of his own generation, shocked into silence by the horrors of the Holocaust. For him, Bontsye is untouchable, almost unmentionable, in the same way that the experience of the Holocaust is something beyond what mere words can convey. The forces of history legitimize Bontsye for Wiesel and make his hyperbolic sufferings into real sufferings that one dare not suggest are anything but the most serious matters. For Wiesel, Samuel and all similar apologists for Bontsye, the irony and satire must be read out of Perets' story, regardless of the original author's intent.

The circumstances shaping the addition of the Prose Frame Story to the book of Job may be much the same. Certainly there is a need expressed in the Prologue/Epilogue to make Job untouchable, a perfect model of the Righteous Sufferer who accepts whatever God gives. This need for a model may not have been an abstract need but rather a concrete necessity for a people trying to find their own way in the face of a history of disaster and tragedy.

While the Poem serves well as a means of giving their anguish an articulate voice, only with the brackets of the Frame Story does it serve to turn this anguish in the desired direction. It has the effect of stripping away the original poet's irony so that Job can become only a reflection of a "bitter reality" that its ancient audience feels compelled to see to the exclusion of anything else. More than this, it becomes again a focus of hope in the midst of despair. Then he who cries out can still be deemed "perfect and upright" and not really rejected by God, even though circumstances might at first suggest otherwise. Moreover, Job's cry to God, which becomes as much of a catharsis to the Jews in ancient times as Bontsye's silence does in modern times, is shown to be a call for mercy that will be answered with a response and a reward, sure to come.

If this understanding of the rationale for the Prose Frame Story is correct, certain aspects of the story can be better understood. For example, one significant and perhaps surprising aspect of the Prose Frame Story is that it makes no effort to justify God the way the Elihu section does. While Elihu would claim that God cannot possibly be unrighteous or—to put it in legalistic terms—guilty, the writer/editor of the prose supplements accepts the proposition that man can receive both good and evil from God. Indeed, as I have suggested above, this concept, forthrightly stated in 2:10, should be properly seen to be Job's credo.[487]

It is interesting to note how the Frame Story deals with Elihu. I have already mentioned that it basically does as much as it can to ignore him because he was not really a part of the folk tradition. But I think that this desire to give Elihu as little standing as possible also reflects a determined effort by the writer/editor of the prose supplements to discount his message to the fullest possible extent. After all, Elihu, in defending God, has to attack Job; and, from the standpoint of the Frame Story, this is completely unacceptable. The author of the Frame therefore indicates that Elihu's message is to be rejected by pointedly noting that God forgave Job's Three Friends but said nothing at all about Elihu. The implication is clear: God has discredited Elihu and all that he has said as well.[488]

This implicit rejection of Elihu is made quite explicit in the *Testament of Job*. The fact that Elihu has not been forgiven by God in the Epilogue is a point the *Testament*'s author does not miss (see 43:1), and he therefore reports that Elihu's attack on Job can only be viewed as having been inspired by Satan (see 41:5). Moreover, there is some indication that the translator of the Qumran Targum of Job (roughly contemporary with the *Testament*) held a similar derogatory view of Elihu's opinions.[489]

Seen in terms of the Bontsye-model, this approach to God, Elihu and Job makes a good bit of sense. First of all, if Job, like Bontsye, was a sacrosanct figure because he was a symbol for the Jews of both their suffering and endurance, one could well understand the desire to protect this figure from criticism. Just as an attack on Bontsye, a portrayal of him as the fool Perets intended him to be, would have the concomitant effect of also labeling the Holocaust generation, whom he had come to represent, as fools, so, too, Jews of an earlier time may have felt that an attack on Job was equally unthinkable for a precisely equivalent reason. Consequently, it would have been natural for them to turn on anyone who would raise his voice in protest against Job. Job's Three Friends perhaps could be tolerated, especially since God was willing to forgive them for the sake of his servant Job. But Elihu was not to be let off so lightly. His attack, in the eyes of those who identified with Job's suffering, would simply be considered too strident and too cruel. Elihu could not be accepted if Job was to be who he had to be.

Beyond this, there is another point to be made about Elihu. From the perspective of those who would make Job an emblem of Jewish strife and tragedy, the Fourth Friend was simply dead wrong about this Righteous Sufferer and God. Just as it is unthinkable today to claim that God acted justly by "punishing" the Jews with the Holocaust, it may well have been unthinkable to say the same thing about the God portrayed in Job: that He acted justly in punishing Job and therefore all of those whom Job had come to represent. Job declares that one receives both good and evil from God, and the generations of Jews who had received more than their share of the latter may not have been willing to condemn Job, and therefore themselves, so that God could be deemed innocent. As Wiesel has so eloquently argued, in the aftermath of disasters innocence is no longer possible—only silence.

At the conclusion of the Poem, Job lays his hands upon his mouth and declares that he will say no more about God and his intentions toward man. This is a conviction that the writer/editor of the prose supplements to Job seems to understand and with which he might well identify. This may be why he refrains from breaking this silence with any Elihu-like justification of God. At best, his intent is only to underscore the more positive aspects of God's incomprehensible nature. Hence, the Epilogue reminds Job's ancient audience: If one can receive evil from God, it should not be forgotten that one can also receive good.

One last aspect of the Frame Story should perhaps be considered from the perspective of the Bontsye-model—the restoration of Job's children. I have already pointed out that this restoration is a flawed conclusion; indeed, if there is one thing that mars the ending of the folktale, as now found in the book of Job, it is the way the children are restored, or rather, not restored. Without doubt, when the new children replace the old, this is represented in the Epilogue as a very positive outcome. But it is also inevitably a somewhat melancholy and difficult finale. The new generation cannot but serve to recall that the generation passed is dead and that they died without sufficient cause. And while God is certainly shown to be merciful to Job, His mercy is not complete. Children have replaced children, but, in this final version of the Joban folktale, there are no miracles of the sort that bring the dead back from the grave.

As I mentioned above, considering how uncomfortable the issues stirred up when Job's murdered children are succeeded by a new generation, one begins to wonder why this is allowed to be part of the story at all. In respect to this, I have already suggested earlier that the exigencies of the folktale itself demanded that if children could not be brought back from the dead, they had to be brought back from somewhere.[490] But there may be more involved here than simply this. It may well be that the first children had to remain dead and the second children had to be born to replace them because this was a reality that the writer/editor of the prose supplements and his ancient audience knew only too well.

In "Bontsye Shvayg" the suffering hero is offered great reward, but there are still the "thousand million" who suffer and die without such divine intervention. And for Jews today the Holocaust simply serves to underscore how prophetically close to the truth this depiction of suffering has proven to be. The distinction between a thousand million and six million is a fine one for any who have seen pictures of the mountains of corpses that the Holocaust produced, and after a certain point, the distinction between such numbers ceases to have any value. Certainly, no one imagines today that these dead can be brought back to repopulate a Yiddish world that no longer exists. That kind of miracle is not to be expected and would be too painful even to imagine. One can only look to the future in which a new generation, escaped by the skin of their teeth, may grow and flourish.

It may have been the same in ancient times. It may have been deemed a pipe dream to imagine that Job's children could come back from the grave. The Jews may have been all too impressed that dead children—be they Job's or their own—remain dead and that the reality of their deaths necessarily makes any appeal to resurrection miracles seem absurd. While there are certainly good theological reasons why resurrection stories were looked at askance in any case,[491] perhaps the most decisive reason that Job's story had to be told with a new generation replacing the old is because this was the sort of limited miracle that Jews could accept and to which they might adapt.

When the writer/editor of the prose supplements added his final harmonic to the Joban counterpoint, he may have felt that it was not appropriate or even seemly to speak of perfect mercy from a completely righteous Deity. He may have been inclined to believe that perfection is not what one hopes for in the aftermath of tragedy: just as Bontsye is willing to settle for his hot, buttered roll in lieu of a perfect and just recompense, so may it be that Jews, both ancient and modern, prefer to focus upon survival of the new rather than insisting upon resurrecting the old. Job's restoration may not have been all one might want, but when seen in the aftermath of a succession of ancient tragedies, it may well have been deemed to be more than enough.

13

Intervening Themes

We must consider one last aspect of Joban counterpoint before this study is drawn to a close. In the preceding discussion we have centered our attention on the writers and editors who have modified the book of Job by adding their supplements to the Poem. But it is also true that the book of Job shows indications that other editorial hands have gone further than this by actually changing the text itself. This editorial intervention constitutes the last and most activist level in the complex of Joban counterpoint. Indeed, it occurs in that gray area of redaction where the text ends and commentary begins. Thus, it is an appropriate way to lead us back to one of the earliest bits of pure commentary on Job known to us, the statement in the Epistle of James, with which we began this study.

The clearest example of this sort of overt modification is found in the Third Cycle of the Joban debate, although, admittedly, it is hard in this particular circumstance to decide how much the alteration is the product of accidental corruption and how much is the work of a determined editor, or, as some have argued, an outraged censor. I have already considered in some detail the specific changes that seem to have been made in this last round of debate.[492] What is important to note here is that regardless of how the text came to be modified, the change does materially alter and soften the characterization of Job found in the Poem and bring his pronouncements more in line with a traditional view. This is particularly true of 24:18 and following and 27:8 and following, both of which are apparently displaced passages now attributed to Job. In each of these speeches, the point made is essentially the same, namely, that those who sin will certainly be punished, which, of course, precisely counters the argument Job has made throughout his debate.

Considering the generally chaotic state of the Third Cycle, it is hard to imagine that the apparent deletions, alterations and displacements that have occurred there are purely the result of a pietistic editor's activity. If this were so, one would expect the editor to have done a far better job of putting things together in some coherent form. Still, if an editor were presented with an already-corrupt text, he might well have decided to attribute to Job the sort of pietistic statements that would tend to restore his legendary image.

In fact, it would not be difficult to imagine that it was the writer/editor of the prose supplements himself who was faced with the task of restoring order to the garbled text now found in chapters 24–27. Assuming this scenario, he might have decided to distribute the rubrics introducing each speech in the Third Cycle in such a way that Job could say what a righteous man *should* say. Perhaps, the writer/editor sincerely seized on this opportunity to read into this text the first stirring in Job of a desire to return to a less-controversial view of man's proper conduct before God, a view that will be further reinforced in the Epilogue.

In any case, whoever chose to attribute more traditional sentiments to Job certainly had a primary goal in mind—to supply an explicit statement from Job's own mouth, proving that he was more accepting of God than otherwise might appear. Nor should we necessarily assume that this editorial decision was made in a calculatedly Machiavellian fashion. From our standpoint, it may seem obviously wrong to attribute to Job pietistic statements that blatantly contradict everything he has stated previously. Nonetheless, the editor who made this decision may well have been *sincerely wrong* after the manner of Aqiba in regard to Song of Songs, or the apologists who see nothing but sincerity and piety in Bontsye's silence.

The other large modification of Job that bears mentioning is actually not found in the Hebrew text of Job—at least in the Hebrew text that has come down through the Masoretic tradition. Rather, it occurs in one of the earliest translations of this book, what has come to be known as the Old Greek version of Job. The most striking thing to notice about the text preserved in this tradition is that it is fully one-sixth shorter than the Hebrew text preserved by the Masoretic editors.[493] Not surprisingly, this overall minus in the Old Greek has attracted considerable scholarly attention, and the case has been made that this apparent abridgement may reflect a pietistic editorial prejudice, a bias that is said to be reflected in the existing renderings of the Old Greek version as well.[494]

Today, however, this view is, by and large, discounted, thanks especially to the careful analysis of the Greek text done by H. M. Orlinsky.[495] H. Heater's comment represents the current scholarly consensus: "Orlinsky's outstanding work on the style of the Septuagint of Job has thoroughly refuted the idea of a broad theological or philosophical bias on the part of the translator. He has demonstrated that many divergences . . . are nothing other than stylistic Greek."[496]

The issue as to why the Old Greek text became abridged is still an open question, probably unresolvable on the basis of our current knowledge of the text-critical history of the book of Job. But for our purposes, the important point to note is that the abridgement of Job, reflected in the Old Greek tradition, seems to be connected less to any attempt to alter the import of the book and reflects more the exigencies involved in translating a difficult Hebrew text. Thus, while intrinsically interesting (and, in its own way, a kind of cultural counterpoint) it is tangential to the concerns of this study.

On the other hand, there are two modifications to the Greek tradition of Job that do seem to be motivated by a desire to bring the figure of Job more in line with a traditional pietistic viewpoint.[497] One is an addition to Job 2:9 in which Job's wife expands on her urging Job to abandon his integrity, curse[498] God and die. She cries out, "How long will you endure and say, look, I will wait a little longer, looking for hope of my salvation?" (2:9a).[499] She then proceeds to elaborate upon her husband's desperate circumstances—the loss of his reputation, the death of their children, the pain and humiliation of his physical afflictions. She also reminds him how horrendous her own circumstances have become; how she must seek charity from house after house and labor all day while overwhelmed by grief. Job's wife seems to have been driven to the point of such despair that in her view, death appears to be the only means of relief. Hence, she urges Job to cry out against God in order that they may be both put out of their misery.

To some extent this addition reflects a desire to include in this version of the Job story an apparently popular, secondary tradition, centered on the trials and tribulations of Job's wife. In fact, this tradition receives an even more elaborate treatment in the *Testament of Job*.[500] But beyond its intrinsic interest, this supplement also serves effectively to reinforce a pietistic view of Job. For in light of this excruciatingly detailed portrayal of the suffering of Job and his wife, the righteous hero's determination to hold fast to his integrity becomes all the more dramatic and heroic.[501]

Even more significant is the addition that the Greek tradition makes to the Epilogue of Job. Part of this supplement supplies a genealogy for Job. Job is identified in an addition to 42:17 with a certain Jobab (see 42:17b), who is then traced through Esau back to Abraham.[502] Thus, the two most prominent biblical heroes, tested by God, are linked not only by the similarity of their stories but also, according to this account, by a bond of blood. In earlier forms of the Joban legend, such as that reflected in the Masoretic tradition, there is no hint of an explicit link between Job and God's Chosen People.[503] One could see that this might prove to be something of an embarrassment, especially for Jews who wished to identify themselves with this archetypical Righteous Sufferer. After all, how could they consider Job to be completely "perfect and upright" if he were not, somehow, a part of the family as well? By giving Job a proper genealogy, this problem could be addressed and a solution neatly supplied.

It is interesting to note that in the *Testament of Job* the association of Job with the Jews is made even more certain in that the second wife Job marries (after the death of his first wife) is none other than Dinah, the only daughter of Jacob. Thus, Job can declare to his children at the beginning of this pseudepigraphal work, "You are a chosen and honored race from the seed of Jacob, the father of your mother [while] I am from the sons of Esau, the brother of Jacob, of whom your mother is Dinah, from whom I begot you" (1:5–6). Clearly, the *Testament* (and the legendary tradition it apparently documents) wishes to make Job and his descendants as Jewish as possible. In all likelihood, it was a similar desire that proved to be the decisive reason for supplying a proper family tree for him in the Greek tradition as well.

But it is the statement supplied in the Greek text immediately preceding this genealogy that reflects a far more dramatic attempt to modify the story of Job and thereby defend it from potential criticism. Here, after bringing Job's life to a close with the statement (also reflected in the Masoretic Text) that "Job came to an end, venerable and full of days," the Greek text adds this addendum: "And it is written[504] that he will again rise with those the Lord raises" (42:17a). This statement has a significant salutary effect on all the most difficult issues raised in the book of Job. As Baskin notes, "In one sentence the central issue of the Book of Job, the existence of unjustified suffering in the universe of a just God, is neatly vitiated. All present wrongs will be righted when we rise again."[505]

In this connection, it is especially important to note how this promise of resurrection is phrased in the Greek supplement to 42:17. It is not just Job who is assured of resurrection; he is simply one among "those the Lord raises." Undoubtedly, Baskin is correct to see this characterization of resurrection as a universal phenomenon which is meant encompass all Righteous Sufferers. This miracle of miracles would then rectify in one stroke all the inequities that the innocent have had to endure since creation.

But this promise may also be meant to address a more specific concern in the story of Job itself. It seems reasonable to suggest that the allusion to others who will be resurrected along with Job is intended to be an explicit reference to Job's original children. Hence, we would see in this statement an attempt late in the editorial development of Job, to redress the one great inequity in the biblical tradition of Job: the loss of the innocent children. And in order to do this, it would seem that the Greek translator returns to the oldest layer in the legend of Job and gives its ancient climax a new authority and therefore a new life. Thus, we find here that the Joban counterpoint has gone full circle: having started with a story of resurrection, it finally returns to it.

Other examples of editorial modification in the book of Job are less dramatic than this and, in nearly all cases, reflect a desire by various editors to make sure that the text maintains a proper respect for God. The most dramatic case of this is found in those texts (Job 1:5, 11; 2:5, 9) where, the possibility of cursing God is broached. Instead of reproducing a baldly blasphemous statement—in which the original Hebrew speaks of cursing God, presumably employing the verb *qll* or *'rr*, "to curse"[506]—*brk*, "bless," is euphemistically substituted. For example, when Job's wife tells Job to "curse God and die" in 2:17, the text actually reads, "bless God and die" (*brk 'lhym wmt*). For the most part, the other ancient versions reflect this same tendency to euphemize, although on occasion the original reading appears to be reflected in some of these early traditions.[507]

Other similar examples can be cited. In Job 7:20, according to the Masoretic tradition, the text has Job declare, *'hyh 'ly lmś'*, "I am a burden to myself." However, scribal tradition indicates that the form *'ly* was changed from an original *'lyk*, and that the unedited reading was "I am a burden unto You [God]."[508] Presumably, a change was made in this instance to avoid the suggestion that any human being could be seen as an actual "burden" to an all-powerful God. Another case is found in the introduction to Elihu's speeches, where the text changes an original condemnation of God into a condemnation of Job (32:3).[509] Similarly, in 34:6, where Elihu characterizes Job as one who claims God has committed falsehood, the text has likely been changed so that it is Job who is now accounted to be a liar instead.[510]

Other examples of this type could be cited,[511] especially if we were to take the various ancient translations of Job into consideration; but in all such instances the impetus for editorial emendation is much the same—a desire to preserve a pious respect for God and to avoid any hint of blasphemy. Such a tendency, of course, should not be viewed as particularly associated with the book of Job. It is better seen as a fairly standard part of postbiblical hermeneutics. If Job seems to attract more than its share of such editorial changes, it is only because, due to the critical nature of its text, it offers more potential opportunities.

There is, however, one particular emendation proposed for Job that is not quite of this type. Moreover, for our purposes, it is particularly insightful. This text is one of the most famous and most oft-quoted texts in the entire book: Job 13:15, which in the King James Version of Job has been enshrined as Job's affirmation of faith: "Though He [God] slay me, yet will I trust in him. But I will argue my ways before Him."

This affirmation of faith on the part of Job is not what it first appears to be. Actually the text, as found in the Hebrew according to the Masoretic tradition, has almost diametrically the opposite meaning as that found in the above "Authorized Translation." It reads, *hn yqṭlny l' 'yḥl 'k drky 'l-pnyw 'wkyḥ*, "If He [God] slays me, I will not wait; still, I will argue my rights before Him." In order to get to the more pietistic version of this verse, one must emend the text; reading *lw*, "to him, for him" in lieu of the negative particle *l'*, "no, not,"—a slight alteration facilitated by the fact that no change need be made in pronunciation. The forms, (*lô* versus *lō'*) are virtually identical from a phonetic standpoint. Hence, *l' 'yḥl*, "I will not wait" is transformed into *lw 'yḥl* "I will wait for/trust to Him."

This proposed emendation is not actually found in the text itself; rather, this tradition is preserved as a marginal note (called a *qere*, or "reading") by the Masoretic editors and can be found in the best and most ancient Masoretic manuscripts.[512] It appears to be reflected in some of the ancient versions of Job as well.[513] Besides these early attestations, it is now clear that this proposed emendation was known in Jewish circles as early as the first century B.C.E. As I have demonstrated in an earlier study, the reading is reflected in the text of the Cave 11 Qumran Targum of Job, the earliest known witness to the biblical text of Job.[514]

It also seems highly likely that the pietistic version of Job 13:15 was also known to the writer of the *Testament of Job* since it seems to be reflected in one of the *Testament*'s passages. In 37:1–5, Baldad/Baldas (= Heb. Bildad) and Job have this exchange:

> And again he [Baldad] said: "Towards whom do you hope?"
> And I [Job] said, "Towards the living God!" (37:1–2)

If the answer to Baldad's question, *epi tinos su elpizeis?*, "Towards whom do you hope?" were given a complete, rather than an elliptical, response by Job, that is, *epi tōi theōi tōi zōnti elpizō*, "I hope towards the living God!" one would have a phrase highly reminiscent of the pietistic version of Job 13:15, especially since *yḥl*, the operative verb in the Hebrew verse, could appropriately be translated as "to hope" as easily as "to wait."

In fact, Baldad uses precisely this sort of phrasing when he continues his questioning of Job in 37:5. He declares, *epi tōi theōi elpizeis?* "Do you hope towards God?" which could easily be answered by the pietistic version of 13:15 in the Hebrew: "To Him I will hope." This is especially true since the operative verb in the *Testament*, *elpizō*, is commonly used in the Septuagint as a reflex of Hebrew *yḥl*, the verb employed in 13:15.[515].

Finally this reading of the text is also discussed in the Mishnah (*Soṭa* 5:5), in a tradition ascribed to Joshua ben Hyrcanus (c. 110–135 C.E.). In an argument in favor of the assumption that Job served God out of love rather than out of fear, the rabbi argued that one must take this text with the pietistic reading *lw 'yḥl* ("I will wait for Him") rather than *l' 'yḥl* ("I will not wait").[516] It also serves as the dying credo of Rabbi Ishmael ben Elisha in Midrash Eileh Ezkerah.[517]

It is clear enough what effect the tradition emending 13:15 has on the interpretation of the verse and, more importantly, what overall effect this reading can have on the picture of Job, especially as found in the Poem. For the emended text would seem to make clear that no matter how much Job vociferously argues his rights in the presence of God, he still maintains his hope and his trust in the Almighty—even though he may be driven to the point of death as a result. Obviously, this reading is useful; for no text could serve more effectively to resolve the apparent contradictions between Job the Patient and Job the Impatient.

But there is another, more subtle point to be considered about this text: Why did it need to be changed? To be sure, as just noted, from a pietistic standpoint many positive results follow from making this slight emendation of the text; but this, in and of itself, is not really a sufficient explanation. There is, after all, nothing blatantly offensive in the unaltered passage—at least, nothing more offensive than in any of a number of passages in the Poem of Job that were left unchanged. In particular, there is no overt impiety towards God reflected in this text, the usual red flag that compels editorial change. We should recall, too, that emendations of this sort were not instituted lightly; in Masoretic circles there was considerable reluctance to tamper, or even to propose tampering, with a biblical text.[518] There had to be strong provocation, an overriding need before such a change could even be suggested. The problem is: in this instance, it is unclear what that provocation would be. It would therefore be fair to say that the change proposed for 13:15 appears to be fairly atypical of normal scribal practice. Note, in this respect, that one would be hard-pressed to find another marginal emendation followed by the Masoretic editors quite like the one they accept for Job 13:15.[519]

So, to return to the question: why then this particular change? To begin with, we should remember that the evidence clearly suggests that this proposed change was not the idea of the Masoretes themselves. They are simply preserving a well-known tradition that we know to have been in circulation at least as early as the first century B.C.E. and probably considerably earlier than that. In a real sense they are indicating that although their received text reads a certain way, there was in this instance another tradition (perhaps even reflected in early manuscripts) that was important enough to be mentioned as an alternate reading.[520]

This relieves the Masoretic editors of direct responsibility for inventing the reading, but we have only succeeded in pushing the question back to the beginning, or slightly before the beginning of the Christian era. Beyond this, if we are to try out a solution for this problem, it may be best to return to a consideration of the unedited reading that prompted the change in the first place, especially the negative verbal phrase in 13:15a, *l' 'yḥl*. This could be variously translated, "I will not wait," "I will not hope."[521] But perhaps we can best understand the proper nuance of this phrase, the particular nuance that the ancient audience of Job heard in 13:15, if we consider the passage as it was heard within the context of the Joban tradition. Especially, we should consider what this phrase means in terms of the most enduring cliché associated with the hero of this tradition: "the patience of Job."

We know that the author of the Epistle of James gave prominence to this phrase, but it is unlikely that he invented it. The "patience of Job" echoes through the *Testament of Job*,[522] and there is no reason to assume that the concept of enduring patience was not a part of the earliest level of the traditional story, the very embodiment of the pietistic ideal it wished to affirm. But if this is so, then it would also be a natural target for the poet of Job to attack and subvert, just as he has done to so many other Joban stereotypes. Perhaps, then, this intent motivates the cutting affirmation that the poet has his Job make in 13:15.

If "Shall we accept Good from God and not Evil?" (2:10) is the credo of Job the Patient, maybe 13:15 is the credo of Job the Impatient and is meant to underline the fact of this Righteous Sufferer's towering impatience. Hence, the best translation may be the one that shows this emphasis most clearly: "Though he slay me, I will not be patient! Regardless, I will argue my rights before Him!"

And this may not be the only instance in which the proverbial "patience of Job" is attacked in the Poem. Consider 6:11, where Job declares, *mh-khy ky 'yhl wmh-qsy ky-"ryk npšy*. In light of the tradition of Job the Patient, this may be best understood, "What is my strength that I should be patient? Or what is my end that my soul should endure?" This would then be Job's disclaimer stating that there is, in truth, no purpose to the proverbial patient suffering of the sort for which this enduring hero is especially famous. The poet would thus be pointedly emphasizing that a mere human hardly has the strength to hold out against divinely ordained punishment, nor is the end (*qs*) that results from such patience worth the effort. For unlike the Job of legend, the poet's righteous man-in-distress has no preordained "happy ending" to look forward to—only destruction and death.

Much the same point is made in Job 14:14. There, as indicated above, Job imagines the possibility of resurrection from the dead.[523] If this were truly possible, he declares, perhaps a heroic endurance would be worthwhile. Verse 14b can be translated in this light as Job's affirmation of this belief: "All my burdensome days I would be patient." But, as we have seen, this is a short-lived, forlorn hope that is quickly overwhelmed by a depiction of the certainty of death. And just as all hope of resurrection dies, so, too, does Job's faith in patience.[524]

But if the Job of the Poem or, better, the writer who created his words has no faith in patience, there were others who did have such a faith. Indeed, in the shadow of ancient tragedies, such a belief in patient endurance may well have been their greatest hope, their basic reason for turning to the book of Job in the first place. And it may have been their desire, their desperate need to preserve this faith at all costs that prompted the rewriting of Job 13:15—certainly, the most clear-cut attack on this most precious icon in the Job tradition.

Actually, the change may well have been considered more properly a reclamation rather than an alteration. After all, by changing but a single letter (and not even altering the sound of the text) an ancient editor could allow Job to reaffirm his ancient credo of 2:10. Certainly, anyone willing to accept both good and evil from his Deity is, without question, also a righteous hero who waits patiently for the Almighty, even in the face of death. Thus with just the slightest of editorial adjustments, the texts in Job 2:10 and 13:15 are shown to say much the same thing. One can well imagine that the possibility of saying so much by doing so little may have been considered an opportunity too fortuitous to be coincidental. The emended reading simply was something that had to be so; and that being the case, the "original" reading simply had to be wrong.[525]

Once more we can see this type of editorial action and the rationale that motivates it echoed in the Bontsye-model. Here, too, we have seen that on occasion, those who saw themselves as preservers of the tradition felt the need to change the text in order to save its "correct" meaning. Thus we find that an Abel or a Perl is prepared to make the slightest change in "Bontsye Shvayg," just an added phrase in one instance, just a dropped phrase in the other, so that the text can more clearly state what it *has to mean*.[526] Note, too, another significant point—that in making their changes, these editors leave the original Yiddish alone. It is only in their popular renditions of the text into English that they feel at liberty to alter the words and make them conform to what, in the light of history in a post-Holocaust world, they must be made to say. Even more to the point, the oral tradition that now surrounds Perets' story is so pervasive that the vast majority of those who know the tale hear it only in one way—as the embodiment of a silent endurance—although, in actuality, it reads quite another way.

Once again, the analogy seems to be useful for understanding the emendation of Job 13:15 and, more broadly, all the changes we have noted above, which constitute this last harmonic in the Joban counterpoint. Note that the change in 13:15 is not really a change at all. The text is as it was; the correction is placed in the margin or, barring this, in a translation or, barring this, in a popularization like the *Testament of Job* or, barring this, in the popular story that one heard told about Job.

This is not to say that there were not overt changes made in the book of Job, either by chance or on purpose, at one point or another. The discussion above has shown that this was so; yet by and large, such was not the dominant tendency—to violate the text *itself*.[527] Nor was it really necessary. Again, the history of "Bontsye Shvayg" is instructive in this regard. The text has always been there to be read, even correct translations and correct criticisms that understand Perets' intent have always been available to guide the uninitiated. But these are not what people choose to read; the satirical message is not what they want to hear. As Perets says, they want their message, but please, without *realism*.

History in the twentieth century has dealt harshly with the Jews; and when they turn to Yiddish literature for insight, they do not seek to find biting, critical lessons that would only serve to rub salt into their wounds. What they seek instead are figures that will remind them of what they have lost, emblematic heroes with whom they can identify and from whose endurance they can derive some sense of hope. The desire to fulfill this need is what makes "Bontsye Shvayg" popular. If its audience could not read these things into Perets' work, they would not read (or at least tell) his story at all.

History has been no less harsh to the Jews in ancient times. They read Job then for the same reason that "Bontsye Shvayg" is read today—to find in its account a figure emblematic of their suffering and loss, someone with whom they could identify and in whose endurance they could also derive some sense of hope. It is for this reason that they wrapped the figure of Job in his cloak of patience just as much Bontsye is wrapped today in his aura of silence.

If, in a case like Job 13:15 or all the other similar cases, they feel the need to adjust the text in order to make the image of their chosen hero a little more perfect, this should not be surprising. History is their vindication: like the Perets-lover, mentioned above, who chose to read "Bontsye Shvayg" as he felt it could only be read, even though this was different from the text before his eyes,[528] so too have generation after generation looked at Job 13:15 and declared, "There, you see, it *does* read 'Though He slay me, yet will I patiently wait for Him.'" So they have read the passage, and so they have read the book.

14

Conclusion: The Joban Fugue

The case I have made above regarding the development of the contrapuntal layers of the book of Job should now be clear. I have argued that it is possible to see a pattern in the development of the tradition of Job strikingly similar to the pattern that shaped the writing of "Bontsye Shvayg" and then continued to shape this Yiddish story's interpretation. This pattern involves the development of a conservative folk tradition embodied in a famous legend. This legend and the pietistic ideals it portrayed provoked the anger of a great literary artist who determined to counterattack its message, utilizing the literary weapon of parody.

But then the forces of history played a trick upon the parodist. The very extremes he so subtly wrote into his text to illustrate the absurdity of the traditional premises themselves became realities as history itself took a turn toward the extreme. Then his parody had to be reread and its interpretation reshaped. What I have called the "Ozymandias effect" worked on the perceptions of the story's audience and caused them to strip from it all hint of parody and irony. Instead, the story that began as an attack upon tradition became the very embodiment of the tradition; the bulwark and focus of hope in the midst of despair.

We have also seen that there are characteristic reactions to parody by those who may have read it in the shadow of tragedy and disaster. Such patterns of reaction can be found in the cultural history of "Bontsye Shvayg" and can also be read into the developing tradition of Job.

Some, like a Madison or the author of the Wisdom Hymn, may recognize an author's original parodistic intent but then self-consciously turn away. They may know what the author intended but feel that now one can only draw out of the text a different message in which the parodistic elements are muted or tacitly ignored. Others like a Greenberg or the Elihu-author may be provoked to protest what they perceive to be an eloquent cry of anguish that has finally gone wrong. They then consider it to be their absolute duty to set the record straight, to make sure no one misunderstands how the message must be interpreted *now*, especially in the light of disastrous events.

Then, there are those like Samuel, Wiesel and the writer/editor of the prose supplements of Job who feel that events have shaped a tragedy for which the story is emblematic, a prophecy before its time. They perceive this tragedy as being beyond explanation; and in trying to come to grips with it, they endeavor to explain nothing. To them it is sufficient to find a reflection of their own sense of anguish in a text

175

that, because it speaks in hyperbole, gives words to that which had otherwise seemed beyond the power of words to convey. They seize upon these words and make them their own.

If, in doing so, they are blind to the irony and satire that gave rise to the words, this is hardly extraordinary. Victims and survivors do not easily grasp or, for that matter, tolerate a depiction of their own situation as ironic or satirical. The "joke" that history has played on them is no parody; hence a story which they see as most clearly reflecting their dilemma cannot be a parody either—only a bitter reality. For them the story becomes a memorial and its protagonists untouchable heroes, beyond irony and beyond criticism. These heroes and their ultimate lot become the focus of their devout attention; for only in the "happy ending" given to these figures can they hope to find their own reconciliation.

Finally there are those like Abel, Perl, and the various editors who have made overt changes to the book of Job. They have gone beyond supplementation and have actually intervened into the text itself, "fine-tuning" it with (usually slight) adjustments that safeguard the text from declaring what it dare not mean and instead serve to allow the text to affirm what it has to say. For the most part they do their work in the margins and only violate the sanctity of the text itself with great reluctance. Still, theirs become the popular renditions—the plays, the reworked stories, the secondary readings (clearly labeled as secondary) and the translations that everybody knows. In this respect, those who modify the text do not lead opinion; instead, they simply place into the text what everyone always thought was there in the first place.

Of course, in the case of the history surrounding Y. L. Perets and his "Bontsye Shvayg" we know what is going on and, in the broadest sense, why things have occurred the way they have occurred. As I have constantly stressed, we have no such luxury when we try to reconstruct the early history of Job. We simply must guess at its background and development. We have no grasp of how the text was really read; whether this or that writer or editor really acted as I have imagined or whether they acted in some entirely different manner. Who knows what crisis or tragedy (if any) motivated this or stimulated that? It's anybody's guess—that is, until one comes to the author of the Epistle of James.

For when we reach James, we finally begin to gain, once more, our footing: at last our critical judgments can be controlled by some sense of the historical context. For example, we know, within reasonable limits, when James' letter was written; even more importantly we know, in general, to whom it was written and the events that shaped both the writer's message and his audience's reaction. Granted, there are still major questions that remain unanswered about the specific history that forms the context for the Epistle of James, but compared to the situation we have faced in regard to the book of Job, there is a relative wealth of information about this New Testament letter and its environment.

What we see in the case of James—especially in regard to its use of the Joban tradition in 5:11—is that it fits the Bontsye-model quite well. We have a community living in the shadow of a great calamity, the loss of their messianic leader, and a succession of further tragedies and disasters that have resulted in the persecutions and deaths of many who have held fast to the faith. James bends his efforts toward explaining all this, especially the intentions of a God who, although merciful, has seemed to show less than perfect mercy and compassion for the ones he has specially chosen as the bearers of His new message of hope.

In the face of all the adversity this community has known, James counsels his brethren that they must endure without complaint, without question; and in order to drive his point home, he turns to what he considers an appropriate emblem of patience from the Bible—indeed, of all the biblical figures, the one who he thinks can fulfill this role better than anyone else: Job the Patient. In fact, from his standpoint, Job is even a better model than an Abraham, because Job was tested beyond what the first patriarch had to endure and still held fast to his integrity; moreover, Job was a gentile and thus proof positive that one need not necessarily be a Jew to have the special merits of chosenness and endurance.

Earlier in this study, I suggested that the author of James had to give precedence to the legend of Job—that which one heard—over the book of Job—that which one read—in order to characterize Job as he does in 5:11.[529] To some extent this remains true; still, in light of our subsequent discussion, it should be clear that this is not entirely the truth. It is completely impossible to accept the proposition that the author of James turned a deaf ear to the book of Job and harkened instead only to a popular account of the story. This viewpoint of James 5:11, seems to reflect the scholarly consensus but in this regard the scholarly consensus is wrong or, at least, not entirely right.

James had to pay attention to the biblical book. It could not be ignored for the simple reason that it supplied the authority that validated his homily about the patience of Job. If the authority came from elsewhere—especially if it came solely from popular hearsay, however ancient—the result would be to undermine the authority of Scripture itself. And it should be clear to anyone who reads James and sees how much he invests in the importance of his biblical canon[530] that this would be the last thing he would wish to do.

More to the point, it is hardly necessary to take the view that James' appeal to the patience of Job steers clear of the biblical text and depends solely upon the authority of ancient legend. Rather, we must recognize that when the author of James reads the book of Job, he harkens to a complex of Joban counterpoint and, out of the aggregate of its harmonies, derives the message he expects to hear.

Perhaps the best way to understand how James listens to Job is to shift our metaphor slightly and think of the book as particular sort of counterpoint—the fugue. In a fugue first one musical line takes up the theme, then, as it continues to progress, a second voice takes up the melody while the first drops down into contrapuntal harmony. As more voices are added in succession, a whole complex of competing musical lines play with and against one another in one of the most complicated forms of counterpoint in the musical repertoire.

To the educated ear it is the way that the melodies and harmonies develop in relationship to one another that is most important—the artistry in the fugue is found in the progress of the counterpoint. Note, in this respect, that a fugue must be distinguished from the far less sophisticated canon or round. In the latter, voice is added to voice in succession, as in the fugue. But then there is no further variation; while the succeeding voices harmonize in counterpoint, they are limited to repeating the same melodies, slightly out of phase with one another, over and over. But the counterpoint in a fugue constantly evolves, with voices changing key, shifting from major to minor (or vice versa), with the gaps between the voices stretched farther apart or pressed more closely together or being themselves interrupted by episodes as voices exit and enter. The term "fugue" comes from Latin *fugo*, "to flee";[531] and this well characterizes the nature of this musical chase of voice after voice in a constantly shifting dynamic of contrapuntal harmonies.

However, to the less sophisticated ear it is difficult and perhaps impossible to keep track of all that is going on. To a popular audience, the harmonies are beautiful and supply the rich background for the musical composition; but what they actually *hear* (or think they hear), for the most part, is the same theme being stressed again and again, as it seems to be "tossed" from one voice to the other—as though the fugue really were a canon after all.

It may be appropriate to see (or hear) the book of Job—built, as it is, over time—as not unlike a fugue. The tradition begins with one theme; then, as time goes on, another theme is scored on top of it, thereby forcing the original theme to take on a new harmonic role; then further themes are added in succession, again requiring the themes that precede to give way and take a different role from what their authors might have originally intended. In this respect, the Joban fugue is less predictable and more adversarial than its musical counterpart. After all, it is a manifestation of historical rather than synchronic counterpoint; and there is not one composer in charge but a succession of composers, bringing to the piece different concerns and different agendas. Still, however the various layers of Job vary or tend to oppose one another, the contrapuntal relationship is still maintained. The same basic universe of motifs is engaged and the beauty of the harmonies never disintegrates into chaos.

We have tried to listen to the voices in Job with a sophisticated ear and have tried to appreciate how one theme plays against another and enriches the evolving composition. But to the less sophisticated ear of a popular audience, the themes are not heard in this highly esoteric manner. James is their representative: for him it is sufficient to search for what he perceives to be the main theme, then to pick it out of the complex of succeeding voices and variations wherever it is to be found— perhaps even to hear it where it really should not be heard.

For James and for the audience he represents, there is little question what the dominant motif in this main theme is: the patience of Job. In his famous pronouncement in 5:11, James, then, is simply reporting what he has heard. He is like a member of a concert audience who has watched the conductor and the orchestra play a piece in accordance with the written score but who cannot be expected to hear the complex of harmonies as the professional musicians hear it. He hears the piece as it strikes his ears, and in this respect he is very much in accord with most in the audience who listen to the piece.

When James and his ancient audience hear the Joban fugue, they pick out the themes that are important to them, the ones with which they can identify—the endurance of the hero, the testing by God, the deeply anguished cries of despair, the hope for a Redeemer who seems even to promise resurrection, the ultimate restoration of the Righteous Sufferer. They may hear the other themes as well;

indeed, how could they do not? But it is not these counterthemes that register in their consciousness; it is not to them that they really *listen*. They only grasp what for them is the clearest melody. The rest plays in the background.

Of course, the Joban counterpoint does not end with the Epistle of James. One could consider how the various rabbis read the book of Job or the patristic fathers, the medieval commentators and so on. Nonetheless, James is as good a place to end as it was to begin this study because, for good or ill, it is James who has set the most decisive mark on Job, if only by default. His is the only overt reference to the book of Job and its protagonist in the New Testament; consequently, when he celebrated the patience of Job, this concept remained fixed from then on as the precedent. Thereafter, especially once the New Testament had authority of its own as the canon that takes precedence over the Old Testament canon, all Christian interpretation of Job had to begin with the assumption that first and foremost, he was the most patient of men.

To be sure, voices always have risen in protest to this viewpoint. Especially, the early rabbis often tended to look at Job askance and were less inclined to grant him the same largess as the early Christian Church wished to bestow upon him.[532] But in the final analysis, this has made very little difference. Christians dictated the shape of Western civilization; therefore it was a single phrase in a minor letter of the Christian canon that carried the day. James urged his audience to remember *tēn hupomonēn Iōb*, "the patience of Job." We continue to heed his advice to this very day.

APPENDIX

The Text and Translation of Y. L. Perets' "Bontsye Shvayg"

The following is a transcription of the Yiddish text of "Bontsye Shvayg" based upon the 1893 edition, with significant variants from the 1901 edition of the story. While this should in no way be considered a "critical"—let alone a "variorum"—edition of the story, it is to my knowledge the most comprehensive listing of story and variants available.

Facing the Yiddish transcription is my own translation, which has greatly benefited from the advice and guidance of Jeffrey Shandler. Nonetheless, any faults or errors are my own. Note that the transcription of "Bontsye Shvayg" has been modernized to reflect the transcription conventions of YIVO (the Yiddish Institute of Study) wherever possible. While I have endeavored in the footnotes to note significant variants in the 1901 edition in translation, not all variants were deemed significant enough or easily translatable. Hence only some 46 variant listing are given in translation, over against 62 in the original.

Bontsye Shvayg![1]

Do, oyf *der* velt, hot Bontsye Shvayg's toyt gor keyn royshem[2] nisht gemakt! Fregt emetsn bekheyrem ver Bontsye iz gevezn, vi azoy er hot gelebt, oyf vos er iz geshtorbn![3] Tsi hot inem dos harts geflatst, tsi di koykhes[4] zenen im oysgegangen, oder[5] der markhbeyn hot zikh ibergebrokhn unter a shverer last . . . ver veyst? Efsher iz er gor far hunger geshtorbn!

A ferd in tramvey zol faln, volt men zikh mer interesirt, es voltn tsaytungen geshribn, hunderter mentshn voltn fun ale gasn gelofn un di neveyle bakukt, batrakt afile dem ort, vu di mapole iz geven . . .

Nor dos ferd in tramvay volt oyf di skhie nisht gehot, es zol zayn toyznt milyon ferd vi mentshn![6]

Bontsye hot shtil gelebt un iz shtil gestorbn; vi a shotn iz er durkh—durkh *undzer* velt!

Oyf Bontsyes bris hot men keyn vayn nisht getrunkn, es hobn keyn koyses geklungen! Tsu barmitsve hot er keyn klingendike droshe nisht gezogt . . . gelebt hot er vi a groy kleyn kerndl zamd baym breg fun yam, tsvishn milyon zayns glaykhn; un az der vint hot'n oyfgehoybn un oyf der anderer zayt yam ariber geyogn, hot es keyner nisht bamerkt!

Baym lebn hot di nase blote keyn shlad[7] fun zayn fus nisht bahaltn; nokhn toyt hot der vind dos kleyne bretl fun zayn keyver umgevorfn,[8] un dem kabrens vayb hot es gefunen vayt fun keyver un derbay a tepl kartoflyes[9] opgekokht . . . es iz dray teg nokh Bontsyes toyt, fregt dem kabren bekheyrem vu er hot'm geleygt!

Volt Bontsye a khotsh matseyve,[10] volt efsher iber hundert yor zi an altertums-forsher gefunen,[11] un "Bontsye Shvayg"[12] volt nokh a mol ibergeklungen in *undzer* luft!

A shotn! Zayn fotografey iz nisht geblibn bay keynem in moyekh, bay keynem in harts; es iz fun im keyn zeykher in keynems moyekh nisht geblibn![13]

"Keyn kind, keyn rind"; elnt gelebt—elnt gestorbn!

Ven nisht dos mentshlekhe geruder, volt efsher emetser a mol gehert[14] vi Bontsyes markhbeyn hot unter der mase[15] geknakt; volt di velt mer tsayt gehot, volt emetser efsher a mol bamerkt, az Bontsye (oykh a mentsh) hot lebedikerheyt tsvey oysgeloshene oygn un shreklekh ayngefalene bakn; az afile ven er hot gor shoyn keyn mase[16] nisht oyf di pleytses iz im oykh der kop tsu der erd geboygn, glaykh er volt lebedikerheyt zayn keyver gezukht! Voltn azoy veynik mentshn vi ferd in tramvay gevezn, volt efsher a mol emester gefregt: vu iz Bontsye ahingekumen?!

---

[1] Bontsye Shvayg.
[2] ayndruk
[3] See subheading "1" in N 201.
[4] *koykhes*
[5] tsu
[6] See subheading "2" in N 201.
[7] tseykn
[8] umgevorfn;
[9] kartofl
[10] a matseyve
[11] eyn altertumforsher zi gefunn
[12] un der nomn "Bontsye Shvayg"
[13] es iz fun im keyn zeykher geblibn!
[14] derhert
[15] last
[16] last

Bontsye the Silent![1]

Here, in *this* world, Bontsye the Silent's death made scarcely an impression![2] Just ask anyone who Bontsye was, how he lived, what caused his death![3] Did his heart give out, did his strength[4] give way, or were[5] his very bones crushed under a heavy load . . . who knows? Maybe he simply died of hunger!

Had a trolley-car horse collapsed, there would have been more notice, newspapers would have written about it, hundreds of people would have gathered from all the streets to gawk at the carcass, even to look over the place where the collapse had happened . . .

Still, the trolley-car horse would never get so much attention if there were a thousand million horses just as there are men![6]

Bontsye lived silently and silently he died; like a shadow passing—passing through *our* world.

At Bontsye's *bris* no wine was drunk, no cups were clinked! At his bar mitzvah he made no elegant speech. . . . He lived like a tiny grey particle of sand on the seashore, among millions of his ilk; and when the wind lifted him up and cast him over to the other side of the sea, no one took notice!

During life the wet earth preserved no track[7] of his footstep; after death the wind knocked over the little marker on his grave, and the grave digger's wife[8] found it far from the grave and cooked a pot full of potatoes[9] over it. . . . It's just three days since Bontsye's death; you can ask the grave digger if he knows where he planted him!

If Bontsye at least had a tombstone, perhaps an archaeologist might find it after a hundred years and "Bontsye the Silent"[10] might yet again resound in *our* air!

A shadow! His image remains etched in no one's mind, in no one's heart, there is no memory of him in anyone's thoughts.[11]

"No kin, no kind"; alone he lived, alone he died!

If not for the human hubbub, someone might yet have heard[12] how Bontsye's bones groaned under the burden;[13] if the world had had more time, someone yet might have noticed that Bontsye (a fellow human being) existed with two extinguished eyes and frightfully hollow cheeks; that even if he had no great burden[14] on his shoulders, he still bent his head to the ground, as though in life he were looking for his grave! Were there as few men as horses on the trolley-line, maybe someone might ask: whatever happened to Bontsye?!

[1] Bontsye the Silent
[2] hardly had an impact!
[3] See subheading "1" in N 201.
[4] *strength*
[5] give way, were
[6] See subheading "2" in N 201.
[7] trace
[8] grave; the gravedigger's wife
[9] potato
[10] the name "Bontsye the Silent"
[11] there remains no memory of him!
[12] detected
[13] load
[14] load

Ven men hot Bontsye in shpitol arayngefirt, iz zayn vinkl in suterine nisht leydik geblibn—es hobn deroyf tsen zayns-glaykhn gevart, un tvishn zikh den vinkl "in-plyus" litsitirt; ven men hot'm fun shpitolbet in toytn shtibl arayngetrogn, hobn oyfn bet tsvantsik oreme kheloim[17] gevart . . . ven er iz aroys fun toytn-shtibl—hot men tsvantsik harugim fun unter an ayngefaln hoyz gebrengt—ver veyst vi lang er vet ruik voynen in keyver? Ver veyst vifl es vartn oyf dem shtikl plats . . .

Shtil geboyrn, shtil gelebt, shtil geshtorbn un nokh shtiler bagrobn.[18]

Nor nisht azoy iz gevezn af *yener* velt! *Dortn* hot Bontsyes toyt a groysn royshem[19] gemakht!

Der groyser shoyfer fun meshiekhs tsaytn hot geklungen in ale zibn himlen: Bontsye Shvayg iz *nifter* gevorn! Di greste malokhim mit di breytste fligl zenen gefloygn un eyner[20] dem andern ibergegebn: Bontsye iz "nisbakesh" gevorn "bishive shel mayle"![21] In ganeydn iz a rash, a simkhe, a geruder: "Bontsye Shvayg! A shpas Bontsye Shvayg!!!"

Yunge malokhimlekh mit brilyantene eygelekh, goldene drot-arbetene fliglekh un zilberne pantoflekh zenen Bontsyen akegn-gelofn mit simkhe! Der geroysh fun di fligl, dos klapn fun di pantoflekh un dos freylekhe lakhn fun di yunge, frishe royzike maylekhlekh hot farfilt ale himlen un iz tsugekumen biz tsum kise-hakoved un Got aleyn hot oykh shoyn gevust az Bontsye Shvayg kumt!

Avrom ovinu hot zikh in toyer fun himl geshtelt, di rekhte hant oysgeshtrekt tsum breytn "Sholem-aleykhem!" un a ziser shmeykhl shaynt azoy hel oyf zayn altn ponem!

Vos redlt azoy in himl?

Dos hobn tsvey malokhim in ganeydn arayn far Bontsyes vegn a gingoldene fotershtul oyf redlekh gefirt!

Vos hot azoy hel geblitst?

Dos hot men durkhgefirt a goldene kroyn mit di tayerste shteyner gezetst! Alts far Bontsye!

—Nokh farn psak fun bezdn shel mayle? fregn di tsadikim farvundert un nisht on kine.

—Oh! entfern di malokhim, dos vet zeyn a proste puste forme! Kegn Bontsye Shvayg vet afile der kateyger keyn vort in moyl nisht gefinen! Der "dyele" vet doyern finf minit!

—Ir shpilt zikh mit Bontsye Shvayg?—

- - - - - - - - -

Az di malokhimlekh hobn Bontsyen gekhapt in der luft un oyfgeshpilt im a zemer; az Avrom ovinu hot im vi an altn kamrat di hant geshoklt; az er hot gehert, az zayn shtul iz greyt in ganeydn; az oyf zayn kop vart a kroyn, az in bezdn shel mayle vet men iber im keyn iberik vort nisht redn—hot Bontsye, glaykh vi oyf in yener velt, *geshvign* far shrek! Es iz im dos harts antgangen! Er iz zikher, az dos mus zeyn a kholem oder a proster toes!

Er iz tsu beyde gevoynt! Nisht eynmol hot zikh im oyf yener velt gekholmt, az er klaybt gelt oyf der podloge, gantse oytsres lign . . . un hot er oyfgekhapt nokh a greserer kaptsn vi nekhtn . . . nisht eynmol hot men in'm a toes gehot, es hot im emets tsugeshmeykhlt, a gut vort gezogt un bald zikh ibergedreyt un oysgeshpign . . .

—Mayn mazl—trakht er—iz shoyn azoy!

---

[17] kranke
[18] A line of dots, marking the end of a section follows this paragraph in the 1901 edition.
[19] ayndruk
[20] eyner hot dem andern
[21] "niskabesh gevorn bishiva shel mayle"!

When Bontsye was taken to the hospital, his corner in the basement did not remain vacant—ten of his kind had waited for it, and the "extra" corner was auctioned off among them; when he was carried off from the hospital bed to the morgue, twenty of the poor infirm[15] had waited for the bed . . . when he was gone from the morgue—twenty were brought in, slain under a collapsed house—who knows how long he will rest in the grave? Who knows how many wait for that pitiful plot . . .

Mutely born, mutely lived, mutely died and more mutely buried.[16]

But it wasn't at all like that in the *other* world! *There*, Bontsye's death made a great impression![17]

The great shofar of Messianic times rang out in all Seven Heavens: Bontsye the Silent is *dead*! The grandest angels with the broadest wings were flying about, and passing[18] the word to one another: Bontsye is to be brought before the Supreme Assembly! In Paradise there is a stir, a thrill, a commotion: "Bontsye the Silent. Can you believe it? Bontsye the Silent!!!"

Young little angels with little sparkling eyes, dainty, golden filigree wings and tiny silver slippers rushed out to meet Bontsye with joy! The whir of the wings, the tapping of the little slippers, the jubilant laughing from the young, fresh, rosy little mouths pervaded all the Heavens, and even God Himself knew that Bontsye the Silent was coming!

Father Abraham sat waiting at the gate of Heaven, his right hand outstretched in a warmhearted "Peace be with you!" and a sweet smile lit up his old face!

What are they rolling across Heaven?

Why, it's two angels wheeling into Paradise an easy chair of pure gold on little wheels for Bontsye's procession.

What just flashed by?

Why, they've just taken in a golden crown set with the most precious jewels! All for Bontsye!

"Before the decision from the Supreme Assembly?" asked the saints in surprise and not without envy.

"Oh!" answer the angels, "that will be no more than a mere formality. Even the Prosecutor will not be able to find an argument against Bontsye the Silent! The 'case' will last but five minutes.

"You do not dare trifle with Bontsye the Silent!"

- - - - - - - - - -

When the little angels had caught Bontsye up into the air and played him a tune, when Father Abraham had clasped his hand like an old buddy, when he heard that his seat was all prepared in Paradise, that a crown was ready for his head, that no undue words would be spoken about him in the Supreme Assembly—Bontsye, just as was the case in the other world, was struck *silent* from fear! His heart skipped a beat. He is convinced that this must be a dream or simply a slip-up!

He is used to both! More than once he had dreamed in the other world that he was picking up money off the floor, huge treasures just lying around . . . and he awoke as wretched a pauper as ever. . . . More than once he had been mistaken for someone else; somebody had smiled at him, said a pleasant word, and then suddenly turned around and spat it out . . .

That's just my lot, he thinks!

[15] sick
[16] A line of dots, marking the end of a section follows this paragraph in the 1901 edition.
[17] had a great impact!
[18] and were passing the word

Un er hot moyre di oygn oyftsuheybn, der kholem zol nisht farshvundn vern; er zol zikh nisht oyfkhapn ergets in a heyl tsvishn shlangn un ekdishn! Er hot moyre fun moyl a klang aroystsulozen, a tnue mit an eyver tsumakhn[22]—men zol im nisht derkenen un nisht avekshlaydern oyf kafakal[23] . . .

Er tsitert un hert nit di malokhims komplimentn, zet nisht zeyer arumtsantsn arum im,[24] er entfert nisht Avrom ovinu oyfn hartslikhen sholem aleykhem,[25] un—gefirt tsum bezdn shel mayle—zogt er im keyn "gut morgn" nisht . . .

Oyser zikh iz er far shrek!

Un zayn shreklikhe shrek[26] iz nokh greser gevorn, az er hot, nisht vilnldik, unter zayn fis derzen di podloge fun bezdn shel mayle! Same alabaster mit brilyanten! "Oyf aza podloge shteyn mayne fis!"—Er vert in gantsn farshtart! "Ver veyst velkhn gvir, velkhn rov, velkhn tsadik men meynt . . . er vet kumen—vet zeyn mayn fintster sof!"

Far shrek hot er afile nit gehert vi der prezes hot befeyresh oysgerufn: "di dyele fun Bontsye Shvayg!" un, derlangndik dem meylets-yoysher di aktn, gezogt: "lez, nor bekitser!"

Mit Bontsyen dreyt zikh der gantser salon, es roysht im in di oyern, nor inem geroysh hert er[27] ale mol sharfer un sharfer dem malekh meyletss zis kol vi a fidl:

—Zayn nomen—hert er—hot im gepast vi tsun a shlank layb a kleyd fun an artist a shnayders[28] hant."[sic][29]

—Vos redt er[30]—fregt zikh Bontsye, un er hert vi an umgedulik kol hakt im iber un zogt:

—Nor on mesholim!

—Er hot zikh keynmol—heybt vayter on der meylets-yoysher—oyf keynem nisht geklogt, nisht oyf Got, nisht oyf layt; in zayn oyg hot keynmol nisht oyfgeflamt keyn funk sine,[31] er hot es keynmol nisht oyfgehoybn mit a pretentsye tsum himl.

Bontsye farshteyt vayter nisht a vort, un dos harte kol shlogt vayter iber:

—On retorik!

—Iev hot nisht oysgehaltn, er[32] iz umgliklikher gevezn———Faktn, trukene faktn!, ruft nokh umgeduliker der prezes.

—Tsu akht tog hot men im male gevezn.

—Nor on realizm!

—A moyel a fusher hot dos blut nit farhaltn——

—Vayter!

—Er hot alts geshvign (firt vayter der meylets-yoysher) afile ven di muter iz im geshtorbn un er hot tsu draytsn yor a shtifmame bakumen . . . a shtifmame a shlang, a marshas . . .

—Meynt men dokh efsher fort mikh? trakht Bontsye—

[22] mit a glid a rir tsu ton
[23] An asterisk note in both versions of the story gives the full spelling, kafakele.
[24] zeyer tantsn arum im,
[25] "sholem aleykhem",
[26] Un zayn shrek
[27] oyern, inm geroysh hert er dokh
[28] shnayders
[29] In both texts of "Bontsye Shvayg" the closed quotation mark appears without a preceding open quotation mark. Presumably, the dashes at the beginning of the paragraph were seen as grammatically equivalent to the quotation marks introducing direct speech. Such flexible punctuation is not unusual for Yiddish of this period.
[30] er?
[31] fun has
[32] er

And he is afraid to lift his eyes, lest the dream disappear; lest he awaken somewhere in a cave, surrounded by snakes and lizards! He is afraid to let a sound pass his lips, to move a limb[19]—lest he be recognized and cast into hell. . . .

He trembles, oblivious to the angels' compliments, blind to their dancing around him; he makes no reply to Father Abraham's warmhearted "Peace be with you," and—when led before the Supreme Assembly—even neglects to wish it "good morning". . . .

He is beside himself from terror!

And his terrible terror[20] is further increased, when he just happens to cast a glance at the floor of the Supreme Assembly beneath his feet! Fine alabaster set with jewels! "And my feet standing on this very floor!"— He is utterly paralyzed! "Who knows what tycoon, what rabbi, what saint they take me for . . . He will come—it will be my doom for sure!"

Out of fright he never even heard when the Presiding Officer sharply called out: "The Case of Bontsye the Silent!" and, handing the files over to the Defense, said: "Read, but keep it short!"

It seems to Bontsye that the entire hall is spinning around him. There is a buzzing in his ears, but then[21] he hears the whisper, becoming clearer and clearer, of the Defending Angel's sweet voice, just like a violin:

"His name," he hears, "suited him like a garment made by the finest tailor's hand for a delicate body."

What's he talking about? Bontsye asks himself, and he hears some kind of impatient voice cut him off and say:

"Come now, cut out the similes!"

"Not once," the Defending Angel goes on, "did he complain about anyone, neither God nor man; not once did a spark of hatred[22] flare up in his eye; not once did he lift it with a claim on Heaven."

Bontsye still cannot grasp a word, and the hard voice once more interrupts:

"Cut out the rhetoric!"

"Job did not endure; he[23] is far less fortunate."

"Facts, dry facts!" the Presiding Officer calls out again impatiently.

"On the eighth day he was circumcised."

"Come now, cut out the *realism!*"

"The bungler of a *moyel* did not staunch the blood . . ."

"Keep going!"

"He always kept silent," the Defending Angel went on, even when his mother died and at thirteen years he got a stepmother . . . a snake, a harpy of a stepmother . . ."

Could it really be possible that he means me? thinks Bontsye.

---

[19] to budge a limb
[20] And his terror
[21] still then
[22] due to hatred
[23] *he*

—On ontsuherenish[33] oyf drite perzonen, beyzert zikh der prezes.

—Zi flegt im zhaleven[34] dem bisn . . . eyernektik farshimlt broyt . . . horflaks far fleysh . . . un zi hot kave mit shmetene getrunkn—

—Tsu der zakh! shrayt der prezes.

—Zi hot im far dos keyn nogl nisht gekargt un zayn bloy-un-bloy[35] layb flegt aroyskukn fun ale lekher fun zayne farshimlt-tserisine kleyder . . . vinter in di greste frest hot er ir borves oyfn hoyf holts gehakt, un di hent zenen tsu yung un tsu shvakh gevezn, di kletslekh tsu dik, di hak tsu shtumpik . . . nisht eynmol hot er zikh di hent fun di staves oysgelinkt,[36] nisht eynmol hot er zikh di fis opgefrirn, nor *geshvign* hot er, afile farn fotr—

—Farn shiker! lakht arayn der kateyger, un Bontsye vert kalt in ale eyvrim—

—nisht geklogt (endikt der meylets-yoysher dem zats).—Un shtendik elnt—firt er vayter—keyn khaver, keyn talmetoyre, keyn kheyder, keyn shokle[37] . . . keyn gants beged . . . keyn fraye minut———Faktn—ruft vayter der prezes.

—Er hot geshvign afile shpeter, ven der fotr hot'n shikererheyt a mol ongekhapt bay di hor in mitn a shneyvintiker vinter nakht[38] aroysgevorfn fun shtub! Er hot zikh shtil oyfgehoybn fun shney un iz antlofn vu di oygn hobn im getrogn . . .

Oyfn gantsn veg hot er geshvign . . . baym grestn hunger hot er nor mit di oygn gebetlt!

Ersht in a shvindldike, nase vesne-nakht[39] iz er in a groyse shtot arayngekumen; er iz areyn vi a tropn in a yam un dokh hot er di eygene nakht in koze genekhtkgt . . .[40] er hot geshvign, nisht gefregt farvos, far ven? Er iz aroys un di shverste arbet gezukht! Nor er hot geshvign!

Nokh[41] shverer far der arbet iz gevezn zi tsugefinen—er hot geshvign!

Bodndik zikhh in kaltn shveys, tsuzamngedrikt unter der shverster last, baym gresten kramp funem leydikn mogn—hot er geshvign!

Bashpritst fun fremder blote, bashpign fun fremde mayler, geyogt fun trotuarn mit der shverster last arop in gasn tsvishn droshken, karetn un tramvays, kukndik yede minut dem toyt in di oygn arayn—hot er geshvign!

Er hot keynmol nisht ibergerekhnt, vifl pud mase[42] es kumt oys oyf a groshn, vifl mol er iz gefaln bay yedn gang far a drayer, vifl mol er hot shir nisht di neshome oysgeshipgn, monendik zayn fardinst, er hot nisht gerekhnt, nisht zayn, nisht yenems mazl,[43] nor geshvign!

Zayn eygene fardinst hot er nisht hoykh gemont! Vi a betler hot er zikh bay der tir geshtelt, un in di oygn hot zikh a hintishe bakoshe gemolt! "Kum shpeter" un er iz vi a shotn shtil farshvundn gevorn,[44] kedey shpeter nokh shtiler oystsubetln zayn fardinst!

---

[33] In Perets' original spelling, *insuniatsyes*, clarified in an asterisk note with *malshines*, i.e., "slander." In the 1901 version, the form is spelled *insuniatsyen*. The spelling here has been normalized to the standard transcription for the term.

[34] kargn

[35] broyn-un-bloy

[36] gelenkn oysrisn

[37] The 1901 edition lacks *keyn shakle*.

[38] vinter-nakht

[39] friling-nakht,

[40] arest ferbrakht . . .

[41] *Nokh* is lacking in the 1901 edition.

[42] last

[43] nisht *zayn*, nisht *yenems* mazl

[44] un er iz farshvundn shtil vi a shotn,

"Leave out insinuations against third persons," chides the Presiding Officer.

"She would begrudge him of[24] any morsel . . . moldy bread from the day-before-yesterday . . . gristle for meat . . . while she drank coffee with cream."

"Keep to the point!" shouts the Presiding Officer.

"She was not so stingy in using her nails on him, and his black-and-blue[25] body used to stick out from his mildewed, bedraggled clothing. . . . Winter, in the severest frost, he was barefoot in the yard chopping up wood for her; and his hands were too immature and too weak, the blocks too thick, the axe too blunt . . . not just once did he sprain his wrist,[26] not just once did his feet freeze; still, he kept *silent*. Even to his father . . ."

"You mean to the drunkard!" the Prosecutor laughs derisively, and Bontsye feels a chill in every limb.

. . . no complaint," the Defending Angel concludes his sentence.

"And always set apart," he continued on, "no friend, no religious upbringing, no schooling, no teaching[27] . . . not one whole garment . . . not a free minute!"

"Keep to the facts!" the Presiding Officer calls out once more.

"He kept silent even later, when his father in a drunken stupor finally seized him by the hair and cast him out of the house in the middle of a snowy, windswept winter night! He quietly picked himself up from the snow and ran off where his eyes led him . . .

"Through the entire journey he remained silent; despite being famished, he only begged with his eyes!

"In what was a reelingly wet, spring night he arrived in a large town; he was absorbed like a drop in an ocean, and yet he spent that very night in jail. . . .[28] He kept silent; he did not ask why or wherefore? On being released, he looked for the hardest work! Still, he kept silent!

"Even more difficult[29] than the work was trying to find it—he kept silent!

"Dripping in cold sweat, utterly weighed down under the heaviest burden, convulsed by the cramps of an empty stomach—he kept silent!

"Besmirched by the filth of strangers; spat upon by the mouths of strangers; chased off the sidewalks into the streets to vie with horse carriages, coaches and trolley-cars, despite the heavy load; staring every minute into the eyes of death—he kept silent!

"At no time did he figure how much of a load he was carrying for a penny, how many times he stumbled doing an errand worth a nickel, how many times he came close to spilling his guts trying to get his earnings; he never considered the difference between his fate and others[30]—he simply kept silent!

"In fact, he never demanded his earnings aloud! Like a beggar he stood himself by the door, the very picture of a dog with pleading eyes! "Come later," and like a shadow he mutely faded,[31] only later to beg even more mutely for his payment!

---

[24] would keep back from him

[25] Literally "blue-and-blue." This was changed in the 1901 edition to *broyn-un-blo*, the common idiomatic equivalent for "black-and-blue," which may suggest that the original reading reflected a simple typographical error.

[26] did he wrench his wrist

[27] "no teaching" is lacking in the 1901 edition.

[28] under arrest . . .

[29] More difficult

[30] *his* fate and *others*

[31] and he mutely faded like a shadow,

Er hot afile geshvign ven men flegt im opraysn fun zayn fardinst, oder areyntsuvarfn im a falshe matbeye . . .

Er hot alts geshvign . . .

Meynt men dokh take mikh! treyst zikh Bontsye.

- - - - - - - - - -

—Eynmol—firt vayter der meylets-yoysher nokh a trunkvaser—iz in zayn lebn a shine gevorn . . .[45] es iz durkhgefloygn a kotsh mit[46] gumene reder mit tseploshete ferd . . . der shmayser iz shoyn lang fun vaytens gelign mit a tseshpoltnem kop oyfn bruk . . . fun di dershrokene ferds mayler shpritst der shoym, fun unter di podkeves yogn zikh funkn vi fun vi a lokomotiv,[47] di oygn blishtshen vi brenendike shturkatsn in a fintsterer nakht—un in kotsh zitst nisht toyt, nisht lebendik a mentsh!

Bontsye[48] hot di ferd farhaltn!

Der gerateveter iz gevezn a yid a bal-tsodke un hot Bontsyen di toyve nisht fargesn!

Er hot im dem gehargetns kelnye[49] ibergegebn; Bontsye iz a shmayser gevorn! Nokh mer, er hot im khasene gemakht; nokh mer——er hot[50] afile mit a kind farzorgt—

Un Bontsye hot *alts* geshvign!

Mikh meynt men, mikh! bafestikt zikh Bontsye in der deye, un hot zikh[51] di hoze nisht an oyg tsuvarfn oyfn "bezdn shel mayle" . . .

Er hert zikh vayter ayn tsum malekh meylets:

—Er hot geshvign afile ven zayn bal-toyve hot in kurtsn bankrotirt un im zayn skhires oykh . . .[52]

Er hot geshvign afile ven dos vayb iz im antlofn un ibergelozt im a kind fun der brust . . .

Er hot geshvign afile mit fuftsn yor shpeter, ven dos kind iz oyfgevaksn un genug stark gevezn—Bontsye aroys tsuvarfn fun shtub . . .

Mikh meynt men, mikh! freyt zikh Bontsye.

- - - - - - - - - -

—Er hot afile geshvign—heybt on veykher un troyeriker der malekhmeylets—ven der eygener bal-toyve hot zikh mit alts oysgeglaykht, nor im keyn groshn skhires nisht tsurik gegebn—un afile demolt, ven er iz Bontsyen (vayter forendik oyf a kotsh mit gumene reder un ferd vi leybn) ibergeforn . . .

Er hot alts geshvign! Er hot afile der politsey nisht gezogt, ver es hot im tsurekht gemakht . . .

- - - - - - - - - -

[45] eyn enderung geshen
[46] af
[47] The 1901 edition lacks *vi a locomotiv*.
[48] Un Bontsye
[49] baytsh
[50] er hot im afile
[51] un hot dokh zikh
[52] zayn loyn nisht batsolt . . .

"He even kept silent when they would dock his pay, or throw him a false coin . . .

"He always kept silent. . . ."

It seems they really do mean me! Bontsye reassures himself.

- - - - - - - - -

"Once," the Defending Angel continues on after a sip of water, "a change came to his life. . . . A coach with rubber tires and runaway horses went flying past . . . the driver already lying far back with his head smashed on the pavement . . . foam spraying from the mouths of the panicked horses, sparks shooting out from the horseshoes as from a locomotive,[32] their eyes blazing like burning torches in a dark night—and sitting in the coach, half-dead, a man!

"Bontsye[33] stopped the horses!

"The rescued fellow was Jewish, a real philanthropist, and did not forget Bontsye's good deed!

"He gave him the slain coachman's place;[34] Bontsye was made into a hack! Beyond this, he arranged his marriage; beyond this: he even produced a child.[35]

"And Bontsye *always* kept silent!"

Me, he's talking about me! Bontsye becomes more certain in his conviction, yet[36] he does not have the confidence to throw a glance at the Supreme Assembly. . . .

He listens some more to the Defending Angel:

"He kept silent even when his patron suddenly went bankrupt and just like that, he had no salary. . . .[37]

"He kept silent even when his wife abandoned him and left him to deal with a nursing baby. . . .

"He kept silent even fifteen years later, when the child had grown up and had become strong enough to throw Bontsye out of the house. . . ."

He really does mean me—me! Bontsye rejoices.

- - - - - - - - -

"He even kept silent," continues the Defending Angel, more softly and sadly, "when the erstwhile benefactor settled his debts with everyone but did not pay him back a penny of his wages—and even then, when (once more zipping by in a coach with rubber tires and horses like lions) he ran Bontsye over. . . .

". . . he always kept silent! He did not even tell the police who it was that had done him in. . . .

- - - - - - - - -

---

[32] The 1901 edition lacks "as from a locomotive."

[33] And Bontsye

[34] He gave him the whip of the slain man;

[35] produced a child for him.

[36] and yet

[37] and did not pay him his wages. . . .

Er hot geshvign afile in shpitol, vu men meg shoyn *shrayen*!

Er hot geshvign afile ven der dokter hot on fuftsn kop[53] nisht gevolt tsun im tsugeyn,[54] un der vakter, on finf kop'—toyshn di vesh!

Er hot geshvign baym goysesn—er hot geshvign in der letster rege baym starbn . . .[55] Keyn vort kegn Got, keyn vort kegn layt! Diksi![56]

- - - - - - - - - -

Bontsye heybt on vayter tsetsitern oyfn gantsn layb. Er veyst[57] az nokhn meylets-yoysher geyt der kateyger! Ver veyst vos *der* vet zogn! Er[58] aleyn hot zayn gants lebn nisht gedenkt. Nokh oyf yener velt hot er yede minut di frierdike fargesn . . . der malekhmeylets hot im alts dermont . . . ver veyst vos der kateyger vet im dermonen!

—Raboysay! heybt on a sharf-shtikhedik-briendik kol—nor er hakt op—

—Raboysay! heybt er nokh a mol, nor veykher un hakt vayter op.

Endlikh hert zikh, fun dem eygenem haldz aroys, a veykh kol vi a puter:[59]

—Raboysay! *Er* hot geshvign! Ikh vel oykh shvaygn!

Es vert shtil—un fun fornt hert zikh a naye veykhe—tsiterdike shtime:

—Bontsye, mayn kind Bontsye! ruft es vi a harfe . . . mayn hartsik kind Bontsye! In Bontsyen tseveynt zikh dos harts . . . er volt shoyn di oygn geefent, nor zey zenen far- fintstert fun trern . . . es iz im azoy zis-veynendik keynmol nisht gevezn . . . "mayn kind" "mayn Bontsye"—zayt di muter iz geshtorbn hot er aza kol un azoyne verter nisht gehert—

—Mayn kind! firt vayter der ov-bezdn—du host alts gelitn un geshvign! Es iz nisht do keyn gants eyver,[60] keyn gants beyndl in dayn layb on a rane,[61] on a blutik ort, es iz nisht do keyn eyn bahaltn ort in dayn neshome vu es zol nisht blutn . . . un du host alts geshvign . . .

Dort hot men zikh nisht farshtanen deroyf! Du aleyn host gor efsher nisht gevust az du kenst shrayen un fun dayn geshray kenen Yerikhes moyern tsitern un aynfaln! Du aleyn host fun dayn farshlofenem koyekh nisht gevust . . .

Oyf yener velt hot men dayn shvaygn nisht baloynt, nor dort iz *oylem hasheker*, do oyfm *oylem hoemes* vest du dayn loyn bakumen!

Dikh vet dos bezdn shel-mayle nisht mishpetn, dir vet es nisht paskenen, dir vet es keyn kheylek nisht oys-un nisht opteyln! Nem dir vos du vilst! *Alts* iz dayn!

Bontsye heybt dos ershte mol di oygn oyf! Er vert vi farblendt fun der likht fun ale zaytn; alts blankt, blishtshet, fun alts yogn shtraln: fun di vent, fun di keylim, fun di malokhim, fun di dayonim! Same zunen![62]

Er[63] lozt di mide oygn arop!

—Take? fregt er mesupek un farshemt!

—Zikher! entfert fest der ov bezdn! Zikher! zog ikh dir, az alts iz dayn, alts in himl geher tsu dir! Kloyb un nem vos du vilst,[64] du nemst nor bay *dir* aleyn!

---

[53] Probably read *kop'*, cf. the next phrase. In the 1901 edition the full writing, *kopekes* is used.

[54] tsugeyn tsu zayn bet,

[55] er hot geshvign bay'm starbn . . .

[56] In the 1901 edition "—*Diksi!*" is indented and made into a separate paragraph.

[57] er veyst,

[58] Bontsye aleyn

[59] See subheading "3" in N 201.

[60] glid

[61] vund

[62] See subheading "4" in N 201.

[63] Un er

[64] See subheading "5" in N 201.

"He kept silent even in the hospital, where you have the right to *cry out!*

"He kept silent even when the doctor would not attend him[38] without a charge of fifteen cents or the attendant change his linen without a charge of five cents!

"He was silent at the last gasp—he was silent at the final instant of death . . .[39]

"Not a word against God; not a word against Man! The Defense rests!"[40]

- - - - - - - - - -

Once more, Bontsye starts to tremble all over. He knows that after the Defending Angel comes the Prosecutor! Who knows what *he* will say! He, himself,[41] had never given a thought about his whole life. In the other world he had forgotten each moment the previous . . . the Defending Angel had brought it all back to him . . . who knows what the Prosecutor may bring back to his mind!

"My lords!" a cutting, stingingly caustic voice starts up, but then he stops short.

"My lords!" he starts up again, but more softly, and again stops short.

Finally there can be heard, coming out from that very same throat, a soft voice, just like butter:[42]

"My lords! *He* was silent! I will be silent, too!"

Everything becomes hushed and in the front can be heard a new, softly tremulous voice:

"Bontsye, my child Bontsye!" it calls like a harp . . . , "my beloved child Bontsye!" Bontsye's heart moans . . . he would surely open his eyes, but they are blotted with tears. . . . He has never had such a good cry . . . "my child," "my Bontsye"—not since the death of his mother has he heard such a voice and such words.

"My child!" continues the Presiding Judge, "you have always suffered and kept silent! There is not a single member, not a single bone in your body without a wound, without a bloody welt, there is absolutely no secret place in your soul where it shouldn't be bleeding . . . and you always kept silent. . . .

"There, no one understood all this. Indeed, you, yourself, perhaps did not realize that you can cry out; and, due to your cry,[43] Jericho's wall can quake and tumble down! You, yourself, did not comprehend the extent of your sleeping power. . . .

"In the other world your silence was not compensated, but that is the *Realm of Lies*, here in the *Realm of Truth* you will receive your compensation!

"On you, the Supreme Assembly shall pass no judgment; on you, it will make no ruling; for you, it will neither divide nor apportion a share! Take whatever you want! *Everything* is yours!"

Bontsye, for the first time, raises his eyes! He is just about blinded by the light on all sides; everything sparkles, everything flashes, beams shoot out from everything: from the walls, from the vessels, from the angels, from the judges! A kaleidoscope of suns![44]

He drops[45] his eyes wearily!

"Are you sure?" he asks, doubtful and shamefaced.

"Absolutely!" the Presiding Judge affirms! "Absolutely, I tell you; for everything is yours; everything in Heaven belongs to you! Choose and take what you wish. You only take what belongs to *you*, alone!"[46]

---

[38] attend him in his bed

[39] he was silent in death . . .

[40] In the 1901 edition, "The Defense rests!" is indented and made into a separate paragraph.

[41] Bontsye, himself,

[42] See subheading "3" in N 201.

[43] that you can cry out; and that, due to your cry

[44] See subheading "4" in N 201.

[45] And he drops

[46] See subheading "5" in N 201.

—Take? fregt Bontsye nokh a mol shoyn mit a zikherer qol!

—Take! Take! Take! entfert men im af zikher fun alle zaytn.

—Nu, oyb azoy—shmeykhlt Bontsye—vil ikh take alle tog in der fri a heyse bulke mit frisher puter!

Dayonim un malokhim hobn aropgelozt di kop farshemt; der kateyger hot zikh tselakht.

"Are you sure?" asks Bontsye once more with growing confidence in his voice.

"Definitely! Absolutely! Positively!" they affirm to him from every side.

"Gee, if you mean it," smiles Bontsye, "what I'd really like is, each and every morning, a hot roll with fresh butter!"

Judges and angels lowered their heads in shame; the Prosecutor burst out laughing.

Abbreviations

AASOR	Annual of the American Schools of Oriental Research
AJSL	*American Journal of Semitic Languages and Literature*
AOAT	Alter Orient und Altes Testament
AOS	American Oriental Society
Bib	*Biblica*
BJRL	*Bulletin of the John Rylands Library*
CBA	Catholic Biblical Association
CBQ	*Catholic Biblical Quarterly*
HTR	*Harvard Theological Review*
HUCA	*Hebrew Union College Annual*
ICC	International Critical Commentaries
IEJ	*Israel Exploration Journal*
JAOS	*Journal of the American Oriental Society*
JBL	*Journal of Biblical Literature*
JCS	*Journal of Cuneiform Studies*
JEA	*Journal of Egyptian Archaeology*
JJS	*Journal of Jewish Studies*
JNES	*Journal of Near Eastern Studies*
JPS	Jewish Publication Society
JQR	*Jewish Quarterly Review*
JR	*Journal of Religion*
JSOT	*Journal for the Study of the Old Testament*
JSP	*Journal for the Study of the Pseudepigrapha*
JTS	Jewish Theological Seminary
JTS	*Journal of Theological Studies*
KARI	*Keilschrifttexte aus Assur religiösen Inhalts*
KTU	*Die keilalphabetischen Texte aus Ugarit* (M. Dietrich, O. Loretz, J. Sanmartín, eds.; Neukirchen-Vluyn: Neukirchener, 1976)
OED	*Oxford English Dictionary* (first edition)
Or n.s.	*Orientalia* (new series)
PBI	Pontifical Biblical Institute
RB	*Revue Biblique*
SBL	Society of Biblical Literature
UF	*Ugarit-Forshungen*
VT	*Vetus Testamentum*
VTSup	*Vetus Testamentum Supplements*
ZAW	*Zeitschrift für die alttestamenliche Wissenschaft*

Dead Sea Scrolls:

1QM	Qumran Cave 1 War Scroll
1QS	Qumran Cave 1 Manual of Discipline
4QtgJob	Qumran Cave 4 Targum of Job
11QtgJob	Qumran Cave 11 Targum of Job
CD	Damascus Document

Rabbinical Writings:

M	The Mishnah
TB	Babylonian Talmud
TP	Palestinian Talmud

NOTES

* E. W. Good, "Job and the Literary Task," *Soundings* 56 (1973): 470–484; esp. 472–473.

** I am using "literary criticism" in the broader sense, rather than in terms of the more narrow definition of "literary criticism" that is often applied to biblical texts by scholars in the field, i.e., as connoting source criticism. J. Barton explains this distinction in the following manner:

> People who come to biblical studies after a training in the study of modern literature are usually puzzled by the sense in which biblical scholars use the term 'literary criticism'. For them, 'literary criticism' is simply the study of literature, especially from the point of view of what in French is called *explication de textes*: the attempt to read the text in such a way as to bring out its inner coherence, the techniques of style and composition used by the author, all that makes it a piece of literary art. In biblical studies the term is used in a much narrower sense. 'Literary' criticism for the biblical scholar is a method used in handling texts that have been produced by amalgamating other, older texts. A good many biblical books, it is thought, were produced in this way; and 'literary' criticism is the attempt to divide them up into their component parts, and then to assess the relative ages of these parts, rather as archaeologists date the various strata of a site.

Cf. *Reading the Old Testament; Method in Biblical Study* (Philadelphia: Westminster, 1984): 20.

1. All quotations from the New Testament are cited according to the standard edition, *Novum Testamentum Graece*; ed., E. Nestle (Stuttgart: 1927, rpt. 1968).

2. Marvin H. Pope, *Job, Introduction, Translation and Notes* (Anchor Bible vol. 15, 3rd revised edition; Garden City: Doubleday, 1973): xv. Note also, for example, H. L. Ginsberg's comment: "The patience of Job is a household phrase in the English language. Yet Job's patience is obvious only in the first two of the forty-two chapters which the book of Job contains" ("Job the Patient and Job the Impatient," *Conservative Judaism* 21 [1967]: 12). Below, I have borrowed the phrasing used by Ginsberg in the title of this article since it effectively captures a sense of the problems one encounters in the book of Job. See also D. B. MacDonald, "Some External Evidence on the Original Form of the Legend of Job," *AJSL* 14 (1898): 137–164; H. A. Fine, "The Tradition of a Patient Job," *JBL* 74 (1955): 28–32, esp. 28–29.

3. Cf. MacDonald's comment (N 2): 139:

> Now of all these virtues the Job of our book can hardly be called a shining example [of patience]. He murmurs with singular emphasis both against his friends and against God. He suffers certainly, and he may even be said to endure, in a sense, but it is not with patience. In fact, to speak of "the patience of Job" is to ascribe to him the one virtue which he is not described as possessing. . . . He was utterly truthful, high-hearted, sincere, keen of insight, firm of purpose, tender of conscience—these are the characteristics by which he lives for us; but among them is not patience.

4. See also, e.g., 2 Cor. 6:4, 2 Thess. 1:4, 4 Macc. 7:22 and more generally *A Greek-English Lexicon of the New Testament and other Early Christian Literature* (W. F. Arndt, F. W. Gingrich, eds.; Chicago: University of Chicago Press, 1957, rpt. 1969): 854 *s. v.* '*upomonē*. For a convenient, comprehensive list of all New Testament uses of *hupomonē*, cf. *Computer Concordance to the New Testament* (Institute for New Testament Research and the Computer Center of Münster University, ed.; Berlin, New York: de Gruyter, 1985): col. 1849. See now C. Haas, "Job's Perseverance in the Testament of Job" in *Studies on the Testament of Job* (M. Knibb and P. van der Horst, eds.; Cambridge: Cambridge University Press, 1989): 117–154, which reached me too late to be incorporated into this study. Note, too, that in the immediately preceding verse in James (5:10), the prophets are cited as an example of "suffering in the midst of endurance" (*tēs kakopathias kai tēs makrothumias*). (For this translation, cf. M. Dibelius, *A Commentary on the Epistle of James* [rev. ed., H. Greeven; M. A. Williams, trans.; Hermeneia; Philadelphia: Fortress, 1976]: 241. On the syntax of the Greek phrase and especially the nuance of *kai* in the context, cf. F. Blass and A. Debrunner, *A Greek Grammar of the New Testament and Other Early Christian Literature* [R. Funk, ed. and trans.; Chicago: University of Chicago Press, 1961, rpt. 1967]: 228, para. 442). This thus sets the immediate context for James' statement about Job.

5. The Epistle of James is probably to be dated roughly between 80 and 130 C.E.; see, e.g., Dibelius and Greeven (N 4): 45–47. We at least have solid indications that the book of Job existed in more or less its canonical form during early Christian times. The targum of Job from Qumran Cave 11 (*siglum*: 11QtgJob), dating no later than the First Century C.E., for example, intermittently covers a fair portion of Job, including the Dialogue of Job with his Three Friends, Job's final long speech at the end of this section, the Hymn to Wisdom, the Elihu Speeches, the Theophany and the Epilogue. Cf., for example, M. Sokoloff, *The Targum to Job from Qumran Cave XI* (Ramat-Gan: Bar Ilan University., 1974). For further discussion of targums of Job see N 527.

6. Compare in this regard Jesus' question to the lawyer in Luke 10:26: "What is written in the law? How do you read [*anaginōskeis*]?" The lawyer understands that he has been asked a question that requires a narrow answer confined precisely to what biblical text would verify the point at issue. Thus, he responds most appropriately by citing the relevant verses (Deut. 6:4, Lev. 19:18). See further on *anaginōskō* in the New Testament, Arndt and Gingrich (N 4): 51. For a complete list of New Testament citations, cf. *Computer Concordance* (N 4): cols. 118–119.

7. Note, for example, that this is precisely what Dibelius and Greeven conclude:

> Continuing along the lines of this martyr-eulogy is v 11, which praises people who were steadfast and then mentions one of the most popular of their number, Job. This might seem strange if one considers the content of the canonical Book of Job, which reports the defiant arguments of its hero with God rather than his patient endurance. Yet the conception of Job as the righteous sufferer, the model of "steadfastness" [*hupomonē*] is older than the Book of Job and goes back to the ancient popular legend of Job who did not sin in spite of all his misfortune.   Dibelius and Greeven (N 4): 245–246.

Similarly, note MacDonald's comment (N 2) 140: "But here, while the form of the reference [in James 5:11] (*ēkousate*) does not prevent it being scriptural, though it permits and even favors it being oral, its matter can leave no doubt that James was not thinking of the Job of his Sacred Books, but of the legendary figure whose story had been in his ears since childhood."

We should note that James is not unique among early Christian writers in focusing solely upon the "patience of Job." For a convenient survey of Christian opinions and commentary on Job, see Judith R. Baskin, *Pharaoh's Counsellors; Job, Jethro, and Balaam in Rabbinic and Patristic Tradition* (Brown Judaic Series 47; Chico: Scholars, 1983): 32–43. Baskin concludes, upon surveying the evidence, that "the rebellious and blasphemous Job is virtually unmentioned in Christian commentary" (p. 35). For a further discussion of later interpretations of the Job legend, stretching into the medieval period, see L. L. Besserman, *The Legend of Job in the Middle Ages* (Cambridge: Harvard University Press, 1979). See also MacDonald (N 2): 140–141 and also his far more extensive discussion of the legendary patient Job in Islamic sources (pp. 141 ff.); also, H.-P. Müller, *Hiob und seine Freunde; Traditionsgeschichtliches zum Verständis des Hiobbuches* (Zürich: EVZ, 1970): *passim.*

8. The Hebrew term *Akedah* is used in Jewish tradition to denote the story of God's test of Abraham by demanding his son Isaac as a sacrifice. The term comes from Hebrew and means "the binding." It is derived from the verb *'qd*, "to bind," the verb used to describe Abraham's action just before laying his son on the altar of sacrifice (Gen. 22:9). A. Segal notes that it is first attested in the rabbinic tractate *Tamid* as a reference to the daily sacrificial lamb offering. He notes that one cannot date its use, based upon current evidence, any earlier than the second century B.C.E.; cf. A. Segal, "The Sacrifice of Isaac in Early Judaism and Christianity," in his *The Other Judaisms of Late Antiquity* (Atlanta: Scholars, 1987): 109–130; esp. 113–114.

9. Shalom Spiegel, *The Last Trial; On the Legends and Lore of the Command to Abraham to Offer Isaac as a Sacrifice: The Akedah*, trans. from the Hebrew edition "Me-Aggadot ha-Akedah," *Alexander Marx Jubilee Volume* (S. Liberman, ed.; New York: 1950; rpt. *The Sacrifice of Isaac; Studies in the Development of a Literary Tradition* [E. Yassif, ed.; Jerusalem: Makor, n.d.,]: unpaged) with an introd. by Judah Goldin (New York: Schocken, 1967). All citations follow the Goldin edition. For the quotation from Rabbi Ephraim's poem (which was first published by Spiegel in this book), see pp. 148–150; ibn Ezra's comment comes from his commentary on Gen. 22:19 and is cited on p. 8; on the "ashes of Isaac," see esp. Spiegel's discussion on pp. 38–44; on the "blood of Isaac," see pp. 45–59. For a convenient survey of modern scholarship on the *Akedah*, see J. Swetnam, *Jesus and Isaac; A Study of the Epistle to the Hebrews in Light of the Akedah* (Rome: PBI, 1981): 4–22 and notes; also, Segal (N 8) and notes.

10. Spiegel, *Trial* (N 9): 57.

11. E.g., ibid., 9–12; for a convenient, recent survey of the *Akedah* in ancient sources outside of Genesis 22, see Swetnam (N 9): 27–85; also L. H. Feldman, "Josephus As a Biblical Interpreter: The *'Aqedah*," *JQR* 75 (1985): 212–252 and notes and D. Marcus, *Jephthah and His Vow* (Lubbock: Texas Tech, 1986): 40–43.

12. Spiegel, *Trial* (N 9): 58.

13. All quotes from the Hebrew Bible are cited according to the standard edition, *Biblia Hebraica Stuttgartensia*, (K. Elliger, W. Rudolph, G. Weil et al., eds.; Stuttgart: Württembergische Bibelanstalt, 1967–1977).

14. Spiegel, *Trial* (N 9): 4. While the following discussion will show that I believe that Spiegel's interpretation of Genesis 22 is correct, we should nonetheless be mindful that his approach is susceptible to the criticism that the "tail is wagging the dog." Spiegel argues that the legendary material found in rabbinical and other post biblical literature reflects the more ancient stratum of tradition and thus even leaves its mark on the biblical text itself. However, one could look at the evidence of Genesis 22 in a contrary fashion. Spiegel's view necessarily depends on small distinctions in the text of this chapter, and to hang so much on so little is always a somewhat risky procedure, especially in biblical criticism. After all, the forces that shape a given biblical text are both complex and subtle and thus open to a variety of interpretations.

One might well argue that the distinctions noted below in Genesis 22 have nothing to do with any presumed ancient traditions; rather, they are simply "peculiarities" that could, for example, be the product of idiomatic Hebrew grammar or of editorial activity. If this is so, then these "peculiarities" could themselves give rise to the interpretations we find in the later legends. In other words, the text would be the catalyst for later traditions, rather than early traditions impacting upon the text. After all, once such "peculiarities" have found their way into a biblical text—for whatever reason—they are then "grist" for the interpretive "mill," especially in rabbinical midrashim. And as Judah Goldin cautions in his introduction to *The Last Trial*, "an ingenious commentator can extract there's no telling what" (p. xv).

Such an argument seems to me altogether unsatisfactory (see my remarks, pp. 22 ff.), and the analysis of the text of Genesis 22 that follows is intended to bolster Spiegel's case in contradistinction to this other view. However, in the final analysis, were I to grant that Spiegel's approach is wrong, this would not profoundly affect my larger argument vis-à-vis the traditional background of the book of Job; nor would it essentially invalidate the manner in which the *Akedah* is employed as part of this interpretation. As will be seen, my case basically depends on the view that a genre of story lies behind not only the *Akedah* and the Job tradition but can be found as early as the Canaanite literature of Ugarit and as late as the Gospels. If this genre of story did not play a direct role in shaping the "peculiarities" of Genesis 22, I would contend that it had a direct effect on the shaping of the legendary material that these "peculiarities" engendered. Thus, we would *still* have a case of an early tradition having impact on a later tradition even though the traditions would seem to counter one another.

I am grateful to my colleague Robert Ratner for sensitizing me to this critical line of attack against Spiegel's view of the *Akedah*.

15. Not only is there a word play between *yaḥdāw and yaḥīd* in Genesis 22, but in verse 19 there is also likely a conscious play between the singular verbs *wayyāšob . . . wayyēšeb*, "he returned . . . he dwelt . . . ." Thus, although the verbs are different in meaning, their identical spelling and their similar pronunciation have the effect of framing the verse—and once again drawing attention to their singular form as well as their singular importance in the narrative.

16. Perhaps this episode is called the *Akedah*, "the binding," in the tradition simply to reemphasize that Abraham never really *did* anything to Isaac; that is, according to the authorized biblical text, the only act that the father could be said to have done to his son was to bind him. Thus, the title *Akedah* demarcates the limit of adverse action against Isaac and thereby emphasizes all the more that nothing was done beyond that limit.

17. Note, for example, E. A. Speiser's comment regarding textual sources for the *Akedah*: "What this amounts to, therefore, is that, on external grounds, *J* was either appended to *E*, or *E* was superimposed upon *J*"; cf. *Genesis; Introduction, Translation, and Notes*, (Anchor Bible, vol. 1; Garden City: Doubleday, 1964): 166. Spiegel discusses the various text-critical theories regarding Gen. 22, cf. *Trial* (N 9): 121–126 and the bibliography cited there. More recently C. Westermann has surveyed the evidence and concluded: "There is virtual unanimity that vv. 15–18 are a later addition to the narrative of 22:1–14,19. The most recent commentators alter nothing here"; cf. *Genesis 12–36; A Commentary* (J. J. Scullion, trans.; Minneapolis: Augsburg, 1985): 363. For the latest survey on the secondary nature of 22:15–18, cf. R. Moberly, "The Earliest Commentary on the Akedah," *VT* 38 (1988): 302–311, which concludes by stating "that the consensus view . . . has not been seriously challenged, and should continue to be maintained as the most likely explanation of the textual peculiarities of structure, style and vocabulary . . . ." (p. 311). On the other hand, for a recent argument in defense of vv. 15–18 being structurally necessary in Genesis 22 and that further labels the view that they are a secondary addition to the text as "untenable," see G. A. Rendsburg, *The Redaction of Genesis* (Winona Lake, IN: Eisenbrauns, 1986): 33–34.

18. The term *yaḥīd* in Genesis 22 is usually translated as "only son," but a more precise translation (especially in light of the fact that Abraham did have another son, Ishmael) would be "only one"; that is, Isaac is the one singled out for special treatment—specifically, he is the one promised to Abraham, the miraculously born male child of the special wife Sarah, he

who is to carry the covenantal blessing. We should understand the term as applied to Jephthah's daughter in a similar manner. For a brief discussion of the use of *yaḥīd* in the Bible and its equivalents in some of the early versions, see Segal (N 8): 125–126.

19. See Louis Ginzberg, *The Legends of the Jews* (7 vols.; Philadelphia: Jewish Publication Society, 1928, rpt. 1968): vol. 6, 203, n. 109. He cites, e.g., David Kimchi's comments on Jud. 11:39 as typical of this viewpoint. For a recent, fuller survey of medieval and modern opinions regarding Jephthah's vow, see Marcus (N 11): 8–9 and notes.

20. The comment was made by Jack Sasson.

21. Yalkut Deut. 26, no. 938; the translation here follows Speigel, *Trial* (N 9): 15. This story of a mother who sacrifices her seven children has a number of versions and permutations. An early source for the tradition is 2 Macc. 7 (also 4 Macc. 8 ff.; esp. 13:12, 15:28, 16:20, and 18:11, where explicit allusions are made to the *Akedah*) and which in turn may have come under the influence of Jer. 15:9. For a listing of other rabbinical versions of this story, cf. Spiegel, *Trial* (N 9): 13–14, note 5; A. Agus, *The Binding of Isaac and Messiah; Law, Martyrdom, and Deliverance in Early Rabbinic Religiosity* (Albany: SUNY Press, 1988): 11–32 and notes. For a recent discussion of 2 Macc. 7, including reference to this theme in pseudepigraphal and other extrabiblical literature, cf. J. Goldstein, *II Maccabees; A New Translation and Commentary* (Anchor Bible vol. 41a; Garden City: Doubleday,1983): 291–304. For a discussion of 4 Macc. 8 ff., see Swetnam (N 9): 44–48.

22. Note in this respect Swetnam's comments ([N 9]: 48) on 4 Maccabees' interpretation of the *Akedah*: "The author of *4 Maccabees* is silent about the atoning value of the Aqedah because for him the Aqedah has no atoning value. And it had no atoning value because there was no shedding of blood. It was a sacrifice (cf. the sacrificial terminology used to describe it), but not a sacrifice which had atoning value. It was, if one will, a sacrifice *manqué*."

23. Spiegel, *Trial* (N 9): 103. Segal ([N 8]: 122) represents a contrary view that "there is no good evidence for a lost *pre-Christian* Jewish tradition of Isaac's resurrection." He therefore comments that "Spiegel's idea that the source of the story is entirely in pagan thought is probably Israeli romanticism and is certainly unfounded in evidence" (p. 110, n. 5). His appeal for concrete evidence must be taken seriously; and if one does not grant that the account in Genesis 22 is itself indicative of such evidence (cf. the discussion above in N 14), one must admit that Spiegel's view could be taken to be no more than an a highly speculative argument from silence.

However, as will be further considered below, there are clear indications that stories of human resurrection were, on the one hand, known from biblical times and, on the other hand, were deemed distasteful within the religious worldview of early Judaism to the point of being specifically suppressed in biblical versions of ancient, popular legends (cf. N 57). Consequently, we might expect precisely stories of this sort to be excluded from "proper" Jewish writings in early, pre-Christian times. Only when the Christian story came to the fore and Jews felt the need to contend against its message would these popular legends once more have been allowed to creep back into the more-official versions of stories preserved in Jewish tradition.

In the final analysis, one can either take a narrow view or a broad view of the question of whether resurrection was a part of the early tradition of the *Akedah*. A narrow view assumes that one can only follow where the evidence specifically leads. Since the evidence shows no definitive use of the resurrection theme in this story before the Christian era, one can only conclude that the theme was absent from the earlier form of the tradition. A broader view recognizes that the available evidence is sparse and probably prejudiced against the resurrection theme. It further assumes that the probability is nonetheless high that the genre of resurrection story was widespread in the biblical world. Especially, it contends that it is more reasonable to assume that resurrection themes had significant impact on pagan, Jewish and finally Christian tradition and than that Jewish tradition (despite all "official" efforts to the contrary) would have been left untouched. Ultimately, there is a degree of aesthetic judgment involved in the broader view as well, namely, that the *Akedah* is a more complete story—as it were, a more elegant story—if one assumes that resurrection always played a role in the shaping of its tradition.

The narrower view must be respected if only because it is the safer, more conservative course. Still, in my view, it should be rejected because there are reasonable counter arguments and especially because, granting Spiegel's view, enables us to follow a far more fruitful line of interpretation than would otherwise be the case.

24. In the period of the Crusader persecutions, precisely this sort of comparison was made between the Abraham of the *Akedah* and the Jewish martyrs; cf. Alan Mintz, *Ḥurban; Responses to Catastrophe in Hebrew Literature* (New York: Columbia University Press., 1984): 84–105, esp. 90–91.

Note that ibn Ezra's criticism of the unauthorized *Akedah* he heard from legend indirectly reflects that tradition's sensitivity to the need to depict Abraham as alone after the slaughtering of Isaac. Ibn Ezra does not speak only of a tradition that shows Abraham slaying Isaac and then the son coming to life again. There is a crucial intermediate step: "Abraham slew Isaac *and abandoned him* (*w'zbw*) and . . . afterwards Isaac came to life again." Naturally, ibn Ezra looks at this in the most negative manner possible and thus disparages the renegade tradition as a story in which a cowardly Abraham abandoned his slain son. But the actual tradition more likely focused on a dramatic moment in which Abraham is completely alone, when he has not so much abandoned his dead son but as himself been seemingly abandoned by all, especially by God. Only then is his test a trial to the full extent. Thus, ibn Ezra's comments may well reflect a version of the *Akedah* that is closer to the original tradition than the account we find in Rabbi Ephraim's poem, where the resurrection of the son comes immediately after the sacrifice.

25. See above, p. 17.

26. *The Oxford English Dictionary* (J. A. Murray et al., eds.; vol. 2; Oxford: Clarendon, 1933, rpt. 1970): 1071 s.v. "counterpoint."

27. Cf. *Encyclopedia Britannica* (vol. 15; Chicago: University of Chicago Press: 1974): 213 s.v. "counterpoint."

28. See ibid., 213–214.

29. This synchronic counterpoint can also be achieved in literature. Note in this respect the critical theories of M. M. Bakhtin, especially his analysis of Dostoevsky as a writer of "polyphonic" works. See his *The Dialogic Imagination: Four Essays* (M. Holquist, ed.; C. Emerson, trans.; Austin: University of Texas Press, 1981); *Problems of Dostoevsky's Poetics* (C. Emerson, ed. and trans; Minneapolis: University of Minnesota Press, 1984). For an interesting discussion of Bakhtin's theories and their relevance to understanding the Dialogue-form in Ancient Near Eastern documents, see S. D. Bolle, *Wisdom in Akkadian Literature: Expression, Instruction, Dialogue* (Ph.D. diss., University of California, Los Angeles, 1982): 110–113; for further bibliography, see the notes thereto. I am grateful to my colleague R. Polzin for drawing my attention to the works of Bakhtin.

30. In the immediately following discussion of the Poem of Job, little will be said about the Elihu speeches (chapters 32–37) since they were almost certainly interpolated into the Poem and are not, in this writer's opinion, as crucial to the overall structure of Job as the other sections of the book. In terms of our musical metaphor, one might call the Elihu speeches more a minor melody than a major theme. Of course, there are other scholars who disagree with this opinion, e.g., R. Gordis (*The Book of God and Man* [Chicago, University of Chicago Press, 1965]: 104–116. We will consider the function of the Elihu speeches within the larger structure of the book of Job later on in this study (see below p. 88 ff. and 145

ff. Likewise, we will defer discussion of the "Hymn to Wisdom" (chapter 28) to a point later in this study (pp. 88 f. and pp. 140 ff).

31. Cf. Job 31. On the function of this explicit use of oath by Job, cf. pp. 107 f.

32. A. Hurvitz, "The Date of the Prose-Tale of Job Linguistically Reconsidered," *HTR* 67 (1974): 17–34.

33. Ibid., 17.

34. Ibid.

35. Ibid., 32–33.

36. For a survey of scholarship on the issue of the relationship of the Prologue/Epilogue and the Poem of Job, see S. Spiegel, "Noah, Danel, and Job," *Louis Ginzberg Jubilee Volume* (New York: American Academy for Jewish Research, 1945): vol. 1, 305–307 and notes; also, H. H. Rowley, "The Book of Job and its Meaning," *From Moses to Qumran* (London: Lutterworth, 1963): 141–183; cf. pp. 151–161; see also Pope, *Job* (N 2): xxiii–xxvi and J. G. Williams, "'You have not spoken the Truth of Me'; Mystery and Irony in Job," *ZAW* 83 (1971): 233–237 for more recent discussions. For the latest bibliography on this issue, see R. J. Williams, "Current Trends in the Study of the Book of Job," *Studies in the Book of Job* (W. E. Aufrecht, ed.; Waterloo: Canadian Corporation for Studies in Religion, 1985): 13–15 and J. Vermeylen, *Job, ses amis et son Dieu; La légende de Job et ses relectures postexiliques* (Leiden: Brill, 1986): 3–28 and notes.

For a convenient survey of opinions on the language of the poetic sections of Job, cf. Pope, *Job* (N 2): xlvii–l. Hurvitz points out that the so-called Aramaisms found in the Poem do not necessarily point to a late date. Early Aramaic rather than the Imperial Aramaic of the Persian period may well have influenced the original language of the Poem. Cf. A. Hurvitz, "The Chronological Significance of 'Aramaisms' in Biblical Hebrew," *IEJ* 18 (1968): 235–236. For further discussion on this issue, see below, pp. 90 ff.

It must be granted that there is a certain degree of "argument from silence" involved in claiming that the poetic portions of Job predate the Prose Frame Story on the grounds that the former show none of the late grammatical traces of the latter. After all, one might simply argue that the distinction between the Poem and the Frame Story reflects a conscious differentiation in style that would be the natural result of an author writing his Prologue/Epilogue in prose and the rest of his work in poetry. Thus, for example, Y. Hoffman has recently contended, "It is only natural to use a lofty, high-flown style in poetry, and it may well be that the writer purposely adopted two different styles in order to differentiate clearly the plot and the discussions" ("The Relation between the Prologue and the Speech-Cycles in Job; A Reconsideration," *VT* 31 [1981]: 162).

Still, in this particular case, the argument from silence is unusually strong for a simple reason: there is no precedence for a linguistic distinction as dramatic as that shown between the prose and poetic sections of Job. In particular, I can think of no case where poetry (or prose) of a late Hebrew period—whether intentionally archaized or not—does not show at least some small grammatical trace of its late date. Consider, in this respect, the non-biblical hymns one finds among the Qumran texts. In all cases, despite considerable effort by their writers/editors to write in the style of biblical Hebrew, unmistakable clues remain that show that the hymns are not ancient but merely archaizing. See, for example, the summary discussion of the *Hodayot* hymns by M. Mansoor (*The Thanksgiving Hymns* [Leiden: Brill, 1961]: 10–32) and supporting bibliography.

The likelihood is remote that there would not be telltale traces of "modernisms" in so large a sample of Hebrew as we find in the Poem of Job if it were of the same late date as the Frame Story. Moreover, we must further consider the unusual dialectical form of Hebrew in which most of the Poem is written. It would be more than simply unusual for the writer to compose his Dialogues in such a dialect—once again, such a shift between normative late biblical Hebrew and so specialized a dialect of poetic Hebrew would be without precedence. Indeed, the more normative poetic standard of the Psalms would seem a far more likely model for a Hebrew poet intent on writing in an archaizing fashion. In fact, we find that the Psalms were a stylistic model for nonbiblical hymns attested among the Dead Sea Scrolls; cf., e.g., J. A. Sanders' comment, "The apocryphal psalms located at Qumran . . . 'want to be' themselves biblical psalms" (The Dead Sea Psalms Scroll [Ithaca: Cornell, 1967]: 11).

An indication of just how "unmodern" the language of the Poem of Job is may be shown from D. A. Robertson's study, Linguistic Evidence in Dating Early Hebrew Poetry (SBL Dissertation Series 3; Missoula, MT: SBL, 1972). Not only does Robertson classify the poetic portions of Job as early, he even argues on linguistic grounds that they are comparable to Deut. 32, 2 Sam. 22 = Ps. 18 and Hab. 3, all of which are texts viewed by scholars as examples of early Hebrew poetry. He tentatively dates the Poem of Job to as early as the eleventh to tenth century B.C.E. (cf. pp. 153–156). While one may reasonably question whether Robertson's absolute dating is correct (especially in light of the dialectical peculiarities of the Job Poem; note, for example, R. J. Williams, op. cit., 23 who labels Robertson's theory as "drastic"), the point is that his analysis turns up no indications of any modernisms of the sort Hurvitz has found in the Frame Story; indeed, just the opposite is the case. Mention should also be made of D. N. Freedman's study of the orthographic characteristics of Job, which leads him to the conclusion that it "was a product of the (North) Israelite diaspora some time in the seventh or early sixth century B.C." ("Orthographic Peculiarities in the Book of Job," Eretz-Israel 9 [1969]: 35–44; esp. p. 43).

Hence, altogether, it is far simpler to assume that the original poetic composition (perhaps not even authored by an Israelite; see. the discussion below, pp. 91 f.) was later brought into more normative Jewish circles and adapted by the inclusion of the Frame Story and other prose formulae in the text as we now find it.

Of course, we should also recognize that there are various textual and therefore linguistic levels within the poem itself. For example, the Elihu speeches in chapters 32–37 appear to represent (at least to the present writer) a different author and a different, more conventional style of Hebrew from that found in the Dialogue between Job and his Three Friends; cf. N 30 and further below pp. 88 f.

37. One should insist upon the qualification with the definite article—"the Satan" (as opposed to the standard translation, "Satan," that one finds, for example, in the King James and Revised Standard Versions)—in Job because this is how the figure is presented in the book. At the time Job was written, "the Satan" was a title ("the Adversary") and not conceived of as a proper name, as appears often to be the case, for example, in the New Testament. This sense of title still persists in our speaking of "the Devil" (from Greek ho diabolos) rather than simply "Devil." For a lengthy discussion of the Satanic concept in the Old Testament, see R. S. Kluger, Satan in the Old Testament (Evanston: Northwestern University Press., 1967); esp. 25–53; see also the discussion in J. Lévêque, Job et son Dieu (Paris: Gabalda, 1970): 179–190 and the supporting bibliography; J. Russell, The Devil; Perceptions of Evil from Antiquity to Primitive Christianity (Ithaca: Cornell University Press, 1977): 174–249. For a recent discussion of Satan, especially in the context of Ancient Near Eastern conflict myths, see N. Forsyth, The Old Enemy; Satan and the Combat Myth (Princeton: Princeton University Press, 1987); esp. 107–123. For the most recent discussion of the evidence on Satan in the Hebrew Bible, cf. P. Day, An Adversary in Heaven; śāṭān in the Hebrew Bible (Atlanta: Scholars, 1988). For the most recent discussion of Satan in the New Testament and early Christianity, cf. J. Russell, Satan; The Early Christian Tradition (Ithaca: Cornell University, 1981). Russell also tracks the development of Satan into modern times in three further works, Lucifer; The Devil in the Middle Ages (Ithaca: Cornell University Press, 1984); Mephistopheles; The Devil in the Modern World (Ithaca: Cornell University Press

1986); *The Prince of Darkness*; *Radical Evil and the Power of Good in History* (Ithaca: Cornell University Press, 1988).

38. Hurvitz, "Date" (N 32): 19–20; see also Gordis (*God and Man* [N 30]: 69), who argues that the dualism implied in the God/Satan correspondence reflects Persian influence. Note, too, in this respect, N. H. Tur-Sinai's (= H. Torczcyner's) argument that the Satan was modeled on the "agent provocateur," the king's spy that one encounters in the Persian court. This is based in part on an assumption (first suggested by S. D. Luzzatto, *Erläuterungen über einen Teil der Prioheten und Hagiographen* [Lemberg, 1876]: 197) of an etymological relationship between *śtn* and the verb *swt*, "to rove about" (cf. Job 1:7, 2:2). Cf. H. Torczcyner, "How Satan Came into the World," *Expository Times* 48 (1936–37): 563–565; idem., "How Satan Came into the World," *Bulletin of the Hebrew University, Jerusalem* 4 (1937): 14–20; N. H. Tur-Sinai, *The Book of Job* (Jerusalem: Kiryath Sepher, 1967): 41–44; also Pope, *Job* (N 2): 9–11; M. Fishbane, *Biblical Interpretation in Ancient Israel* (Oxford: Clarendon, 1985): 450–451, n. 7; Forsyth (N 37): 114. The origins of this role in the royal court may have Neo-Babylonian antecedents; see A. L. Oppenheim, "The Eyes of the Lord," *JAOS* 88 (1968): 173–180. For a differing view, see Kluger (N 37): 29–34.

39. It has been often argued that the absence of any reference to Satan in the Poem does not "prove" that the prose and poetic sections of Job come from different hands and different periods. Once again, Hoffman's argument, in this respect, can be taken as representative: "The disregard of Satan in the speeches is also well explained by the literary conventions of the book; Job and his Friends know nothing about the wager [between God and Satan], and by ignoring Satan the author brings into focus the real existential problem dealt with in the dialogues." (Hoffman [N 36]: 162–163).

Such an argument as this seems, at least to me, difficult to maintain. Considering what a dominating figure the Satan is in the Prologue, one would expect some manner of acknowledgment of his role in the drama of the Poem. Simply because Job and his Friends are unaware of the "wager" between the Satan and God, it does not necessarily follow that no reference to his role would be found in the colloquy between Job and his Friends. After all, the reader of Job is acutely aware of the role of the Satan in Job's distress, and it would be expected that the author would wish to underscore the distinction between what Job and his Friends know and what has been withheld from them by the use of indirect reference to the actions of the Satan. For example, we might expect Job or his Friends to speculate on whether Job's distress might have something to do with some manner of Satanic influence on the Heavenly Council.

Besides this, the omission of all mention of the Satan in the Epilogue (see the further discussion, p. 26 f.) is even more difficult to explain along the lines Hoffman has argued above. One might with difficulty contend that due to Job and his Friends' ignorance, no mention of the Satan is appropriate in the Poem, but the Epilogue returns to the expanded perspective of "omniscient narration" with which the book began in the Prologue. Within such a universal purview an ultimate return to the scene of the Heavenly Council where the "wager" was made and an assessment of its result would seem not only expected but virtually required.

The only easy way to explain this extraordinary omission is to assume that the Satan episode in the Job story is a later interpolation.

40. Hurvitz supplies a list of such phrases that occur elsewhere in the Bible "only in connection with personalities mentioned in the Pentateuch." (Hurvitz, "Date" [N 32]: 31 with n. 50). Note also N. Sarna, "Epic Substratum in the Prose of Job," *JBL* 76 (1957): 13–25.

41. Hurvitz, "Date" (N 32): 31.

42. Note, in this connection, 42:11 which speaks of *kl-hr'h 'šr hby' yhwh 'lyw*, "all the

evil which the LORD brought upon him [Job]," a statement often noted by scholars as suggesting an older level of the Job story in which the Satan played no role. For this and other potential markers of an earlier version of the Job story embedded in our extant Prologue/Epilogue, see, e.g., Spiegel, "Noah, Danel, and Job" (N 36): 324–330 and notes. For a more recent discussion, see Vermeylen (N 36): 3–28.

43. See, e.g., P. K. McCarter, Jr.'s observation in *II Samuel; A New Translation with Introduction and Commentary* (Anchor Bible vol. 9; Garden City: Doubleday, 1984): 508 and the bibliography cited there in reference to the unknown cause for God's wrath. As regards *wysp*, it is also quite likely that this term has an editorial function, signalling that the following section is to be understood as an appendix to 2 Samuel, not in its proper chronological place in the narrative. See, e.g., ibid., 509, 516–517.

44. See, e.g., Hurvitz, "Date" (N 32): 19.

45. I have followed the translation in Ginzberg (N 19): vol. 1, 272–273; for other sources of this story, see Ginzberg, vol. 5, 248–249, n. 228. Note especially the following account in Jubilees 17:15–18 where Mastema, who is labeled as the chief of demons in Jub. 10:8, takes on the Satanic role:

And it came to pass . . . that words came in heaven concerning Abraham that he was faithful in everything which was told him and he loved the Lord and was faithful in all affliction. And Prince Mastema came and he said before God, "Behold Abraham loves Isaac his son. And he is more pleased with him than everything. Tell him to offer him (as) a burnt offering upon the altar. And you will see whether he will do this thing. And you will know whether he is faithful in everything in which you test him."

And the Lord was aware that Abraham was faithful in all of his afflictions because he tested him with his land, and with famine. And he tested him with the wealth of kings. And he tested him again with his wife, when she was taken (from him), and with circumcision. And he tested him with Ishmael and with Hagar, his maidservant, when he sent them away. And in everything in which he tested him, he was found faithful. And his soul was not impatient. And he was not slow to act because he was faithful and a lover of the Lord.

For this reading of the passage, see O. S. Wintermute, "Jubilees (Second Century B.C.); A New Translation and Introduction," in *The Old Testament Pseudepigrapha* (James H. Charlesworth, ed.; 2 vols.; Garden City: Doubleday, 1983, 1985): vol. 2, 90. See also, R. H. Charles, *The Book of Jubilees* . . . (London: 1902): 120–122; idem, *The Apocrypha and Pseudepigrapha of the Old Testament in English*; vol. 2, *Pseudepigrapha* (Oxford: Clarendon, 1913; rpt. 1973): 39.

Note that the name "Mastema" is equivalent to Hebrew *mśtmh*, "hatred, animosity, hostility" (cf. Hos. 9:7,8, 1QS 3:23, and esp. 1QM 13:4, CD 16:5 where the phrase *ml'k mśtmh* is employed) which may be derived from *śtm*, possibly a biform of *śtn* (cf. Kluger [N 37]: 26–29; Forsyth [N 37]: 182). Regardless of its etymology, it is certainly a variant Satanic title (cf., e.g. *Supplementum ad Lexicon in Veteris Testamenti Libros* [L. Köhler and W. Baumgartner, eds.; Leiden: Brill, 1958]: 169). For further discussion of Mastema, cf. Forsyth (N 37): 182–192, 199–202.

It is noteworthy that when this account lists the tests of Abraham previous to the sacrifice of Isaac, God alone is depicted as the agent of testing. Only in this last trial is there a need to inject the Satan as a buffer between God and the trying of his righteous servant. In part, this may be because of the serious nature of what the traditions usually take to be the final challenge to Abraham's integrity; but also, the clear Joban overtones to this trial likely caused it, in particular, to be reformulated in the image of the book of Job's Prologue.

A somewhat similar theme may be found in Pseudo-Philo's *Biblical Antiquities* 32:1–2.

In this account the instigators of the *Akedah* are the angels who are jealous of God's favored treatment of Abraham. In order to demonstrate Abraham's faithfulness to these envious angels, God asks him to sacrifice his son. Abraham's exemplary behavior then becomes the occasion of God's triumphant declaration (32:4): "You shall not slay your son, nor shall you destroy the fruit of your body. For now I have appeared so as to reveal you to those who do not know you and have shut the mouths of those who are always speaking evil against you." For this reading of the passage, cf. D. J. Harrington, "Pseudo-Philo (First Century A.D.)" in Charlesworth, (N 45): 346; cf. further the discussion in Swetnam (N 9): 48–56. The jealousy of the angels for Abraham is also mentioned in *Genesis Rabbah* 55:4.

46. Following the *ketiv*; see the following discussion.

47. Cf. Spiegel, "Noah, Danel, and Job," (N 36): 305–355; also M. Noth, "Noah, Daniel und Hiob in Ezechiel XIV," *VT* 1 (1951): 251–260; R. G. Albertson, "Job and Ancient Near Eastern Wisdom Literature," *Scripture in Context II* (W. Hallo, J. Moyer, L. Perdue, eds.; Winona Lake, IN: Eisenbrauns, 1983): 214–215.

48. Spiegel, "Noah, Danel and Job," (N 36): 319. For a different view of the oracles here in Ezekiel 14, see Moshe Greenberg, *Ezekiel 1–20; A New Translation with Introduction and Commentary* (Anchor Bible 22; Garden City: Doubleday, 1983): 261–263. It seems to me that Greenberg has missed the point when he argues (p. 258) that Spiegel is "misguided" in focusing on the children of the three heroes. Greenberg contends that the focus on the children is meant to be a "thinly veiled" reference to the actual sons and daughters of the Exiles. But, assuming Greenberg were correct, Spiegel's argument should hardly be seen as in opposition to his view. Indeed, Spiegel's interpretation would seem more to reinforce Greenberg's argument than to detract from it.

Mention also should be made of the comments of W. Zimmerli, (*Ezekiel 1, A Commentary on the Book of the Prophet Ezekiel, Chapters 1–24* [Hermeneia; Philadelphia: Fortress, 1969]: 315) who thus criticizes Spiegel: "[When he] deduces from Ezek 14 a tradition in which Dan(i)el and Job redeemed their sons from corruption by their piety, he is schematizing the tradition much too strongly." To begin with, Zimmerli's comment somewhat misrepresents Spiegel in that the latter never argues that the piety of Danel, and Job saved their respective children from corruption. Rather, it is the children's lives that were ransomed through the righteousness of their respective fathers. The only further point Zimmerli makes is that "Ezekiel was here speaking in a universal way of the divine righteousness, which inevitably concerns every man, whether Israelite or not. . . ." In fact, this latter point is completely consistent with Spiegel's view.

The advantage of Spiegel's interpretation is, of course, that it explains *in specific terms* why these particular figures—Danel, Noah and Job—were singled out and brought forward by Ezekiel instead of seeing their use here as coincidental or ad hoc. Moreover, there is a clear genre of story that one can isolate in this and other Ancient Near Eastern legends, a story type with which Ezekiel was familiar and which he could use to tie these three heroes of righteousness together as he does. This latter point is one I have tried in particular to emphasize; and, in doing so, I hope that I have bolstered Spiegel's view.

49. Perhaps this is why the operative verb in Gen. 7:13 is singular (*b'*) rather than plural (contrast *wyb'w* and *hb'ym*, the plurals used respectively in 7:15,16 in reference to the animals). The text seems so structured as to emphasize that only Noah really counts here. It is he who enters the Ark, and all the others are allowed to pass under the shelter of his singular presence which is signaled by the singular verb. In fact, this seems precisely the opposite of the circumstance we discussed above (pp. 18 ff.) in Gen. 22:19. There, the singular verb *wyšb* (contrasted by the immediately following plurals *wyqmw wylkw*) emphasized the absence of the son; here the singular verb *b'* (followed immediately by a list of Noah's entourage) emphasizes that they are all together, thanks to the merit of Noah.

50. See, e.g., Spiegel, "Noah, Danel, and Job," (N 36): 307–310 and especially the bibliography cited therein.

51. Ibid., 310–318; esp. 310–311, n. 1 for a convenient listing of early bibliography on the text. More up-to-date bibliographies, translations and philological discussions of the text may be found in *Textes Ougaritiques*; vol. I, *Mythes et légendes* (A. Caquot, M. Sznycer and A. Herdner, eds.; Paris: Cerf, 1974): 401–458 and *Mitos y leyendas de Canaan segun la tradicion de Ugarit* (G. Del Olmo Lete, ed.; Madrid: Cristiandad, 1981): 327–401. For the most recent and best overall analysis of the Aqhat story at Ugarit, see S. B. Parker, "Death and Devotion: The Composition and Theme of *AQHT*," *Love and Death in the Ancient Near East*; *Essays in Honor of Marvin H. Pope* (J. H. Marks and R. M. Good, eds.; Guilford, CT: Four Quarters, 1987): 71–83. The most reliable and accessible English translation is still that of H. L. Ginsberg ("Ugaritic Myths, Epics, and Legends" in *Ancient Near Eastern Texts* [J. B. Pritchard, ed.; 3rd ed.; Princeton: Princeton University Press, 1969]: 149–155); see also M. D. Coogan, *Stories from Ancient Canaan* (Philadelphia: Westminster, 1978): 27–47; J. C. L. Gibson, *Canaanite Myths and Legends* (Edinburgh: Clark, 1977): 103–122; J. C. de Moor, *An Anthology of Religious Texts from Ugarit* (Leiden: Brill, 1987): 224–273.

52. Cf. Parker (N 51): 82.

53. Spiegel, "Noah, Danel, and Job," (N 36): 316; see also Albertson (N 47): 215, who even apparently reconstructs an episode in which "It began to rain and Anath breathed the breath of life into the nostrils of Aqhat." This "climax," although presented as part of the known story of Danel and Aqhat, is not attested in the Ugaritic text. We should note in passing that Ezekiel makes mention of Danel in one other instance, Ezek. 28:3, where this ancient hero is invoked as one of the great masters of Wisdom. However, this passage offers no significant further insight into the Danel tradition known to Ezekiel relevant to our concerns here.

54. Note, however, Parker's caution: "I do not find in an internal analysis of the poem, nor in the structural analogues to its major components, any grounds for concluding that the sequel would have told of the resurrection of Aqhat." But Parker does not exclude such a possibility, and, moreover notes, "Possibly there were other versions of the tale in which Aqhat did return to life." Cf. (N 51): 82.

One potential, indirect indication that the Aqhat story ended (at least in some version) in a climactic resurrection of the son is that according to the Ugaritic account Aqhat's death is seen to have a direct impact on the fertility of the land; that is, when Aqhat dies, the land seems to die with him, overcome by drought. Since it seems reasonable to assume that the land is restored to fertility at the conclusion of the story, there would seem a natural parallel between its ultimate restoration and that of Aqhat. Certainly, it would make quite an appropriate denouement if on the resurrection of Aqhat from the dead, the land also came back to life again. For a consideration of how this thematic idea may function within the Poem of Job, cf. pp. 130 ff.; also N 407.

55. For the quote from Spiegel, see "Noah, Danel and Job" (N 36): 319. Note also Gordis' comment (*God and Man* [N 30]: 69): "In the form in which it was familiar to Ezekiel's contemporaries of the sixth century B.C.E., the tale doubtless told how the righteous Job, because of his piety, had been able to save his children from death as Noah did, or had brought them back from the nether world as Dan'el had." It is interesting to note that in Islamic legends, the story of Job involves God giving back his selfsame children to him. See the sources (including the Qur'an) cited by MacDonald (N 2): 142 ff.; also, more recently, Müller, *Hiob* (N 7): *passim*.

56. A revealing instance in which the authorized Job story has been adjusted in a popular rendition to obviate the problem of Job's children occurs (perhaps not surprisingly) in a modern paraphrase of "Bible stories" for children. At the conclusion of this children's version

of Job, the Epilogue is summarized: "And God healed Job and brought his children and his servants and all his animals back to him and Job marveled at the greatness of the Lord." (L. Hayward, *Bible Stories from the Old Testament* [New York: Grosset & Dunlap, 1987]: 87). Here, the storyteller rethinks the story so that it goes the way it *should* go in order to be "suitable" for children. For a discussion of similar slight alterations of text, cf. pp. 77 ff. and pp. 166 ff. I am grateful to Mary Pinkerson for drawing my attention to this children's version of Job.

57. If the reconstructions presented here of the *Akedah*, Job and Danel legends are correct, then in all three cases we are dealing with stories in which the human children of the designated heroes are first murdered and then resurrected from the dead. Nonetheless, the authorized, biblical versions of these legends (as respectively represented in Genesis, Job and Ezekiel) go to some pains to eliminate all direct mention of any aspect of human resurrection. Moreover, there is no other story in the Old Testament corpus where an overt account of human resurrection may be found. Such a systematic exclusion of what in all likelihood was a popular and widespread genre of story is probably best explained as due to theological prejudice of the various biblical writers and editors who ultimately became the arbiters of the Canon (cf. below Ns 99, 101).

We can only speculate as to why stories of human resurrection would have been distasteful to these arbiters, but the strongest possibility is that such stories were too intimately associated with pagan motifs, especially those depicted in stories of dying and rising gods. See, e.g., the discussion by H. Birkeland, "The Belief in the Resurrection of the Dead in the Old Testament," *Studia Theologica* 3 (1949): 60–78.

The Christian myth makes precisely this sort of association when it essentially fuses these related story-genres: compounding a story of a dying and rising god with that of the resurrection of a human child of the hero. As I will argue (pp. 34 f.), it is precisely this association that makes the Job legend so important to the author of the Epistle of James.

58. The way the children are introduced in 42:13 also may be of some significance. We are presented with a simple statement of possession: *wyhy-lw šbʿnh bnyn wšlwš bnwt*, "And Job had seven sons and three daughters." In fact, the statement may be a bit too simple. We are never actually told where these children come from; we are never told, for example, that Job knew his wife and that she conceived and bore to him his second family. The children are just *there*, along with the sheep, camels, etc. Of course, we can only surmise that they are new children born to Job to replace the ones who died. Yet I wonder whether there could be an intentional ambiguity here. Perhaps by not stating precisely where the seven sons and three daughters come from the story can thereby allow its readers to imagine that they are the selfsame children that the ancient tradition says were restored to Job. Thus, the authorized narrative can allude to the more ancient tradition, just as the *Akedah* does when it shows us Abraham returning alone to Beer Sheva.

Beyond this, there is another point to consider. When Job's fortunes are restored, he receives double what he had before—with one exception. Even though the logic of the circumstance might lead us to expect him to gain 14 sons where before he had seven, and (perhaps) six daughters where before he had three, instead he receives back precisely the same number of offspring as he had lost at the beginning of the story. Once more, this equal compensation may indirectly allude to the more ancient version of the story; for clearly the number of children lost and regained must match if they are to be seen as the *same* children after all. To double the number would serve to undercut this potentiality; and therefore, it may well be significant that the version of the Job story we find reflected in the Epilogue refrains from doing this.

59. Spiegel makes an interesting argument that the element of prayer in the Epilogue (42:10 cf. 42:8)—"which seems alien and irrelevant" in the immediate context—also reflects

a trace of the earlier story beneath the authorized version. He speculates that in the original story it was an act of selfless prayer that served as the reason for the turn in Job's fortune:

> Himself in woe and want, Job continued in his uprightness to "strengthen feeble knees" and "uphold him that was falling" (4:4) or even redeem the sinner "through the cleanness of his hands" (22:30), traits apparently taken over from the old folk-tale. A particularly poignant example of self-abnegation probably served as the climax of the story, when Job, mindless of his own misery, invoked mercy upon some one else, praying $b'd\ r'hw$ ["on behalf of a friend"] for a fellow creature in pain. Then or only then, all the world, even Job's adversary in heaven, had to acknowledge with one voice: $hnm\ yr'\ 'lhym$ ["he selflessly reverences God"].

Once Job showed this act of charity, God could see what a truly righteous man he was and thus end His test of Job. In particular, Spiegel notes that the retention of the singular $r'hw$ "his friend"—rather than the expected plural $r'yw$ "his friends"—in the Epilogue is a signal of this older layer of the story. This singular simply had to be retained because it constituted the ancient turning point of the story: "The original conclusion (42:10) was too often quoted and too well-known to permit any modification or deviation." Thus, again we may see the composer(s) of the Prologue/Epilogue paying homage to the contrapuntal theme that plays beneath the authorized tale. Even if—contextually speaking—the singular "his friend" makes no sense (or rather can only be made sense of with considerable exegetical effort), it *had to be there.* Otherwise the story would not be the story. Cf. Spiegel, "Noah, Danel, and Job" (N 36): 326–330.

60. In saying this, I do not necessarily mean to imply that in *all* early versions of the Job legend a single deity tested Job. It seems to me quite possible that in other versions of this story (and, more broadly, in this genre of story) there may have been a conflict between competing gods over the righteousness of Job (or such Job-like heroes). In such a story type, one god would defend the righteousness of the protagonist, while the other (perhaps equal in strength or status) would try to subvert his righteousness, presumably by sending on him all manner of misfortunes and plagues.

Such a story type might not be too dissimilar from Aesop's fable, "The Northwind and the Sun." In this story the Northwind and the Sun argue over which of them is strongest. They determine to settle the matter by seeing who can make a man remove his coat. First, the Northwind blows fiercely; but the more it beats down upon the man, the more determinedly the man clings to his coat. When the Sun's turn comes, the heat of its warmth is more than enough to make the man willingly shed his coat. Thus, the Sun wins the contest of strength through its essentially beneficent warmth after the Northwind has failed in its hostile, windy attack. (For this fable, see Fable 18 in the Greek version preserved by Valerius Babruis [third century C.E.]; English version: *Aesop's Fables Told by Valerius Babrius* [D. B. Hull, trans.; Chicago: University of Chicago, 1960]: unpaged.)

The aforementioned Ugaritic tale of Aqhat and Danel may reflect something along similar lines. Note that the object of favor, Aqhat, could be seen as "a bone of contention" between two deities, Baal and Anat. While the former endeavors to support Aqhat in every manner, the latter tries first to tempt him and then to destroy him. Indirectly, Aqhat thus might be seen as the occasion for a test of strength between god and goddess (and perhaps, in more universal terms, between male and female). A related, though not identical, genre of text may be the sort of "contest" fables found in Akkadian literature, e.g., "The Tamarisk and the Palm," "The Fable of Willow," "Nisaba and Wheat," "The Ox and the Horse" and "The Fable of the Fox." For a comprehensive collection of these texts including translations, see. W. G. Lambert, *Babylonian Wisdom Literature* (Oxford: Clarendon, 1960; rpt., 1975): 150–212; see further, the discussion of the genre in Bolle (N 29): 148–163. Note, particularly,

Bolle's discussion of the similarity of these stories to the fables of Aesop (pp. 161–162); also R. J. Williams, "The Fable in the Ancient Near East," in *A Stubborn Faith* (E. C. Hobbs, ed.; Dallas: Southern Methodist University Press, 1956): 3–26; J. H. Hayes, *Old Testament Form Criticism* (San Antonio: Trinity University Press, 1977): 245–247; 253–256.

If a "Northwind and the Sun" story type also lies behind the legend of Job, the later insertion of the Satan into the story not only might serve to buffer God from his evil but could also act as a faint echo of a divine conflict or test of strength between god and god. Possibly one might consider the story of Jesus temptation in the wilderness (Mark 1:12; Matt. 4:1–11; Luke 4:1–13) in a similar manner.

61. It is not surprising that Abraham was also used in early Christian writings as a type for all Christians to follow, very much in the same manner as Job. For a recent discussion, see Segal (N 8): esp. 119 ff.

62. See, e.g., Rom. 10:4, 1 Tim. 1:5 and more generally Arndt, Gingrich (N 4): 819, n. c. In the LXX the verb *teleō* is used to render Hebrew *klh* (cf. Ruth 2:21) and *šlm* (cf. Neh. 6:15); see E. Hatch and H. Redpath, *Concordance to the Septuagint* (Oxford: Clarendon, 1897): 1342 s.v. *telein*.

63. See, e.g., Luke 1:33, 1 Pet. 4:7 and, more generally, Arndt and Gingrich (N 44): 819, nn. a,d. In the LXX *telos* commonly translates Hebrew *qṣ* and *swp*; see, e.g., Jud. 11:39, 2 Sam. 15:7; Eccles. 3:13, Dan. 6:26 (Theodotion); cf. Hatch and Redpath (N 62): 1344 s.v. *telos*. See also the comments in Dibelius and Greeven (N 4): 246–247.

64. There is likely another reason why Job was singled out by the author of James as *the* example of patience, as opposed to other potential examples like the Suffering Servant of Second Isaiah: because he was a gentile. As a gentile, he could serve as proof positive that one need not be a Jew to be a model of the sort of fortitude that God requires of the righteous. This falls in line with the standard early Christian understanding of Job. As Baskin notes, "Patristic exegetes are unanimous that Job was a gentile," and comments further: "Since Christianity was a religion which sought to encompass all peoples, the portrayal of saintly pagans, biblical and non-biblical, as gentile witnesses to the coming Incarnation of Christ played an important part in the early theology of the Church. . . ." She quotes appropriately in this connection Gregory the Great's comment on Job's gentile origin: "It is not without cause that the life of a just pagan is set before us as a model side by side with the life of the Israelites. Our Savior, coming for the redemption of Jews and gentiles, willed also to be foretold by the voices of Jews and gentiles." (Baskin [N 7]: 32, 33, 35. The comment of Gregory the Great is from his *Moralia on Job*; Preface, section 5 (cf. *A Library of Fathers of the Holy Catholic Church* (Oxford: Publisher, 1844–50) vol. 18, 18. The translation follows Baskin.

65. I would like to acknowledge the help of Dr. Abraham Zygielbaum of the Hebrew Union College, Jewish Institute of Religion, Los Angeles and Dr. Janet Hadda of the Department of Germanic Languages, UCLA, both of whom generously gave of their time and expertise to help guide me through "Bontsye Shvayg" and the broader milieu of Yiddish literature. I also must mention Dina Abramowicz, librarian of the YIVO Institute for Jewish Research who made the facilities of the institute's library so very accessible to me. Special thanks must go to Jeffrey Shandler, who did vital research on my behalf at YIVO; and finally to Rena Fisher, who did some research on my behalf at the National Yiddish Book Center in Amherst.

The edition of record for the Yiddish of "Bontsye Shvayg" utilized in this study is the first edition: Y. L. Perets, *Literatur un leben; ayn zammelbukh far literatur un gezelshaft aroysgegebn durkh Y. L. Perets* (Warsaw: Perets, Funk, 1894): 1–22. A second version of this story, the changes in which were probably made by Perets himself, appeared in Y. L. Perets, *Shriften yubileum oisgabe* (Warsaw: Halter, 1901): 38–46; a volume which was published to honor Perets' 50th birthday and the 25th anniversary of his career as a writer (cf. further below, N 201). All subsequent editions and translations appear to rely on one or the other of these versions as their authority. Among other Yiddish editions of "Bontsye Shvayg" consulted for this study, the following are the most notable: L. Wiener, *Yiddish Literature in the Nineteenth Century* (New York: Scribners, 1899): 332–353 (transliterated Yiddish text with facing English translation); Y. L. Perets, *Ale Verk* (David Pinsky, ed.; 11 vols.; New York: CYCO, 1947): vol. 2, 412–420; *Y. L. Perets in nayntsntn yorhundert*; (S. Rollansky, ed.; Buenos Aires: Ateneo Literario en el Instituto Cientifico Judio: 1967): 149–159.

The translation of "Bontsye Shvayg" employed in this study is based on the 1894 version of the story. Other translations primarily consulted are "Bontzye Shweig," in I. L. Peretz, *Stories and Pictures* (Helena Frank, trans.; Philadelphia: JPS, 1936): 171–181. "Bontche Shweig," in idem., *Three Gifts and Other Stories* (H. Goodman, trans.; New York: Book League, 1947): 23–30; "Bontsha the Silent," in *A Treasury of Yiddish Stories* (Hilde Abel, trans.; I. Howe, E. Greenberg, eds.; New York: Viking, 1954): 223–230; "Silent Bontche," in Maurice Samuel, *Prince of the Ghetto* (Philadelphia: JPS, 1948): 75–83; "Bontshe the Silent" Y. L. Perets, *Bontshe the Silent* (A. S. Rappoport, trans.; Philadelphia: Paul/McKay, n.d.): 13–22; "Silent Bontsia," in *As Once We Were* (E. T. Margolis, ed. and trans.; Los Angeles: Acme, 1951): 208–219; "Buntcheh the Silent," in *In This World and the Next*; *Selected Writings of I. L. Peretz* (M. Spiegel, ed. and trans.; New York: Yoseloff, 1958): 58–65. Where it may be useful, alternate translations from these other versions will be cited in the notes. For the most comprehensive listing of all English translations of "Bontsye Shvayg," and Perets' other stories, see U. Weinrich, "Guide to English Translations of Yitshok Leybush Peretz (1851?–1915)"; *The Field of Yiddish* (U. Weinrich, ed.; New York: Columbia University Press, 1954): 292–299.

We will follow the convention utilized by YIVO and the Library of Congress for transliteration of Yiddish. For a convenient overview of this transcription system, see, e.g., U. Weinrich, "Note on the Transcription, Transliteration, and Citation of Titles," ibid: vi–viii; also, idem., *College Yiddish*; *An Introduction to the Yiddish Language and to Jewish Life and Culture* (5th ed.,; New York: YIVO, 1981): 25–29; and esp. idem., *Modern English-Yiddish Yiddish-English Dictionary* (New York: Schocken, 1977): xx–xxv and throughout the text for *loshn-koydesh* words (i.e., words derived from Hebrew). Note especially "Perets" as opposed to the "Peretz" one often finds in the literature. There appear to be as many variant spellings of "Bontsye Shvayg" as there are editions of the story or critical comments thereon. For the sake of simplicity, one transcription—"Bontsye Shvayg"—will be used in all citations. Where necessary, the spelling of this title will be conformed to this transcription in translations or other quotations, excluding article titles. See further D. N. Miller, "Y. L. Perets' 'Bontsye Shvayg': Perspectives on Passivity," *Slavic and East European Journal* 18 (1974): 45, n. 1.

66. The only serious critical study known to me is that of D. N. Miller (see Miller [N 65]: 45 n. 1). According to Miller, "Interpretive close readings of 'Bontsye Shvayg' have not appeared in the relevant critical literature, which restricts itself to bibliography and biographical matters or to paraphrase" (ibid., 46 n. 5). As far as I am aware, this is generally an accurate statement. There are, however, other studies that do briefly consider "Bontsye Shvayg" in the context of Perets' work and the broader topic of Yiddish literature. Various such studies will be considered as they become relevant.

67. Also note Job 16:19–20, which invokes an intercessor who would act as Job's defender before God, just as an angelic defender speaks on behalf of Bontsye before the Heavenly Tribunal. Note especially that 16:20 utilizes *mlysy*, which might be translated "my advocate, defender" (on various problems and interpretations of the reading, see, e.g., the

summary discussion in N. Habel, *The Book of Job*; *A Commentary* [Old Testament Library; Philadelphia: Westminster, 1985]: 265–266; see further pp. 320 f.). This seems to be reminiscent of the Hebrew-Yiddish *meylets-yoysher* (lit. "defender of the right") which Perets uses as the title for Bontsye's Advocate. An even more striking passage in Job which might also inform the background of "Bontsye Shvayg" may be 33:23, where Job's erstwhile friend Elihu declares: *'m-yš 'lyw ml'k mlyṣ 'ḥd mny-'lp lhgyd l'dm yšrw*, "if he has an angel to represent him, a defender—one out of a thousand—to affirm a man's uprightness" (see further, pp. 155 f.). In fact, this is the only instance in the Bible where the Hebrew terms Perets uses to characterize Bontsye's Defender (*ml'k, mlyṣ, yšr*) occur together.

Another biblical antecedent that may have directly or indirectly informed "Bontsye Shvayg" is Zech. 3:1–10. Here, according to the traditional Hebrew text, the high priest Joshua is judged before the LORD in what appears to be a heavenly tribunal. Zechariah sees Joshua "before the angel of the LORD [*lpny ml'k yhwh*] and the Satan standing at his right side to accuse him [Joshua] [*whśṭn 'md 'l ymynw lśṭnw*]" (Zech. 3:1). The Satan functions in this instance as a divine accuser, a prosecutor; cf. Ps. 106:9, where a similar judicial proceeding is portrayed (although in that instance with no divine overtones to *śṭn*, "accuser, prosecutor"). In some respects, the "angel of the LORD" appears to be more a judge acting on behalf of God than anything else (see, e.g., D. L. Petersen, *Haggai and Zechariah 1–8* [Old Testament Library; Philadelphia: Westminster, 1984]: 190–191). Still, since the text in vs. 2 depicts the LORD speaking for Himself (see also 3:7 ff.) and since the "angel of the LORD" acts in favor of mercy for the sinful Joshua (3:4), the scene can be interpreted as depicting the angel as Defender, the Satan as Prosecutor and the LORD as merciful Judge. As such, the scene in Zechariah is an obvious source that could affect stories that, like "Bontsye Shvayg," show a soul in judgment before God with an angelic Defender and Satanic Prosecutor in judicial contention. For a fuller discussion of the Zechariah passage, see, e.g., ibid., 186–214; Kluger (N 37): 139–147; C. L. and E. M. Meyers, *Haggai, Zechariah 1–8; A New Translation with Introduction and Commentary* (Anchor Bible vol 25B; Garden City: Doubleday, 1987): 178–227.

Of course, in making reference to these biblical passages, I do not wish to imply that they are the only, or even the primary, influences informing this story of a heavenly trial of a human soul. Clearly, this is a stock Yiddish genre that is used, for example, by Perets in a number of his short stories (see the following discussion where several such stories are noted).

68. Wiener (N 65) translates *on a rane, on a blutik ort*, "without wounds, without a spot of blood. . . ."

69. Wiener (ibid.) translates *"es zol zayn toyznt milyon ferd vi mentshn"* somewhat more paraphrastically, ". . . if there were as many millions of them in existence as there are men"; see further, N 201.

70. This is also Miller's view, see (N 65): 43.

71. Note Abel's paraphrastic translation (Howe and Greenberg, *Treasury* [N 65]: 230), which makes Perets' implicit remark an explicit statement: "There in that other world, no one understood you. You never understood yourself. You never understood that you could have cried out and that your outcries would have brought down the world itself and ended it."

A striking parallel to this concept occurs in an early rabbinical account of the martyrdom of ten great rabbis at the hands of an archetypical Roman tyrant. In this account, one rabbi after another is tortured and murdered—and in each instance the rabbis remain steadfast in their faith in God, certain of their reward in the world to come. The most dramatic moment comes in the account of the martyrdom of the Second Century rabbi, Ishmael ben Elisha: "The emperor immediately ordered his servant to strip the skin off Rabbi Ishmael's face. When they reached the spot on his forehead where he used to place his phylacteries, Rabbi

Ishmael groaned with such terrible bitterness that the heavens and the earth trembled. He groaned a second time and the Throne of Glory trembled." This leads to the most dramatic point in the account where the fate of God's creation quite literally trembles in the balance: "A *bat kol* [i.e., an oracular voice] declared from heaven, "If I hear one more word in protest, I shall destroy the entire universe and return it to chaos and void!" When Rabbi Ishmael hears this, the story notes that he ceased groaning and "became silent," explaining that he was not crying out for himself but only due to the loss of the privilege of laying on phylacteries. This leads to a final query from the tyrant and a heroic response from the rabbi:

"Yet you still trust in your God!" said the emperor.

"Let him kill me if He will," said Rabbi Ishmael. "I shall still hope in Him."

Perhaps not surprisingly, these last lines are taken from Job 13:15, perhaps the most famous, traditional affirmation of faith in the popular conception of the book of Job (see further pp. 170 ff.). While it is hardly certain that Perets was familiar with this specific story, it is quite probable that martyrological accounts of this type were known to him and stood in the background of his "Bontsye Shvayg." The translation here follows D. Roskies, "The Ten *Harugei Malkhut*," in *The Literature of Destruction; Jewish Responses to Catastrophe* (D. Roskies, ed.; Philadelphia: JPS, 1988): 63–64; also 49–50; see further D. Stern, "Midrash Eleh Ezkerah," *Fiction* 7 (1983): 69–98. For the original, see A. Jellinek, *Bet ha-Midrash: Sammlung* (Jerusalem: Wharman): vol. 2, 64–72.

A somewhat similar theme that may lie in the background of "Bontsye Shvayg" is the Jewish folk legend that there are unknown, hidden *ṣaddīqīm* (just men), upon whom the fate of the entire world depends. For a discussion of this legend, see G. Scholem, "The Tradition of the Thirty-Six Hidden Just Men," *The Messianic Idea in Judaism* (New York: Schocken, 1971): 251–256.

72. One might argue that the "impatient voice . . . hard voice" that interrupts the Defending Angel's speech is that of the Prosecuting Angel rather than the Presiding Officer of the Assembly. Indeed, Abel is clearly of this opinion as her free translation of the story shows. Where in the Yiddish it simply states ". . . and the hard voice once more interrupts: 'Cut out the rhetoric!' " (*un dos harte kol shlogt vayter iber: On retorik!*), she translates "The harsh voice of the prosecuting angel broke in once more. 'Never mind the rhetoric please!' " (Howe and Greenberg, *Treasury* [N 65]: 226). Nonetheless, the only figure clearly identified as delivering orders relevant to the conduct of the trial is the Presiding Officer: "The Presiding Officer sharply called out '. . . Read, but keep it short' "; " 'Facts, dry facts!' the Presiding Officer calls out again impatiently"; " 'Leave out insinuation against third persons,' chides the Presiding Officer"; " 'Keep to the point!' shouts the Presiding Officer"; " 'Keep to the facts!' the Presiding Officer calls out once more." Granted, the Prosecuting Angel does clearly intervene once, but then only with a snide remark about Bontsye's father being a drunkard. But the whole tenor of this mocking remark—" 'You mean to the drunkard!' the Prosecutor laughs derisively"—is completely different from the peremptory orders barked by the "hard voice." Moreover, Bontsye's reaction to the Prosecutor's remark, "And Bontsye feels a chill in every limb," seems to suggest that this is a new voice which Bontsye hears now for the first time and then reacts so strongly to. It is therefore more likely that the previously heard "hard voice" is that of the Presiding Officer rather than that of the Prosecutor. See also Miller (N 65): 43.

73. *Dayonim un malokhim hobn aropgelozt di kop farshemt; der kateyger hot zikh tselakht.* Note some alternate translations. Goodman: "The Prosecuting Angel laughs aloud." (N 65): 30; Margolis: "Over the bowed heads of the shamed and silent Heavenly Hosts a sardonic shout rang high and clear. The prosecutor was shaking with laughter." (N 65): 219; Samuel: "The prosecuting attorney broke into a laugh" (N 65): 83; Rappoport: "Abashed, angels and judges drooped their heads; whilst the accuser burst out into laughter." (N 65): 22;

Abel: "Then the silence is shattered. The prosecutor laughs aloud, a bitter laugh." Howe and Greenberg, *Treasury* (N 65): 230.

74. For the Yiddish version of *Oyb nisht nokh heker* (written in 1900) see Pinsky (N 65): vol. 5, 134–39. This translation is taken from Goodman, (N 65): 17.

75. It is interesting to cite S. Pinsker's comments on the final scene, in this connection: ". . . the resulting tableau of Bontsye among the angels causes them to 'bend their heads in shame at this unending meekness they have created on earth.' The sentimentality of the tale served to suggest possibilities of holiness and piety beyond even those sponsored by the official religion." (*The Schlemiel as Metaphor* [Carbondale: Southern Illinois University Press, 1971]: 65). What is particularly striking is not so much what Pinsker says as what he does not say: nowhere in his remarks does he mention the laugh of the Prosecutor. Rather, he appears to have interpreted the story as though this laugh were not of any significance; indeed, as though it did not occur in the story at all. This is noteworthy on two counts: first, because the interpretation to which he comes without the prosecutor's laugh in consideration, is precisely the pietistic view we have suggested would result; second, because he has (unconsciously?) factored the laugh out of the story altogether. As we have suggested, the Prosecutor's laugh can only intrude on a pietistic interpretation such as Pinsker presents. Only by tacitly ignoring its force can Pinsker proceed to his interpretive conclusions. This then would clearly suggest that the pietistic interpretation would have been best served if Perets had not let the prosecutor laugh. We will return to a consideration of Pinsker's interpretation below, pp. 75 f.

76. M. Waxman, *A History of Jewish Literature from the Close of the Bible to Our Own Days*, vol. 4, *From Eighteen-Eighty to Nineteen-Thirty-Five* (New York: Bloch, 1941): 500. A somewhat similar point is made by Howe and Greenberg:

> The skepticism is sharpest in Perets' single most famous story, "Bontsye Shvayg" in which this archetypal *kleyne mentshele* (little, little man) . . . evokes from the heavenly prosecutor a "bitter laugh," as if shamed before the paltriness of human desire. Perets—and here he does seem a little like Kafka—touches in this story on one of the major themes of modern literature: the radical, hopeless incommensurability between morality and existence, the sense of a deep injustice at the heart of the universe which even the heavens cannot remedy. (I. Howe, E. Greenberg, *Selected Stories: I. L. Peretz* (New York: Schocken, 1974): 18; similarly stated by Howe and Greenberg in "The World of I. L. Perets," *Commentary* [January, 1974]: 48.)

The translation employed in *Selected Stories* is Abel's (pp. 70–77), the same one employed in their earlier book (*Treasury* [N 65]). Of course, Abel's interpretive translation, "bitter laugh" (see N 73)—conveys precisely the nuance Howe and Greenberg see here.

We will return to a consideration of Howe and Greenberg's remarks and Abel's translation below, pp. 70 f.; 77 f.

77. For *Der meshulekh* (written in 1890) in Yiddish, see Y. L. Perets, *Far kleyn un groys* (*For Small and Large*) (Vilna: Kletskinb, 191–): 255–267. For a translation in English, see, e.g., Frank (N 65): 101–113. C. A. Madison has also noted the comparison and contrast of Shemayah to Bontsye (*Yiddish Literature; Its Scope and Major Writers* [New York: Ungar, 1968]: 112–115; see also idem, "Isaac Loeb Peretz," *Poet Lore* [1928]: 73–106; esp. pp. 85–88). For a further consideration of the implications of Madison's use of this comparison, see below, pp. 73 ff.

78. Waxman (N 76): 500.

79. Pinsker (N 75): 64; see below pp. 75 f.

80. This is also in line with the opinion expressed by R. Wisse, *The Schlemiel as Modern Hero* (Chicago: University of Chicago Press, 1971): 22; Ruth Adler, *Women of the Shetl*

through the Eyes of Y. L. Peretz (Rutherford: Fairleigh Dickinson University Press, 1980): 39; Miller (N 65): esp. 45; D. G. Roskies, "The People of the Lost Book; A Cultural Manifesto," *Orim* 2 (1986): 20, 23. Madison (*Yiddish Literature* [N 77]: 115) voices a somewhat similar opinion but tempers this by calling Bontsye's attitude "fatalistic" rather than foolish and concludes that "he [Perets] loved the poor porter and sympathized with . . . [his] naive piety, artless mind . . . and simple wholesomeness"; see also "Perets" (N 77): 87–88; see further my discussion on pp. 73 f. On other more optimistic interpretations of the conclusion of "Bontsye Shvayg," see p. 59.

81. We may wish to make an exception in respect to the Prosecutor; for it seems quite possible that Perets wished to suggest that this Satanic angel had an inkling that Bontsye was not all that he appeared to be even before our hero made his request for a hot roll with fresh butter. The Prosecutor begins his response to the Defense's speech apparently with the intent of giving a full refutation. But when he stops short and in "a soft voice, just like butter" (*a veykh kol vi a puter*) decides to be silent, too, there is a sense of slickness to this nonresponse: perhaps this Satan is not necessarily thwarted by his awe of our hero's presumed piety. Rather, it may be that he suddenly realizes what Bontsye really is and that the *best* way to defeat Bontsye is to let him speak for himself; for in no other manner can the true identity of this schlemiel be so startlingly revealed.

It may well be, however, that Perets had second thoughts about leaving this potential nuance in his story and took steps to change the wording accordingly in the revised edition of "Bontsye Shvayg" that appeared in 1901. For a fuller discussion, see below N 201.

82. I am grateful to my student Jeff Tamura for bringing this last point to my attention.

83. This is not the only case in which Perets uses the last phrase in a short story to compel the reader to alter his view of the story as heretofore presented. Consider the last lines of his story "The Three Gifts" (*Dray matones*). This, too, is a highly sentimentalized tale focusing on the piety of three Jewish martyrs. The three gifts alluded to in the story's title are each a representation of the ultimate piety to which each martyr clings, even at the point of death. These gifts are presented to Heaven by a wandering soul who has been instructed to "fly down . . . close to the world of the living and see what is happening there. And if you see anything there that is extraordinarily beautiful and good, seize it and fly up; it will be a gift to the Saints in Paradise. . . ." The soul, who has yet to gain entry into heaven, is told, "And be assured, when you have brought three gifts, the gates of Paradise will open to you."

When the last of the three gifts has been duly presented by the wandering soul to the Saints, the story comes to a happy conclusion: "The Saints in Heaven intercede on her behalf: The gates of Heaven are opened to her after the three gifts." But this is not where Perets ends his story. Rather, just as in "Bontsye Shvayg," he appends a final phrase that inevitably alters the entire cast of his theme: "And the Saints announce: 'Really beautiful gifts, surpassingly beautiful. . . . They are of no use whatever, but they are surpassingly lovely!'" For the original Yiddish, see Y. L. Perets, *Folkstimlikhe geshiktn* (*Folk-like Stories*) (Warsaw: Proges, 1908): 13–24. The translation here is from Goodman (N 65). Howe and Greenberg comment, "This concluding sentence can make the head reel; it comes as a shock of dissociation, perhaps despair, regarding the very purities of martyrdom Perets has celebrated." ("World," [N 76]: 43–48; esp. 47).

In fact, the concluding phrase makes one rethink "The Three Gifts" and consider whether the martyrdom depicted therein is truly worthy of praise. In this respect, the story's ironic ending makes it far closer in theme to "Bontsye Shvayg" than would first seem to be the case. As Roskies notes, "The Three Gifts" is best seen as a story that "mocked the most hallowed concept of all—*kiddush haShem* or martyrdom" ("Lost Book" [N 80]: 20).

84. See Pinsker's criticisms, cited above on pp. 40 f.

85. Note that in a popular, dramatic rendition of "Bontsye Shvayg" by Arnold Perl, the

objections of the Presiding Officer are explicitly depicted as being brushed aside by no less than the Presiding Officer, himself. Perl adds a final interruption by the Presiding Officer not found in the original story. Including stage directions, it reads:

PRESIDING ANGEL. Could I suggest, please—time is—(*The Angels murmur in protest. The Presiding Angel is reached too.*) No, you go ahead. (A. Perl, *The World of Sholom Aleichem; A Play* [New York: Dramatists Play Service, 1953]: 19.)

86. Note that Perets italicizes "realizm" (i.e., in the convention of Yiddish/Hebrew printing, he spaces out the letters) in order to give the term particular emphasis. Wiener (N 65) translates: "Pray, without realism"; see also Miller (N 65): 43 who translates "No realism!" Other translations: "We want no realism!" (Frank [N 65]: 175); "Such realistic details are unnecessary" (Abel; see Howe and Greenberg, *Treasury* [N 65]: 226); "But no realism, please" (Samuel [N 65]: 79).

87. Miller ([N 65]: 43) also believes that this comment is meant as a broader comment on the proceedings.

88. A similar point is made by A. A. Roback in *I. L. Peretz; Psychologist of Literature* (Cambridge: Sci-Art, 1935): 297–298.

89. Waxman (N 76): 496. It might be argued that there is a chronological problem involved in taking this position; that is, since "Bontsye Shvayg" is one of Perets' earlier stories, it cannot be simply compared to his more pietistic pieces, which tend to come later. However, it is certainly true that other of Perets' more traditional stories were written early, e.g., "The Messenger," cited above. By the same token, a number of Perets' other satirical stories are written a good deal later than "Bontsye Shvayg," e.g., "The Three Gifts"; see N 83.

90. See, e.g., Waxman's discussion of these stories as satire, (N 77): 496–497. For *Di frume kats* in Yiddish, see Perets, *Kleyn un groys* (N 78): 27–30; for an English translation, see, e.g., Margolis (N 65): 227–230; for *Der golem* in Yiddish, see Perets, *Kleyn un groys*: 46–47; for an English translation, see, e.g., I. Howe in Howe and Greenberg, *Treasury* (N 65): 245–246. For the Yiddish of *Der brilliant* see Pinsky (N 65): vol. 15, 96–103. According to Weinrich, "Guide" (N 65, "This last short story has not yet appeared in English translation." See provisionally Waxman's summary of the story in Waxman (N 76): 496–497.

91. For *Simkhe shebesimkhe* (written in 1912) in Yiddish, see Pinsky (N 65): vol. 5, 252–257. Weinrich lists only one translation of "Joy within Joy," that of Samuel (N 65): 179–181; see Weinrich (N 65): 295, cf. 298. More recently, a new translation by Shlomo Katz has been published under the title "Joy Beyond Measure" in Howe and Greenberg, *Selected Stories* (N 76): 78–82. The translation here follows Samuel. See also Waxman (N 76): 505.

92. See Samuel (N 65): 187.

93. Note the comments of Hersh D. Nomberg, a novelist and admiring colleague of Perets, made in connection with his anthology *Folstimlikhe geshiktn*, but equally applicable to all Perets' hasidic stories: "In *Folkstimlekhe geshiktn* the two chief traits in Perets' creativity were united: the hasidic fervor which was in his very nature, and the return to his people, the striving for openheartedness and artlessness which he attained only after searching long and wandering about on his and others' ways and paths." ("Master of a Literary Generation" in *The Golden Tradition; Jewish Life and Thought in Eastern Europe* [L. S. Dawidowicz, ed.; New York: Holt, Rinehart & Winston, 1967]: 296.

Note also the comment of Jacob Glatstein:

With all the strength of his artistic personality, Perets sought the ideal of artistic anonymity in his folkloric tales. He wanted, as it were, to give these tales back to the people, but in the process of giving them back the words took on wings. Stripping the text to what seemed a primitive simplicity, he raised it up from the mere two-dimensionality of the folk-voice and imparted to it an additional dimension of mind. Every tale gained something in the process. The color and flavor of a modern story-teller was added to their biblical clarity, and they became neo-biblical moral fables of a newer form of Judaism—Hasidism. (J. Glatstein, "Peretz and the Jewish Nineteenth Century," in *Voices from the Yiddish* (I. Howe and E. Greenberg, eds.; R. Sanders, trans.; Ann Arbor: University of Michigan Press, 1972): 51–63; esp. 61.

We should further note that the turn towards the hasidic genre in Perets' writing represented a notable departure from the earlier Yiddish literature of writers who, like Perets, came out of the tradition of the *Haskala* (Jewish Enlightenment). More typically, Yiddish was seen within the context of the *Haskala* movement as the best means to attack and satirize the ideals of hasidism. Yiddish writing was thus seen primarily as a limited tool of education for the masses but not as an appropriate medium for true, "literary" writing. Hebrew was the language for this. While, as we will see, Perets held to the idea that Yiddish and satire were important tools for education (see below, Ns. 141, 142) he also self-consciously tried to raise Yiddish and Jewish/hasidic traditions into the rank of true literature which had intrinsic value. See the extensive discussion by Dan Miron (*A Traveler Disguised; A Study in the Rise of Modern Yiddish Fiction in the Nineteenth Century* [New York: Schocken, 1973]: *passim*; esp. 39–40; 60–63.

94. As noted above (N 65) "Bontsye Shvayg" first appeared in the anthology *Literatur un lebn* in 1894. Roback ([N 88]: 136) suggests that Perets had already written the story before 1891 and had read it privately to various gatherings. He gives no reference in support of this claim.

95. Note in this respect Ginsberg's comment: ". . . even in the final stage of its evolution, the tale of Job the Patient is simple. In its most primitive state, Job is super-Abraham. In its ultimate stage, he is an ultra-super-Abraham" ("Patient" [N 2]: 15). It will be clear to anyone familiar with Ginsberg's interpretation of "Job the Patient/Job the Impatient" how much the following argument owes to his original insights, an indebtedness I wish formally to acknowledge here.

96. Note that Ginsberg anticipates this argument:

It is, or ought to be, obvious that in these chapters [the Poem of Job] a great genius has taken advantage of a chink in the armor of the orthodox doctrine of retribution, in order to drive a wedge into it. Tradition itself admits that Job, though blameless, suffered for a time. It therefore occurred to our poet to make Job, at the height of his suffering, a mouthpiece for a protest against the prevailing doctrine. So our poet switched the roles traditionally assigned to Job and his friends. Job becomes the protestant and his friends become the champions of orthodoxy. (Ibid., 15.)

The best argument in favor of the Friends-role's being part of the traditional Job legend may be that they also have a part to play in the Prologue/Epilogue. On the other hand, their presence there may simply reflect the influence of the Poem on the later refiguring of the folktale. Of course, it is also possible that there was a Friends-role in the original story that was partially reformed in the prose frame story under the influence of the Poem; see, e.g., Spiegel's argument cited above, N 59.

97. We should not exclude the possibility that the "Friends" were genuine comforters to Job in some version of the legendary tradition. In at least one version of the Job story, the so-called *Life of Job* of Aristeas, this is precisely how they are depicted; see below N 109. Still, if this is so, the irony of their role in the Poem is no less marked. For then we would have the

case of the traditional comforters necessarily converted into attackers of a Job that is no longer silent. Thus, once again the Friends would be converted into Anti-Friends for purposes of parody.

98. For a convenient survey of various proposals along these and similar lines regarding the meaning of the book of Job, see Rowley (N 36): 170–173 and notes; for a more recent discussion, see Williams, "Current Trends" (N 36): 24–27.

99. In the discussion that follows, I will be using *canon* in a fairly flexible sense to mean the biblical books that were generally accepted first by Jews and later by Christians as authoritative for religious practice. In using *canon* in this manner, I do not wish to imply that there was agreement in every detail between various Jewish and Christian bodies as to what constituted the canon or, for that matter, what constituted the canonical version of Job. Such was clearly not the case. Still, one can fairly speak of a broader consensus, at least, vis-à-vis the "Old Testament" Canon (excluding the Apocrypha) and, in particular, the canonical version of Job. It is to this broader consensus that I shall refer when applying the label canon to biblical writings. Some specific differences between canonical versions of Job and the implications of these variants will be considered further below.

For a discussion of the importance of looking at the canonical framework of biblical books, see James A. Sanders, *Torah and Canon* (Philadelphia: Fortress, 1972) and for a more recent general discussion, see idem., *Canon and Community; A Guide to Canonical Criticism* (Philadelphia: Fortress, 1984) and now most recently *From Sacred Story to Sacred Text* (Philadelphia: Fortress, 1987).

100. See above pp. 14 f.

101. I have already noted my agreement with Hurvitz that the language of the prose brackets in the book of Job must be dated to the period of late biblical Hebrew, i.e., the period of such books as Chronicles, Esther, etc. (see above, pp. 26 ff.). Beyond this, I will be intentionally vague about who should be understood to have redacted the book of Job and at what date (or, more likely, dates) the redaction(s) occurred. I will also be equally vague in regard to exactly who made the decision or series of decisions that brought Job and the other biblical books into the canon or at what date(s) such decisions took place. Our specific knowledge of the process of redaction and canonization of the Bible in general and Job in particular is far too limited for this process to be characterized in any but the most general terms. For a discussion of the problems involved with dating the book of Job, see, e.g., Pope, *Job* (N 2): xxxii–xl. On the date of the closing of the Canon, vis-à-vis the third division of Scriptures, the Writings, see S. Z. Leiman, *The Canonization of Hebrew Scripture; The Talmudic and Midrashic Evidence* (Hamden: Archon, 1976): esp. 26–50, 131–135. In general, I concur with Leiman's view that the canon of the "Old Testament" had already been closed in normative Jewish circles "through out the first centuries before and after the Christian era" (p. 135).

102. *Pseudepigraphal* is a designation used by scholars to label those ancient texts of a "biblical" type that never ultimately achieved canonical status (see N 99) within Judaism or Christianity. A collection of the Pseudepigrapha (lit. "false writings") in English translation was made some time ago by R. H. Charles (see [N 45]); more recently an expanded and updated collection of pseudepigraphal books has appeared, edited by J. H. Charlesworth (see [N 45]).

103. The Greek text of this work is available in a critical edition: *Testamentum Iobi; Apocalypsis Baruchi Graece* (S. P. Brock, J.-C. Picard, eds.; Leiden: Brill, 1967). A more accessible Greek text with English translation is *The Testament of Job* (R. A. Kraft *et al.*, eds.; Missoula, MT: Scholars, 1974). Most recently, a new English translation, and running commentary with an excellent introduction and bibliography has been published by R. P. Spittler, "Testament of Job; A New Translation and Introduction" in Charlesworth (N 45):

vol. 2, 829–868. See further, Baskin (N 7): 29–32; Besserman (N 7): 41–51; H. Cavallin, *Life After Death; Paul's Argument for the Resurrection of the Dead in 1 Cor 15; Part 1, An Enquiry into the Jewish Background* (Lund: Gleerup, 1974): 160–163; John J. Collins, "The Testamentary Literature in Recent Scholarship" and "The Testament of Job," in *Early Judaism and Its Modern Interpreters* (R. A. Kraft and G. W. E. Nickelsburg, eds.; Philadelphia: Fortress, 1986): 276–277 and supporting bibliography thereto; idem, "Testaments," *Jewish Writings of the Second Temple Period* (M. E. Stone, ed.; Philadelphia: Fortress, 1984): 349–354 and esp. the bibliography on p. 354; G. W. E. Nickelsburg, *Jewish Literature between the Bible and the Mishnah* (Philadelphia: Fortress, 1981): 241–248 and notes; E. Urbach, *The Sages; The World and Wisdom of the Rabbis of the Talmud* (I. Abrahams, trans.; Cambridge: Harvard University Press, 1987): 411 and 867–868, n. 68. See now the collected essays in Knibb and van der Horst (N 4); esp. R. Spittler, "The Testament of Job: a History of Research and Interpretation," 7–32. This volume reached me too late to be considered in this study.

104. *Testament of Job* 27:2–5. The translation here follows Spittler, (N 103): 851. For a discussion of the wrestling image employed by this and other early Christian commentators to connote the struggle of Job with Satan, see M. Poliakoff, "Jacob, Job, and Other Wrestlers: Reception of Greek Athletics by Jews and Christians in Antiquity," *Journal of Sport History* 11 (1984): 48–65, esp. 49–54. I am grateful to my colleague Ronald Hock for drawing this reference to my attention.

105. *Testament of Job* 27:7. The translation here follows Spittler, (N 103): 851. Note that the Greek terms for "endurance" and "patience" once again find echoes in the Epistle of James 5:11; see the discussion above in N 4.

106. *Testament of Job* 18:6. The translation follows Kraft (N 103): 41. I have borrowed the terminology of Spittler here ([N 103]: 846, n. d) in calling this passage the "parable of the beleaguered sailor."

107. *Testament of Job* 6:4–11. The translation follows Spittler, ibid., 841.

108. Baskin (N 7): 32.

109. There also exists a literary work called the *Life of Job*, written by Aristeas (not necessarily to be identified with the author of the famous Letter of Aristeas) and quoted by Eusebius in *Praeparatio Evangelica* 9.25, 430d–431. The picture of Job apparently found in this work falls in line with the traditional viewpoint and with that found in the Testament of Job. He, too, is a patient sufferer who endures a testing by God. The Friends in this case act as genuine comforters. Eusebius continues in his remarks on the *Life*: "While he was being comforted, he [Job] said that even without comfort he would be steadfast in piety in such trying circumstances. God, amazed at his high courage, freed him from illness and made him master of many possessions." For the text, see C. R. Holladay, *Fragments from Hellenistic Jewish Authors*, vol. 1, *Historians* (Chico: Scholars, 1983): 268–273; also, Robert Donan, "Aristeas the Exegete" in Charlesworth (N 45): vol. 2, 859; Baskin (N 7): 29 and esp. 139, n. 93; P. W. van der Horst, "The Interpretation of the Bible by the Minor Hellenistic Jewish Authors," *Mikra; Text, Translation, Reading and Interpretation of the Hebrew Bible in Ancient Judaism and Early Christianity* (M. Mulder and H. Sysling, eds.; Philadelphia: Fortress, 1988): 543.

Mention should also be made of the Book of Tobit, especially in the tradition preserved in the Vulgate. Tobias, the hero of this book in the Apocrypha, is depicted as a virtuous and pious man, very much after the model of Job. Early in the account, he is blinded. At that point Jerome's rendering of Tobit includes an added comment over the Greek tradition where the implicit reminiscence of the Job theme is made explicit and explained as a trial of Tobias' patience: "In fact, this temptation therefore the Lord permitted to occur to him so that an example of his patience [*patientiae eius*] might be given to posterity just like that of holy Job [*sancti Iob*]" (2:12). In the account that follows, Tobias remains steadfast, despite the challenges of kinsmen. Again Jerome's version adds a phrase where these challenges are compared to those of the "kings" who castigated Job (2:15). Naturally, Tobias, like the traditional Job, remains steadfast and does not cry against God (*non est contristatus contra Deum*) for the blow that he has endured (2:13). More generally, it seems clear that to a large extent, the story of patient Job (probably in a tradition also reflected in some of the additions to the Septuagint version of Job; see below pp. 339 ff.) served as a model for a number of episodes in the book of Tobit. For a discussion of this issue, see D. Dimant, "Use and Interpretation of Mikra in the Apocrypha and Pseudepigrapha," in *Mikra*, op. cit., 417–419.

For the citation from the Vulgate, see *Biblia Sacra iuxta Vulgatam Versionem* (R. Weber, ed.; Stuttgart: Württembergische Bibelanstalt, 1969). For a fuller discussion of the passage in Tobit and its relationship to the *Testament of Job*, see Besserman (N 7): 34–35.

110. See the discussion by Spittler as well as the supporting bibliography (N 103): 833–834; also Collins, "Testaments" (N 103): 353; Baskin (N 7): 30. A full history of the discussion of the date and provenance of the *Testament of Job* can be found in Spittler's comprehensive "Annotated Chronological Bibliography," Kraft (N 103): 17–20.

111. Spittler (N 103): 829.

112. By employing the singular here, I do not wish to imply that the *Testament of Job* in its entirety was necessarily the composition of a single individual. Certainly, a good case can be made for the view that there is more than one editorial level to this work (see, e.g., ibid., 833–834). Still, I tend to believe that it is, by and large, the composition of a single individual. In any case, whether one author or several authors and redactors should be posited for the *Testament of Job*, the issues we are considering here remain largely the same.

113. This count is based upon the list of cited references that Spittler supplies in the margin of his translation and commentary on the Book of Job; see ibid., 839–868. His list, however, is almost certainly not comprehensive; thus, "over 60" specific references is probably a most conservative estimate.

114. The fact that no records of such debates on the sanctity or canonicity of Job are preserved in the early rabbinical writings should not be cited as "proof" that such debates never did occur. We should recall that very few debates by the rabbis of *any* sort along this line are preserved in respect to the Jewish Canon. This likely indicates that by the beginning of the Common Era, all essential canonical issues, by and large, had long been settled, just as Leiman suggests in his consideration of this issue (see N 101). Given such a circumstance, any full-blown debate on the appropriateness of a book's position in the canon would likely have seemed close to being blasphemous by the rabbis. Even if such debates did occur, pious compilers and editors of the rabbinical traditions might well have hesitated to include very much of this sort of material in the various haggadic or halakhic compendia. Thus, we should not be so much surprised that debate on Job's sanctity or canonicity is not to be found; rather, we should consider ourselves fortunate to be the recipients of any such, similar debates from this early time.

115. For a convenient recent survey on various specific interpretations of the Song of Songs, especially recent scholarly attempts to characterize more precisely its genre, see Marvin H. Pope, *Song of Songs; A New Translation with Introduction and Commentary* (Anchor Bible vol. 7C; Garden City: Doubleday, 1977): 89–229; esp. 192 ff.

116. R. Gordis, *The Song of Songs and Lamentations* (rev. ed.; New York: Ktav, 1974): 1.

117. See Tosefta, Sanhedrin 12:10.

118. TB Sanhedrin 101a.

119. That is, the tannaitic rabbis active in the first two centuries C.E. We are focusing our attention on these Jewish leaders in particular simply because only the records of their disputes (as opposed to those of other Jewish religious groups or sects) have come down to us in reference to the appropriateness of particular books being in the canon. I do not wish to imply, however, that the decisive rulings on which books were to achieve canonical status

and which were to be excluded came down solely (or even partially) from the early rabbis or their *direct* predecessors. The evidence on the process of canonization of the Hebrew Scriptures is too limited for one to reach such a conclusion. Nonetheless, we will, once more, operate under a working assumption similar to one I have already stated above (see N 99): specifically, that despite the obviously wide range of specific opinions that divided Jewish groups in the Maccabean period and later, there was nonetheless a broader consensus on how to characterize God's relationship to Israel and an individual's proper pietistic stance vis-à-vis the Deity.

120. We should take some care in defining precisely the sense of *mṭm' 't hydym*, "defiles the hands," as used by the rabbis in reference to scriptural (and other) writings. For a comprehensive list of all the relevant references as well as a full discussion of the proper sense of this technical phrase as used by the rabbis, see Leiman (N 101): 102–120. Leiman contends that the expression is used to connote whether a text was sacred, (i.e., divinely inspired) or not. Nonetheless, it is possible for a text to be canonical (i.e., authoritative for religious practice) without being inspired in this manner. As regards Song of Songs, however, the issue is of less importance. As we shall see, the rabbis (especially Rabbi Aqiba) defended the appropriateness of Song of Songs presence in the Bible on the grounds that it was indeed inspired. Thus, for all intents and purposes, the distinction between sacredness and canonicity affects our discussion very little.

121. See M Yadayim 3:5; the translation largely follows Leiman, (N 101): 105–106.

122. In saying this, I do not mean to imply that at the time of Aqiba the question of whether Song of Songs should be admitted into the canon was at issue. As noted above, I am inclined to agree with Leiman that the decision on the canonicity of Canticles was made much earlier than this (see N 101). Rather, Aqiba's remarks (and for that matter the remarks of those rabbis who debated whether Song of Songs "defiled the hands") are in reference to the status quo. The issue is not whether Song of Songs should be admitted into the canon but rather, in consideration of the fact that it is in the canon, how does one justify its presence there?

123. Pope, *Song of Songs* (N 115): 92.

124. I do not wish to imply that the view that Perets' story is a satire is at all new. Clearly, as is already indicated in various sources cited above (see Ns 80, 93 in reference to Miller [N 65], Wisse [N 80], Adler [N 80], Roskies, "Lost Book" [N 80] and Madison, *Yiddish* [N 77]; idem, "Peretz" [N 77]; note, as well, Roback [N 88]): 290–298) this has long been understood in many critical circles. Still, to my knowledge, no study has gone into the detail of how the satiric parody works. Indeed, outside of Roskies ("Lost Book," 20), no scholar to my knowledge has specifically classified "Bontsye Shvayg" as a parody.

125. Wiener (N 65): 210–211. Note, too, that Wiener's judgment and interpretation of "Bontsye Shvayg" probably did a great deal to set the popular perception of this story. Roback ([N 88]: 294–295) comments, "Bontsye Shvayg was one of the earlier tales of Perets. At first it passed unnoticed in the Jewish literature. It was only after Professor Wiener (of Harvard University) in his *History of Yiddish Literature in Nineteenth Century* translated this story in the chrestomathy, which he appended to his work, that Bontsye Shvayg became a widely-circulating reference."

126. Samuel (N 65): 74. We will return to a consideration of Samuel's interpretation of "Bontsye Shvayg" later in this study; see pp. 71 ff. Also note S. W. Baron, who states that Perets "depicts how Bontsye Shvayg, meek and unassuming in life, is ultimately recognized in Heaven in his truly tragic grandeur." (*The Russian Jew under the Tsars and Soviets* [New York: MacMillan, 1976]: 153.) Consider, too, the comment of A. Posy in *Mystic Trends in Judaism* (New York: Jonathan David, 1966): 187, which comes close to Wiener's view but at the same time places "Bontsye Shvayg" in a far more expansive context:

He [Perets] takes us into a fantastic world which is all spirit, spirit that pushes everything material aside, and prevails, even when it loses the struggle on the physical plane. It is that extraordinary world where the heart rules over the mind, a world that treads out the path for the Messiah. But it is not an invented world. It is reality, a world where the essence of Judaism has its home, and to which—robed in modern dress—the present new generation could adjust itself.

127. See above p. 40.

128. See the discussion above in N 75 and further, pp. 75 f.

129. Wisse (N 80): 22; see also Roskies comments, "Lost Book," (N 80): 23.

130. There are, of course, many examples where the "Ozymandias effect" has resulted in the misapprehension of satire. One case that is particularly insightful is the song "Sonny Boy," made popular by Al Jolson in the movie *The Singing Fool* in 1929. As David Ewen notes:

"Sonny Boy" was the first song written for the talking screen that became a giant success. It was a last-minute replacement for another number which was judged unsuitable. Jolson frantically telephoned [Bud] De Sylva, [Lew] Brown and [Ray] Henderson from California, reaching them in Atlantic City, New Jersey, where they were working on a show. Jolson urged them to write a special number that would fit in with the plot of the movie: a widowed father who is deeply devoted to his little son who dies. De Sylva, Brown and Henderson wrote their song hastily, passing it off to Jolson as a serious effort at sentimental balladry, but actually intending its maudlin lyric and saccharine melody to satirize sentimental songs. Jolson took it seriously and sang "Sonny Boy" in the film where it became so popular that it was largely responsible for the giant box-office draw of the picture. See David Ewen, *All the Years of American Popular Music* (Englewood Cliffs, NJ: Prentice-Hall, 1977): 382.

While one cannot convey here the weeping melody (carried primarily by yet another saccharine violin!) nor the tearful, "Mammy"-type delivery Jolson always gave to the song, the lyric can well convey the flavor of the satirical parody by which the writers mocked Jolson and his public—a singer and an audience whose hearts fed all the more eagerly:

Climb upon my knee, Sonny Boy!
Though you're only three, Sonny Boy!
You've no way of knowing,
There's no way of showing,
What you mean to me, Sonny Boy!

When there are grey skies,
I don't mind the grey skies,
You make them blue, Sonny Boy!

Friends may forsake me,
Let 'em all forsake me!
I still have you Sonny Boy!

You're sent from heaven,
And I know your worth,
You've made a heaven
For me here on earth!

When I'm old and grey, dear,
Promise you won't stray dear,
For I love you so, Sonny Boy!

Finally, after a sentimental musical refrain, a final verse concludes the song:

> And the angels grew lonely,
> Took you because they were lonely!
> Now I'm lonely too, Sonny Boy!

(© 1955 Chappell & Co., Stephen Ballentine Music Publishing Co. and Ray Henderson Music; all rights reserved; used by permission.)

131. Pinsker (N 75): 64–65.

132. Madison, *Yiddish Literature* (N 77): 115; also idem, "Perets" (N 77): 88.

133. See above, p. 72.

134. For a recent, convenient survey of this period, see S. Ettinger, "The Modern Period" in *A History of the Jewish People* (H. H. Ben-Sasson, ed.; Cambridge: Harvard University Press, 1976): 881–890. See further, e.g., S. Dubnov, *History of the Jews* (M. Spiegel, trans. and rev.; London: Yoseloff, 1973): vol.5, pp. 512–588; idem, *History of the Jews in Russia and Poland* (I. Friedländer, trans.; Philadelphia: JPS, 1916): vol. 2, 154–473; vol. 3 esp. 7–31; 66–120; Dawidowicz (N 93): esp. 39–69; Baron (N 126): 26–153; G. Israel, *The Jews in Russia* (S. L. Chernoff, trans.; New York: St. Martin's, 1975: 31–117; C. S. Heller, *On the Edge of Destruction; Jews of Poland between the Two World Wars* (New York: Columbia University Press, 1977): 13–45; J. Frankel, *Prophecy and Politics; Socialism, Nationalism, and the Russian Jews, 1862–1917* (Cambridge: Cambridge University Press, 1981): esp. 49–132. For the cultural and literary background of the period, note especially, Miron, *Traveler* (N 93); D. G. Roskies, *Against the Apocalypse* (Cambridge: Harvard University Press, 1984): esp. 53–108; Mintz (N 24): 109–154.

135. Dawidowicz (N 93): 46–47.

136. Ibid., 47; see also, e.g., Mintz (N 24) 110–111; Roskies, *Apocalypse* (N 134): 65.

137. See, e.g., Dawidowicz (N 93): 48.

138. Ibid.

139. For a survey of the entire period, see S. Liptzin, *The Flowering of Yiddish Literature* (New York: Yoseloff, 1963); for Perets, esp. 98–116. I have employed the phrase "flowering of Yiddish literature" in conscious imitation of Liptzin.

140. In connection with this, note the observations of Glatstein (cited from Howe and Greenberg, *Voices* [N 93]: 54):

> Deep down, Jewish life had not yet shaken out of its long slumber—at least not until Perets consciously set out to create *a Jewish nineteenth century* shortly before the century was over. In Yiddish he reconstituted its general inquietude and fever, its mass of problems. And in that consists his strength and achievement, for Perets brought us into the marching ranks of the world as conscious Jews. He joined us to the great ebb and flow of the world at large. Creating a whole Jewish century, he wove it into the cultural history of the world.

Note also the observations of Roskies regarding the turn to Hasidism at the end of the nineteenth century:

> [At] the end of the nineteenth century, we find Jewish political action suddenly turning inward in the wake of reaction and repression in Tsarist Russia. Political Zionism and the Jewish Labor Bund, officially launched in the same year (1897), shared the realization that the Jewish Problem had somehow to be addressed from within. This lent credence to a reassessment, among other things, of Hasidism, as an invaluable and indigenous cultural resource. To be sure, the image of Hasidism . . . was colored by a romanticism as much as the earlier battle [which gave rise

to the *Haskala* movement] had been fought in the name of rationalism. Thus abstracted, Hasidism became the ideal vehicle for expounding the new "isms" of the twentieth century without foregoing a commitment to tradition.

(D. G. Roskies, "The Emancipation of Yiddish," *Prooftexts* 1 [1981]: 29.)

141. Of course, Perets was not the only major writer of Yiddish and Hebrew in his time to turn to satire and parody as a means of exposing the dangers of an unthinking turn to piety in response to the pogroms of the 1880s. In fact, satire and parody were common genres employed in Yiddish writing, and, in this respect, Perets was following long standing tradition (see above, Ns 80, 93). Note, in this connection, the discussion of parody in Yiddish literature in general, particularly in the works of S. J. Abramowitsch (via his persona, Mendele Moykher-Sforim) by Miron, *Traveler* (N 93): 1–129; esp. 51–63; see also idem., "Folklore and Anti-folklore in the Yiddish Fiction of the Haskala," *Studies in Jewish Folklore* (F. Talmage, ed.; Cambridge: Association for Jewish Studies, 1980): 219–249; Roskies, *Apocalypse* (N 134): esp. 63–78. Note, further Mintz's discussion of the Hebrew works of Abramowitsch (*Beseter ra'am*, "Secret Thunder" and *Hanisrafim*, "The Beggars"), Saul Tchernichowsky (*Barukh mimagentsah*; "Baruch of Mainz") and Ch. N. Bialik (*Ba'ir haharegah*, "In the City of Slaughter"; for a recent translation, see A. M. Klein in Roskies, *Destruction* [N 71]: 160–168) as satires that attacked the pious, martyrological response of Eastern European Jewry (as especially manifest in Jewish "Lamentations-type" writing) to the pogroms (Mintz [N 24]: 117–154). These same works (and others) are also similarly discussed by Roskies, *Apocalypse*, op. cit.

142. There can be little question that Perets self-consciously chose to write in Yiddish in order to reach and educate the broader mass of Jews. Thus Madison ("Perets" [N 77]: 76) notes, "Perets realized from the beginning that Yiddish, crude and rudimentary as it seemed for literary purposes, was the only language with which to address the Jewish mass. He adopted it, therefore as his own mode of expression. In 1890 he wrote: 'We want to educate the people, and we need to write in Yiddish because we have about three million souls who understand only Yiddish.'" The quote comes from Perets' essay "Education" (*Bildung*), his preface to the first volume of the *Yidisher bibliotek* of 1890—probably very near to the time when "Bontsye Shvayg" was written. Elsewhere in the same preface Perets further stated:

Our program is education. We want to educate the people: to turn fools into wise men; to make educated persons out of fanatics, out of idlers and ne'er-do-wells—workers; useful, respectful people that work for themselves and thereby benefit us all. . . . We say simply: We Jews are people like all people! We have virtues, we have faults. We are neither gods nor devils, but people. And human beings need to educate themselves, to learn understanding, to become wiser, better, finer with every passing day.

(The translation here basically follows Madison, "Perets" [N 75] but also benefits from the guidance of Jeffrey Shandler. For the Yiddish, see Pinsky [N 65]: 3–17; for a complete translation of the essay in English, see *Stories from Peretz* [ed., S. Liptzin; New York: Hebrew, 1947]: 214–221.)

The emphasis here on turning fools into wise, educated men, religious fanatics into intelligent believers and on seeing Jews as no specially chosen saints (or devils) are clearly themes that "Bontsye Shvayg" endeavors to speak to. Moreover, when, after a hiatus of two years as a publisher and editor, Perets turned specifically to this education in Yiddish with the publication of his anthology *Literatur un lebn* (N 65) in 1894, the theme of "Bontsye Shvayg"—the first story in the anthology—was clearly foremost in his mind. This is particularly manifest in the way he began the introductory article in this work: "After two years of silence [*shvaygn*], I return to Yiddish literature." As Sh. Niger states, further quoting from this same preface: "Perets could not, or, more correctly, was no longer forced to *be silent* [*tsu shvaygn*] in his literary and cultural activities, and once again he put forth his call to the Jewish intelligentsia and with this argument, that 'four million Jews must remain here, and for these four million one must work *in situ*, and the intelligentsia must, to that end, make as its chief goal the education of the folk.'" See Sh. Niger, *Y. L. Perets* (Buenos Aires: Yiddish Cultural Congress, 1952): 225; cf. 226. Once again, I am grateful to Jeffrey Shandler who aided me in translating Niger from the original Yiddish.

Finally, we should note that Perets was not only willing to write but to act on his beliefs as well. For this reason he met with numerous socialist groups and taught them by reading his stories. Indeed, at one such meeting in 1899 he was arrested by the authorities and served several months in jail. According to Esther Hautzig, one of the stories he read at this meeting was "Bontsye Shvayg" (*"The Case Against the Wind" and Other Stories by I. L. Peretz* [Esther Hautzig, ed. and trans.; New York: Macmillan, 1975]: xii).

143. Mintz notes that a similar misreading was made of a Tchernichowsky's satire, "Baruch of Mainz" (see above N 141) by its contemporary audience. In particular, one section of the poem presents a series of curses, based on biblical models, that the protagonist, Baruch, hurls at the brutal gentiles who perpetrated the pogroms. Mintz comments, "By itself this section was one of the high points of the poem for the contemporary audience, those who were able to read it in its uncensored version; its malediction of the Gentiles was daring for the literary conventions of the times, both externally and internally imposed, and it had the effect of giving vent to pent up rage." Roskies (*Apocalypse* [N 134]: 82) makes a similar observation: "Hailed as a prophetic response to the Kishinev pogrom, this most accessible of Tchernichowsky's narrative poems . . . soon occupied a central place in the secular liturgy of the Zionist movement." But Mintz further notes, "Yet read within the sequential context of the poem, this rage against the Nations . . . is undercut by irony: While the Nations do indeed deserve to be damned, we know that Baruch's project of damnation has originated in his need to alleviate his own guilt." (Mintz [N 24]: 127–128).

144. Another Perets story, "The *Shabes-goy*" underscores a similar point. In this case Perets depicts a poor Jew—Yankele by name—who is continually beaten by the *Shabes-goy*, a gentile whose job it is to do small chores that are forbidden to Jews on the Sabbath for the community in Chelm. When Yankele seeks the advice of the Chelmer rabbi, the rabbi counsels passivity. Moreover, the rabbi tries to place the blame for the problem of Yankele's mistreatment everywhere but on the *Shabes-goy*. Finally, when the problem becomes too difficult to handle easily, the Chelmer rabbi reaches what seems to him the only possible conclusion: Yankele must leave the community. Moreover, the *Shabes-goy*, the rabbi concludes, must also finally be dealt with—but in a rather unusual manner: "Now, in order to appease his resentment, and with the object of redeeming the entire community from dire peril, let us give the *Shabes-goy* a raise, a larger portion of the Sabbath loaf, and *two* drinks of brandy instead of one. And what else? Perhaps he'll have compassion!" Perets obviously wants his readers to understand how absurd the advice of the Chelmer rabbi is. After all, everyone knows how simple-minded the people of Chelm are! Still, he concludes the story with a caution that seems all too pertinent in the time of the pogroms: "You're laughing? Still, there is a little of the Chelmer rabbi in each of us."

For the story in Yiddish, see Pinsky (N 65): vol. 9, 49–63. For this translation by Etta Blum the only one in English to my knowledge, (see Weinrich [N 65] who does not note any other translation), see Howe and Greenberg, *Selected Stories* (N 76): 49–57. See also the discussion in Madison, *Yiddish Literature* (N 77): 108–109.

145. Another example in which Perets has piled on the qualifiers for parodistic effect involves the description of the seat being prepared for Bontsye's procession upon his entry into heaven. The idea that a saint, especially a martyred saint, would have special seating in Paradise is well established in Jewish legend. Note, for example, how Rabbi Eleazar ben

Shamu'a's comments to his students on the final end for martyred saints at the conclusion of the *Harugei Malkhut* passage of Midrash Eileh Ezkerah: "My children, I also behold the soul of each and every righteous creature purifying itself in the water of Shiloah in order to enter the heavenly academy in purity this day. . . . Each and every angel will bring golden thrones upon which the righteous souls will all sit in purity." (The translation follows Roskies, *Destruction* [N 71]: 69; for further discussion of the "Thrones of Paradise" see, e.g., Ginzberg, *Legends* [N 19]: vol. 5, 418–419.)

There can be little doubt that it is a legendary figure of this nature that lies in the background of Perets' description of the golden throne being prepared for Bontsye in Paradise. But note that he qualifies this traditional symbol by making it not merely a golden throne but actually an "easy chair" (*fotershtul*) of finest gold, and if that is not enough, he adds to it a set of wheels! Thus an archetypical reward for the purest of saints is turned into an ever so slightly absurd ambulatory armchair—that can only make one wonder (at least in retrospect) just how saintly Bontsye really is.

146. It seems altogether likely that Perets structured his story's conclusion to play off of a common folkloric genre. In this type of story the protagonist is offered anything he wishes. Instead of being greedy and asking for the greatest material gain, the hero proves his worthiness and humility by asking for the least rather than the most he could have. Often in such a story, the wise but humble request of the hero is contrasted with the foolish, greedy demand of an antagonist—the former being rewarded for his humility, the latter being punished for his avarice.

Such a genre of story manifests itself as early as the famous tale of Solomon's request for Wisdom in 1 Kings 3:4–15 and certainly existed in hasidic folk legends with which Perets was likely familiar. B. Orenstein briefly surveys the literature on Perets' use of hasidic legend, even citing a possible specific precedent for Bontsye's request in a story ascribed to Baal Shem-Tov, in *I. L. Peretz's Bontche Shweig and V. G. Korolenko's Makar's Dream; a Comparative Literary Study* (Montreal: Jewish Cultural Club, 1965): esp. 35–42 and notes.

Of course, the irony here is that Perets parodistically inverts the normal correspondences of the genre, a reversal first signaled (as just noted) by the piling up of the qualifiers of *bulke* (i.e., "roll") in Bontsye's request, and then confirmed by the Prosecutor's laugh. After all, a key point in the standard form of the story is that the hero is either clever or sincerely humble. If the protagonist is clever, then he realizes that there is a "trick" in the offer to have anything he desires. He accordingly circumvents the trap by asking for the least instead of the most (knowing that the most will then be granted to him). If the protagonist is sincerely humble, then out of his pure simplicity he asks for little or nothing at all—never dreaming that a great reward will be granted because of this humility. One can, for example, see elements of both sagacity and humility in Solomon's request. Perets injects the Prosecutor's laugh at the conclusion of his story in order to underscore that Bontsye has neither of these characteristics; rather, he is both stupid and greedy.

For a discussion of a fairy-tale type, encompassing similar themes, see R. Darnton, *The Great Cat Massacre* (New York: Basic, 1984): 60; also A. Aarne and S. Thompson, *The Types of Folktale; A Classification and Bibliography* (2d ed.; Helsinki: Academia Scientiarum Fennica, 1964): 122, see tale-type 330.

I am grateful to Prof. Dov Noy for pointing out to me the relevance of this folkloric genre to "Bontsye Shvayg."

147. See Esther Hautzig, *"The Seven Good Years" and Other Stories of I. L. Peretz*, (Philadelphia: JPS, 1984): 8.

148. The image of Isaac as both sacrifice and survivor was a guiding influence on Elie Wiesel when he focused on the term "holocaust," as a term connoting burnt offering, religious sacrifice, to characterize the Jewish genocide by the Nazis. For Wiesel, the *Akedah*

always serves as the backdrop for the Holocaust. For a full discussion of Wiesel's coining of "The Holocaust" and the implications thereof, see Z. Garber and B. Zuckerman, "Why Do We Call the Holocaust, 'The Holocaust'? An Inquiry into the Psychology of Labels" in *Remembering for the Future; Papers to be Presented at an International Scholars Conference to be Held in Oxford, 10–13 July, 1988; Theme 2; The Impact of the Holocaust of the Contemporary World* (Oxford: Pergamon, 1988): 1879–1892; also in slightly different form in *Modern Judaism* 9 (1989): 197–211.

149. Interview with Heywood Hale Broun in 1974 in I. Abrahamson, "Introductory Essay," *Against Silence; The Voice and Vision of Elie Wiesel* (3 vols.; ed., I Abrahamson; New York: Holocaust Library, 1985): vol. 1, p. 56. See further Abrahamson's comments pp. 54–58. The concept of silence as the only possible response to incomprehensible wrong is a major theme in Wiesel's novel, *The Oath*.

150. L. Edelman, "The Use of Words and the Weight of Silence," interview of Elie Wiesel in *National Jewish Monthly* (November, 1973) in Abrahamson (N 149): vol. 2, 82; see also Abrahamson, "Introductory Essay," ibid., vol. 1, 56.

151. E. Wiesel, "From Holocaust to Rebirth," Herbert R. Abeles Memorial Address, 39th General Assembly of the Council of Jewish Federations and Welfare Funds, Kansas City Missouri, November 14, 1970 in Abrahamson (N 149): vol. 1, 239.

152. "Victims of God," review of *Selected Stories by I. L. Peretz*, ed. by I. Howe and E. Greenberg; *The New Republic* (September 21, 1974); cited in Abrahamson (N 149) vol. 2, p. 321. It might be assumed that Wiesel has meant this statement to be taken as ironical; however, it seems to me more likely that he wishes to view Bontsye's words as emblematic of the sort of understatement that he himself has always strived for in his own writing. Indeed, in one description of the creative process in his writing, Wiesel has characterized the process very much in the image of a Bontsye who is at first silent and then speaks as little as possible:

> Before I write I must endure the silence, then the silence breaks out. In the beginning there was silence—no words. The word itself is a breaking out. The word itself is an act of violence; it breaks the silence. We cannot avoid the silence, we must not. What we can do is somehow charge words with silence. If one of my novels is only words, without silence, I do not even reread or publish it. The unspoken is as important as the spoken: the weight of silence is necessary. (H. A. Walker, "How and Why I Write," interview with Wiesel in *Journal of Education* [Boston University, Spring, 1980]; in Abrahamson [N 149]: vol. 2, 119.)

153. Elie Wiesel, *Night* (New York: Avon, 1969): 63.

154. Ibid., 112–113.

155. This is also true of the story "The *Shabes-goy*," mentioned above (see N 144). Once again, events of the twentieth century have validated as reality what Perets meant to be seen as patently absurd. In this case it is the reality of the policy of appeasement to Hitler in the years before the invasion of Poland that transforms Perets' story from satire into a history before its time. One can hardly laugh so easily at the Chamberlain-like decisions of the Chelmer rabbi after the British and French appeasement to the demands of Hitler at Munich.

156. Hautzig, *Wind* (N 142): xiii. Note in this connection Darnton's discussion of French eighteenth century peasant stories, which emerged against a cultural and social background of desperate poverty and want ([N 146]: 33):

> Wishing usually takes the form of food in peasant tales, and it is never ridiculous. . . . Once supplied with magic wands, rings, or supernatural helpers, the first thought of the peasant hero is always for food. He never shows any imagination in his ordering. He merely takes the *plat du jour*, and it is always the same: solid peasant fare. . . . Usually the peasant raconteur does not describe the food in detail. Lacking any notion

of gastronomy, he simply loads up his hero's plate; and if he wants to supply an extravagant touch, he adds, "There were even napkins."

157. Once again, this point has been made by Wiesel who characterizes Bontsye as someone continually victimized: "Poor Bontsye: he doesn't even know what to yearn for, how to dream of something good, something beautiful. But who is to blame? Mankind, which has humiliated him too long? God who did not intervene soon enough? Whatever shame emerges in that tale does not belong to Bontsye but to the others, all the others." (Wiesel, "Victims" [N 152]: 322.) I am particularly grateful to the late Dr. Abraham Zygielbaum, himself a survivor of the Nazi concentration camps, for sensitizing me to the need to see Bontsye as victim rather than a fool in a post-Holocaust world.

158. Roskies, "Lost Book" (N 80): 23.

159. See above, p. 61.

160. It is notable that Perets' "The Three Gifts" (see N 83) was similarly subverted in the Holocaust environment. Roskies comments,

> . . . the archetype of martyrdom that it sought to burlesque was simply too strong. The readers of Yiddish now faced ever-greater tests of their collective will and they needed modern texts to help them cope with unwarranted suffering. And so Perets' story was pressed into action and never more forcefully than during the Holocaust. Dina Abramowicz, the chief librarian at the YIVO Institute, recalls that in the Vilna ghetto the story was read as a call to arms! ("Lost Book" [N 80]: 23.)

161. Note, in this connection, the Czech novelist Josef Bor's *The Terezin Requiem* (E. Pargeter, trans.; New York: Knopf, 1963), a semifictional account of a performance of Verdi's *Requiem* by the Jewish inmates of Theresienstadt, narrated from the standpoint of the conductor, Raphael Schächter. As S. D. Ezrahi notes in her discussion of this work (*By Words Alone* [Chicago: University of Chicago Press, 1978]: 19),

> The Requiem is, on the night of the performance, transformed by these artists into a cry of protest: Schäcter takes the liberty of amending the libretto by answering the four pianissimo notes of the finale—the conciliatory "libera me" ["release me"]— with a defiant fortissimo "libera *nos*," ["release *us*"] delivered by the entire orchestra and choir as four fighting blows (the three short and one long strokes of Beethoven's Fifth Symphony).

For this alteration of Verdi, Schäcter begs forgiveness: "O Saint Verdi in heaven, forgive me my sin; if you had been in a concentration camp you, too, would composed your finale differently. . . ." (Bor, op. cit., 83.)

162. E. Greenberg, "Y. L. Perets un Bontsye Shvayg in Varsaver Getto" in *Di lange nakht* [*The Long Night*] (New York: Lipkaner Besaraber sosayeti, 1946): 16–19.

163. Ibid., 17, stanza 11. This picture of Job on the ash heap was somewhat altered to a depiction of Job on a dunghill in the Septuagint. Of course, this scene became proverbial in depictions of the Job legend; see the discussion in Besserman (N 7): 38–39 and note especially his collection of artistic representations of Job on his ash heap or dunghill from the medieval period (116–128).

164. See below, N 167.

165. Greenberg, "Perets un Bontsye" (N 162): 18; stanzas 18, 19–20. In Yiddish the passage reads:

Kh'vil its fun zikh aroysshrayen alle yorn shvaygn
Kh'vil du zolst a tsung, zolst its mir loshn gibn!
. . . .
Tsu zayn an eydes, vi s'hot di velt geshvign, vi geshvign s'hot der boyre

Ven m'hot undzer shtam gekoset—kind un keyt, dem evyen vi dem yosher!
—Bashafer mayner, ruf oyfsnay di gantse velt tsu a din-toyre,
Nor loz mikh, dem eybikn shvayger, zayn atsind zeyer melets yosher!

Loz mikh oyfefenen di eybik-farsolesene lipn,
Vos zaynen a lebnlang geven mit shavygenish farziglt!
Loz mikh oyfpraln das harts, vos hot a lebnlang gekhlipt
In shvaygenish—oyf toyznt riglen fest farriglt! . . .

Once again, I am grateful for the guidance of Jeffrey Shandler in translating passages here and below from this poem into English.

166. Ibid., stanzas 21–22. The Yiddish reads:

Zayn yomer shteygt, un geyt ariber in a vildn voyen,
Zayn kol shlogt-op atsind vi volf-un-toyb gebrum.
Biz der morgn nemt zikh tsindn mit fibershn shegeon—
Un Perets yomert un Bontsye yomert—un s'glivert der arum.

Eykoh yoshboh bodod hoir rabbosi om hoysah kalmonoh . . .
Hazos hoir sheyomru kelilas yofi mosus l'kol ho'orets . . .
Tsevy yidn shokln zikh baym shayn fun an oysgayendiker levone,
Fun gantser shtot geblibn zaynen Bontsye un Y. L. Perets.

Note that the first two lines in stanza 22 (printed in boldface in the original edition) quote in Hebrew from Lamentations 1:1 and 2:15 respectively, where the destruction of Jerusalem by the Babylonians is bewailed.

167. In the poem Greenberg has Bontsye demand this change of role from *bashafer mayner* (lit. "creator, mine"). There is, in all likelihood an intentional ambiguity that the poet wished to establish by this particular phrasing. Contextually, the "creator" involved could be Perets. Note, in this respect that Perets is specifically designated as Bontsye's creator (*zayn bashafer*) in line one of stanza thirteen. In this case Greenberg's Bontsye demands of his artistic creator a rewrite of his story with the roles therein reassigned. But on a more expansive level, the referent may also be seen as God, the Creator of all, who has just been unambiguously invoked above at the beginning of the stanza, the poet using the Hebrew *boyre* (Creator) rather than the Yiddish *bashafer*.

168. See N 166.

169. Howe and Greenberg, *Selected Stories* (N 76): 18; also idem., "World" (N 76): 48. A fuller quotation of their remarks appears in N 76.

170. Ibid. They specifically state that, in writing "Bontsye Shvayg," Perets "does seem a little like Kafka"; In "World" ([N 76]: 48) they also make passing mention of Nietzsche.

171. Note, in this respect, that when Howe and Greenberg put together their largest collection of Yiddish stories, they dedicated their work "to the Six Million." Thus, it would seem clear that they view their work in Yiddish literature as an homage to the victims of the Holocaust and that the historical reality of the Holocaust was a strong (if not the strongest) motivating factor informing their efforts. See *Treasury* (N 65); dedication page.

172. See above, p. 66 and Ns 152 and 157. It is noteworthy that Wiesel's comments on "Bontsye Shvayg" were in a review of an anthology of Perets' stories edited by Howe and Greenberg—one in which their interpretation of the story is given a clear exposition. Nowhere does Wiesel suggest that his view of Perets' story is at variance from that of Howe and Greenberg; indeed, the entire tenor of his review suggests that he endorses their depiction without significant reservation.

173. See p. 66.

174. Wiesel, "Victims" (N 152): 322.

175. Ibid.
176. Ibid; for a fuller quotation of his remarks see N 157.
177. Ibid.
178. See the quotations cited above, pp. 65 ff. and in N 152.
179. See Samuel (N 65): 74; cited in part above on p. 59. Note that he also classifies *Dray matones* ("The Three Gifts") in the same manner, ignoring the irony of the story's conclusion; see above Ns 83 and 160.
180. Samuel (N 65): 7.
181. Ibid.
182. Ibid., 6.
183. Ibid., 6–7.
184. Ibid., 8–9.
185. Ibid., 7–8.
186. Ibid., 9–10.
187. See Madison's article "Perets" (N 77), written in 1928 as well as his larger study *Yiddish Literature* (N 77), written in 1968. Also, see above (N 80) where Madison's temporizing remarks on "Bontsye Shvayg" were previously mentioned.
188. Madison, *Yiddish Literature* (N 77): 115.
189. Ibid.
190. See above, p. 40.
191. Madison, *Yiddish Literature* (N 77): 115.
192. Madison makes a similar statement about the figure of Bontsye in his 1928 article: "Yet Perets loved the poor man [i.e., Bontsye], even as he loved the old messenger. He sympathized with his whole-hearted piety, with his simple thinking and with his human wholesomeness. And he was grieved because Bontsye was taken advantage of by mean and unscrupulous people; and the poetic justice he deals him in heaven he deals him with his heart." (Madison, "Peretz" [N 77]: 88).
193. See the discussion above, pp. 41 ff.
194. See Madison, "Peretz" (N 77): 88.
195. Madison, *Yiddish Literature* (N 77): viii.
196. We should also remember that even before the Holocaust, East European Jewry had been subjected to an ever growing cycle of violence. Roskies' comments are cogent:

> In all the pogroms of 1881–1883, fewer Jews were killed than in Kishinev during Passover of 1903; the forty-nine casualties of Kishinev, in turn, paled before the 800 dead in the pogroms of 1905–1906 (over 300 in Odessa alone). And in the 726 pogroms that broke out in 1905–1906 fewer than half as many Jews were murdered than in Proskurov on February 15, 1919. After that, the numbers hardly matter, we may accept Simon Dubnow's figure of 60,000 dead in the Ukrainian civil war of 1918–1919 or go as high as the 250,000 of the other estimates. (*Apocalypse* [N 134]: 82.)

Quite obviously, these progressively murderous blows had to have an impact on the popular conception of Bontsye and would appear to have had a direct effect upon Madison's judgment of the story even in his critical comments before the onset of the Holocaust.
197. See pp. 40 f.; also N 75.
198. Pinsker (N 75): 65, 66.
199. Ibid., 64.
200. Ibid., iv.
201. The alterations in the text of "Bontsye Shvayg" discussed here are to be distinguished from the changes made in the story between the editions of 1894 and 1901 (see

above, N 65). To my knowledge, no study of Perets or "Bontsye Shvayg" has drawn attention to these alterations; nor have I been able to uncover any specific documentary evidence by which to determine whether the changes instituted in the 1901 version of the story were Perets' own revisions or rather reflect the efforts of an editor.

Nonetheless, it seems altogether likely that the revisions were made by Perets himself. For one thing, considering that the 1901 collection was done in Warsaw in honor of the author's 50th birthday and his 25th year as a writer, it seems scarcely credible that any alteration in "Bontsye Shvayg" would have been done without his approval. More likely, the changes in the text reflect the author's own refinements, which he desired to get on record in this Jubilee edition. We should note, too, that from 1901 forward it is this revised edition of Perets' story that essentially becomes the edition of record—the edition that, for example, Pinsky reproduced in his compendium of all of Perets' writings, *Ale verk* (see N 65) and on which most translations of the story have since depended.

Besides, in all cases, the changes found in the 1901 edition really *are* refinements. In my opinion, they all—without exception—have the effect of tightening up the narrative and heightening the impact of its message. Since these revisions sensitively enhance "Bontsye Shvayg," it is hard to believe that such careful changes could have come from anyone else but Perets. Finally, we should note that the revisions are fairly extensive. Altogether, excluding minor spelling variations, I have collated some 77 specific changes between the editions of 1894 and 1901. Once again, it is difficult to assume that anyone but the author himself would have taken such liberties with the text. For a comprehensive collation of the changes between the 1894 edition and the 1901 edition of "Bontsye Shvayg," consult the appendix.

Most of the revisions made to "Bontsye Shvayg" in the 1901 edition are minor (e.g., small adjustments in word choice or syntax); however, several are more substantial and thus worthy of specific mention. They are as follows:

1. Part of the introductory paragraph of the story:

   1894: *Fregt emitsn bekheyrem ver Bontsye iz gevesn, vi azoy er hot gelebt, af vos er iz geshtorbn!*

   Just ask anyone who Bontsye was, how he lived, what caused his death!

   1901: *Fregt emitsn bekheyrem:* ver *Bontsye iz gevesn,* vi *azoy er hot gelebt, af* vos *er iz geshtorbn!*

   Just ask anyone: *who* Bontsye was, *how* he lived, *what* caused his death!

2. The comparison of men to tramway horses in the first part of the story:

   1894: . . . *es zol zayn toyznt milyon ferd vi mentshn!*

   . . . if there were a thousand million horses just as there are men!

   1901: . . . *es zol zayn azoy fil ferd vi mentshn—toyznt milyon!*

   . . . if there were as many horses as men—a thousand million!

3. The introduction to the third, climactic attempt by the Prosecuting Angel to initiate his challenge to Bontsye's integrity:

   1894: *Endlikh hert zikh, fun dem eygenem haldz aroys, a veykh kol vi a puter* . . .

   Finally there can be heard, coming out from that very same throat, a soft voice, just like butter . . .

   1901: *Endlikh hert zikh, fun dem eygenem haldz aroys, kimat a veykh kol* . . .

   Finally, there can be heard, coming out from that very same throat, what almost seems a soft voice . . .

4. The description of what Bontsye sees just before he responds to the Presiding Judge near the conclusion of the story:

1894: *Er vert vi farblendt fun der likht fun ale zaytn; alts blankt, alts blishtshyet, fun alts yogn shtraln: fun di vent, fun di keytlim, fun di malokhim, fun di dayonim! Same zunen!*

He is just about blinded by the light on all sides; everything sparkles, everything flashes, beams shoot out from everything: from the walls, from the vessels, from the angels, from the judges! A kaleidoscope of suns!

1901: *Er iz vi farblendt; alts blankt, alts blitst, fun alts yogn shtraln.*

He is just about blinded; everything gleams, everything flashes, beams shoot out from everything.

5. The Presiding Judge's urging Bontsye to ask for his reward from Heaven at the conclusion of the story:

1894: *Kloyb un nem vos du vilst, du nemst nor bay dir aleyn.*

Choose and take what you wish. You only take what belongs to *you*, alone!

1901: *Voren alts vos do blankt un blitst iz nor an opshayn fun deyn farshvaygener gutkeyt; an opglants fun dayn neshomeh! Du nehmst nor bay dir aleyn!*

For all that gleams and flashes is only a reflection of your mute goodness; a reflection of your soul! You only take what belongs to *you*, alone!

In the instances of revisions cited here, Perets has reworked his story either to simplify and therefore intensify the impact of the narrative line (examples 2 and 4), to draw a more dramatic picture of Bontsye's wretched circumstance (example 1), or to sharpen the dramatic irony of his satire (examples 3 and 5).

These last two revisions are particularly noteworthy. In the first case (example 3) Perets appears to have decided to alter slightly the role of the Prosecuting Angel. As we noted above (see N 81), when this Satanic accuser responds in a voice "soft as butter," Perets leaves an implication that the Prosecutor has not been entirely fooled by the silence of Bontsye. In the 1901 edition, the Prosecutor is not so depicted, rather he too is shown to be a reluctant convert who must accede to Bontsye's victorious piety in a "what almost seems a soft voice."

The alteration in the second case (example 5) is even more dramatic. In the earlier version the Presiding Judge states that Bontsye may ask for whatever he wants, since everything belongs to him in any case. However, in the revision Perets adds an extra phrase in which the Presiding Judge further clarifies the justification for this largess on the part of Heaven: because "all that sparkles and flashes is only a reflection of your [Bontsye's] mute goodness, a mirror of your soul." In other words, Perets draws special attention to the fact that it is the presumed piety of Bontsye—a goodness that comes from his silence (*fershavygener gutkeyt*)—that is the reason all Heaven wishes to reward him. This addition thus allows the writer to lay on one more oversentimental statement by which to emphasize just how misguided the view of Heaven is. And, as usual, there is an undercurrent of irony. The depiction of Bontsye's goodness as a reflection that sparkles and flashes also carries connotations of a blinding mirage. What all Heaven sees is not Bontsye's true self but a false reflection thereof—the moral equivalent of an optical illusion.

Overall, the changes Perets apparently made in his story served his purpose well. But we should also recognize that these changes can be double-edged—especially the latter two just discussed above. That is, they can be all too easily shorn of their satirical purpose by an audience intent on canonizing Bontsye. When this is done, they may be read as yet further confirmation that Bontsye was meant to be the very model of pious goodness, not merely a reflection of the purest of souls but a mirror which a traditional audience could hold up and in which they might see the "goodness" in themselves.

202. That is, the translation found in Howe and Greenberg's popular anthology of Yiddish Literature, *Treasury* (N 65) and also reproduced in their *Selected Stories* (N 76).

203. Perl N 85. The second part of this drama (pp. 15–21) is a reworking of "Bontsye Shvayg." This play was first presented on Broadway in 1953 and has had numerous productions, even including a televised rendition, since then.

204. Overall, Abel's translation may be properly criticized not only for being needlessly paraphrastic but also for seriously misconstruing Perets' intentions in a number of instances. Note, in this respect, that Miller labels this treatment "the most accessible . . . but unfortunately not satisfactory for serious reading . . ." since it "takes unwarranted liberties with the sense of the Yiddish text"; (N 65): 46, n. 3; see also n. 7. I have already noted two instances in Abel's translation of broad paraphrase that can therefore be misleading (see Ns 71 and 72). In another particularly notable instance Abel misjudges the syntax of a phrase and gives a drink, which Perets meant for the Defending Angel, instead to Bontsye. The Yiddish simply reads, *Eynmol—firt vayter der meylets-yoysher nokh a trunkvaser—iz in zayn lebn a shine gevorn* [1901 edition: *an enderung geshen*], " 'Once,' the Defending Angel continues after a sip of water, 'a change came to his [Bontsye's] life.' " Abel renders: " 'Once,' the defending angel went on, 'Bontsye crossed the roadway to the fountain for a drink, and in that moment his whole life was miraculously changed.' "; see Miller, op. cit., n. 8.

For an earlier discussion of paraphrase in Perl's work, see N 85.

205. See above, p. 58 and N 73.

206. See Howe and Greenberg, *Treasury* (N 65): 230; idem., *Selected Stories* (N 76): 77. A shorter excerpt of Abel's rendering is cited above in N 73.

207. See pp. 70 f.

208. I have touched upon the connection of Abel to Howe and Greenberg previously; see above, N 76.

209. On the image of Abramowitsch as Mendele, the "grandfather" of Yiddish literature, a persona that Sholom Aleichem developed and fostered, see Miron, *Traveler* (N 93): 28–33.

210. Perl (N 85): 15.

211. Ibid., 21.

212. See above, pp. 20 f.

213. Perl (N 85): 15.

214. Miller (N 65): 46; cf. nn. 2, 9; see also Roskies' comments, "Lost Book" (N 80): 20.

215. Of course, the argument I am making here is vulnerable to an obvious criticism— that there is no reason to assume that "our perspective," that is, the perspective presented in this study, is any less influenced by historical forces than any other. Why should it be assumed, therefore, that this viewpoint shows less prejudice than the ones rejected above as "wrong"?

I can only admit the validity of such a criticism; but I can also offer an apology in defense of my view. The apology is based on a midrash in *Lamentations Rabbah* and its interpretation by Alan Mintz. The midrash reads as follows:

> Rabbi used to expound the verse "The Lord laid waste without pity" [Lam. 2:2] in twenty-four ways. R. Yohanan could expound it in sixty. Could it be that R. Yohanan was greater than Rabbi? Rather because Rabbi was closer in time to the destruction of the Temple, he would remember and stop to weep and console himself. He would

begin again only to weep, console himself and halt. R. Yohanan, because he was not close in time to the Destruction of the Temple, was able to continue to expound without pause. (*Midrash Echa Rabbati* [ed., S. Buber; Vilna, 1899]: 100.)

The dilemma posed by this midrash is, as Mintz notes, "How is it possible that Rabbi Judah the Prince, called simply Rabbi, the compiler of the Mishnah and the preeminent sage of the period, could be bested in interpretive ingenuity by R. Yohanan his disciple. . .?" But the Midrash has an explanation. Rabbi Judah lived close to the times of the horrific Bar Kokhba conflict (132–135 C.E.) whereas Yohanan was of the following generation. Therefore, as Mintz puts it, Yohanan was "not burdened by the same weight of memory" as Rabbi Judah and could proceed to expound the scriptural passage with far greater freedom; Mintz (N 24): 50–51; the translation from Lamentations Rabbah follows Mintz.

By the same token, I would not claim any superior ability to interpret Perets and "Bontsye Shvayg" over the critics cited above. However, what I would claim is that they, like Rabbi Judah, are, by and large, one generation closer to catastrophe than I am and thus burdened by a weight of memory that can only be less for me. If the perspective presented here is consequently less constrained by the forces of historical memory than the views of those who were closer to the Holocaust, it is only because the perspective is longer and the passions cooler.

216. See above, pp. 56 f.

217. See pp. 57 f.

218. For a recent discussion of the structure of Ecclesiastes with bibliography, see B. S. Childs, *Introduction to the Old Testament as Scripture* (Philadelphia: Fortress, 1979): 580–589; esp. 584–586.

219. R. B. Y. Scott, *Proverbs, Ecclesiastes; A New Translation with Introduction and Commentary* (Anchor Bible vol. 18; 2d ed.; Garden City: Doubleday: 1981): 191.

220. The term *qoheleth* the Hebrew designation for the author of Ecclesiastes, is not a proper name but rather a title (cf. 8:12 and probably 7:27 where the definite article is used: *hqhlt*, "the Qoheleth"). The designation probably connotes "one who assembles, gathers together" either students or collections of wise sayings for instruction—quite possibly both. The traditional designation from the King James Version—"the Preacher"—is an attempt to render *ekklēsiastēs*, "leader of the Church," the Greek term used in the LXX as a reflex of *(h)qhlt*; see G. W. H. Lampe, *A Patristic Greek Lexicon* (Oxford: Oxford University Press, 1976): 433 s.v. *ekklēsiastēs*. For a convenient, brief discussion of the term, see, e.g., Scott (N 219): 192–193 and, most recently, J. L. Crenshaw, *Ecclesiastes; A Commentary* (Old Testament Library; Philadelphia: Westminster, 1987): 32–34.

221. Reading *ktwb* as an infinitive rather than a passive participle.

222. Of course, it is certainly possible to assume more than one level of redaction reflected in the epilogue of Ecclesiastes; that is, we might assume that 12:9–11 represents one editorial hand while verses 12–14 reflect the activity of another editor; see, e.g., Crenshaw, *Ecclesiastes* (N 220): 189–190. However, whether there is or is not more than one editor involved really affects the approach presented here very little. The situation is essentially analogous to the one we considered above in reference to the redactional levels of Genesis 22 (cf. pp. 22 ff.). The important issue is that the ostensibly contrary views of verses 9–11 and 12–14 remain within the text; and, as Childs declares, "the crucial issue focuses on determining the effect of the epilogue on the interpretation of the book regardless of whether the addition derives from one or two editorial layers"; see Childs [N 218]: 585 and the bibliographical references cited there.

223. On the difficulties of *ky-zh kl-h'dm*, see, e.g., Charles F. Whitley, *Koheleth, His*

Language and Thought (Berlin, New York: de Gruyter, 1979): 105. I have adopted an approach that essentially follows R. Gordis, *Koheleth, the Man and His World; A Study of Ecclesiastes* (3d ed.; New York: Schocken, 1968): 355.

224. Scott (N 219): 194.

225. See, e.g., Leiman (N 101): 104–106 for a citation of the relevant references in the rabbinical literature.

226. See the discussion above, pp. 26 ff.

227. For a bibliography on this issue, see Rowley (N 36): 173–174 and notes; for a more recent survey, see Williams, "Current Trends" (N 36): 22–24 and notes. Note also the judicious survey of this issue in Pope, *Job* (N 2): xxxii–xl. His overall conclusion (p. xl) underscores the difficulties involved in dating Job: "The fact that the dates proposed by authorities, ancient and modern, span more than a millennium is eloquent testimony that the evidence is equivocal and inconclusive."

228. See, in this respect, the arguments of Hoffman cited above (Ns 36, 39). It is particularly noteworthy that one of the most recent full commentaries of Job to appear— Habel, *Job* (N 67)—essentially argues for the unity of the book of Job, primarily on literary grounds. He declares, "The book of Job reveals an underlying structure which gives coherence to the work as a literary whole" (p. 35; cf. his further discussion, pp. 35–69). Note also J. G. Janzen's discussion in his recent commentary, *Job* (Interpretation; Atlanta: John Knox, 1985): 15–24. For a defense of this "literary" approach to the Book of Job, regardless of whether it was composed by a single author or not, see Alan Cooper, "Narrative Theory and the Book of Job," *SR* 11 (1982): 35–44; also Cooper's review of Habel in *Theodolite* 7 (1986): 4–6. For a consideration of some weaknesses in this argument, see below N 230.

229. Note in this respect that even Robert Alter, one of the leading proponents of the "literary" approach to the interpretation of the Bible, nonetheless, accepts the "scholarly consensus that there are composite elements in the Book of Job, that it is not all the work of one hand." In particular, within the Poem of Job itself he further grants, ". . . there is fairly general agreement among scholars that [there are] interpolations for which the original Job poet was not responsible." (*The Art of Biblical Poetry* [New York: Basic, 1985]: 87.)

230. D. N. Freedman, "The Elihu Speeches in the Book of Job; A Hypothetical Episode in the Literary History of the Work," *HTR* 61 (1968): 51–59; see also, e.g., Pope, *Job* (N 2): xxvii–xxix. Stylistic departures also mitigate against the view that the Elihu speeches were written by the original Job poet; see the careful discussion of this issue by E. Dhorme, *A Commentary on the Book of Job* (H. Knight, trans.; London: Nelson, 1967): xcviii–cx; esp. civ–cv. An interesting (although, in my opinion, unconvincing) attempt has been made by Gordis to defend the Elihu speeches as coming from the same hand as the rest of the Poem of Job despite the problems outlined here. He argues, "The style of the Elihu chapters is by no means totally different from the rest of the book, but it does exhibit variations. These are entirely explicable by the assumption that the Elihu section emanates from the same author writing at a later period of his life." (*God and Man* [N 30]: 110). For a survey of the scholarly discussion on the Elihu speeches, see Rowley (N 36): 146–151; for more recent discussions and bibliography, see Williams, "Current Trends" (N 36) 16–17; Vermeylen (N 36): 23–24 and notes.

Arguments along the lines of Habel (*Job* [N 67]: 36–37) that the Elihu speeches should be seen as part of the original composition of Job because they are "an integral part of the structure of the book" (see also his more detailed comments in "The Role of Elihu in the Design of the Book of Job," in *In the Shelter of Elyon; Essays on Ancient Palestinian Life and Literature in Honor of G. W. Ahlström* [W. B. Barrick and J. R. Spencer, eds.; Sheffield: JSOT, 1984]: 81–98; esp. 92–96) are vulnerable to an obvious criticism. Even granting that the Elihu speeches serve an integral role in the structure of Job as we now have it, this does not necessarily prove that they must therefore have been authored by the same writer who composed the rest of the Poem. The integration of the Elihu speeches into the greater structural whole could just as easily have been done "after the fact" by an author who perceived a weakness or inadequacy in the original structure of the book and then proceeded to address this problem with the addition of the Elihu texts.

Consider, in this respect, as an analogous example, another illustrious Ancient Near Eastern literary composition, the Gilgamesh epic. Few would deny that the prologue to the epic (tablet 1, lines 1–26) or the extended discussion of the flood by Utanaphistim are now integral parts of the structure of this work. (For the most up-to-date translation of these passages, see M. Kovacs, *The Epic of Gilgamesh* [Stanford: Stanford University Press, 1989]: 3–4, 97–103; see also E. A. Speiser, "Akkadian Myths and Epics" in Pritchard [N 51]: 61, 91–97.) Yet the empirical evidence is considerable that neither section was a part of the Old Babylonian version of Gilgamesh. Only in the later editions of the epic were these sections interpolated into the text. Still, as J. H. Tigay declares, "Though the editors of these [later] versions made their own creative contributions to the epic both in the poetic rephrasing of older poetic passages and in the composition of new lines and sections, they were clearly transmitting in revised form a text that was essentially the work of an earlier author." ("The Evolution of the Pentateuchal Narratives in Light of the Evolution of the *Gilgamesh Epic*," *Empirical Models for Biblical Criticism* [J. H. Tigay, ed.; Philadelphia: University of Pennsylvania Press, 1985]: 21–52; esp. 35–42; the quotation is on p. 39; see further, the more detailed discussion in Tigay's *The Evolution of the Gilgamesh Epic* [Philadelphia: University of Pennsylvania Press, 1982]: *passim*, esp. 140–158; 214–240). It is not unreasonable to assume that a similar process of interpolating development might have acted on the book of Job and brought the Elihu speeches (as well as other additions) into its structural framework.

231. Pope, *Job* (N 2): xxvii. See the discussion and scholarly survey of Rowley (N 36): 166–169; for a more recent discussion, see Lévêque (N 37): 593–606; Vermeylen (N 36): 13–15. Again, Habel ([N 67]: 38–39) can be considered representative of those who defend the Hymn to Wisdom as authored by the original Job poet on literary-structural grounds.

232. See, e.g., the summary discussion by Pope, *Job* (N 2): xxviii–xxix. For a more detailed consideration and bibliography, see Rowley (N 36): 164–166 and notes; for more recent surveys, see Williams, "Current Trends" (N 36): 17; Vermeylen (N 36): 24–27 and notes.

233. Another proposed interpolation sometimes suggested by scholars is chapters 29–31, Job's final speech. See, e.g., R. J. Williams' declaration: "I submit that chapters 29–31, as more than one scholar has maintained, are likewise secondary" ("Theodicy in the Ancient Near East," *Canadian Journal of Theology* 2 [1956]: 22). For a survey of various scholarly theories regarding additions to Job, see Rowley (N 36): 167–169; see further the various proposals by Vermeylen (N 36): *passim*; esp. 15–23 and his conclusion, 80–81.

234. For the moment we will consider this issue outside of the text-critical problem of the relationship between the book of Job as found in the Masoretic text tradition versus and that in the LXX text tradition. For a consideration of this latter issue, see below, pp. 167 ff. and esp. N 493.

235. Note, too, that there are a number of philological and textual difficulties in this passage, which may indicate that it has undergone some corruption as well as misplacement. See, e.g., the discussions by S. R. Driver and G. B. Gray, *A Critical and Exegetical Commentary on the Book of Job* (ICC; 2 vols.; Edinburgh: Clark, 1921): vol. 1, 211; Dhorme, *Job* (N 230): xlv–xlvi; Pope, *Job* (N 2): 195; even Habel (see *Job* [N 67]: 357–358), who generally hesitates to argue against the integrity and the overall unity of Job (see above N 230), feels constrained in this instance to accept the likelihood that the text has been corrupted and misplaced. In contrast, for a recent defense of the integrity of the Third Cycle, see D. Wolfers, *Dor le Dor* 16 (1987/1988): 217–226.

236. Note, in this respect, that the first line of Bildad's speech (25:2a), "Dominion and awe are with him" (*hmšl wpḥd 'mw*), has no clear referent; that is, the antecedent of "him" is unexpressed. Moreover, in the following two verses this lack of specificity continues. Only in verse 4a is it finally made clear that Bildad's speech refers to God (*wmh yṣdq 'nwš 'm-'l*, "How then can Man seem just to God?"). No other similar construction, in which the antecedent follows a pronoun to which it refers, can be found in any of Job's or his Friends' previous speeches. This appears to be a clear indication that originally there were other verses preceding the first preserved verse of Bildad's speech. Presumably, somewhere in these missing verses the now lacking antecedent was originally to be found. See, e.g., Driver and Gray (N 235): vol. 1, 214–215; Dhorme, *Job* (N 230): 368. For a similar example, also apparently from a misplaced speech in the Third Cycle, see below, N 238. Note that the Targum of Job from Cave 11 (9:4) at Qumran is sensitive to this lack of antecedent in Job 25:2 and translates "with him" as "with God," undoubtedly using vs. 4a as a guide (cf. Pope, *Job* [N 2]: 181; B. Zuckerman, *The Process of Translation in 11QtgJob; A Preliminary Study* [Ph.D. diss.; Yale University, 1980]: 297).

237. See, e.g., the remarks of Driver and Gray (N 235): vol. 1, 216.

238. The situation here is analogous to that noted above for chapter 25 (cf. N 236); namely, the referent in vs. 6a ("Naked is Sheol before Him," *'rwm š'wl ngdw*) and in the following verses is unquestionably God. Still, the entire passage is left without a grammatical antecedent; that is, nowhere in the text is God specifically mentioned. Once again, this points to the likely conclusion that Job 26:5–14 represents only a fragment of what was once a longer doxology.

239. This does not mean that scholars have not made heroic efforts to do precisely this. For a survey of scholarly efforts to rework the Third Cycle of speeches in the Poem of Job, see, e.g., Rowley (N 36): 162–164 and the bibliography cited therein.

240. See p. 26 and N 36.

241. R. H. Pfeiffer, "Edomitic Wisdom," *ZAW* 44 (1926): 13–25 esp. 17–22. Pfeiffer also cites earlier scholarly antecedents to this proposal (p. 17); see also Pfeiffer's "The Dual Origin of Hebrew Monotheism," *JBL* 46 (1927): 193–206.

242. Cf. especially Obad. vs. 8, Jer. 49:7; see more generally, the discussion by Pfeiffer, "Edomitic Wisdom" (N 241): 13–14. Note that Pfeiffer is careful to make a distinction between the Prose Frame Story and the Poem of Job: "It is by no means certain that the Volksbuch of Job, in its present form, was written by the author of the dialogue. The poem is based on the old story, but not on its extant transcription, which may very well be the work of a Jew." Nonetheless, Pfeiffer argues, the "Edomitic character" of the folktale, for instance, the association of Job with the "land of Uz" (*'rṣ 'wṣ*, Job 1:1); the "sons of the East" (*bny-qdm*, Job 1:3); and also the fact that Job's friend Eliphaz is a Temanite (Job 2:11, etc.), may once again reflect the original context of the legend which inspired the Poem. See ibid., 13, 17.

243. See the general discussion in Tur-Sinai, *Job* (N 38): viii–li and throughout his verse-by-verse commentary.

244. The most prominent advocate of this theory has been A. Guillaume, *Studies in the Book of Job with a New Translation* (J. MacDonald, ed.; Leiden: Brill, 1968): esp. 1–15; also idem, "The Arabic Background of the Book of Job," *Promise and Fulfillment: Essays Presented to S. H. Hooke* (F. F. Bruce, ed.; Edinburgh: Clark, 1963): 106–127. Also note the earlier study, F. H. Foster, "Is the Book of Job a Translation from an Arabic Original?" *AJSL* 49 (1932–1933): 21–45.

245. Note, in this respect, the survey and evaluation by J. Barr, "The Book of Job and Its Modern Interpreters," *BJRL* 54 (1971): 35; see also Williams, "Current Trends" (N 36): 9–10.

246. *Northwest Semitic* is the technical designation used by linguists to classify the family of Semitic languages (especially ancient languages) in the area of Syria-Palestine (on *Syria-Palestine*, see the following note). These include the so-called Canaanite languages, of which Hebrew is the most prominently studied, as well as the Aramaic languages. For an overview of these languages and dialects during the biblical period, see most recently, W. R. Garr, *Dialect Geography of Syria-Palestine, 1000–586* B.C.E. (Philadelphia: University of Pennsylvania Press, 1985): 1–14 and notes. For earlier discussions of Northwest Semitic, cf., for example, W. L. Moran, "The Hebrew Language in Its Northwest Semitic Background," in *The Bible and the Ancient Near East; Essays in Honor of William Foxwell Albright* (G. E. Wright, ed.; Garden City: Doubleday, 1965): 59–84; H. L. Ginsberg, "The Northwest Semitic Languages," *Patriarchs; The World History of the Jewish People* vol. 2 (B. Mazar, ed.; New Brunswick: Rutgers University Press, 1970): 102–124.

247. Note Garr's comments at the conclusion of his survey of the dialect geography of ancient Northwest Semitic dialects (Garr [N 246]: 227):

> This analysis of shared innovations provides the basic information necessary to establish a dialectal continuum of N[orth]W[est]S[emitic] spoken in Syria-Palestine. Like a color spectrum, the continuum is bordered by two polar extremes. Between these extremes lie dialects with intersecting linguistic elements, whose overall character displays greater affinities to one or the other pole. The result is a series of closely interrelated dialects which form a dialect chain.

I have employed the term *Syria-Palestine* as the specific geographic designation for the area in which the ancient Northwest Semitic languages and dialects were spoken in conformity to conventional linguistic custom.

248. In this respect, it is interesting that scholars have noted linguistic affinities between the language of the Poem of Job and that of the texts recently discovered at Deir Alla in Jordan (c. eight to seventh century B.C.E.; on the dating, see, e.g., the paleographic discussion by Jo Ann Hackett, *The Balaam Text from Deir 'Alla* [Harvard Semitic Monographs 31; Chico, CA: Scholars, 1980]: 9–19). For a discussion of these affinities, see, e.g., J. Hoftijzer and G. van der Kooij, *Aramaic Texts from Deir 'Alla* (Leiden: Brill, 1976): *passim*, esp. 275–276 with n. 14. The Deir Alla dialect, like the dialect found in the Poem of Job, has stirred considerable debate as to its proper linguistic classification; for a discussion and survey of opinions, see, e.g., B. Halpern, "Dialect Distribution in Canaan and the Deir Alla Inscriptions," in *Working with No Data; Semitic and Egyptian Studies Presented to Thomas O. Lambdin* (D. Golomb, S. Hollis, eds.; Winona Lake, IN: Eisenbrauns, 1987): 119–139. As Garr states, "Examination of the Deir Alla dialect has yielded classifications as Old Aramaic, Ammonite, South Canaanite, Midianite, and Gileadite" ([N 246]: 2). More properly, the Deir Alla dialect should be viewed as falling within the dialect spectrum somewhere between Hebrew and Moabite, on the one hand, and Aramaic on the other (ibid., 229).

249. This is not to say that the Poem of Job does not make reference to other divine beings known from other Canaanite texts, especially those discovered at Ras Shamra (ancient Ugarit) in Syria. Note, e.g., the focus upon the divine dragon (*tnyn*), sometimes called Leviathan or Rahab (see Job 3:8, 7:12, 9:13, 26:12–13, 41:1 ff.); Yam, the god of the sea (7:12, 26:12, see also 3:8; note, e.g., the discussion in Pope, *Job* [N 2]: 30); Resheph, depicted as an engenderer of pestilence (Job 5:7; note Pope's translation: "Man, indeed, is born for trouble, And Resheph's sons wing high."; see ibid., 41, 42–43; note also the discussion in W. J. Fulco, *The Canaanite God Resep* [New Haven: AOS, 1976]: 58); and Behemoth, apparently a divine, bovine monster perhaps not all that dissimilar to the "Bull of Heaven" encountered by Gilgamesh (Job 40:15 ff.; see Pope, op. cit., 320–323); possibly

also Mot, the god of Death (Job 18:13; see once again, Pope's comments, ibid., 135; N. Sarna, "The Mythological Background of Job 18," *JBL* 82 [1963]: 314–318; also further below, p. 119). The famous phrase in Job 38:7 ("When the morning stars sang together, and all the sons of God shouted for joy," *brn-y ḥd kwkby bqr wyry'w kl-bny 'lhym*) also appears to be a reference to a divine pantheon with numerous deities (see, e.g., Pope, op. cit., 292).

Still, in fairness, it must also be noted that a number of similar references can be found throughout the Bible, especially in the Psalms and in the prophetic literature.

250. An important point bearing on this issue involves the names utilized for the deity throughout the Poem of Job. With one problematic exception (Job 12:9; also note the use of *'dny* in 28:28 [discussed below, p. 138 with N 423]), nowhere is the special, Israelite/Jewish national name of God, *Yhwh*, ever employed in a poetic passage. This omission represents strong (if circumstantial) evidence that the religious-cultural milieu for the original Poem of Job may well have been distinct from that in which the rest of the Bible evolved. The fact that the Prose Frame Story and the short phrases introducing each speech in the Poem employ *Yhwh* at every obvious opportunity, lends credence to the assumption that they are secondary interpolations that the Poem attracted once it had found it way into more normative Israelite/Jewish circles (see below, pp. 138 ff.).

For a discussion of the divine names in Job, see, e.g., Dhorme, *Job* (N 230): lxv–lxxii. On the secondary nature of Job 12:9, see, e.g., B. Duhm, *Das Buch Hiob* (Freiburg: Mohr, 1897): 67; Dhorme, *Job* (N 230): 175. The fact that there is a reminiscence of Isa. 41:20 in Job 12:9 has caused some scholars to argue that this is a conscious quotation of the former by the latter (e.g., R. Gordis, *The Book of Job; Commentary, New Translation and Special Studies* [New York: JTS, 1978]: 138). On the other hand, it is just as easy to argue that the use of *Yhwh* in Job 12:9 is a simple harmonization that could have occurred quite late in the textual history of Job. See the discussion immediately below.

251. Note, in this connection, the intriguing discussion of typological change by F. M. Cross, "Alphabets and Pots: Reflections on Typological Method in the Dating of Human Artifacts," *Maarav* 3 (1982): 121–136. In the course of developing postulates for typological analysis he argues, "the discipline of typological analysis does not operate merely on the assumption of change or innovation in time. Equally important is a paired postulate: that a typological sequence always reveals a continuity of types. Each emergent type is related to, and continuous with its antecedent type" (p. 127).

As an example relevant to this point, Cross cites the development of Israelite religion (p. 131):

> The religion of Israel has been conceived of as a unique, isolated phenomenon, radically or wholly discontinuous with its environment. . . . The claim that Israelite religion "was absolutely different from anything the pagan world ever knew" to quote the late, great Yehezkel Kaufmann is now being swept away under an avalanche of archaeological evidence. But his claim never should have been made. It violates fundamental postulates of scientific historical method. The empirical historian must describe novel configurations in Israel's religion as having their origin in an orderly set of relationships which follow the usual typological sequence of historical change.

252. I am treating "biblical Hebrew" as a unit here only for the sake of convenience. I certainly do not mean to imply that one can view the Hebrew of the Bible in a monolithic fashion. Clearly (despite efforts at standardization and leveling by later editors), there are a number of dialects and styles discernible under the broader umbrella of biblical Hebrew. The point I wish to make here is that the Hebrew of the Poem of Job is distinct enough to be set against the entire aggregate of other Hebrews subsumed under "biblical Hebrew."

253. Note especially the similarity of Job 3 and Jeremiah 20:14–18 which has been utilized by scholars as a basis for assuming a direct dependency of one on the other and thus as grounds for dating Job. See, e.g., S. Terrien, who states: "On est general d'accord pour decouvrir en Jeremie le terminus *a quo*" for the composition of Job (*Job* [Paris: Delachaux & Niestle, 1963]: 24). We will consider Job 3 more closely below, pp. 123 ff.

254. For a survey of opinions on the relationship of Second Isaiah to Job, see Williams, "Current Trends" (N 36): 22–23. Note especially the detailed discussion by S. Terrien, "Quelques remarques sur les affinites de Job avec Le Deutero-Esaïe," *VTSup* 15 (1966): 295–310; also Pfeiffer, "Dual Origin" (N 241): 202–206; idem., *Introduction to the Old Testament* (London: Adam & Charles Black, 1952): 467 ff.

255. Note, e.g., the suggestion that Ps. 8:5–7 is utilized and parodied in Job 7:17–18. Fishbane, for example, argues that the "exegetical revision" of the former by the latter is "sharp and clear."; see (N 38): 285.

256. Numerous examples can be cited of scholars assuming that the book of Job was an Israelite creation without even considering otherwise. For example, no less an authority than H. L. Ginsberg has forthrightly stated, "I am sure . . . that the author was a Jew, 100 percent" (Ginsberg, "Patient" [N 2]: 25) primarily because he views the book's focus upon issues of injustice in the world as peculiarly Jewish (p. 28). Note, similarly, the comments of T. Jacobsen, who sees Job as the product of "the religious genius of Israel" (*The Treasures of Darkness; The History of Mesopotamian Religion* [New Haven: Yale University Press, 1979]: 163) and F. M. Cross, who remarks, "There is a sense in which Job brought ancient Israelite religion to an end" (*Canaanite Myth and Hebrew Epic* [Cambridge: Harvard University Press, 1973]: 344; see also his further comments, pp. 344–346). For a recent discussion that works without further comment from this same assumption, see J. G. Janzen, "The Place of the Book of Job in the History of Israel's Religion," in *Ancient Israelite Religion; Essays in Honor of Frank Moore Cross* (P. D. Miller, P. D. Hanson and S. D. McBride, eds.; Philadelphia: Fortress, 1987): 523–537.

Pope, on the other hand, responds, "Without wishing to detract from ancient Israel's merited praise for concern about social justice and sensitivity to injustice . . . it does not seem reasonable to deny the possibility of this basically human reaction to non-Israelites" (*Job* [N 2]: xlii).

257. See above N 233.

258. The same point applies, of course, to the issue of whether the Behemoth/Leviathan section of the Theophany is a secondary addition. In a future study I hope to present a detailed consideration of this latter part of God's speech and its form and function within the Poem of Job. Suffice it to say here that I not only believe that the Theophany acted as the climax of the original Poem of Job but also that the Behemoth and Leviathan passages form a dramatic and thematically appropriate conclusion to the Theophany. For a recent defense of the Behemoth/Leviathan speeches as the "culminating images" of the Theophany, see Alter (N 229): 106–110.

259. Of course, once we speak of "Wisdom" in the Ancient Near East, there arises the question of how to define what this means. I am inclined to follow the view of G. Buccellati ("Wisdom and Not: The Case of Mesopotamia," *JAOS* 101 [1981]: 35–47; esp. 44) that Wisdom is best viewed as a tradition rather than as a literature. This is not to say that there is no "Wisdom Literature" but rather that Wisdom is better grasped in terms of a cultural phenomenon that had an effect on a broad range of literatures, even including texts not normally thought to be Wisdom works. For a recent discussion of the definition of Ancient Near Eastern Wisdom, including a survey of scholarly opinions, see Bolle (N 29): 12–43.

260. Sometimes an influx of new information can well illustrate the difficulties involved in isolating traditions played on in the Poem of Job. For example, only with the discovery of the Ugaritic tablets was it finally made clear that Leviathan/Rahab, alluded to several times in the Dialogue and, of course, the major focus of attention in Job 40:25 ff., was a fierce, supernatural, seven-headed dragon known from Canaanite legend, rather than a representation of an Egyptian crocodile, as many scholars had previously surmised; see the discussion by Pope, *Job* (N 2): 329 ff. On the other hand, the figure of Behemoth (40:15 ff.) is not known to us from attested extrabiblical material (not counting references to Behemoth in late sources, e.g., various pseudepigraphal texts or Jewish legend, which undoubtedly draw on Job as their primary source of information). Pope (ibid., 320 ff.) endeavors to make a case, based on context and circumstantial evidence, that Behemoth is a divine bull much like the Bull of Heaven from the Gilgamesh story. This may well be true, but the problem is that there is no specific evidence to muster in favor of the point. Until an ancient text (Canaanite or otherwise) comes to light, chronicling a saga of Behemoth (or similar beast), we will be basically unable to understand exactly how the poet was using the "Behemoth-tradition" (assuming there actually was such a tradition), because we do not *know* this tradition. On the other hand, such a presumed tradition would have certainly been well known to the Job poet's ancient audience; hence, the manner in which he manipulated this motif would also have been clear to them.

261. Sometimes also called the *Acrostic Poem*; see discussion below in N 293.

262. The edition of record for the *Theodicy* is that of Lambert, *Wisdom* (N 60): 63–91, which includes both a transcription of the text (with variants) and a translation. Other easily accessible translations are those of R. D. Biggs in Pritchard (N 51): 601–604 and of H. Schmökel in *Near Eastern Religious Texts Relating to the Old Testament* (W. Beyerlin, ed.; J. Bowden, trans.; Philadelphia: Westminster, 1978): 133–137 (containing only excerpts). For a listing of all published editions of this work in Akkadian, see Lambert's introduction, op. cit., esp. 68–69. For his remark on the text probably being known as late as the Seleucid period, see p. 63. We will rely on his text and translation (with further reference to the recent transcription/translation by Bolle [N 29]: 284–309) in the discussion that follows. For further discussion and bibliography on the *Theodicy* especially in reference to Job, see H.-P. Müller, *Das Hiobproblem* (Darmstadt: Wissenschatliche Buchgesellschaft, 1978): 51–53; Lévêque (N 37): 23–31 and notes. Also note the discussions in J. Gray, "The Book of Job in the Context of Near Eastern Literature," *ZAW* 82 (1970): 251–269; esp. 256 ff.; J. L. Crenshaw, "Popular Questioning of the Justice of God in Ancient Israel," *ZAW* 82 (1970): 381–395; Williams, "Theodicy" (N 233): 14–26; Bolle, op. cit., 195–230; and Albertson (N 47): 225–226 as well as the respective, supporting bibliographies.

263. For a consideration of specific parallels of this nature, see, e.g., Gray (N 262): 256–258; Crenshaw, "Popular" (N 262): 386–388; Lévêque (N 37): 24–27.

264. See, e.g., Job 9:23–24 versus Theodicy, lines 70–71; Job 21:7–13 versus Theodicy, lines 50–53.

265. See Job 4:7–8 versus *Theodicy*, lines 60–64.

266. See Job 17:1–7 versus *Theodicy*, lines 29–33.

267. In speaking of the "author" of the *Theodicy*, I do not mean categorically to exclude the possibility that this work was the product of more than one creative mind. Still, scholars generally assume that the *Theodicy* is essentially the work of a single writer (or, at least, I am not aware of a contrary opinion), and, moreover, the acrostic in the *Theodicy* even identifies who that author is; see below, the discussion in N 293.

268. Of course, it might be argued that the author of the Poem of Job was familiar with the *Theodicy* and was writing his work in conscious imitation of this particular, undoubtedly famous text. One point in favor of this assumption is that nowhere else in Mesopotamian

literature has a text in precisely this Dialogue-form ever turned up. Still, we should recall that literary texts (let alone Wisdom texts) are rare finds among Mesopotamian literature. The fact that no other Job-like Dialogue has been discovered is probably best attributed to happenchance rather than to the assumption that no similar texts existed. In fact, Lambert does make mention of at least one other text (apparently Middle Assyrian), which he declares "is clearly a dialogue, and the little that remains suggests a debate similar to the *Theodicy*" (*Wisdom* [N 60]: 90–91). However, considering that only a few phrases from this text are preserved without any clear context or continuity, it would be highly speculative to label this as another definite example of a Dialogue similar to Job. Mention should also be made of a text catalogued as RS 25.130, discovered at ancient Ugarit and published by J. Nougayrol in *Ugaritica* 5 (C. F. A. Schaeffer *et al.*, eds.; Paris: Geuthner, 1968): 291–297; see also Lévêque (N 37): 45–47. Nougayrol argues that this is a Dialogue text very similar to the *Theodicy* and, for that matter, Job (p. 292). It focuses on Ea/Enki, the god of Wisdom in Mesopotamia, and upon the sad lot of mankind, who, the text declares, has very little joy in life (lines 18', 20'). However, it is not clear from what remains whether the text is a Dialogue or, for that matter, whether it may be a Righteous Sufferer's Appeal.

There is one strong argument against the assumption that the *Theodicy* was the specific model employed by the poet of Job. If the *Theodicy* were the *only* Dialogue-model for Job, we might expect a much closer textual dependency of the latter on the former. (Contrast, in this respect, the relationship between the *Testament of Job* and the book of Job, where this close dependency is unmistakable; see the discussion above, pp. 51 f.) But such a dependent connection is not manifest between the *Theodicy* and Job; while both Dialogues touch on much the same themes, they do so in their individual ways. Thus, I am inclined to agree with Gray ([N 262]: 255) that the similarities in these texts "reflect the conventional language of the Plaint of the Sufferer . . . and are variants of this common literary type."

We should note in this connection the study of P. Skehan, "Strophic Patterns in the Book of Job," *CBQ* 23 (1961): 125–142. He argues that the lines in the Job Poem (especially in chapters 4–14) show a consistent patterning of 22 or 23 lines and that this constitutes "the deliberate equivalent of an acrostic based on the series of letters that make up the Hebrew alphabet" (p. 126). If so, this acrostic patterning—also manifest in the *Theodicy* (see below, N 293)—may be a convention used for Dialogue texts and thus another indication of the poet's adherence to the genre.

There is one other Mesopotamian text that appears in a kind of Dialogue-form. This is the so-called *Dialogue of Pessimism*. (For the text and translation, see Lambert, *Wisdom* [N 60]: 139–149; Biggs' translation in Pritchard [N 51]: 600–601; Bolle [N 29]: 311–317; E. A. Speiser, "The Case of the Obliging Servant," *JCS* 8 (1954): 98–105; cf. also Lévêque [N 37]: 27–29 and notes; Bolle, op. cit., 239–253 and notes.) In this text a master proposes first to do one thing and then to do its opposite. To each proposal, his slave gives immediate endorsement and proceeds to justify first the pro and then the con of the action. Finally, at the conclusion of this absurd litany of contrary proposals, the master asks the slave, "What then is good?" The slave responds that they should both have their necks broken and their bodies thrown in the river (lines 81–82). The *Dialogue of Pessimism* seems to highlight the hopelessness of the lot of mankind; and in doing so, it certainly touches on themes of Joban dimension. Still, the tenor of this text is quite different from that of Job or, for that matter, any other text within the Wisdom tradition. Hence, we should be cautious of an approach that sees this text as essentially the same sort of Dialogue found in Job or the *Theodicy*. The most prominent point in common between the *Dialogue of Pessimism* and the Joban Dialogue may be that they both appear to share a satirical purpose; see below, N 418.

Mention can also be made of the "contest fables" discussed above (see N 60). These, too, are in Dialogue-form, pitting one entity against another. But these contest texts show only a tenuous relationship to either Job or the *Theodicy* beyond the fact that they are all Dialogues between disputants.

Finally, we should note in passing that there is a sort of Dialogue-form in an Egyptian Wisdom text, the *Dispute over Suicide*, that depicts a man engaged in discussion with his soul as to whether life is worth living. (For the text, see J. A. Wilson's translation in Pritchard, op. cit., 405–407; R. O. Faulkner, "The Man Who Was Tired of Life," in *The Literature of Ancient Egypt* [W. K. Simpson, ed.; New Haven: Yale University Press, 1973]: 201–209; M. Lichtheim, *Ancient Egyptian Literature* vol. 1, *The Old and Middle Kingdoms* [Berkeley: University of California Press, 1973]: 163–169; for an earlier treatment, see A. Erman, *The Literature of the Ancient Egyptians* [trans., A. M. Blackman; London: Methuen, 1927]: 86–92; for a survey of scholarship see R. J. Williams, "Reflections on the *Lebensmünde*," *JEA* 48 [1962]: 49–56; also note the discussion in Lévêque op. cit., 63–67, esp. the bibliography cited on p. 63, n. 1.) This text does touch on a number of themes that are also found in Job (see Lévêque's discussion, ibid.) and the genre of text used here may have some relationship to the Dialogue-form in the Job Poem and the *Theodicy*. Still, once more, the emphasis in the *Dispute over Suicide* is a good deal different from that we find in either the *Theodicy* or the Job Poem. In particular, nowhere is the issue of the god's role in the plight of man ever an issue in this Egyptian work; see Williams, "Theodicy" (N 233): 18; Crenshaw, "Popular" (N 262): 380, n. 5.

Perhaps the only thing we can say about the Dialogue-form, as attested in the various texts discussed above, is that it seems in one way or another to be associated with a wide variety of texts that come out of the Wisdom tradition. As Buccellati suggests, "the correlation between wisdom themes and dialogic form is a very meaningful one: the dialog, pure and simple, emphasizes the unfolding of thought process viewed dynamically in its becoming"; see (N 259): 39.

269. I am making a distinction between texts of this nature and a very similar group of incantation texts from Mesopotamia as represented in the collection made by W. G. Lambert, "Dingir SA.DIB.BA Incantations," *JNES* 33 (1974): 267–322 and app. "Hittite Parallels," (by H. G. Güterbock), 323–327. Lambert notes that these texts are often (although not always) entitled "incantation for appeasing an angry god" (p. 267). I see these texts as somewhat different for two essential reasons. First, they are specifically incantations, i.e., texts recited, usually as part of a ritual, to relieve affliction. In such cases the assumption is that the recitation itself has efficacy. While the appeal texts below have a somewhat similar thrust, they are never specifically labeled as incantations, nor is it ever implied that their recitation is inherently efficacious. Second, in these incantations, the sufferer usually confesses his sin and often grants man's inherently sinful nature. In this respect, the appeal texts are distinctive, since the sufferer is deemed to be righteous.

On the other hand, while this distinction is useful, it should not be considered absolute; in particular, we should not assume that because an incantation is "cultic" while an appeal text is "Wisdom," they do not share many common values. For a discussion of this issue, see Bolle (N 29): 74–77. In fact, we will return to these incantation texts below as possible models utilized by the poet of Job (p. 115).

270. Again, we will rely on the transcription and translation of Lambert, *Wisdom* (N 60): 21–62 with reference to the more recent transcription/translation of Bolle (N 29): 362–395. For other easily accessible translations, see Biggs in Pritchard (N 51): 596–600; Schmökel in Beyerlin (N 262): 137–140 (excerpts only). See further, E. Dhorme, "Ecclesiastes ou Job?" *RB* 32 (1923): 5–27; Müller, *Hiobproblem* (N 262): 49–51, 57 ff.; Lévêque (N 37): 20–23 and the respective bibliographies cited therein; Gray (N 262): 254–256; Williams, "Theodicy" (N 233): 15–16; Albertson (N 47): 224–225. Further additions to the text of *Ludlul* have recently been published by D. J. Wiseman, "A New Babylonian Poem of the Righteous Sufferer," *Anatolian Studies* 30 (1980): 102–107.

271. See, e.g., Lambert, *Wisdom* (N 60): 27; Gray (N 262): 254; Pope, *Job* (N 2): lxi. Others have dubbed this text the "Babylonian Qoheleth"; see, e.g., the discussion by Dhorme, "Ecclesiastes" (N 270) and Lévêque (N 37): 23.

272. See, e.g., the parallels noted by Dhorme, "Ecclesiastes" (N 270); Gray (N 262): 254–255; Lévêque (N 37): 21–23.

273. The translations here and below follow both Lambert, *Wisdom* (N 60) and Bolle (N 29).

274. The complete text was published along with a translation by S. N. Kramer, " 'Man and His God'; A Sumerian Variation on the 'Job' Motif," in *Wisdom in Israel and in the Ancient Near East Presented to Professor Harold Henry Rowley* (VTSup 3; M. Noth and D. W. Thomas, eds.; Leiden: Brill, 1960): 170–182; see also Kramer's translation in Pritchard (N 51): 589–591; Schmökel's translation in Beyerlin (N 262): 140–142 (excerpts only); see further, Müller, *Hiobproblem* (N 262): 55–56 and notes; Lévêque (N 37): 31–33 and notes; also Bolle (N 29): 237–239; Albertson (N 47): 222–224. Kramer (op. cit., 170) suggests that the composition of this text could go back as early as the Third Dynasty of Ur (c. 2000 B.C.E.).

275. This text is generally known by its accession number in the Louvre, AO 4462. It was originally published by J. Nougayrol, "Une version ancienne du 'Juste Souffrant,' " *RB* 59 (1952): 239–250; see further W. von Soden, "Zum altbabylonischen Gedicht von schludlos Leidenden," *Or* n.s. 26 (1957): 315–319; J. Bottéro, "Le problème du mal en Mésopotamie ancienne: Prologue à un étude du 'juste souffrant,' " *Recherches et documents du Centre Thomas More* 77, no. 7 (1977); Bolle (N 29): 230–239; Müller, *Hiobproblem* (N 262): 53–54; Lévêque (N 37): 29–31; Gray (N 262): 259–261. We should note that this text is both difficult and fragmentary, making not entirely certain how it should be understood in detail. See Lambert's cautionary remarks in *Wisdom* (N 60): 10–11, n. 1.

276. The edition of this text (RS 25.460), along with a translation was once again published by J. Nougayrol in Schaeffer (N 268): 265–273; see also Müller, *Hiobproblem* (N 262): 56 and the discussion and summary by Gray (N 262): 262–264. Although this text dates from the 14th century B.C.E., Nougayrol suggests that its original composition could be considerably earlier, and the locus for its composition in Mesopotamia (p. 267). Note, in this respect, that this text is addressed, as is *Ludlul*, to Marduk (lines 15, etc.). Nonetheless, it is significant that the attested version of this text comes from Ugarit, since this directly demonstrates that Wisdom works of this nature were definitely known within the Syria-Palestine geographical locus where Job was likely written.

277. We certainly should not exclude the possibility that a genre of text existed within the Ancient Near Eastern Wisdom tradition that, like Job, also incorporates aspects of both Dialogue and Appeal. Considering how limited our sampling of known Wisdom texts of this type is, this would hardly be surprising. Nonetheless, no such prototype encompassing both these motifs is attested. Job is the only known example. It has been argued (see, e.g., Gray [N 262]: 259; Lévêque [N 37]: 29) that AO 4462 (see N 275) involves not only a Sufferer and his god but a Friend as well. This may be so, in which case this text would then be the closest to the specific form we find in Job. Still, considering how fragmentary the text is, this cannot be certainly affirmed. The lines attributed to this so-called Friend might just as easily be interpreted as spoken by an impersonal narrator (see, e.g., Lambert, *Wisdom* [N 60]: 11, n. 3; Bolle [N 29]: 230–232).

Barring the discovery of further relevant textual data, the question of whether the Job poet created an expansive form from two related genres or was simply following an already established hybrid pattern must remain moot. Still, if the Job poet did create a hybrid Dialogue/Appeal form, this would be consistent with the pattern of his literary creativity. As we continue this discussion, I hope to demonstrate that the Job poet was an innovator who liked to combine types and genres; indeed, this drawing on a variety of different literary motifs is a hallmark of parody, since it gives the artist more points against which to play a satiric counterpoint. See the discussion below, pp. 136 ff.

278. See the discussion above, pp. 66 ff. and below, pp. 170 f. It is interesting to note that rabbinical discussions of the merits of Abraham versus Job are sensitive to the issue of the silence of the former over against the vocal complaint of the latter in the canonical version of the Job story. In fact, this distinction allows the first century rabbi, Yohanan ben Zakkai to fault Job's piety in comparison to the piety of Abraham because Job only obeyed due to his fear of divine punishment while Abraham obeyed out of genuine love of God (see M. Sota 5:5). Note too the similar sentiments of Aqiba who notes that "Abraham was silent when punished" whereas Job "complained when punished" (Tractate Semahot 8; Midrash Tehillim 26:2). Accordingly, in Aqiba's view, Job could not be a saint-of-saints; rather, he must be seen as one of the Flood generation, who must serve a 12-month punishment in Gehenna at the dawn of the Messianic age for his faults (see M. 'Eduyyot 2:10).

Of course, it is precisely because Job is vocal that he can be taken to task by the rabbis in this manner. Had he been seen simply as Job the Silent, then, no distinction could have been made between him and Abraham. In fact, the third century rabbi, Hanina bar Papa makes precisely this point (Pesiqta Rabbati 190a): "Had he [Job] not complained, then just as we now say, the God of Abraham, the God of Isaac and the God of Jacob, so we would have said, and the God of Job." See further, the discussion of these and related passages in Baskin (N 7): 10 ff.; Urbach (N 103): 406 ff.

279. See above, pp. 69 ff. There may be some manner of literary conceit involved in the poet's choice of the Dialogue/Appeal form as well; that is, the poet may have felt that if one is going to write a great poem, one must use sophisticated forms after the "grand manner," employing the appropriate genres known in the Wisdom tradition for their ability to display artistic language in the most bravura fashion. One is reminded that Milton also felt a similar need when he wrote *Paradise Lost*. He believed that in order to justify God's ways to man, one could not rely on the simple prose style one finds, for example, in the story of Adam and Eve in Genesis or, for that matter, in his own religious treatise, *De doctrina Christiana*. Rather, one could only recast this story as an "adventurous song," quite literally of epic proportions, that attempts "things unattempted yet in prose or rhyme" (Book 1, lines 13, 16). Just as Milton turned to the literary forms of classical epic as the organizing structure for his reworking of the story of Adam and Eve, so too may the Job poet have felt the need to turn to the most "classical" forms of his own culture, the great literary genres exemplified in the Ancient Near Eastern Wisdom tradition and exemplified in the Dialogue/Appeal texts we have been discussing above.

280. It is sometimes argued that the formulations used by the poet of Job, especially his use of the dialogue, shows little intellectual progress. Note Pope's comments (*Job* [N 2]: lxxv), which can be considered representative:

> Actually it is scarcely appropriate to call this section of the book a dialogue. There is not here the give-and-take of philosophical disputation aimed at the advancement of understanding and truth. Rather each side has a partisan point of view which is reiterated *ad nauseam* in long speeches. There is no real movement in the argument. Attempts to find progression in the debate and subtle differences in the character and personality of the three friends are labored and unconvincing.

Of course, the same criticisms could be leveled at any of the texts we have been discussing. One searches in vain for an "intellectual" progression in the Dialogue of the *Theodicy*, nor can one see a true development of argument in the speeches of *Ludlul*. However, as Bolle has pointed out, the problem may be more with our definitions and expectations than with the texts themselves. In reference to Dialogue, she notes ([N 29]: 97), "We approach all dialogues unconsciously expecting certain elements to be present and then we grow uncomfortable and disgruntled if those elements are lacking. . . . I think that, without consciously reflecting upon it, we simply use the standard of Platonic dialogue to measure Job and Mesopotamian dialogues."

Such a chauvinistic approach inhibits appreciation of Job (and the other Dialogue/Appeal texts we have discussed) in their own terms because it fails to appreciate what were the standards of Ancient Near Eastern high literary style. In fact, Pope may well have touched on the best characterization of this high literary style when he described works of this sort as typically full of "long speeches" "reiterated *ad nauseam*." I think the Dialogue/Appeal forms are better understood precisely in this sense—as essentially reiterative rather than linearly progressive; that is, sophistication in writing in Ancient Near Eastern texts like the Poem of Job, *Ludlul* or the *Theodicy* was equated with the author's ability to rework his basic points in elegant elaborations, often to an hyperbolic extent.

The pleasure derived by an ancient audience in this form of literary expression may be something akin to that we find in listening to a musical piece of theme and variations. To be sure, there is a progression of sorts in this manner of musical composition, as first one nuance and then another is drawn out of the basic theme (and I think one could make a case that Dialogue/Appeal texts "progress" in much the same manner), but this is a cyclic progression that ultimately turns back on itself. The variations are only truly understood as a kind of counterpoint always anchored to the underlying melody that defines the dimensions of the musical universe in which the composition exists.

281. Kramer (N 274): 171.

282. E.g., Williams, "Theodicy" (N 233): 19 ff.; Gray (N 262): 256 ff.

283. See Williams, "Theodicy" (N 233): 21, who makes precisely this comparison; also Gray (N 262): 260–261. For the best discussions of the lament form in Job, see C. Wéstermann, *The Structure of the Book of Job; A Form-Critical Analysis* (C. A. Muenchow, trans.; Philadelphia: Fortress, 1981): 31–66 and Lévêque (N 37): 329–437. Westermann states (p. 31) quite correctly that the "lament comprises by far the most prevalent element in the Book of Job."

284. See pp. 48 f.

285. See p. 49.

286. This assumes that the *Theodicy* does reflect a standard Dialogue-form within Ancient Near Eastern Wisdom traditions. Nonetheless, we should be mindful of a point noted above (see N 268); namely that this is the *only* clear example of a "Job-like" Dialogue attested outside of Job itself. Certainly, any discussion of "standard" or "typical" forms that, on final analysis, is based upon only one example, is inherently speculative. Thus, the assumptions and argument that follow should be viewed in this light.

287. *Theodicy*, lines 56–57, 67–68.

288. See above, pp. 81ff. This interpretation of the *Theodicy* largely follows the arguments made by Bolle. She comments on the conclusion:

It is true that the friend's tone has changed in his concluding speech when he admits that the sufferer may have a legitimate case. But the sufferer's final words of trust in his god and goddess, not apparent at any other place in the poem, confirm the thesis of the friend. For, finally, the sufferer indicates his intentions to concentrate on what *is* eternal despite what he sees and experiences in his everyday life. If the friend has opened himself up at the conclusion, this is no less true for the sufferer. Through the dialogue, a true compromise and resolution has been effected. Questions were asked by the sufferer, replies given by the friend. The discussants have achieved harmony dialogically. ([N 29]: 225–226.)

A similar point could be made about the critical arguments expressed in appeal-texts such as *Ludlul*.

289. For further discussion of this issue, see below, N 293.

290. Perhaps even here there is an ironic undercurrent in the poet's use of the verb *l'h*, "to be weary." This verb also has the nuance "be impatient" (see Isa. 1:14; Jer. 6:11, 15:6 [niphal]; note also the causative [hiphil] in the sense "exhaust the patience of"; see Isa. 7:13; Mic. 6:3; note esp. Job 16:7a where *hl'ny*, "He has exhausted me," not only carries a sense of physical weariness but also of exhausted patience). When Eliphaz asks, Could it be that Job might be growing a bit impatient? the expected answer should be, Of course not! After all, Job is the very epitome of what patience is. In this connection, it may also be significant that Eliphaz begins his speech with the verb *nsh*, "to test, to try," the very same verb that initiates the divine test in the *Akedah*: *wyhy 'ḥr hdbrym h'lh wh'lhym nsh 't 'brhm*, "Thereafter, God tested Abraham" (Gen. 22:1). This may well be a reference to the test of Job in the traditional story. We expect that if Eliphaz is going to "try" Job, the latter will endure, as usual, in stoic silence. But here, at the outset of the Dialogue, the poet has already begun to signal that this is a new sort of Job, quite different from his traditional prototype. Indeed, three verses after Eliphaz has posed his "polite" question to Job, he supplies an answer as well, once again using *l'h* (4:5): *ky 'th tbw' 'lyk wtl'h*, "But now it [disaster] comes upon you and you are impatient!"

291. For the range of meaning for *'ml* "trouble, strife" in Job, note its use in 3:10; 4:8; 5:6, 7; 7:3; 11:16; 15:35.

292. The translation here follows the interpretation of Pope. See his discussion in *Job* (N 2): 99.

293. The fact that Appeal texts, such as *Ludlul bēl nēmeqi*, show a divine response whereas our one definitive example of a Dialogue text, the *Theodicy*, ends without an answer from the Sufferer's deity might argue in favor of seeing a dramatic distinction between the genres of Appeal and Dialogue. This appears to be Lambert's view, at least in so far as his interpretation of the *Theodicy* is concerned. He argues that the lack of a divine response in the *Theodicy* makes the conclusion "pathetic," essentially because it portrays mankind as the product of divine whim rather than divine concern. The gods have put mankind in an untenable position, because "whatever evil men do . . . is done because the gods made them that way" (Lambert, *Wisdom* [N 60]: 65). If this negative view of life is the essential message in the *Theodicy*, then it would be better linked to texts like the *Dialogue of Pessimism* or Ecclesiastes rather than, as I have argued, with texts within the Appeal genre such as *Ludlul*.

As is clear from the discussion above, I do not share Lambert's view of the *Theodicy*. Instead, I think that there is an implicit but unmistakable sense of hope at the foundation of this dialogue. When the Sufferer appeals to his patron deities at the end to give him aid, I do not believe that this is meant to be seen as a pathetic gesture. Granted, the *Theodicy* does, as Lambert says, show that mankind is completely at the gods' mercy, but it also clearly suggests that the gods can also be merciful to men, that righteous suffering is, in its own peculiar way, a precious gift of the gods, reserved for their most special servants.

There may be one concrete indication that this pious view is the one intended in the *Theodicy*. The poem is written as a "sentence acrostic"; that is, the initial syllable in each of the 11 lines of a given stanza is always the same; and when they are combined in succession, they read as a message. (For a discussion of acrostics, a well known literary device in Ancient Near Eastern, not to mention classical, composition, see Bolle [N 29]: 195–199 and notes and, most recently, W. Soll, "Babylonian and Biblical Acrostics," *Bib* 69 [1988]: 305–323.) In the case of the *Theodicy*, the sentence acrostic may be translated as follows: "I *Saggil-kinam-ubbib*, the incantation priest, am a worshipper of God and king." This statement not only apparently identifies the author of the *Theodicy* and tells us his profession, but, more importantly, it serves as a kind of credo—an affirmation by this priest of his faith in the world order as represented by the gods and their divine representative on earth, the king. I find it difficult to assume that the writer of the *Theodicy* could, on the one hand, declare his loyalty to god and king and, on the other, intend to subvert this loyalty by writing a pessimistic composition that underscores the hopelessness of man's plight under divine control. Rather, I think the better assumption is that this is a pious statement that also informs the basic theme of the *Theodicy*: the necessity that man submit to the gods, appeal for their mercy, and hope for restoration from strife. If one believes in god and king, one can only assume that truly righteous suffering ultimately must gain reward, and it is to such a reward that the *Theodicy* looks forward.

Note, in this connection, Soll's comment on the Theodicy:

> While the text of the poem is largely a complaint, the acrostic which gives the poem its structure is an assertion of the author's goodwill towards the social order in the divine and human spheres. One could say that the acrostic text which proclaimed his loyalty gave him greater freedom (both inwardly and in the eyes of others) to voice his complaints and doubts. The acrostic thus constitutes the framework in which the problem of innocent suffering is explored. The acrostic gives the poet scope for sustained reflection, and allows him to explore the questions of theodicy without having to resolve them or abandon his social and religious loyalties.

Cf. ibid., 316–317.

294. The bite of this sarcasm is reinforced in the immediately following verses, when God mockingly challenges Job to demonstrate his wisdom: *w'š'lk whwdy'ny . . . hgd 'm-yd't bynh . . . ky td'*, "I will ask you and you make known to me! . . . Expound, if you know understanding! . . . Surely you must know!" (38:3b, 4b, 5a). In all these verses the poet plays upon *yd'*, "to know," with telling effect. Although Job has only words *bly-d't*, "without knowledge" (38:2), he is challenged to make things known, for certainly he must have the knowledge; without doubt he must know. How else would he *dare* to speak as he has to God?

295. Of course, if one takes the Epilogue of Job as part of the original poet's work, then there is an ultimate restoration scene as part of the author's original conception. However, as our discussion above has indicated, I believe that there are solid grounds for assuming that the Prose Frame Story was appended to Job after the poem was written (see above pp. 25 ff.). Hence, in this discussion I have built my argument on the assumption that one should not factor the restoration in the Epilogue into an analysis of the Poem. This restoration scene must rather be taken as part of the course of action involved in incorporating the Poem of Job into the book of Job. We will consider this issue further below, pp. 157 ff.

296. B. Gemser, "The *Rib*- or Controversy-Pattern in Hebrew Mentality," in Noth and Thomas (N 274): 120–137; esp. 134–135.

297. There are, however, various texts in which the deity is invoked as a judge and advocate for an individual who has been wronged. In the Bible these occur especially among the Psalms, in particular, lament Psalms (e.g., 35:1, 43:1). Similar sentiments also are to be found in Mesopotamian prayers and incantation texts. See the discussion, ibid., 126–127, which surveys biblical and Mesopotamian writings utilizing this theme, as well as the bibliography thereto. In any case, the manner in which the poet of Job develops his legal metaphor is considerably different from how this theme is conventionally presented in prayers and incantations—which is not to say that he is unaware of the type or that he did not bring themes of this nature into play in his work. This latter point will be considered further below, pp. 115 f.

298. This can be demonstrated by surveying the various studies cited above, which have

been so helpful in clarifying the Dialogue/Appeal and its relationship to Job. Lévêque (N 37) extensively discusses the theme of the Righteous Sufferer in Ancient Near Eastern and classical literature (pp. 13–116). However, nowhere in this excellent discussion is any attempt made to "link up" to the legal metaphor. Likewise, in the studies of Gray (N 262) and Williams ("Theodicy" [N 233]), no consideration of the legal metaphor will be found. On the other hand, the study of Gemser (N 296), which focuses on legal terminology in Job, makes no mention of the Dialogue/Appeal texts. Similarly, other recent studies involving extensive discussion of the legal metaphor in Job, make no mention of these texts. See, e.g., J. J. M. Roberts, "Job's Summons to Yahweh: The Exploitation of a Legal Metaphor," *Restoration Quarterly* 16 (1973): 159–165; S. H. Scholnick, *Lawsuit Drama in the Book of Job* (Ph.D. diss.; Brandeis University, 1975; Ann Arbor: University Microfilms, 1987); idem, "The Meaning of *Mišpaṭ* in the Book of Job," *JBL* 101 (1982): 521–529; idem, "Poetry in the Courtroom: Job 38–41," in *Directions in Biblical Hebrew Poetry* (E. R. Follis, ed.; Sheffield: JSOT, 1987): 185–204; M. B. Dick, *Job 31: A Form-critical Study* (unpublished Ph.D. diss.; Johns Hopkins University, 1977); idem, "The Legal Metaphor in Job 31," *CBQ* 41 (1979): 37–50. On the other hand, this is not always the case. Note, in this respect, Crenshaw, "Popular" (N 262); esp. 389, and Habel, (*Job* [N 67]: 45) who try to consider how the legal metaphor and the Dialogue/Appeal form interact with one another.

299. In considering the Joban use of *rīb*, a degree of caution should be exercised. In order to study this and other legal terms found in Job, we must rely, for the most part, on biblical texts, since they supply the most extensive, directly comparable, semantic evidence. Yet in accordance with a point we have considered above (pp. 90 ff.), we cannot be at all certain that the Poem of Job was written in the same Israelite/Jewish cultural milieu as other biblical texts containing juridical terminology. While I believe that the term-to-term correspondences between Job and other biblical texts are clear enough for us to assume that they are mutually illuminating, it should emphasized that this is, nonetheless, a working assumption and not a foregone conclusion. In any case, we should not simply grant that the juridical milieus alluded to in Job and in various other biblical passages are identical—that, as it were, the poet of Job and the biblical prophets passed essentially the same bar examination. Still, it seems reasonable to accept the proposition that whatever the specific cultural background of the Poem of Job, its author shared a broad, legal heritage that is also reflected in other biblical texts.

300. For a survey of the uses of *rīb* in the Hebrew Bible, see Gemser (N 296); J. Limburg, "The Root *RYB* and the Prophetic Lawsuit Speeches," *JBL* 38 (1969): 290–304 and his more detailed discussion in *The Lawsuit of God in the Eighth-Century Prophets* (Th.D. dissertation, Union Theological Seminary, VA, 1969; Ann Arbor: University Microfilms, 1974): 53–126; also Scholnick, *Lawsuit* (N 298): 103–175 as well as the bibliographies cited in these respective studies. For a broader consideration of the history of scholarship on the use of *rīb*, see Limburg, *Lawsuit*: 1–52; K. Nielsen, *Yahweh as Prosecutor and Judge* (*JSOT* Sup. 9; Sheffield: JSOT, University of Sheffield, 1978): 5–26 and notes.

301. Limburg, *Lawsuit* (N 300): 90.

302. Scholnick, *Lawsuit* (N 298): 109. The following discussion closely follows the observations of Scholnick and the debt owed to her scholarly insights is acknowledged forthwith.

303. Ibid., 112–114; see also Limburg, *Lawsuit*, (N 300): 97–100. Scholnick argues (op. cit., 161, n. 24) that *rbym* in Exod. 23:2, usually translated "multitude, many, majority," should more properly be understood in this context as "elders," i.e., men with power and influence. Thus, the sense of *l' thyh 'ḥry-rbym* (etc.) would be, "You shall not side with the mighty" as opposed to "You shall not side with the many." In either case, the force is much the same: you shall not show partiality, whether for the powerful or for the mob over a weaker individual.

304. Scholnick defines *rīb* accordingly:

A study of *ryb* . . . reveals that the root refers to a verbal dispute which may be settled privately between the individuals involved or publicly with the help of community officials. When solved by means of intervention or arbitration, the dispute, the *ryb* becomes a lawsuit. Hebrew law requires that the proceedings be conducted with impartiality so that a fair decision may be reached. The basic elements then for a judicial settlement of a *ryb* are rather simple: two contending parties, a public accusation by one party of an offense committed by the other and a group of individuals standing in the community (the elders or, in difficult cases, priests or magistrates) who hear the case and arrive at a decision. (Ibid., 126–127.)

305. The treaty involved is the Sefire Treaty. For the best overall treatment of this series of texts, see J. A. Fitzmyer, *The Aramaic Inscriptions of Sefire* (Rome: PBI, 1967). The use of *ryb* occurs in stela 3, lines 17, 26. For the interpretation of these passages, cf. Limburg, "Root" (N 300): 299–300; idem, *Lawsuit* (N 300): 114–126; Scholnick, *Lawsuit* (N 298): 118–119. Although a cognate of the term *rīb* does not occur in Mesopotamian legal contexts (cf. the comment of A. L. Oppenheim, cited by Limburg, *Lawsuit*, op. cit., 89, n. 42), essentially the same correspondences outlined for this proceeding can be documented among the Akkadian civil proceedings. For a convenient summary, see Dick, "Legal Metaphor" (N 298): 41–44.

306. This is, in fact, essentially the translation given, for example, in the Revised Standard Version: "But how can a man be just before God?" and in the old Jewish Publication Society Version (Philadelphia: JPS, 1917): "And how can man be just with God?"

307. The subject and object of *y'nnw* are ambiguous in the context. It is possible to see God as the subject and man as the object, in which case the correct translation would be "He would (not) answer him." In this case the point is, should man attempt to file a legal complaint against God, God would not respond to it. (For this interpretation, see, e.g., Dhorme, *Job* [N 230]: 126; Habel, *Job* [N 67]: 179.) On the other hand, if man is the subject and God the object one would translate: "he could (not) answer Him." Then the point is that man has little prospect of a successful defense against an all-powerful deity's cross-complaint or cross-examination. This latter interpretation would then prefigure the course of events in the Theophany. (For this interpretation, see, e.g., Tur-Sinai, *Job* [[N 38]: 154, Pope, *Job* [N 2]: 68).

I am inclined to follow the first interpretation, taking the verb in the legal sense of "to reply (to a complaint)." See the discussion in Scholnick, *Lawsuit* (N 298): 166 n. 75 and the more general discussion of *'nh* as a judicial term, pp. 227–237. This makes for a more logical development in the context: if one makes a complaint, then the defendant refuses to respond.

308. The sense of the phrase *ṣdq 'm-'l* is, "to be vindicated in a court proceeding against God." Note, in particular, that the preposition *'m*, "with," designates an opponent-at-law. One might say that it has the same sense as "versus" in a legal case, e.g., "the case of X vs. Y." A translation like that employed by Pope, "be acquitted before God" (cf. Pope, *Job* [N 2]: 68) is misleading since it implies that God is the judge in the legal suit rather than a colitigant. The phrase probably should be related to *ryb 'm*, "make a complaint against"; see further, Limburg, "Root" (N 300): 296; idem, *Lawsuit* (N 300): 71–72; 77–78.

It seems altogether likely that the poet's use of the preposition *'m* was intended not only to establish the legal nuance of the phrase, but also to contrast with the near parallel of Eliphaz's declaration in 4:17a. That passage essentially matches Job's statement word-for-word except that the preposition employed is a form of *mn* rather than *'m*. The preposition *mn*, "from, away from," connotes separation; hence, Eliphaz's statement might be characterized as emphasizing that man is too remote from God to hope to aspire to His standards of righteousness. By changing to *'m* for Job's declaration, the poet emphasizes that there should be equality between man and God within a legal context, the sort of equal footing that any two conflicting parties should have before a judge in a court case.

309. Dick ("Legal Metaphor" [298]: 39–41) points out that there may be a presumption of sinfulness for any man who has fallen ill. This is especially well documented in Mesopotamian texts. In particular, he further notes that "there are even Mesopotamian texts which describe in the language of the court man's suffering as legal judgment of guilt." He cites in this connection (following Gemser [N 296]: 127, n. 1), an Assyrian incantation text (see below, N 331) which constitutes an appeal to Shapash, the Mesopotamian god of justice: "In the (legal) cause of the illness which has seized me, I am lying on (my) knees for judgment. Judge my cause; give a decision for me!" (cited from E. Ebeling, *KARI*, 184 R, 1, lls. 19 ff.).

310. Reading with many exegetes *hnhw* (possibly reflecting a haplography under the influence of the initial *waw* in the following form) for the grammatically difficult phrase ending *hnh*. See, e.g., Dhorme, *Job* (N 230): 138; Pope, *Job* (N 2): 72.

311. For a discussion of *mšpt* in Job as well as in other biblical contexts, see Schlonick, "*Mišpat*" (N 298): *passim*; idem, *Lawsuit* (N 298): 264–306. In translating *mšpt* as "legality" here, I have tried to use a term that captures the sense "justice" and "litigation," which both seem to be part of the nuance of the term in this context.

312. Dhorme, (*Job* [N 230]: 138) argues that *yw'ydny* has specific judicial connotations; however, Scholnick cautions that the evidence is lacking from other contexts to establish that the causative form of this verb is a technical legal term (*Lawsuit* [N 298]: 280). Whether Dhorme's assumption is correct or not, contextually the sense appears to have a specifically judicial nuance, "set a date for me in court"; compare 9:32: *ky-l'-'yš kmwny "nnw nbw' yḥdw bmšpt*, "for He is not a man like me that I could challenge: Let us enter into court together."

313. Alternatively, read the particle *l'* as *lū'* rather than as the negative particle *lō'*, in which case the statement would be taken subjunctively: "Would that there were a judge between us. . . ." This interpretation appears to be reflected in the LXX and the Peshitta versions of Job; see, e.g., Dhorme, *Job* (N 230): 144; Pope, *Job* (N 2): 76.

314. For the difficulties involved in understanding the precise sense of *kn-l' 'nky 'mdy* (lit., "it is not so: I with me"), see, e.g., Pope, *Job* (N 2): 76–77. It is possible that *'nky 'mdy* might be some manner of idiomatic colloquialism; in any case, I have translated what I believe is the essential force of the phraseology.

315. It is sometimes argued that there is a logical progress, or at least a design, in the poet's development of the legal metaphor in the book of Job. Note, for example, Habel's schematic outline and general discussion, *Job* (N 67): 54–57, which, however, encompasses the entire book into the presumed legalistic design. While it is certainly reasonable to grant that the legal argument comes to a head in chapter 31 (see the discussion below), I find it less convincing that the legal aspect of the Poem truly progresses in a linear fashion throughout the Dialogue. Rather, as I have discussed in more general terms above (see N 280), the legalisms utilized by Job seem to me better characterized in terms of a recycled metaphor— variations on the juridical theme—that reflects the poet's high literary style.

316. Cf., Dick, "Legal Metaphor," (N 298); idem, *Job 31* (N 298): *passim*.

317. The term translated here "cross-complaint" is *spr* (lit., "document, writing"). I have tried to give this a specific legal nuance, i.e., as a legal document designed to enter a countersuit in response to Job's initial filing of a grievance.

318. The last phrase in this verse is difficult due to the apparent perfect tense of the verb "to write" (*ktb*). This would seem to require a past tense, hence, the translation "he has written." I have taken the phrase as an adverbial accusative, juxtaposed to the direct object ("me"), which clarifies how God should respond to His opponent-at-law. However, the tentativeness of this interpretation of the syntax cannot be overemphasized; in fact, no matter how one interprets this text, serious difficulties are encountered.

In context, a jussive tense (read *yktb*?; see, e.g., Gordis, *Job* [N 250]: 355) would certainly make a smoother reading, and thus many have rendered the verb in translation, sometimes without explanation. See Pope, *Job* (N 2): 227, "Let my opponent write a document"; also, e.g., Habel, *Job* (N 67): 425. Another proposal by Dick, "Legal Metaphor" (N 298): 47, n. 48, to understand *ktb* as a "precative perfect" could conceivably be correct; still, it seems more to be an effort to "explain away" an otherwise difficult form than anything else. For other explanations involving the assumption that part of the verse has been inadvertently dropped, see, e.g., Driver and Gray (N 235): vol. 1, 274–276; G. Fohrer, "The Righteous Man in Job 31," in his *Studien zum Buche Hiob* (Berlin: de Gruyter, 1983): 78, n. 2. Fortunately, whatever the precise grammatical nuance of the phrase, the overall sense is largely unaffected.

319. See the discussion on pp. 98 f. and note, e.g., Westermann, *Structure* (N 283): 38–42; Fohrer, "Righteous Man" (N 318): 80–81.

320. Dick, "Legal Metaphor" (N 298): 46–47.

321. I wonder whether this chronicle of crimes that Job has never committed is meant to play off similar litanies of sinful behavior like those found in Mesopotamian collections of incantations of expiation such as the one called *Shurpu*, "Burning." (For the edition and translation of *Shurpu*, see E. Reiner, *Šurpu*; *A Collection of Sumerian and Akkadian Incantations* [Graz: Archiv für Orientforshung (Beiheft 11), 1958]; note especially her introductory discussion, 1–6; see also H. Zimmern, *Beiträge zur Kenntnis der Babylonischen Religion* [Leipzig: Hinrichs, 1901; rpt. Leipzig: Zentralantiquariat der DDR, 1975]: 1–80.) Bolle desscribes how such texts are typically structured:

> . . . the narrator, usually the priest performing the rituals and incantations, addresses a deity. A man could commit an offense either unwittingly or in full cognizance of what he has done. Because many times he does not know what exactly he has done, the narrator will list all possible transgressions of the sufferer, although it is clear that he could not have committed so many offenses. But because the sufferer does not understand what he has done, the priest lists all possibilities; then when the prescribed ritual is performed, all possible guilt will be absolved. (Bolle [N 29]: 168–169.)

This long confession of sins, along with the concomitant rituals, might be said to be a strategy to "conjure up" a deity and evoke his merciful intercession. The sufferer admits to anything and everything sinful and then prays for absolution. But in Job, the poet has his Sufferer do precisely the opposite: Job exhaustively lists sin after sin, not in order to confess and plead for mercy but rather to deny culpability and demand justice. In a sense, Job's oath becomes an incantation-of-sorts, designed to compel his deity to respond, but on legal, rather than cultic, grounds.

Other scholars have suggested a potential connection of Job 31 to *Shurpu* (see the discussion and bibliography in Fohrer, "Righteous Man" [N 318]: 84), but Fohrer objects that the texts are not really comparable because they are such different genres (ibid.). However, this is not a major objection if, as I have suggested, the poet is utilizing the form for the purposes of parody. This would simply be another case where he has reached out for yet another genre whose conventions he can twist around to serve his broader thematic goals.

Mention should also be made of the negative confessions of sins that some scholars have seen as a possible informing influence on Job 31. See the discussion by P. Humbert, *Recherches sur les sources égyptiennes de la littérature saptientiale d'Israël* (Neuchâtel: Secretariat de l'Université, 1929): 75–106, esp. 91–96; Fohrer, op. cit.

322. See the overall discussion in M. Tsevat's "The Meaning of the Book of Job," *HUCA* 37 (1966): 73–106; esp. 77–79; rpt. in his *The Meaning of the Book of Job and Other*

Biblical Studies (New York: Ktav, 1980): 1–37; esp. 6–7; the quotation is from p. 78 (rpt. p. 6). See also S. H. Blank, "An Effective Literary Device in Job XXXI," *JJS* 5 (1960): 105–107; idem, "The Curse, Blasphemy, the Spell, and the Oath," *HUCA* 23 (1950–51): 73–95; esp. 91–92.

323. Dick, "Legal Metaphor" (N 298): 49.

324. For a recent discussion of the legal aspects of God's final speech, see Scholnick, "Poetry," (N 298).

325. In this connection Scholnick declares (*Lawsuit* [N 298]: 300–301): "Job had earlier . . . asked for God's participation in the suit either as plaintiff or defense. Here God chooses to provide testimony and let Job give the counter-testimony. The important point to be made is that, according to Job's definition of *mspṭ* ["justice, legality"] as the settlement of disputes in a human court of law, justice is being done with God's entrance in his lawsuit.

326. Hence, the title of her dissertation, *Lawsuit Drama in the Book of Job* (N 298); note also her summary on p. 264.

327. A king (*melek* in Hebrew) being defined as an hereditary ruler or one who claims hereditary rule, as opposed to a ruler who gains authority through any other means.

328. This point has been extensively discussed in the scholarly literature. See, most conveniently, Scholnick's discussion in "*Mišpaṭ*" (N 298); idem, *Lawsuit* (N 298): 266 ff. and the bibliography thereto.

329. The translation here follows S. N. Kramer, "Lipit-Ishtar Lawcode," in Pritchard (N 51): 159. Note also the concluding remarks of this king: "Verily in accordance with the tr[ue word] of Utu (= Shapash, the god of justice), I caused [Su]mer and Akkad to hold to true justice. I, Lipit-Ishtar, the son of Enlil, *abolished* enmity and rebellion; made weeping, lamentations, outcries . . . taboo; caused righteousness and truth to exist; brought well-being to the Sumerians and the Akkadians . . . (ibid., 161).

330. The translation follows T. J. Meek, "The Code of Hammurabi" in ibid., 164. At the conclusion of the prologue Hammurapi further states, "When (the god) Marduk commissioned me to guide the people aright, to direct the land, I established law and justice in the language of the land, thereby promoting the welfare of the people" (ibid., 165).

331. The text, published by S. N. Kramer, *Sumerian Literary Texts from Nippur* (AASOR 23; New Haven: ASOR, 1944): text 149 rev II, 8 ff., is quoted by Gemser (N 296): 126, cf. further, 126–127 n. 1 for reference to a collection of similar texts. Dick cites a similar example ("Legal Metaphor" [N 298]: 49), where king Yarim-Lim of Aleppo appeals to Shapash against the king of Dir: "Let Shapash investigate my conduct and yours, let him judge." For the text, see G. Dossin, "Une lettre de Iarim-Lim, roi d'Alep, à Iasub-Iaḥad, roi de Dir," *Syria* 33 (1966): 66; cf. lines 5–6.

332. From col. 3 of the *Epic of Tukulti-Ninurta I* (late 13th Century B.C.E.), in the edition of R. C. Thompson, "The British Museum Excavations at Nineveh," *Annals of Archaeology and Anthropology* 20 (1933): 124–125 (Thompson's column 4), lines 3–15. I am following here the interpretive line of J. Harvey, who has connected the biblical *rîb* with international law manifest in Mesopotamian and Hittite texts of this sort. See "Le 'Rîb-Pattern,' requistoire prophétique sur la rupture de l'alliance, *Bib* 43 (1962): 172–196, esp. 180; idem, *Le Plaidoyer prophétique contre Israël àpres la rupture de l'alliance* (Bruges: Desclée de Brouwer, 1967): esp. 120. See also the discussion of Harvey's thesis by Limburg, *Lawsuit* (N 300): 23 ff. The translation here follows Limburg, p. 27; also note the remarks of Nielsen (N 300): 14–19.

It is not my intention here or in the discussion that follows on prophetic lawsuits in the Bible to become involved in the complicated issue of the specific *Sitz im Leben* (life setting) of these various types of legal or quasi-legal pronouncements. For our purposes, it is sufficient to confine analysis to a consideration of the roles of the parties in dispute (i.e., as judge, plaintiff, enforcer, defendant, etc.), since it is these roles *themselves* (rather than their specific contexts) that the poet of Job also works with and manipulates for his own purposes.

333. See Thompson (N 332): 26, col. 3 (Thompson 4), lines 27–29, 35–38. The translation here follows Thompson; see also Limburg, *Lawsuit* (N 300): 252.

334. For the most detailed analysis of this passage in terms of its legalistic import, cf. Limburg, *Lawsuit* (N 300): 190–218, which also considers much of the more recent scholarly discussion of the passage; cf. further, Nielsen (N 300): 32–38.

335. Lit., "oath/curse and lie." I have taken this as expressing essentially a single idea, i.e, perjury; see the discussion by Limburg, *Lawsuit* (N 300): 210–211.

336. The verb employed here, *'bl*, usually means "mourn." However, in this particular context, as occasionally elsewhere, this form must be etymologically connected instead with Akkadian *abālu*, "to dry up" (see the *Chicago Assyrian Dictionary*; vol. A, Part 1 [Chicago: Oriental Institute, 1964]: 29 ff. s.v. *abalu* B). See, e.g., the discussion in F. I. Andersen and D. N. Freedman, *Hosea; A New Translation with Introduction and Commentary* (Anchor Bible vol. 24; Garden City: Doubleday, 1980): 339; also Limburg, *Lawsuit* (N 300): 212–213. This does not mean, however, that the nuance "mourn" for *'bl* is not to be read into Hosea's phraseology. It is probable that there was an intentional word play here: Even as the land withers, so too does it mourn.

337. Nielsen (N 300): 33. See also Limburg's remarks (*Lawsuit*, [N 300]: 216–217): "This model also explains the identity of Accuser and Judge, in that if the maker of this accusation via messenger [the prophet] happens to be a suzerain, he can appeal to no higher authority to make a judgment."

The situation portrayed here is probably best characterized in terms of Lewis Carroll's poem, "The Mouse's Tail," from *Alice in Wonderland*, which in the original version actually zig-zags like a mouse's tail:

> Fury said to a mouse,
> That he met in the house,
> "Let us both go to Law,
> *I* will prosecute *you*.—
> Come, I'll take no denial;
> We must have a trial:
> For really this morning
> I've nothing to do."
> Said the mouse to the cur,
> "Such a trial, dear Sir,
> With no jury or judge
> Would be wasting our breath."
> "I'll be judge, I'll be jury,"
> Said cunning old Fury:
> "I'll try the whole cause.
> And condemn you to death."

338. See, e.g., the observations of Roberts (N 298): esp. 162 ff. who speaks of the "flaw" that "lies at the [legal] metaphor's roots" (p. 165).

339. See Job 9:32, where Job makes precisely this point: *ky-l'-'yš kmny 'nnw nbw' yḥdw bmšpṭ*, "For he is not a man like me against whom I could testify (when) we both go to court." It is true that there are several occasions in biblical texts where the possibility of a suit with God is broached. For the most thorough discussion of these passages, see Scholnick, *Lawsuit* (N 298): 122–127; also Gemser (N 296): 133–134. In all cases but one, the absurdity of such a course of action is emphasized. Jer. 2:29 catches quite well the sense of folly connected

with any attempt to enter into a suit with God. There, God chastises his chosen people: *lmh trybw 'ly klkm pš'tm by*, "How dare you bring a suit unto me: All of you have transgressed against me!" This is the typical situation: a party (usually Israel), manifestly guilty of sin, making a false accusation of unjust treatment by God. Quite obviously, from a legal standpoint, there is no case here—the "charges" against God could only be summarily dismissed due to their lack of merit.

The use of the preposition *'l*, "unto," in connection with *ryb* in Jer 2:29 may be significant. The exact nuance of *ryb 'l* ("to complain unto"?) is difficult to determine (see Limburg, *Lawsuit* [N 300]: 80–81), but it seems less adversarial than *ryb 'm* or *ryb 't* which appears consistently to mean "complain against" (see N 308; also, Scholnick, op. cit., 78). This less hostile phrasing may therefore represent a circumlocution in order to avoid any implicit disrespect for the Deity—i.e. by suggesting that one might have equal standing with God in court. (Note, in this respect, that Elihu almost reproduces the phrasing in Jer. 2:29 when he questions Job [33:13]: *mdw' 'lyw rybwt*, "Why have you made accusations unto God?" This is just the sort of respectful rubric one might expect from this self-styled defender of the Deity.)

The only clear case that might be brought forward as an example of a righteous man bringing suit against God is Jer. 12:1. There the prophet declares, *ṣdyq 'th yhwh ky 'ryb 'lyk 'k mšptym 'dbr 'wtk*, "Innocent are You, LORD, if I bring a suit unto You. Still, I would make a case against You." These are bold words for a prophet of God—especially *mšptym 'dbr 'wtk*, a phrase used elsewhere in Jeremiah only in an adversarial context (see, e.g., W. L. Holladay, *Jeremiah 1*; *A Commentary on the Book of the Prophet Jeremiah, Chapters 1–25* [Hermeneia; Philadelphia: Fortress, 1986]: 40, 376; idem, "Jeremiah's Lawsuit with God," *Interpretation* 17 [1963]: 280–287; esp. 281). Still, the force of Jeremiah's sentiments is softened by the context of the phrase. Note that once again, the less contentious *ryb 'l*, is used; moreover, the prophet wants to make clear immediately that were God actually to be tried, He would be swiftly exonerated. Most significantly, as soon as Jeremiah contemplates making a case against God (on the grounds that God does not punish the wicked; see 12:1b–2), the prophet withdraws the motion, preferring instead to plead to God that He act to punish evildoers (12:3). Jeremiah would seem to be acknowledging here that since God is the power behind the law, He must be depended on to see that all evildoers are ultimately punished as the law requires. The prophet must depend on his faith in this basic assumption rather than try to argue his case. Consequently, at best, we have here a suit contemplated but never really instituted (see Holladay, "Lawsuit," op. cit., 284–285; Scholnick, op. cit., 124–125).

340. Only once is there a clear reference to the legal metaphor in the speeches of the three friends, when Eliphaz declares (22:4): *hmyr'tk ykyḥk ybw' 'mk bmspṭ*, "Because He [i.e., God] fears you, will He arraign you, enter into court with you?" But in this case Eliphaz is mocking Job and his demand for a court proceeding with God; he only makes reference to Job's legal metaphor in order to underscore what seems to him its essential absurdity. See the discussion by Scholnick, *Lawsuit* (N 298): 282; Habel, *Job* (N 67): 338.

341. In this respect I disagree with Scholnick who believes that the Friends accept the legal metaphor (*Lawsuit* [N 298]: 128).

342. Or alternatively, "He has cast his net around me." See, e.g., the discussion in Habel, *Job* (N 67): 291.

343. There is almost certainly a legal nuance to the verb *'nh* in verse 7a and to the noun *mšpṭ* in 7b. One might more broadly paraphrase: "Look, I cry out that I am the victim of a crime, but I am not able to get any testimony on my behalf. I cry out for help but I can't get a day in court."

344. The reading in verse 9a, as it stands in the Hebrew, would seem to mean "Woe to him who would lodge a complaint against his Maker—a pot/potsherd with the earthen pots/potsherds." I have followed the interpretation in the RSV, reading *ḥrś* (participle,

"engraver,") for *ḥrśy* and understanding *ḥrś 'dmh* (lit., "cutter, fabricator of clay") as a rubric for "potter." Others emend 9b, reading *p'lw* ("its maker") for *p'lk* ("your work") and render, "Does the clay say to its fabricator, 'What are you doing?' or (to) its maker, 'This lacks handles.'" For a discussion of the reading, see, e.g., C. R. North, *The Second Isaiah* (Oxford: Clarendon, 1964): 153. However one understands the construction of the passage, the overall meaning is clear. Similar sentiments are expressed in Isa. 10:15: "Does the axe vaunt itself over the one who wields it? or the saw aggrandize itself over the one who uses it? As though the rod raised up him who lifts it or as though the staff lifted the man" (lit., "one who is not wood").

345. For a similar use of the potter/pot figure, see Jeremiah 18:1 ff.; also note Job 10:9, which plays off the same idea. Roberts cites Ps. 143:2 as containing a similar sentiment. He notes that entering into litigation with God "normally designates an experience to be avoided if possible. The Psalmist prays to be delivered from it: 'Do not enter into judgment with your servant . . . for no living being can be right before you.'" See (N 298): 160.

346. The legal situation presented here is reminiscent of the parable by Franz Kafka, "Zur Frage der Gesetze," i.e., "The Problem of the Laws" (in F. Kafka, *Parables and Paradoxes* [N. Glatzer, ed.; New York: Schocken, 1961]: 154–159). In this Kafkaesque vignette, a narrator discusses the laws of his country, "which are not generally known" but which have profound impact upon everyone's life. The actions of the nobility, who control the laws, have been minutely studied in order that the legal system that guides their actions might be extrapolated therefrom. But, the narrator declares, "When in accordance with these scrupulously tested and logically ordered conclusions we seek to orient ourselves somewhat towards the present and the future, everything becomes uncertain, and our work seems only an intellectual game, for perhaps these laws that we are trying to unravel do not exist at all." Some have argued, the narrator continues, that the law is whatever the nobility do; but most believe that the reason the laws are not understood is because of man's inherent inadequacy to comprehend the law. It is suggested that the logical course would be to challenge the nobility, repudiating both them and the law. In fact, any party that would do this would unite the people behind them. But Kafka concludes, "No such party can come into existence, for nobody would dare to repudiate the nobility. We live on this razor edge. A writer once summed the matter up this way: The sole visible and indubitable law that is imposed upon us is the nobility, and must we ourselves deprive ourselves of that one law?"

347. The many philological problems in this passage have been discussed at length in the scholarly literature. It is very difficult to make much sense of the Hebrew as it stands, and virtually all modern commentators opt for some manner of emendation. Fortunately, however one understands the phrasing, the overall meaning is clear.

I read and restore the Hebrew as follows:

> *gm-'th hnh-bšmym 'dy*
> *wśhdy bmrwmym*
> *mlyṣy r'y 'l-'lwh*
> *⟨'lyw⟩ dlph 'yny*
> *wywkḥ lgbr 'm-'lwh*
> *wbn-'dm lr'hw*

A few clarifications on the text and translation presented here are appropriate. I read *mlyṣy* as a singular noun, "my advocate"; I also take *'l-'lwh* with the otherwise short stich of verse 20a rather than as the beginning of 20b and assume that *'lyw* has dropped from the beginning of 20b through a haplography; cf. the LXX's *enanti de autou*. For this line of interpretation, see, e.g., Pope, *Job* (N 2): 125; Habel, *Job* (N 67): 265–266. I have employed angled-brackets in the text and translation to indicate where this restoration has been made.

Note that, in my understanding of the text, the added *'lyw*, "unto him" would refer to the advocate, not to God.

348. Again, this is one of the most notoriously difficult passages in the book of Job. Especially difficult to interpret are verses 26–27, for which there are a wide range of scholarly interpretations. We will return to a consideration of this passage, including verses 26–27, below, pp. 132 ff. For a specific philological discussion of these two verses, see N 409. Fortunately, once more, the general sense of the passage as it relates to the legal metaphor is fairly clear even if the details are open to a broad range of interpretations. For a recent, brief survey of opinions, see Habel, *Job* (N 67): 292–294; also J. K. Zink, "Impatient Job; An Interpretation of Job 19:25–27," *JBL* 84 (1965): 147–152. For a comprehensive survey of early interpretations of this passage, see J. Speer, "Zur Exegese von Hiob 19:25–27," *ZAW* 25 (1906): 47–140.

349. Habel, *Job* (N 67): 306; see also, e.g., Lévêque (N 37): 467–497 and the bibliography thereto; W. A. Irwin, "Job's Redeemer," *JBL* 81 (1962): 218–229; esp. 218–219 and the references cited there; also H. Ringgren, "*g'l*," in *Theological Dictionary of the Old Testament* (G. Botterweck and H. Ringgren, eds.; Grand Rapids: Eerdmans, 1977): 350–355; esp. 355.

350. See Williams, "Theodicy," (N 233): 24.

351. I.e., *dîni dîn(a) purussāiā purus(a)*; see Gemser (N 296): 126 and the discussions above, N 309 and p. 109.

352. Note also Lam. 3:58, *rbt 'dny ryby npšy g'lt ḥyy*, "You have pleaded my own case, Lord, You have redeemed my life!" and similar sentiments expressed in Prov. 23:11 and Jer. 50:34. The association of *g'l* with *ryb* in all these instances indicates that it can have specifically legal connotations.

The discussions of *g'l/gō'ēl* and its various nuances of meaning in the Bible are voluminous in the scholarly literature and we cannot hope to make a comprehensive survey here. For an overview with particular reference to Job 19:25, see, e.g., Dhorme, *Job* (N 230): 283; Pope, *Job* (N 2): 146; Lévêque (N 37): 487–488; Gordis, *Job* (N 250): 205–206; Habel, *Job* (N 67): 303–308; Gemser (N 296): 126; A. R. Johnson, "The Primary Meaning of √*g'l*," *VTSup* 1 (1953): 67–77 (which, however, does not discuss Job 19:25); Irwin, "Redeemer," (N 349); Ringgren, "*g'l*" (N 349). Ringgren's characterization the legal nuance of *g'l* may be considered representative: ". . . the *gō'ēl* could appear as a helper in a lawsuit to see that justice was done to his protege" (ibid., 352).

353. See also Isa. 34:9; 51:22, Jer. 51:36. All of these texts have been noted by Gemser (N 296): 126; see also Lévêque (N 37): 487–488. Even in the more typical Prosecutor/Judge pericopes, God can be depicted as an advocate; see Limburg's discussion of Isa. 3:13–15, *Lawsuit* (N 300): 132–160; esp. 146–147, 152, 157–160.

354. I have already voiced my reservations against making this assumption above in N 299. One strong reason to conclude that there is not this sort of *direct* connection between the poet's and the prophets' legal metaphor falls in line with criteria considered in that note, namely, that there is no overt textual connection between the Poem of Job and the various relevant prophetic pericopes; that is, there is no concrete indication that the Job poet was citing Isaiah, Jeremiah, Amos, Hosea, etc. or that they were citing him. At best, we would probably have to grant that the author of Job was familiar with the prophetic tradition preserved in the Bible in general terms rather than in specific instances. But even this is best seen as more a possibility than a certainty.

355. The verb *hdk*, taken as an imperative, "mow down!" occurs only here in the Bible. The translation is conjectural, based on context alone. For further discussion, see, e.g., Habel *Job* (N 67): 552–553.

356. See p. 108.

357. Note Scholnick's comment about the use of *mšpṭ* in Job:

A look at the author's use of the word for justice, *mišpaṭ*, shows that the definition changes during the course of the work and through these changes he is able to dramatize Job's search for the meaning of justice. The poet presents two dimensions of the word: the juridical and the executive. Job and his friends draw their definitions from the sphere of the court, while God understands it as executive sovereignty, the prerogative of the ruler. Much of the tension of the drama grows out of this difference in understanding justice. (*"Mišpaṭ"* [N 298]: 521.)

358. Note, e.g., that N. H. Tromp, in his study *Primitive Conceptions of Death and the Netherworld in the Old Testament* (Rome: PBI, 1969) makes 126 specific references to the Book of Job (see the index references, pp. 226–227). Only the Psalms are more extensively considered (see pp. 227–230).

359. For a discussion of the concept of death in biblical texts, see, e.g., ibid.; R. Martin-Achard, *From Death to Life* (J. P. Smith, trans.; Edinburgh: Oliver & Boyd, 1960): esp. 16–47; W. Eichrodt, *Theology of the Old Testament* (J. A. Baker, trans.; Philadelphia: Westminster, 1967): vol. 2, 210–228; G. Von Rad, *Old Testament Theology* (D. Stalker, trans.; New York: Harper & Row, 1962): 387 ff.; H. Ringgren, *Israelite Religion* (D. Green, trans.; Philadelphia: Fortress, 1966): 239–247; L. H. Silberman, "Death in the Hebrew Bible and Apocalyptic Literature," *Perspectives on Death* (L. O. Mills, ed.; Nashville, New York: Abingdon, 1969): 13–32; L. R. Bailey, "Death As a Theological Problem in the Old Testament," *Pastoral Psychology* 22 (1971): 20–32; J. C. Burns, "The Mythology of Death in the Old Testament," *Scottish Journal of Theology* 26 (1973): 327–340; K. Spronk, *Beatific Afterlife in Ancient Israel and in the Ancient Near East* (AOAT 219; Neukirchen-Vluyn: Neukirchener, 1986): *passim*, esp. 29–64, 86–236. For further references, note the extensive bibliography in Spronk's book, pp. 348 ff.

360. For a convenient translation of the Akkadian account of Ishtar's descent into the Netherworld, see E. A. Speiser, "Descent of Ishtar to the Netherworld," in Pritchard (N 51): 106–109; for a translation of the Sumerian version of this story, see S. N. Kramer, *Sumerian Mythology* (Philadelphia: University of Pennsylvania Press, 1961): 83–96; more recently, idem., "The Descent of Inanna," in D. Wolkstein and S. N. Kramer, *Inanna; Queen of Heaven and Earth* (New York: Harper & Row, 1983): 52–89. Note, in particular the climax of the encounter of Ereshkigal and Inanna, as rendered by Kramer:

Then Ereshkigal fastened on Inanna the eye of death.
She spoke against her the word of wrath.
She uttered against her the cry of guilt.

She struck her.

Inanna was turned into a corpse.
A piece of rotting meat,
And was hung from a hook on the wall. (Ibid., 60.)

361. For a discussion of Mot in the Ugaritic texts, see, e.g., P. Watson, *Mot the God of Death at Ugarit and in the Old Testament* (Ph.D. dissertation; Yale University; 1970; Ann Arbor: University Microfilms, 1971); M. H. Pope and W. Röllig, "Syrien. Die Mythologie der Ugariter und Phönzier," *Wörterbuch der Mythologie* band I; *Götter und Mythen im Vorderen Orient* (H. W. Haussig, ed.; Stuttgart: Klett, 1965): 300–302; Tromp (N 358): *passim*, esp. 98 ff. For the most up-to-date bibliography, see Del Olmo Lete (N 51): 131 ff.

Of course the most death-oriented culture in the Ancient Near East is that of Egypt. However, as seems to be the case elsewhere (e.g., vis-à-vis the Righteous Sufferer motif and the legal metaphor), the poet of Job seems to draw less on the cultural/religious milieu of Egypt than on that of Mesopotamia and Syria-Palestine. In any case, there appears to be no direct and obvious connections between the way death is considered in Egypt and in the Poem of Job.

362. See *KTU*, text 1.5, col. 2, lines 2–4. For a convenient translation of the entire text, see Ginsberg in Pritchard (N 51): 138–139; Coogan (N 51): 75–115 esp. 106 ff.; see further, Caquot, Sznycer and Herdner (N 51): 237–252; Del Olmo Lete (N 51): 213–222; also the discussion on pp. 131–143; Watson (N 361): 46 ff.; de Moor, *Anthology* (N 51): 71–72. In making this translation, I have followed the readings of A. Herdner in *Corpus des tablettes en cunéiformes alphabétiques* (Paris: Geuthner, 1963): 33, which I have further confirmed by personal inspection of the text.

For a full discussion of all the Ugaritic texts in which Mot plays a role, see Watson, op. cit., *passim*, esp. 32–135, 172–221 for the conflict between Mot and Baal. For a discussion of biblical reflections of the "jaws of death," see ibid., 268–269; Tromp (N 358): 104–106; T. H. Gaster, *Thespis; Ritual, Myth and Drama in the Ancient Near East* (New York: Harper Torchbooks, 1961): 206–207.

363. See above, N 249.

364. See, e.g., the discussion of this point by Burns (N 359): 327–340, esp. 333–336.

365. For a convenient discussion of *Sheol*, see T. H. Gaster, "The Abode of the Dead" in *The Interpreter's Dictionary of the Bible* (G. A. Buttrick, et al., eds.; Nashville: Abingdon, 1962): vol. 1, 787–788. See also Tromp (N 358): 21–23; Martin-Achard (N 359): 36–47; Spronk (N 359): 66–71 and the bibliography discussed therein.

366. See Job 3:17 and, especially, 1:21 and the comments made, e.g., by Pope (*Job* [N 2]: 16, 32).

367. For similar sentiments in Job, see 10:21–22; 14:10–12.

368. The text is taken from an Old Babylonian recension of Gilgamesh (tablet 3, lines 1–5,) which adds material to tablet X of the standard Assyrian recension. The translation here essentially follows Kovacs (N 230): 85 n. 1; see also Speiser, "Akkadian" in Pritchard (N 51): 90; see further, e.g., Spronk (N 359): 96 ff. and the sources cited therein.

369. See *KTU* 1.17 col. 6, lines 25–29, 34–38. For a translation within the broader context, see Ginsberg, "Ugaritic" in Pritchard (N 51): 149–155; esp. 151; Coogan (N 51): 32–47; esp. 36–37; de Moor, *Anthology* (N 51): 233–240, esp. 238–239. For more detailed discussion and philological analysis, see, e.g., Caquot, Sznycer and Herdner (N 51): 399–458; esp. 431–433; Spronk (N 359): 151 ff. For a discussion of the passage demonstrating man's inability to be immortal, see, e.g., B. Vawter, "Intimations of Immortality and the Old Testament," *JBL* 91 (1972): 158–171; esp. 164–165.

The idea that no mortal can achieve immortality should not be used as an argument against a reconstruction of the Aqhat epic in which the slain hero is brought back to life (see above pp. 20 ff.) A distinction must be made between mortal resurrection and immortality. The former connotes a restoration to life but does not necessarily presume that he whose life has been renewed will then continue to live forever. Thus, an Aqhat or an Isaac might well be resurrected—a wondrous miracle in and of itself. But this resurrection is, nonetheless, a miracle with a time limit. Mortal resurrection only allows those who experience it to fill out their days and then finally die in their old age rather than be cut down in their youth before their time.

Of course, once in a great while there was an exception to the rule that no man could become immortal. In the Mesopotamian legends, the hero of the Flood Story, Atra-hasis or Utanaphistim seems to be such an exception; within biblical traditions, Enoch and Elijah also manage to escape death through divine intervention.

370. See, e.g., Bailey (N 359): 24–25.

371. See, e.g., Martin-Achard (N 359): 19, 31.

372. It is also possible that the next verse, the meaning of which is uncertain, also extends the death imagery; see the discussion in Tromp (N 358): 55–56. Tromp's interpretation of the verse has been accepted (with slight modification) by Pope, who renders 17:2: "The Mounds loom before me, On the Slime-Pits my eye dwells" (*Job* [N 2]: 127 and comments, p. 128). For a more traditional interpretation, see, e.g., Gordis, *Job* (N 250): 180. He renders: "Indeed, there are mockers all about me, and my eye must abide their provocations" (p. 172).

373. The Hebrew phrase in verse 12b reads 'wr qrwb mpny ḥšk (lit., "Light is near from before darkness"). The problem here is how exactly to understand qrwb, "near," in the context. Various explanations and emendations have been proposed (see, e.g., the discussions in Dhorme, *Job* [230]: 253; Driver and Gray [N 235]: 113; Gordis, *Job* [N 250]: 184).

The translation of verse 12 in the new Jewish Publication Society Bible (*Tanakh*; *A New Translation of the Holy Scriptures According to the Traditional Hebrew Text* [Philadelphia: JPS, 1985]: 1363), "They say that night is day, / That light is here—in the face of darkness" is attractive in that it makes good sense in and of itself. But it is hard to fit this statement, apparently taken as an observation by an impersonal third party, within the broader context of Job's speech. A simpler explanation may be that light is "near" in the sense of being closed in, before an all-encompassing darkness. The sense would be that light must stay close and therefore "give ground" from before the dark. The overall figure in verse 12 would thus portray everything going topsy-turvy. Night is turned into day and, conversely, light gives ground before darkness.

374. The form bdy, translated "gates," is problematical; see, e.g., the discussion in Dhorme, *Job* (N 230): 255; Pope, *Job* (N 2): 131; Gordis, *Job* (N 250): 185 for various scholarly explanations. I have opted for the long proposed explanation that the form be connected with bdym, "bars" (i.e., "gates") as in Hos. 11:6.

375. Reading this verb, with many commentators, nḥt, following the LXX, as first common plural from the root nḥt, "we will descend." See, e.g., Pope, *Job* (N 2): 131; Dhorme, *Job* (N 230): 256; Habel (N 67): 264.

376. Tablet 2, lines 112–115. The translation here follows Lambert, *Wisdom* (N 60): 46; see further, Bolle (N 29): 378, 379. For a discussion of similar figures of death in Mesopotamian literature, see, e.g., Burns (N 359): 330–331.

377. The death-oriented description continues through 88:13. See also, e.g., Ps. 18, esp. 18:5; Ps. 22, esp. 22:16; Ps. 28, esp. 28:1; Ps. 69, esp. 69:3.

378. Lévêque makes a comparison of lament figures in chapter 6 that also occur among passages in the Psalms, see (N 37): 332–333, n. 3. Also note the discussion in Westermann, *Structure* (N 283): 50–51.

379. Reading with virtually all commentators hwty (as in 30:13) for the otherwise unknown hyty. See, e.g., Pope, *Job* (N 2): 50; Habel (N 67): 139.

380. The meaning of l'w, which occurs only here and in Prov. 20:25, may mean "to speak rashly." For a discussion of various possibilities, see, e.g., Driver and Gray (N 235): vol. 2, 35; Dhorme, *Job* (N 230): 76.

381. The verb sld, employed here, is unique to this passage in Job. The meaning is highly conjectural and based as much on context as on various proposed etymologies and renderings in the other ancient versions. For a survey of interpretations, see, e.g., Driver and Gray (N 235): vol. 2, 38–39; Dhorme, *Job* (N 230): 82.

382. The following passage, Job 6:10c, ky-l' kḥdty 'mry-qdwš, would seem to mean, "because I have not suppressed the utterances of the Holy One." This could make some reasonable sense in the context. Job would seem to suggest that, though he wishes God to destroy him, he still wants to make it clear that this would be the punishment of the innocent; for Job has never tried to deny God's words.

Still, there are reasons for thinking that the passage may be secondary. First, it does not parallel anything, as is usually the case for poetic lines in the Poem of Job. The poet normally writes parallelistically paired or sometimes tripled lines which usually reinforce one, another. The third line of vs. 10 does not fit this general pattern and thus invites the suggestion that it is an interpolation. More significant is the use of $qdw\check{s}$, "Holy One" as an epithet for God. This is hardly without precedent in the Bible (cf., e.g., Dhorme, *Job* [N 230]: 82); still, this is the only instance where this title is used in Job. Once more, this would seem evidence in favor of an assumption that the term part of a glossator's addition. In any case, whether 6:10c is an addition or not has little effect upon the argument presented here.

383. That this verse might be meant ironically to foreshadow the Theophany, where, when Job does at last gain his confrontation with God, he is compelled to fall silent, should not be excluded.

384. For a discussion and analysis of the form of Job's curse, see, most recently, Habel, *Job* (N 67): 102–106.

385. For a discussion of Job 3 as a lament, see, e.g., Westermann, *Structure* (N 283): 37–38 and notes; also, Lévêque (N 37): 333–344. Note Westermann's verse-to-verse comparison of the Jeremiah and Job passages and his comment: "The two passages are remarkably similar to one another, coinciding in almost every respect." (p. 60, n. 12).

386. Ibid., 60. I am more doubtful of Westermann's assumption that this particular lament type had a "fixed preliterary form." This could very well be; however, it is equally possible and, I suspect, more probable that this is a *literary* form, especially in consideration that the structures of the "curse-the-day" lament in Jeremiah 20 and Job 3 are so strikingly similar.

387. See the discussion of this passage above in N 339.

388. See pp. 95 ff. and N 293 A similar point could be made about Psalm 88. Although this psalm is nothing but lament, without the turn to appeal one finds elsewhere in other similar texts, nevertheless, I believe that the appeal is implicit; indeed, one can only wonder why it would be among the lament psalms of the Bible if it were otherwise.

389. That a death-wish sentiment might play an archetypical role in the relationship of a prophet to God is perhaps indicated, in that at least two other biblical prophets, Elijah and Jonah, express precisely this desire to their Deity.

Elijah does so at a very dark moment in his prophetic career, while fleeing from the wrath of Jezebel toward an exile in the wilderness from which there would seem to be no recourse. Finally Elijah declares, "Take my life, for I am no better than my fathers!" (1 Kgs. 19:4). But it is just at this desperate moment that God acts in Elijah's favor—stimulated by the prophet's plea *in extremis*—first, giving him physical sustenance (19:5–8) and then further sustaining him through the profoundest revelation of the divine presence (19:8 ff.); cf. also the somewhat similar circumstances in Gen. 25:22, 27:46, 30:1.

Jonah twice expresses his desire to die—first, after he discovers that God has decided, after all, not to destroy Nineveh (Jonah 4:3) and again after God has destroyed the plant that had given His prophet shade from the sun (4:8–9). In both instances Jonah is sent reeling into a despair that culminates in a demand that God put an end to His prophet's existence.

In all likelihood, the author of Jonah is utilizing Jonah's death-wish in an ironic fashion. Note, in this respect, that it seems slightly absurd that Jonah should go into such paroxysms of grief simply because God has robbed him of his shade from the sun. Hence, it is doubtful that we are supposed to take Jonah's desire to die seriously: much more likely, it is simply a pose. Just as this reluctant prophet pretends that he is sorry for the death of the plant when what he really misses is its shade (4:9–10), so too he histrionically voices a desire to die when what he truly wants is to gain God's pity and support.

Jonah's death-wish is thus best understood as a burlesque of the sort of despair exemplified in Jeremiah's and Elijah's desire to die. But at the base of this satirical play on prophetic despair there probably is an element of truth. It may not be all that unusual for prophets to get so desperate that they would voice a demand to die or even wish that they had never been born. Still, in the final analysis, this, too, is really a pose, although of an entirely earnest sort. Just as we have seen in the case of Jeremiah and Elijah, it is a drastic means of getting divine attention and ultimately a redress of grievance. If the author of Jonah can use such a figure so effectively, one wonders whether, by his time, the prophetic death-wish might have come to be viewed as a cliché.

390. Still, there may well be an ironic undertone to Eliphaz's initial remark; see the discussion above, N 290.

391. Book 1, lines 258–263.

392. In saying this, I do not necessarily mean to imply that according to the view expressed in the Poem, God is out of his jurisdiction in the netherworld. While such an assumption is explicit in Canaanite myths like the Ugaritic Baal cycle or in *Innana/Ishtar's Descent*, at best these traditions probably have a subliminal effect on the conception we see expressed in Job. In this respect, the *Paradise Lost* analogy is helpful. In Job, as in Milton's epic, it is not so much that God cannot exert control over the netherworld, but rather that He does not care to do so. Certainly, in other biblical texts there is little question of God's control over *Sheol*, and, although we cannot be certain that the poet of Job was specifically familiar with such texts, we should not necessarily assume that the concept was foreign to him. Indeed, considering the sort of omnipotent God he portrays throughout his work, there is good reason to think otherwise.

393. There is one passage where Job appears to ask for reprieve and pardon; but a closer look at the text shows that things are not quite what they would appear to be. The passage in question is 7:21a where Job asks God, "So why do You not pardon my transgression and take away my iniquity?" Already, this text seems at odds with the sense of Job's overall disputation. After all, the whole point of Job's argument is that he is innocent; so why, all of a sudden, does he begin to talk about his transgression ($p\check{s}'$) and his iniquity ('wn), as if he really *were* a sinner who merited punishment? I suspect that Habel is on the right track when he sees this passage as a "mock plea" for pardon from a bogus sin (cf. 7:20) that Job might be imagined to have committed. As Habel suggests, this request for pardon is best characterized as "a taunt rather than a traditional affirmation of trust in God's mercy and confession of guilt" (see Habel, *Job* [N 67]: 166).

In line with this, the second half of the verse makes sense in terms of the analysis of the death-motif I have presented above. Job says (7:21b), Forgive my sin, "for then I might lie down in the Dust, and You [God] would seek me, but I would no longer exist." Once more, we have an illogical and disjunctive turn in Job's discourse. Where the conventional expectation would be for Job to plead, "Forgive me so that You may rescue me," instead, he says, "Forgive me, let me die, so You can no longer find me." This then, reinforces the manner in which the poet utilizes the death-wish motif, by portraying a Job who really wishes to elude God, even if he must go to that one, final hiding place of mankind in order to do so.

394. In this connection, note Ringgren's comment: "But besides such statements [emphasizing the permanency of death] we find, even in the earlier period, isolated [biblical] passages looking forward to a resurrection of the dead." (*Israelite* [N 359]: 322).

395. There can be little question that in late biblical writings the concept of resurrection from the dead was stimulated at least in part by the influence of Iranian religion and thought. Ringgren's observation (ibid., 323) on this point is, however, cogent: "In this realm one must reckon with a comparatively powerful influx of Persian ideas, which suggest that the doctrine of the resurrection also drew its inspiration from this quarter. It must be remembered, however, that the earliest text shows definite features of the ancient Canaanite syncretism. It is likely that we have here one of the pillars on which the doctrine of the resurrection was based. In any event, Persian influences cannot explain everything." See also the extensive

discussion of this point in Martin-Achard (N 359): 186 ff. Most recently, Spronk has resurveyed the evidence and reached this conclusion regarding the influence of Persian religion on the biblical conception of resurrection: "Persian influence is not regarded anymore as a crucial factor in this development. It probably was restricted to the influence of some elements of the Persian conceptions upon the way in which the Jewish eschatology was developed"; (N 359): 57–59, 125–129; the quotation is on pp. 58–59.

For a general discussion of the concept of resurrection in the Ancient Near East and its effect on the Hebrew Bible, see, e.g., ibid., 49 ff.; Ringgren, op. cit., 322–323; Birkeland (N 57): 60–78; J. Wijngaards, "Death and Resurrection in Covenantal Context (Hos. VI 2)" *VT* 17 (1967): 227–239; Vawter (N 369): 158–171. For the concept of resurrection in later Jewish thought, see Cavallin (N 103); G. W. E. Nickelsburg, *Resurrection, Immortality, and Eternal Life in Intertestamental Judaism* (Cambridge: Harvard University Press, 1972). The most extensive, recent discussion of the concept of resurrection in the Ancient Near East is Spronk, op. cit. See further, the cautionary remarks regarding some of Spronk's conclusions in the review by M. Smith and E. Bloch-Smith, *JAOS* 108 (1988): 277–284.

396. Cf., e.g., similar figures in Ps. 90:4–5; 103:15–16; Isa. 40:6–7. See also Habel, *Job* (N 67): 240.

397. I suspect, with many commentators, that vs. 4 is a gloss. For a discussion of the pros and cons on this issue, see, e.g., Dhorme, *Job* (N 230): 195–196; Pope, *Job* (N 2): 106–107; Habel, *Job* (N 67): 240. I also wonder whether vs. 3, with its sudden switch to a first-person object (*'ty*, often emended in the commentaries to *'tw*; see, e.g., Dhorme, op. cit., following the reading in the LXX, Vulgate and Peshitta) and its shift to juridical terminology is out of place. In any case, the argument presented here is not appreciably affected, whether these verses are taken to be original to the Poem or not.

398. For the text, see *KTU* 1.6, col. 3, lines 4–9. For a translation in the broader context, see Ginsberg, "Ugaritic," in Pritchard (N 51): 140; Coogan (N 51): 112; Gibson (N 51): 77; de Moor, *Anthology* (N 51): 91. Just how we are to understand the so-called "Seasonal Pattern" as depicted in the Ugaritic myths centering on Baal is a much-debated issue. Still, few scholars in the field of Ugaritic studies would deny that the story of Baal's conflict with Mot was seen by its ancient audience as having a direct connection with an agricultural alternation between fertility and drought.

For a sustained consideration of the Baal/Mot conflict as reflecting an annual seasonal pattern, see J. C. de Moor, *The Seasonal Pattern in the Ugaritic Myth of Ba'lu* (Neukirchen-Vluyn: Butzon & Bercker Kevelaer, 1971) where all the relevant texts are discussed; see also Spronk (N 359): 145 ff. The reader should be cautioned, however, that neither de Moor's, nor any other scholar's specific model for fitting the Baal texts into the broader framework of the agricultural/religious life at Ugarit has achieved scholarly consensus. In particular, it is open to serious question whether the cycle of death and renewal depicted in the Baal texts is meant to represent an annual agricultural progress of seasons. For a recent discussion of the "Seasonal Pattern" interpretation, vis-à-vis the Baal texts at Ugarit with extensive bibliography, see M. Smith, "Interpreting the Baal Cycle," *UF* 18 (1987): 313–339, esp. his criticism's of de Moor's approach, 314–316; also Smith and Bloch-Smith (N 395): 278 ff.

A similar assumption of a connection between agricultural death and renewal and a dying/rising god possibly also informs the Tammuz/Dumuzi cult, which, as we know from Ezek. 8:14, was present in the biblical milieu. For a discussion of the cult, see, e.g., T. Jacobsen, "Toward the Image of Tammuz," in *Toward the Image of Tammuz and Other Essays on Mesopotamian History and Culture* (W. L. Moran, ed.; Cambridge: Harvard University Press, 1970): 73–101.

399. See the discussion above, N 54.

400. Of course, once more we could appeal to a psychological explanation. God would

then be like a dieter who hides sweets so that he will not be able to get to them easily. Again, there is likely an element of truth in this sort of psychological explanation, but such a narrow approach seems to be insufficient to do justice to the poet's intentions here.

401. See above, pp. 223 ff.

402. See pp. 220 ff.

403. See e.g., Terrien, *Job* (N 253): 151; Gordis, *Job* (N 250): 205; Habel, *Job* (N 67): 308.

404. Cf. Tromp's discussion of the term, (N 358): 85–91 and the bibliography cited therein. For the most detailed discussion of the resurrection theme as applied to the Redeemer passage in Job 19, see Lévêque (N 37): 478 ff. who also supplies extensive bibliography; for a more recent discussion, see Spronk (N 359): 310–315. For a specific discussion of "dust" in the Poem of Job, see Lévêque, op. cit., 481, n. 1.

405. It is precisely because of the apparent allusion to Baal, found here in Job, that Williams believes that the Redeemer *is* Baal, not merely created, as it were, in his image. See above p. 114 and Williams, "Theodicy," (N 233): 24.

406. Usually in such stories, at least in so far as they occur in the Bible, God is shown to be in conflict with the god of the oceans, Yam, or the great sea dragon, Leviathan. No overt references to a conflict with Mot occur among the biblical texts. Whether this reflects happenchance or a systematic suppression of such material is hard to determine, although I suspect the latter is more likely than the former. In any case, it is not so much the substance of the story type that concerns us here as the form, which, regardless of who is the champion and who the enemy, is largely the same.

407. It is also quite possible that in some version of the Aqhat/Danel legend, it is Baal who is instrumental in bringing Aqhat back to life. Note, in this respect, that Baal also plays a crucial role in gaining a son for Danel in the first place after his wife had been previously barren. Note, too, that when Anat offers Aqhat eternal life (see the passage cited above, p. 120), she compares herself with Baal "when he brings to life" (*kyḥwy*). In a like manner she boldly affirms, "so I too can bring to life" (*aḥwy*). See *KTU* 1.17 col. 6 lines 30, 33; for this understanding of the passage, see Spronk (N 359): 151 ff., esp. 155; also Smith and Bloch-Smith (N 395): 278–279.

Still, we should also recognize that there is considerable debate as to whether Job 19:25 ff. purports to represent resurrection or not. For a discussion of this issue, including considerable bibliography, see Lévêque (N 37): 479–489.

Recently, M. Barré has made an interesting argument that if correct, would make the resurrection theme in this passage unmistakable. He notes that in vs. 25, the terms *ḥy* and *qwm* (as verbal roots, "to live" and "to arise, stand," respectively) constitute a common pair used in poetic contexts (likewise, their semantic equivalents *balāṭu* and *tebû* in Akkadian). He further notes that in "*all* attested instances of the formulaic pair [there is] the same setting-in-life—that of healing/resurrection. Therefore, if the pair does occur in this verse [19:25]— and that does not seem open to question—we should expect it to refer to healing or resurrection as well." He therefore offers the following translation of the verse:

> I know that my redeemer can restore life/health,
> And that (my) guarantor can raise up from the dust [=netherworld].

Barré also makes mention of the fact that one of the attributes of Marduk in *Ludlul* is that he can restore to life. In tablet 4 line 33, the Righteous Sufferer declares, "Who but Marduk can restore the dead to life?" and similar sentiments are also voiced in lines 29 and 35. Job's Redeemer would then be depicted here in much the same terms. See "A Note on Job XIX 25," *VT* 29 (1979): 108–110. For the passages in *Ludlul*, see Lambert, *Wisdom* (N 60): 58–59; Bolle (N 29): 390–393.

This is attractive, however it does require some adjustment/emendation of the text (read $g'lyhy = g'ly\ yhy$ for $g'ly\ hy$ and $yqm = y\bar{a}q\bar{i}m$ for $yqwm$), and it also discounts the parallel in the Ugaritic myths cited above. I therefore hesitate to adopt this interpretation, although it may well be that the pairing may reflect at least an indirect allusion to resurrection. Nonetheless, we should never assume that tradition constitutes a kind of literary strait jacket that necessarily inhibits a writer's ability to manipulate a theme with considerable freedom. In this respect, Habel's comments on Barré's approach (*Job* [N 67]: 293) seem to me quite on the mark: "It is valuable to recognize traditional word pairs, since they highlight the underlying polarity of the text. But the life/death polarity is evident without making the emendations proposed. Moreover, authors adapt word pairs to their specific purposes."

408. Like virtually every term in these verses, various alternative readings and interpretations have been offered for *'hrwn* in vs. 25b. M. Dahood in "Hebrew-Ugaritic Lexicography IX," *Bib* 52 (1971): 346 has taken the term substantively as an epithet parallel to $g\bar{o}'\bar{e}l$, "Redeemer." He therefore translates it as "the Ultimate." Pope, (*Job* [N 2]: 146) also takes the term as a substantive, but renders it as "Guarantor" based on the rabbinical usage of the term *'hr'y*. I am inclined to preserve the adverbial sense of the term. Note in this connection Habel's sensible observation: "the expression *'ah^aron* is not a standard epithet for God, and unless there are cogent reasons to the contrary the term should be retained as an adverb"; *Job* (N 67): 305.

409. Any attempt at translation of these verses must be considered provisional and tentative. I have tried to to read the text, as much as possible, without emendation. Beyond this, a brief philological explanation may be in order. I have taken *'hr*, "after," in a temporal sense, in coordination with *'hrn* of the previous half verse. The term *z't*, "this," in vs. 26a poses syntactic problems no matter how it is rendered. I have been inclined to follow the view that this term modifies *'wry*, "my skin." If the reading is correct as it stands, perhaps the disjunctive position of *z't* is used to give the pronoun a dramatically emphatic force, hence, the translation "my very skin"; see, e.g., T. H. Meek, "Job xix 25–27," *VT* 6 (1956): 102. The sense of *mbśry*, "from my flesh," would seem to be "from (within) my flesh." It is also possible to read the preposition (m-<mn) as connoting separation, "without my flesh." That is, Job, although stripped of his skin and flesh, essentially a skeleton, still sees God; see, e.g., Habel, *Job* (N 67): 293. For further consideration of this possible reading of the phrase, see N 411. It is hard to determine whether vs. 27b is part of this same thought as vv. 25 ff. or not. Conceivably, it could be a misplaced half-verse, as is apparently the case with vv. 28–29; see, e.g., Pope, *Job* (N 2): 147. If 27b is to be taken together with the previous passage, it might be understood as an implicit adverbial qualification of 27ab; that is, it relays Job's condition even as he is seeing God with his own eyes. My translation of this half-verse tries to convey a sense of this adverbial nuance. If one reads the earlier phrase *mbśry* as "from my flesh," 27b would connote that this flesh is decomposed; if one reads *mbśry* as "without my flesh," 27b simply reinforces the image of a Job worn down to the very bone. On the other hand, one could just as easily take the passage as simply an outburst of despair at the conclusion of Job's speech.

410. It has been argued that *l'd* in vs. 24b should be read as "for a witness" rather than "forever," reading *'ēd* for *'ad*. Then the text would be translated, "carved as a witness in the rock." For bibliography on this proposal, see, e.g., Dhorme, *Job* (N 230): 282.

411. My interpretation is not appreciably altered if the phrase *mbśry*, "from my flesh," is taken to mean "without my flesh" as some commentators have suggested (see above N 409). In that case the poet presents a picture of a truly disembodied Job—without skin, without flesh, literally worn down to the bare bones. A scene of resurrection comes to mind that is reminiscent of this scene of a Joban skeleton rising from the grave—Ezekiel's vision of the valley of dry bones (chap. 37). Of course, in that instance the bones that Ezekiel's message

raises from the dead, do not simply come together; but sinews, flesh and skin are overlaid on them and the breath of life enters them (37:7 ff.). Just as in Paul's declaration in First Corinthians, the dead are "changed," and their bodies renewed. The Joban image of a resurrection without flesh and skin can only be seen as a grisly counterpoint to this stereotypical picture of the triumph over death. I am grateful to D. N. Freedman for pointing out to me the relevance of the Ezekiel passage to the picture of resurrection in Job 19:23 ff.

412. One is reminded, in this connection, of the famous short story by W. W. Jacobs, "The Monkey's Paw." In this story a man and his wife obtain a mummified monkey's paw that has been enchanted by an old fakir who wanted "to show that fate ruled people's lives, and that those who interfered with it did so to their sorrow." The enchantment allowed the possessor three wishes.

The man therefore wishes for 200 pounds, a wish granted when their son dies, after being horribly mangled in the machinery at his workplace. The company, in order to avoid litigation, offers precisely this amount in compensation.

Ten days later, while in the depths of mourning, the couple realize that they still have two more wishes left. So at the wife's frenzied urging, the husband makes the fateful second wish: "I wish my son alive again."

After a while there is a knocking at the door, at first very quiet and then a pounding, louder and louder. While the wife runs to meet her son, the husband suddenly realizes what he has done: he has wished back a living corpse, and it is this mangled, decomposed thing, banging for admittance to his home, that would enfold his wife in its cold embrace. While the mother frantically tries to unlock the door, her husband does the only thing he can do to save them all: he makes his third and last wish—to send the dead thing come alive again back where it belongs; back to the grave.

For the story, see, e.g., *Black Water; The Book of Fantastic Literature* (A. Manguel, ed.; New York: Potter, 1983): 511–521. I am grateful to my colleague David Tool for drawing my attention to "The Monkey's Paw" in connection to the Joban concept of resurrection.

413. The translation follows Kovacs (N 230): 3–4; tablet 1, lines 8–13, 16–19, 22–26, see also tablet 11, lines 314–319 (pp. 107–108).

414. For example, a number of scholars have noted how the poet of Job utilizes doxologies, i.e., hymns in praise of God, in a parodistic fashion. This is especially clear in chapter 12:13–25. Note Habel's comment, *Job* (N 67): 216: "As scholars have recognized, 12:13–25 has the form of a hymn extolling God's wisdom and power. Its orientation, however, is satirical, since all the deeds of God reflecting his wisdom and authority are negative." Thus, although the poet chooses stereotypical figures in this and other doxologies (see, e.g., 9:5–13) to "praise" God, the figures employed stress the destructive attributes of God, thereby turning the hymn into a "counterdoxology" that tends to undercut the standard convention. For further discussion of doxologies in Job, cf., e.g., Lévêque (N 37): 312–328, Westermann, *Structure* (N 283): 72–79; J. L. Crenshaw, "The Influence of the Wise upon Amos; The 'Doxologies of Amos' and Job 5 9–16, 9 5–10," *ZAW* 79 (1967): 42–52.

For a survey of recent studies on irony and satire in the book of Job, see Williams, "Current Trends" (N 36): 18–22.

415. J. L. Crenshaw, *Old Testament Wisdom; an Introduction* (Atlanta: John Knox, 1981): 120. Note also Westermann's comment that some scholars "contend that so far as literary form is concerned, the Book of Job is utterly unique"; *Structure* (N 283): 1 and the collection of such opinions on p. 14, n. 2. Westermann himself classifies the Book of Job as a drama. This is not an inappropriate descriptive term, especially as Westermann uses it, i.e., to connote "an occurrence, an event" that the poet "works into the framework of a narrative" (p. 6). Still, by defining Job in this more impressionistic fashion and eschewing the sense of drama "in the firmly fixed literary sense" (ibid.) we really have yet another restatement that

Job is a thing unto itself, not easily classed with other literary works from the Ancient Near East.

416. Note, for example, that Yiddish satirists typically ranged all over their cultural milieu in search of targets to mock, precisely as suggested here. Indeed, their satires are often so detailed and all-encompassing that they have now become one of the primary sources for study of folkloric elements in east European Jewish culture before the turn of the century. Miron considers this issue in some detail. He notes, "with a typically anatomical intent they [Yiddish satirists] set about analyzing and recording various facets of the vast panorama of traditional Jewish behavior: Jewish dress, Jewish superstition, rites of passage, holidays, rituals, domestic life, patterns of sexual behavior, cultural characteristics of various professions, jokes, proverbs, curses, dialectic idiosyncrasies, and so on." Satire had to encompass all of these elements because it was precisely these aspects of Yiddish culture that in the eyes of the satirists, held the Jews back from assimilation into the broader European culture. Miron observes that these various folkloric elements in Yiddish society

> embodied Jewish specificity in its most obvious forms; it included all the factors—material, behavioral, and verbal—which set the Jew apart, and which made him for the non-Jew a stereotype, both hateful and ridiculous. Obviously, it had to be erased. Jews had to change their language with their dress, modify their intonation as well as their customs, shed the encrustation of specific cultural identity which had solidified around them in the course of long centuries of separate corporate-like existence in a feudal society. For that purpose, folklore itself had to be attacked, satirized, taken apart, and anatomized away. (Miron, "Folklore" [N 141]: 220–221.)

417. See the discussion on pp. 44 f.

418. An interesting example of an Ancient Near Eastern satirical literary work is the *Dialogue of Pessimism*. As Speiser notes, "one could make out a case for listing Jonathan Swift as a spiritual descendant of our ancient author" ("Case" [N 268]: 105) in this instance. Although, as noted above (N 268), this work is not directly comparable to the dialogue form of the Poem of Job; on the other hand, it does show certain affinities to the parodistic elements we have been considering in the current discussion. Note, in this respect, that the author of the *Dialogue* presents theme and countertheme, as the master first proposes one position and then its opposite, with the slave adding his fervent agreement, no matter what his master proposes. It is also significant to note the range of materials encompassed, as the satire turns from topic to topic (e.g., from traveling to banqueting to hunting to legal accusation to criminal activity to love and so on). Finally, especially significant is Speiser's observation that the author of the *Dialogue of Pessimism* apparently ranges all over the literary-cultural scene (even lifting a phrase from Gilgamesh) to quote "clichés and copy book maxims" for the purpose of lampooning them in this exchange between master and slave (ibid., 104–105).

Still, although it seems probable that the *Dialogue of Pessimism* was meant to be broadly humorous, nonetheless, this parody of the master-slave relationship probably has a far more serious underlying intent—to emphasize that every thought or action can be reasoned both pro and con and that as a result, any attempt to find an ultimate purpose or meaning in the efforts of humanity can only prove to be futile.

419. For a discussion of the various debates over the significance of the "day of the LORD" in Amos and elsewhere, see, e.g., H. W. Wolff, *Joel and Amos* (Hermeneia; W. Janzen and S. D. McBride, eds.; C. A. Muenchow, trans.; Philadelphia: Fortress, 1969): 254–257 and the sources cited therein. Note that however scholars choose to understand Amos' use of the "day of the LORD," there is general agreement that he is lampooning a standard "woe" oracle by turning it against Israel rather than against Israel's enemies. Of

course, he uses the same sort of misdirection in the opening series of oracles: first, by portraying God as condemning Israel's enemies, as prophets are conventionally supposed to do (Amos 1:2–2:5) but then reversing his field by showing that God also condemns Israel itself (2:6 ff.), thus turning the stereotypical oracle against foreign nations on its head. Likewise, the prophetic claim that God hates and despises ritual and sacrifice, first promulgated by Amos (e.g., 6:21 ff.) but then taken up by the prophets that follow, must also be seen as a case of playing a counterpoint against the stereotype. The people may think that God loves and even demands ritual and sacrifice, but, on the contrary, the prophets declare, this is precisely what he hates and rejects.

420. See above, p. 84.

421. See the discussion above, pp. 87 ff.

422. This motto is also cited in Prov. 9:10; Ps. 111:10; and Sir. 1:14 (cf. 1:11–30), 19:20, 25:10–11. In Ben Sira's writings, the concept that the "awe of the Lord" is the most fundamental principle of Wisdom can rightly be considered one of the organizing principles of the book. See. e.g., the discussion in A. A. Di Lella and P. W. Skehan, *The Wisdom of Ben Sira* (Anchor Bible vol. 39; Garden City: Doubleday, 1987): 78 ff.

Certainly, an argument could be made that this proverb had much broader circulation than just the biblical environment in which it now occurs. Thus, like similar potential "parallels" between Job and other biblical texts, it should not be considered decisive proof of a specifically Jewish/Israelite context for chapter 28 (see further, the discussion on pp. 91 f.). Still, in this particular instance I think that the frequency with which this tenet is identified with the biblical attitude toward Wisdom has to be taken seriously. Indeed, it would be fair to argue that this motto is the very embodiment of the biblical Wisdom credo and arguably the most famous of all Wisdom statements in the Bible. While such evidence cannot be said to be airtight "proof" that any text that uses this phrase therefore must be Israelite/Jewish in origin, it would be fair to say that the available evidence generally favors this assumption.

Of course, there is a question as to whether this phrase is part of a secondary addition to the Hymn to Wisdom. For a consideration of this issue, see pp. 143 ff.

423. See, e.g., Lévêque (N 37): 595 and especially note 3 which gives a thorough list of studies that consider this issue. Note also, in this connection, that vs. 23 utilizes *'lhym* for "God," the normal Israelite/Jewish term in contradistinction to *'l* and *'lwh* which are the common terms for "God" in Job. See Lévêque's comments, ibid.

424. The name also occurs in 1 Sam. 1:1; 1 Chron. 12:21, 26:7 and 27:18; and in no such case is the name associated with a foreign individual. There are six further attestations of the name from ancient inscriptions, and, in all cases, their provenance would seem to be the environs of Jerusalem; see J. H. Tigay, *You Shall Have No Other Gods; Israelite Religion in the Light of Hebrew Inscriptions* (Harvard Semitic Studies 31; Atlanta: Scholars, 1986): 48. For a discussion of the forms of the name Elihu/Eliyahu, see, e.g., Dhorme, *Job* (N 230): 473; Pope, *Job* (N 2): 241–242; J. D. Fowler, *Theophoric Personal Names in Ancient Hebrew; A Comparative Study* (Sheffield: University of Sheffield Press, 1988): 129–130; 179–180; 336, 342. Note, in contrast, that the names of Job's three other friends, have no Israelite/Jewish associations.

425. See 1 Chron. 2:9, 25, 27; Ruth 4:19 and, e.g., the discussion ibid., 242.

426. See pp. 81 ff.

427. M. Greenberg, "The Redaction of the Plague Narrative in Exodus," *Near Eastern Studies in Honor of William Foxwell Albright* (H. Goedicke, ed.; Baltimore: Johns Hopkins University Press, 1971): 243–252; esp. 245.

428. See Tigay, "Evolution" (N 230): 35 ff., esp. his remarks on Greenberg's theoretical, redactional model, p. 45.

429. If we were to assume that other sections of Job (e.g., the Theophany or some part

thereof) have been interpolated into the book (see. p. 89), they would fit into Greenberg's model as well. In that case, we would recognize such supplements as being so chronologically close to the original poem that they are integrated into the work with little noticeable disjunction. In fact, it is precisely for this reason that one cannot find certain grounds that they are interpolations at all.

430. See pp. 88 f.

431. Reading with the $qere$, $pnynym$ for the anomalous $pnyym$. For a discussion of this term, which connotes some manner of precious red stone (see Lam. 4:7); see for example, Driver, Gray (N 235): vol. 1, 241; Pope, Job (N 2): 204; Habel, Job (N 67): 391. Various proposals have been made for this with "coral" being the most popular alternative to rubies. In the absence of decisive evidence one way or another, I have opted for the traditional translation.

432. See also Prov. 8:10–11.

433. Some commentators emend 'rkh, "its price," to $drkh$, "its way," and translate along the lines of "no man knows its way"; see, e.g., Dhorme, Job (N 230): 406–407; Habel, Job (N 67): 390. Pope proposes translating 'rk as "abode," basing his understanding of the term on a presumed Ugaritic cognate; see Job (N 2): 203.

434. If, as has been argued above, the Poem of Job and the Hymn to Wisdom, which has been interpolated into it, are chronologically earlier than the Prose Frame Story, one could always contend that the writer of the Prologue lifted the phrasing from 28:28 and placed it in the Prologue. Conversely, if 28:28 is a late gloss added to the Hymn, the process could have been the reverse, i.e., the glossator of the Hymn might have used the phrasing of the Prologue to guide his addition to the Wisdom Poem. My inclination, however, is to follow neither of these scenarios. I suspect, instead, that the description of Job as one who "fears God and shuns evil" was a fixed part of the old folk story itself. This phrase was then preserved in the later rendition of the Prose Frame Story and also was alluded to in 28:28.

435. See, conveniently, Lévêque, (N 37): 595, esp. the sources cited in n. 3.

436. The Wisdom Hymn might even be seen as a complete pietistic adaptation of an earlier, more critically minded poem, which was then added to the conclusion of the Dialogue.

437. See pp. 73 ff.

438. See the discussion above, p. 88.

439. Cf. Habel, "Role" (N 230): 88; for his fuller discussion, see esp. 88–96. See also, idem, Job (N 67): 36–37; 443 ff. and J. W. Wheedbee, "The Comedy of Job," $Studies in the Book of Job$ ($Semeia$ 7; R. Polzin and D. A. Robertson, eds.; Missoula: SBL, 1977): 19–20; D. A. Robertson, "The Comedy of Job: A Response," in ibid. 43; note also Cooper's approving comments of Habel's interpretation, "Review" (N 228): 5; but note as well his criticisms of Wheedbee, "Narrative Theory," (N 228): 42.

440. Habel, Job (N 67): 36–37.

441. Note, e.g., how Habel deals with Elihu's comment in 32:18, which he translates, "For I am bloated with arguments / And wind distends my belly." Habel sees this as a fairly vulgar play upon the earlier comment by Eliphaz (15:2) that Job has "windy knowledge": "Unwittingly Elihu characterizes himself as a windbag and a constipated fool by appropriating the sarcastic language chosen by Eliphaz to taunt Job. The inner compulsion to speak, which was experienced by Jeremiah as the fire of God's word burning within (Jer. 20:9), is transformed by Elihu into a need to relieve himself of the wind building up in his body" (ibid., 444). While such a reading of the passage is certainly possible, this is not the kind of subtle figure we have seen earlier in the Poem. Rather, it would be a blatant play on the earlier text—a literary pratfall. On the other hand, the figure need not necessarily be taken in

such a scatological sense. Rather, it can be read "straight" as the sincere passion of Elihu as he gives vent to his anger. Note, in this respect, the translation in the Revised Standard Version, which conveys Elihu's statement without a hint of the broad, vulgar humor that Habel finds here: "For I am full of words; / The spirit within me constrains me."

442. See pp. 111 f.

443. Habel makes an intriguing argument that *'p* as employed here by Elihu is meant to have a double meaning, not only connoting "also," as we have noted, above but also "anger," which is spelled in precisely the same manner. He comments, "While *'ap-'ani* is a common emphatic idiom of self-assertion, the words themselves suggest a hidden rendering of "I am anger." If this double entendre is intentional, we have a hidden allusion to the true character of Elihu in the poet's wording of Elihu's own apology." (Habel, *Job* [N 67]: 443–444).

444. Pope, *Job* (N 2): xxvii. For an approving consideration of Elihu's point that suffering can be disciplinary, see W. A. Irwin, "The Elihu Speeches in the Criticism of the Book of Job," *JR* 17 (1937): 39–40.

445. For a convenient summary and interpretation of Elihu's use of legal terminology, see Scholnick, *Lawsuit* (N 298): 291–300.

446. See ibid., 291; idem, "*Mišpaṭ*" (N 291): 525.

447. My inclination is to follow Scholnick's interpretation here and see the term *mwkyḥ* as connoting a legal advocate; see Scholnick, *Lawsuit* (N 298): 321, n. 83. Note in this respect that here the term is used in context with *'nh*, "to respond," which definitely connotes an advocacy role. Habel, in contrast, interprets the term in a more neutral fashion as connoting "arbiter" who should "process Job's case"; cf. *Job* (N 67): 441, 452, probably under the influence of the use of *mwkyḥ* in Job 9:33. However, as I have argued above (pp. 223 ff.), even in Job's appeal in 9:33 and elsewhere for legal aid, he really does not desire an impartial intercessor but rather a divine Judge-Advocate, who is partisan in Job's favor.

448. For this legalistic interpretation of *dbry* (lit., "my words"), see Scholnick, *Lawsuit* (N 298): 221.

449. For a discussion of the legal nuances here, see, e.g., ibid., 196–197, 221; Habel, *Job* (N 67): 463–465. Note that similar legalistic phrasing occurs in Job 13:6, 18; 23:4.

450. Note, e.g., 33:8 ff.

451. See 35:4, where Elihu declares, "I will make a (legal) response to you, and to your friends as well!"

452. See Scholnick, "*Mišpaṭ*" (N 298): 525; *Lawsuit* (N 298): 293–294. I have essentially adopted her translation here and followed her interpretation of *bḥr*, translated here as "to consider," and *mšpṭ*, rendered as "(legal) case."

453. Scholnick would even read *ṭwb*, the Hebrew term for "good," as "defensible." For her rationale, see "*Mišpaṭ*" (N 298): 525, n. 7; *Lawsuit* (N 298): 294–295.

454. See ibid., 295; Habel, *Job* (N 67): 431.

455. There is considerable debate over how to read and interpret the verb employed here, *'kzb*, according to the Masoretic tradition. With Pope (*Job* [N 2]: 256) and Dhorme (*Job* [N 230]: 510–511) I have followed the LXX which reads *epseusato=ykzb*, lit., "he lies," i.e., a third-person masculine singular verb instead of the first-person common singular verb found in the MT. Presumably, the text was changed in the Masoretic tradition so as not to impugn falsehood to God; see C. McCarthy, *The Tiqqune Sopherim and Other Theological Corrections in the Masoretic Text of the Old Testament* (Orbis Biblicus et Orientalis 36; Freiburg, Göttingen: University of Freiburg and Vandenhöck & Ruprecht, 1981). For interpretations with *'kzb*, see, e.g., the discussion in Scholnick, *Lawsuit* (N 298): 295; Habel, *Job* (N 67): 475. For objections to the interpretation usually employed if the Masoretic reading is followed, i.e., "I am accounted a liar," see Pope's and Dhorme's comments, op. cit. However

one reads the text in this instance, the overall force of the argument is not materially affected. See further, p. 169.

456. The form $ḥṣy$ is grammatically anomalous in the text. I have emended to $ḥṣyw$, "his darts." For recent discussions of various alternative interpretations, see, e.g., Scholnick, *Lawsuit* (N 298): 322, n. 95; Habel, *Job* (N 67): 475. The basic meaning of the passage is clear regardless of how the form is taken.

457. See also, 34:35–37.

458. See also 35:1 ff.; 36:1 ff.

459. Or alternatively the "Innocent-Mighty," since $ṣdyq$ can carry the nuance of both "just, righteous" and "(legally) innocent." Undoubtedly, the Elihu-writer wishes both nuances to be encompassed by $ṣdyq$ in the context.

460. Freedman ("Elihu" [N 230]) has made the intriguing argument that each of the Elihu speeches was "intended to be placed separately at strategic points in the Dialogue" (p. 57) and that the Elihu author "composed the four speeches as part of a general plan to reorganize the Book of Job" (p. 58). If Freedman is correct, his interpretation would dovetail nicely with the arguments made here. For then each of Elihu's speeches would serve as an immediate commentary at the end of each cycle of speeches by which to take the Three Friends' arguments and reformulate them in legal terms. Thus, the Elihu author could effectively show that his view is compatible with that of the Friends but that it extends their arguments by putting them on a proper legal footing.

461. Of course, the Friends *are* explicitly rebuked in the Epilogue where God declares that they have represented him falsely (42:7–8). But since, according to the approach to Job presented here, this addition to the book should be seen as being later than the Elihu section, this should not directly affect the Elihu-author's view of the Friends as found in the Poem of Job.

462. We should not exclude the possibility that the Elihu-author wrote some form of this introduction himself and that this was later adapted and incorporated by the editor (or editors) of the Prose Frame Story.

463. The Masoretic tradition actually reads $wyršy'w$ 't-'ywb, "and they condemned Job," at the end of 32:3, as do the other ancient versions. However, this is one of the 18 *tiqqunne sopherim*, "emendations of the scribes," where rabbinical tradition says that the text has been intentionally altered in order to eliminate a reading that is ostensibly impious toward God. In this instance, the original reading is said to have been $wyršy'w$ 't-$h'lhym$. I have followed most modern commentators in accepting this as the original text. See, e.g., Pope, *Job* (N 2): 242; Habel, *Job* (N 67): 442. For a discussion of this scribal practice, see McCarthy (N 455); I. Yeiven, *Introduction to the Tiberian Masorah* (E. J. Revell, ed. and trans.; Masoretic Studies 5; Missoula: Scholars, 1980): 49–51; for an older discussion, see, e.g., C. D. Ginsburg, *Introduction to the Massoretico-Critical of the Hebrew Bible* (rpt. with a Prolegomenon by H. M. Orlinsky; New York: Ktav, 1966): 347 ff., esp. 361. For a specific discussion of this proposed emendation of the scribes, see McCarthy, op. cit., 115 ff.; op. cit., 50. See, further discussion in this study on p. 169 ff.

464. See Alexander Pope's "An Essay on Man" lines 289–294.

465. This is especially manifest again in chapter 34, cf. verses 2, 4, 10, 34; but note as well 36:19, 23.

466. See pp. 68 ff.

467. As I have also noted, the same motivation lies behind Pinsker's attack on "Bontsye Shvayg"; see above, pp. 75 f.

468. See above, p. 150.

469. The form *pd'hw* is unclear, although the context leaves little doubt of the meaning here. I have read with many commentators *pr'hw*, "spare him. . . ." For a discussion of the form, see, e.g., Dhorme, *Job* (N 230): 502; Habel, *Job* (N 67): 458.

470. See, e.g., the comments by Pope, *Job* (N 2): 251; Habel, *Job* (N 67): 470.

471. See above, N 67.

472. See N 83.

473. See the discussion above, pp. 60 f.

474. There are sound reasons to assume that the rubrics introducing the various speeches in the Joban debate are secondary rather than an original part of the Poem. For one thing, it should be noted that it is hardly unusual to find dialogic narratives in Ancient Near Eastern texts where the speakers are not designated explicitly in the text. The most obvious such example is the *Babylonian Theodicy* (see N 262). In this exchange between Righteous Sufferer and Comforter, there are no introductory narrative statements like we find in Job, e.g., "The Righteous Sufferer/the Friend spoke and said. . . ." Instead, the change of voice must be inferred from the context alone. Similarly, in the *Dialogue of Pessimism* (see N 418), which chronicles the exchange between a master and his slave, there are no introductory formulae to indicate change of speaker (e.g., "the master said . . . then the slave said . . ."). At least one similar example can be cited from the Bible. It is usually assumed that the Song of Songs represents a dialogue between two lovers and perhaps may involve other voices as well. (For a discussion of this dialogic interpretation of Canticles, see. e.g., Pope, *Song* [N 115]: 34 ff.). But, again, no rubrics are given to designate the various speakers. The change of voice must be inferred from the context.

This is not to say that all examples of dialogue lack explicit phrasing designating the speakers. For example, in the Mesopotamian contest fables (see N 60), the dialogic exchanges do have explicit introductory rubrics, and the same thing can be said about the Egyptian text, Dispute over Suicide (see N 268).

There are really two strong indications that the introductory dialogue formulae in Job are secondary. First, in the Theophany they employ *Yhwh*, a name found elsewhere only in the Prose Frame Story and completely absent from the Joban speeches themselves (see N 250). Second, the shift in form of the dialogue formula in the Third Cycle of the Joban debate seems to be trying to deal with the textual corruption/correction of the text, an indication that the dialogue already had a textual history before these introductory elements were added to them (see, further, the discussion on pp. 89 f.).

475. For convenience I will refer to the "writer/editor" in this and similar instances; but, in doing so, I do not wish to exclude the possibility, already noted above, that there was more than one editorial hand involved in composing the Frame Story. Still, even if more than one editor/writer were involved, the view presented is essentially the same; so no significant distortion of meaning comes from letting one "writer/editor" stand for all.

476. The discussion of the bringing of gifts to Job in vs. 11 can also be seen in this light.

477. See pp. 47 f. and Ns 59 and 96.

478. Of course it is quite possible to argue that the entire Elihu section, including his prose introduction, was added to the book of Job after the Prologue and Epilogue were added. Then the Elihu section would be the final, significant editorial layer to the Job story. There is, however, reason to think otherwise. Since the Elihu-writer tends to follow the text and argument of Job and his Friends so carefully, if he also knew of the Prologue/Epilogue, one might expect that he would make specific reference to it as well. In particular, one might have looked for an allusion to the Satan. The fact that there is no hint of a reference to the Frame Story or to the Satan is strong evidence that the Elihu-writer did not know of the Job legend in

the form we now find in the book of Job. It also suggests, by the way, that the Satan probably played no role in the form of the legend of Job with which the author of Elihu was familiar.

479. See pp. 139 f.

480. See pp. 51 f.

481. Note that the first 27 chapters of the *Testament* deal with an elaboration of the Prologue, while 28–38 are given over to the Debate between Job and the Three Friends. Chapters 41–43 concern Elihu but also include a summary discussion of the Theophany as well (see chap. 42). Hence, out of the 53 chapters in this work, just 14 are employed to cover the Poem of Job.

Such an attitude toward the book of Job persists into the modern day. A typical treatment of this sort is Archibald MacLeish's version of Job in modern dress, his play *J.B.* MacLeish devotes most of his interest to the Prologue and Epilogue and the issues engaged therein. Once again, little attention in the play is given to the debate between Job and his Friends per se. Needless to say, MacLeish betrays no awareness that the Poem of Job might have any ironic or parodistic elements. Cf. further, B. Zuckerman *Perspectives on the Book of Job: A Comparison of Milton's and MacLeish's Views of the Work with a Modern Critical View* (Princeton Univ. senior thesis, 1969): 117–183.

482. See p. 97.

483. The fact that there is a narrative frame to the Poem of Job may also be significant. At least one other Appeal text has a somewhat similar framework, namely the so-called "Sumerian Job" (cf. N 274). Although the text is fragmentary, Kramer notes that it begins with a narrator who "introduces the unnamed individual who, upon being smitten with sickness and misfortune, addresses his god with tears and prayers" (Kramer [N 274]: 172). The text therefore begins as a third-person narrative and then switches to first-person when the Sufferer himself is making his anguished appeal. At the conclusion, the text again switches to third-person narrative that, as Kramer notes, constitutes "the 'happy ending' where the poet informs us that the man's prayer did not go unheeded, and that his god accepted the entreaties and delivered him from his afflictions" (ibid.). Nougayrol suggests that a similar framing device may be used in AO 4462 (see "Juste" [N 275]: 249; also Gray [N 262]: 259), but the evidence in favor of this assumption is less clear.

In any case, if a narrative framing device was part of the genre of Dialogue/Appeal, at least in some versions, then the use of the Frame Story in Job also would serve to reinforce the pietistic stereotype typical of such a text. Presumably, the structure in such a text would be: a. Prologue, narrated in the third person, introducing the righteous victim and describing the onset of his suffering; b. Poem, in which the victim, speaking in the first-person, makes his complaint (perhaps also engaging a friend in dialogue); c. Conclusion, in which a third-person narrative shows the "happy ending" where the god appears and mercy is granted.

By adding a Prologue and Epilogue that respectively mirror "part a" and "part c" of the Dialogue/Appeal structure, the writer/editor of the prose supplements to Job leaves the impression that "part b" should also be taken in a conventional manner. Thus he acts once more to bring the text in line with this conventional form of a Dialogue/Appeal and thus also emphasizes that the complaining Job should be seen as a typical Righteous Sufferer who is granted relief rather than as the opposite of this—as the poet of Job intended him to be.

484. See p. 59.

485. See pp. 71 ff.

486. See pp. 66 f.

487. See pp. 46 f.

488. One might argue that if the writer/editor of the Prose Frame Story found Elihu so distasteful, he could just as easily have excised this section entirely. But this is easier said

than done. It is doubtful that the prose supplementer of Job saw the Elihu speeches as a separate interpolation. To him it was a part of the Poem, and to violate the integrity of the Poem in any significant way was something he would hesitate to do. If Elihu was already deeply rooted in the tradition of the Poem known to the writer/editor of the Prose Frame Story, then he simply could not be "crossed out." The best one could do would be to blunt his attack as much as possible, to see his arguments as a false start that one might read and consider but that one must also reject, just as God had done.

489. One of the clearest indications of this is found in 11QtgJob 4:2 = Job 21:3b versus 11QtgJob 21:1, 9 = Job 32:10, 17. In this instance the translator has apparently switched the phrasing in similar passages. Where Job 21:3b reads *dbry*, taken as "my [Job's] words," the targumist renders [*m*]*nd'y*, "my knowledge." Hence, where the original has Job say to the Friends, "After my words, you may mock on," the Qumran Targum reads, "[After] my [in]sights, you may mock on." Conversely, where, in the Elihu speeches, the Hebrew used to describe Elihu's remarks is *d'* (which the targumist apparently understands as "knowledge"), the translator renders with *mly*, "my words." Hence where the Hebrew reads (according to the targumist's understanding), "I [Elihu] will expound my insights" (Job 32:10b, 17b), the translation in 11QtgJob reads, "I will expound my words."

This would seem to suggest that the translator has made a calculated transposition with a particular intent. He thereby implies that Job's arguments are best viewed as "insights" rather than mere "words"; while, conversely, Elihu's remarks should be seen only as mere "words" of no special insight. If this interpretation is correct, it is a clear indication that the translator of 11QtgJob desired to upgrade Job and downgrade Elihu much after the manner found in the *Testament of Job*. For a more detailed discussion of the translations in the Qumran Targum, see Zuckerman, *Process* (N 236): 139–141.

490. See p. 32.

491. See N 57.

492. Cf. pp. 89 f.

493. There actually is no example of the Old Greek text preserved among any of the early LXX (or LXX dependent) manuscripts. All such manuscripts are "Hexaplaric"; that is, they reflect the influence of the version of Job edited by the early Christian father, Origen (third century C E.), as part of his Hexapla edition of the Bible, which was reputedly laid out in six columns. In preparing his Greek text of Job, Origen filled out the Old Greek essentially to the length of the Hebrew tradition, primarily relying on another early Greek translation of Job, attributed to Theodotion (second century C.E.). The LXX versions now reflect this hybrid tradition.

There are various criteria by which to determine what actually constitutes the shorter Old Greek version of Job. It is particularly fortunate that Origen marked the additions he made to the text of Job with asterisks in the Hexapla, and some manuscripts preserve (at least in part) these editorial markings. While the evidence may be uncertain at one point or another, overall, there is a broad scholarly consensus as to what constitutes the Old Greek text of Job and what does not. For the most reliable guide, see the critical edition of the LXX version of Job, J. Ziegler, *Septuaginta vetus testamentum graecum*, vol. 11, 4; *Iōb* (Göttingen: Vandenhöck & Ruprecht, 1982). This also serves as the edition of record for this study. For a discussion of the Hexapla itself, see S. Jellicoe, *The Septuagint and Modern Study* (Oxford: Clarendon, 1968): 100–133. For a more specific discussion of the Hexaplaric version of Job versus the Old Greek, see, e.g., Ziegler, op. cit., 60–133; Zuckerman, *Process* (N 236): 23–36 and the sources cited therein; also H. Heater, *A Septuagint Translation Technique in the Book of Job* (Washington: CBA, 1982): 7–8 with nn. 41–45.

494. The most prominent proponents of the argument in favor of an editorial bias in the Old Greek are G. Gerleman, *Studies in the Septuagint I: Book of Job*; (Lund: Lunds Univer-

sity Press, 1946); H. S. Gehman, "The Theological Approach of the Greek Translator of Job 1–15," *JBL* 68 (1949): 231–240; D. H. Gard, *The Exegetical Method of the Greek Translator of the Book of Job* (Philadelphia: SBL, 1952). For a more detailed discussion of the history of criticism on this issue, see H. M. Orlinsky, "Studies in the Septuagint of the Book of Job; Chapter I," *HUCA* 28 (1957): 53–73.

495. Ibid.; also "Studies . . . II," *HUCA* 29 (1958): 229–271; "Studies . . . III," *HUCA* 30 (1959): 153–167; "Studies . . . III (Continued)," *HUCA* 32 (1961): 239–268; "Studies . . . IV," *HUCA* 33 (1962): 119–151; "Studies . . . V," *HUCA* 35 (1964): 57–78; "Studies V [Continued]," *HUCA* 36 (1965): 37–47. Orlinsky never published a conclusion to this series.

496. Heater (N 493): 4; see also the comments of E. Tov, *The Text-Critical Use of the Septuagint in Biblical Research* (Jerusalem: Simor, 1981): 52. This is not to suggest that a case cannot be made that there is, on occasion, some bias revealed on the part of the translator of the Old Greek. Note, in this respect, Urbach's criticism of Orlinsky's thesis (N 103): 866–867, n. 66. In particular, modifications seem to occur as part of a tendency to avoid depicting God in a less-than respectful-fashion. Nonetheless, considerable caution must be exercised in making use of comparisons, and all potential examples must be judged on a case-by-case basis.

For example, recently Baskin has revived an argument that Job 14:14 is translated into Greek in such a way that the rendering no longer reflects doubt about resurrection (cf. Baskin [N 7]: 28). Orlinsky, on the other hand, has strenuously argued that the reason this passage was altered had nothing to do with any editorial bias at all; see "Studies . . . I" (N 494): 67; also idem., "The Hebrew and Greek Texts of Job 14.12," *JQR* 28 (1937–1938): 63 ff. If examples like this are disputed, other examples seem more clear cut, e.g., the shift from "the sons of God" (*bny 'lhym*) to "my angels" (*aggeloi mou*) in the LXX rendering of Job 38:7b. For a discussion of the passage, see, e.g., B. Zuckerman, "Two Examples of Editorial Modification in 11QtgJob," in *Biblical and Near Eastern Studies; Essays in Honor of William Sanford LaSor* (G. A.Tuttle, ed.; Grand Rapids: Eerdmans, 1978): 269; for another similar example, see the discussion in this study of the LXX rendering of 36:14b on pp. 270 ff.

Overall, one should not look in the Greek tradition for a major shift in viewpoint; still, where the viewpoint is shifted, there can be little question that the slant is toward a more pietistic presentation.

497. It might be fairly argued that a discussion of these additions to the text of Job should be more properly grouped with the supplements to the Poem, considered in the previous section of this study. Nonetheless, I feel that these additions are more properly grouped under the heading of editorial modifications rather than supplements. For one thing, they occur as part of a translation, as opposed to an intervention into the Hebrew text per se; and there are clear indications that they were added as secondary commentary to what was already perceived to be, essentially, a canonical text of Job. This is, for all intents and purposes, explicitly stated in the case of the addition to Job 42:17, which is cited on the basis of secondary authority (see Ns 503, 504, below); and in the case here, the rationale for supplying a commentary, beyond what the text itself says, is not difficult to determine (cf. p. 168 with N 501).

Overall, the distinction between these additions and those discussed above can be seen this way: In the earlier examples cited above, the authors were intent on supplementing the Poem of Job; thus their additions should be seen as a part of the evolution of the canonical form of Job. In these instances, one is dealing with essentially a postcanon phenomenon, where editors are trying to add commentary to the *book* of Job.

498. On the euphemistic handling of this "curse," in the Hebrew text, according to the Masoretic tradition as well as in the other ancient versions, see p. 169.

499. All designations of additions to this text and to 42:17, below, follow the versifications assigned in Ziegler's edition of the LXX of Job (N 493).

500. See, e.g., the comments of Spittler (N 103): 831.

501. It should also be recognized that this additional commentary is added here to explain—and, at least to some extent, to mitigate—the actions of Job's wife. By showing her horrific circumstances in greater detail, her urging that Job curse God is then seen to be the desperate plea of a woman whose troubles have caused her to take leave of her senses. This is probably also the way her description is meant to be taken in 2:10—as being like women who are *aphronōn* (= Hebrew *hnblwt*): not so much "foolish" as "crazy, insane."

Another indication of a desire in the Greek tradition to soften the wife's culpability may be reflected in the apparent circumlocutionary phrasing of her plea made to Job: *alla eipon ti rēma eis kurion*, "But say something towards God," presumably over against an original Hebrew that, in all likelihood, simply employed *qll/ 'rr 'lhym*, "Curse God!"

502. This is based on Gen. 36:33–34, where Jobab is mentioned as the second ruler in Edom. This tradition is also known from the *Testament of Job* (see 1:1,6, etc.) and apparently was also known to the author of the *Life of Job* (cf. N 109). The connection of Job to Jobab is apparently made due to the similarity of their names as well as the fact that like Job, Jobab was a figure from patriarchal times. See, e.g., Baskin (N 7): 29.

503. Note that the Greek translator explicitly states that this tradition is cited on the basis of a secondary authority "from the Syriac book" (*ek tēs suriakēs biblou*); cf. 42:17b). It is now unclear exactly what this "Syriac" (presumably = Aramaic) book is, but it seems doubtful that it was viewed as being an authoritative (i.e., canonical) source on a par with the Hebrew text (or texts) of Job on which the Greek translator based his translation. See further, Dhorme, *Job* (N 230): xvii–xviii.

504. The use of *gegraptai*, "it is written," again indicates that the authority for this statement is taken from a secondary source, although in this instance it is unclear whether the "Syriac book," mentioned in vs. 17b, is the specific authority alluded to (see N 503). Note that the LXX renderings of both 14:14 and 19:25–27 may also reflect an affirmative attitude toward resurrection; see the discussion by Cavallin (N 103): 105–106. Not surprisingly, we find the *Testament of Job* also touching on a theme found in the Greek tradition, since it also refers to Job's resurrection (see, e.g., 4:9). For further discussion see ibid., 160–163.

505. Baskin (N 7): 29.

506. See, e.g., Dhorme, *Job* (N 230): 4–5; Blank, "Curse" (N 322): 83–84; and for the most extensive recent discussion, McCarthy (N 455): 191–195.

507. See, e.g., Dhorme, *Job* (N 230): 4, 7–8, 17, 19 for a convenient discussion of how the various versions handle the curse phrasing. One might argue (e.g., as does Habel, *Job* [N 67]: 88) that the writer/editor of the Prose Frame Story employed this euphemism himself. Still, the fact that there are other apparent instances in Job where the text has been changed to avoid an impious reference to God (see the following discussion) and where it is more difficult to see the reading as original supports the assumption that this is an instance of editorial change (see McCarthy [N 455]: 195). In 1 Kgs. 21:10, 13; (possibly also Ps. 10:3; however, note, e.g., McCarthy's caution, ibid., 192, n. 149) a similar euphemistic usage of *brk* seems to be employed (see, e.g., Pope, *Job* [N 2]: 8). For a fuller discussion of this euphemism, including other possible examples, see Blank, "Curse" (N 322): 83–85.

508. This is one of the *tiqqunne sopherim*, "emendations of the scribes" (see above N 463). The unemended reading may be preserved in the LXX (note, however, Yeiven's caution [N 463]: 51). See further, for example, McCarthy (N 455): 79 ff.; Ginsburg (N 463): 360–361; Dhorme, *Job* (N 230): 110.

509. Another reputed emendation of the scribes. This text has already been discussed above, N 463.

510. The reading before emendation appears to be preserved according to the tradition in the LXX. This passage is discussed above, N 455.

511. There is also the curious example of the forms spelled $r\check{s}'ym$ in 38:13, 15, "evil ones." According to scribal practice within the Masoretic tradition, the letter $'ayin$ is suspended above the line in both these words, apparently indicating that it was not originally written in the text but was added subsequently. There are two other cases of suspended letters according to the Masoretic tradition ($'wtwt\ tlwywt$; the others are in Judg. 18:30, Ps. 80:14; see, e.g., Ginsburg [N 463]: 340–341; McCarthy [N 455]: 225–226; Yeiven [N 463]: 47). The reason the original form $r\check{s}ym$ had to be emended is unclear. G. R. Driver in his study, "Two Astronomical Passages in the Old Testament," JTS 4 (1953): 208–212, has suggested that reference is being made here to astronomical constellations or possibly comets. The arguments in favor of this are not, however, convincing. Nonetheless, it is quite possible that some manner of perceived impropriety prompted the emendation, although exactly $what$ is unclear on the basis of the evidence currently available. On the other hand, the original reading may simply reflect a phonetic misspelling, due to the weakening of the pronunciation of the laryngeal $'ayin$ to zero (a phenomenon documented in some of the Dead Sea Scrolls), which was then corrected back to the proper historical spelling (see Yeiven, op. cit.; McCarthy, op. cit., p. 226 n. 161 and the sources cited therein).

512. The marginal $qere$ is preserved, for example, in the Masorah notes of both the Aleppo Codex (see $The\ Aleppo\ Codex\ Provided\ with\ Massoretic\ Notes\ and\ Pointed\ by\ Aaron Ben\ Asher$ [M. H. Goshen-Gottstein, ed.; Jerusalem: HUBP, 1976]: "$tqmw$" [= p. 546]) and in Leningrad Codex B19a (see $Pentateuch,\ Prophets\ and\ Hagiographa;\ Codex\ Leningrad B19a$ . . . [D. S. Löwinger, ed.; Jerusalem: Makor, 1970]: vol. 3, 147).

513. Aquila, the Vulgate, and the Peshitta all reflect the same reading as found in the $qere$ of the Masoretic tradition. The LXX appears to have read a volitive particle $l\bar{u}/l\bar{u}'$. Cf., for example, the discussion in Dhorme, Job (N 230): 187.

514. Cf. Zuckerman, "Two Examples" (N 496): 272–274. The text involved actually is the Qumran Targum's rendering of 34:31. But in that instance, the translator appears to have substituted the phrase from 13:15 (essentially in its Hebrew form) for Elihu's more strident comment about Job. This, too, indicates that for the translator of 11QtgJob, the pietistic version of 13:15 already was well known and already had special authority and importance. On the date of 11QtgJob, see idem., "The Date of 11QtgJob; A Paleographic Consideration of Its $Vorlage$," JSP 1 (1987): 57–78.

515. According to Hatch and Redpath (N 62): 453–454, $elpiz\bar{o}$ is used 13 times as the equivalent of yhl ($piel$ and $hiphil$ in the LXX). This makes it the most common reflex for this verb in this Greek tradition; see further, E. Dos Santos, $An\ Expanded\ Hebrew\ Index\ for\ the Hatch-Redpatch\ Concordance\ to\ the\ Septuagint$ (Jerusalem: Dugith, n.d.): 80. To my knowledge, the connection of this passage in the $Testament$ to the pietistic version of Job 13:15 has not been previously noted.

516. See further, N 278. For a discussion of the passage, see, e.g., R. Gordis, $The Biblical\ Text\ in\ the\ Making;\ A\ Study\ of\ the\ Kethib-Qere$ (rev. ed. with prolegomenon; New York: Ktav, 1971): 50–51; idem., Job (N 250): 144; Urbach (N 103): 408; Baskin (N 7): 19–20.

517. See the discussion above, N 71.

518. Cf. Gordis' caution that this emendation cannot be considered merely an attempt by the Masoretes to alter the text of Job simply because then it would conveniently serve a pietistic end: "The Qere is not 'an ingenious emendation of the Masoretes.' It cannot be too strongly stressed that modifying a text was definitely not a Masoretic purpose or activity. . . . Far more heterodox passages in our book and elsewhere were left unmodified by the Masoretes, whose self-imposed task was the $preservation\ of\ the\ received\ text$ [Gordis' italics]" (Gordis, Job [N 250]: 144).

519. Note, in this connection, that Gordis, in his listing and classification of all Masoretic examples of *ketiv/qere* characterizes the reading in Job 13:15 as "unclassified." See *Biblical Text* (N 516): 150–152, list 81.

520. For a general discussion of this tendency in the Masoretic text (especially in respect to *ketiv/qere*), see S. Talmon, "Double Readings in the Masoretic Text," *Textus* 1 (1960): 144–184; also idem., "The Three Scrolls of the Law that Were Found in the Temple Court," *Textus* 2 (1962): 14–27.

521. For a consideration of other potential interpretations, see, e.g., Driver and Gray (N 235): vol. 2, 84–85; Gordis, *Job* (N 250): 144; Habel, *Job* (N 67): 225.

522. See pp. 50 ff.

523. See the discussion of the passage above, pp. 130 ff.

524. Other uses of *yḥl* in Job may be seen in the same light. Note especially that Elihu seems to be playing off this same theme in 32:11, 16. In both these verses he affirms that like the proverbial patient Job he has waited while Job and his Friends argued their point and counterpoint. But finally he has had enough. Like the Job of the Poem, he will be patient no more. As he declares in vs. 17, he is now bound and determined to speak his mind.

If these verses do reflect a play on the patience-of-Job cliché, it would indicate that the Elihu-author is just as aware of this theme as is the poet of Job and that the stereotype exerted a powerful influence in his time as well the later period of the writers of the *Testament of Job* and the Epistle of James.

For a consideration of another potential play on the patience theme in the Poem, see N 290.

525. We might even press this argument further. It seems at least conceivable that the emendation of *l'* to *lw* may not, in the final analysis, really be an emendation at all; that is, it may be that the phrase "Though he slay me, I will (patiently) wait for Him" really *was* the genuine reading or at least a genuine phrase from out of some version of the ancient Joban folk tradition. The author of the Poem may then have taken this well-known phrase and twisted it into a parody, converting *lw* to *l'* and thus turning the Joban credo of patience inside-out: "Though he slay me, I will not be patient!" This would have been a parodistic flourish having the maximum devastating effect; for it would sound like the standard Joban credo, but would mean precisely the opposite.

If this is so, then the pietistic reading in 13:15 should not be viewed as a conversion of the text but rather more as a retroversion to the original, traditional phrase, which, presumably, was still well known in the popular, folk tradition of Job. This would help make sense of the preservation of this reading as a *genuine* variant, known to the rabbis of the Mishnaic period and would also explain the retention of this reading in a tradition known to, and preserved by, the Masoretes. After all, it could then be reasonably argued that in "changing" the reading in 13:15, no real change was actually made. This was simply a case of putting things right again.

526. See pp. 77 ff.

527. It may be more than simply a coincidence that two out of the three clearly targumic texts found among the Dead Sea Scrolls are targums of Job, namely the Cave 11 Targum of Job (see N 5) and the few fragments constituting the extant Cave 4 Targum of Job (siglum: 4QtgJob) (cf. *Discoveries in the Judaean Desert* vol. 6 [J. T. Milik, ed.; Oxford: Clarendon, 1977]: 86–90). We should also note that in the only attested discussion of a specific targum in the early rabbinical literature (Tosefta Shabbat 13:2; cf. TB Shabbat 115a; TP Shabbat 16:1), the particular targum under discussion is a targum of Job. In that instance Rabban Gamaliel (80–110 C.E.) is noted to have been reading a targum of Job, which reminded R. Halafta that Gamaliel's grandfather, Gamaliel the Elder (30–70 C.E.) had once been brought a targum that he subsequently ordered to be hidden. In this latter instance the targum in question was, once again, a targum of Job. Moreover, the one citation of a targumic passage known from the

Talmud is a rendering of Job 5:10 (see TB Nazir 3a; for further discussion of Job targums in rabbinical literature, R. Weiss, *The Aramaic Targum of Job* [Tel Aviv: Tel Aviv University, 1979]: 1–36 [Hebrew] and English summary, iv–v).

We can only wonder why a good deal of the evidence we have of written targums from the period of the early rabbis centers upon targums of Job? One probable reason is that the Hebrew of Job, even at this early time, must have been recognized as being notoriously difficult to read and comprehend. Hence, if any biblical text cried out for a popular translation so that it would be more widely accessible in the vernacular of the day, Aramaic, it would certainly have been Job. Moreover, it would not only be because of the difficult nature of the language that targumic renditions of Job were called for. In all likelihood the controversial issues raised in Job were also deemed to require special handling, especially in more popular translations that would make Job more broadly available to the Jewish community in rabbinical times. We might suspect that it was in translations of this nature that various small adjustments were often made in order to conform the text to pietistic standards.

On the other hand, it is also quite likely that more straightforward renderings of Job were made in targumic form. After all, 11QtgJob and 4QtgJob, insofar as they are preserved, are fairly accurate renderings that contain relatively limited editorial adjustments. In fact, it may even be partly for this reason that Gamaliel the Elder wished to hide away the targum that was brought before him; that is, he may have deemed the targum too correct to be exposed to the uninitiated. Note in this connection TB Megillah 3a which suggests a divine injunction against translating any of the biblical *Ketuvim* or Writings into the vernacular.

It is also likely that Gamaliel did not like the idea that any biblical text should be committed to writing in the vulgar language of the time and that this also prompted his suppression of the targum brought to his attention (note, in this respect, Leiman [N 101]: 176–177, n. 331).

Regardless, it does seem fairly reasonable to assume that when the rabbis thought of a biblical targum around the beginning of the Common Era, the stereotypical example would seem to have been a targum of Job. And this at least supports the assumption that the Job that known to the popular audience of that time was likely Job in translation as opposed to Job in the hard-to-read original Hebrew.

528. See p. 80.

529. See pp. 32 f.

530. By which I mean the "Old Testament" portion of Scripture. Whether he would have conceived of the Christian writings as part of the biblical canon is not at issue here. Nor is it important, for purposes of this argument, to know what version (or versions) of the Bible James employed. I am more concerned with how he viewed the authority of the Bible his Christian community inherited from Jewish tradition. In this respect, note that he cites the authority of Scripture several times (2:8, 23; 4:5) and quotes liberally from "Old Testament" books, all indications that the authority of this material was taken by him to be a matter of course.

531. Cf. *OED* (N 26): vol. 4, pp. 585–586.

532. For a convenient survey of the range of early rabbinical opinions on Job, see Baskin (N 7): 7–26. She comments (p. 25):

> There is no rabbinic consensus on Job. Even those who grant his good qualities cannot deem him, a gentile and a blasphemer, the equal in righteousness with an Israelite. Some Sages, out of a general sense of hostility towards perceived sectarians as well as the gentile nations, do their best to stress his iniquities and denigrate his rewards. Even the glorification of Job as a model Israelite . . . may have as much to do with scoring points against Christian argument as genuine esteem for the character himself.

Index of Authors

Dhorme, E. (continued)
N313, N352, N373, N374, N375, N380,
N381, N382, N397, N410, N424, N433,
N455, N469, N503, N506, N507, N508,
N513
Dibelius, M., N4, N5, N7, N63
Dick, M., 10, 107, 108; N298, N305, N309,
N316, N318, N319, N323
Di Lella, A., N422
Dimant, D., N109
Donan, R., N109
Dos Santos, E., N515
Dossin, G., N331
Dostoevsky, F., N29
Driver, G. R., N511
Driver, S. R., 10; N235, N236, N237, N318,
N373, N380, N381, N431, N521
Dubnov, S., N134, N196
Duhm, B., N250

Edelman, L., N150
Eichrodt, W., N359
Elliger, K., N13
Emerson, C., N29
Erman, A., N268
Ettinger, S., N134
Eusebius, N109
Ewen, D., N130
Ezrahi, S., N161

Faulkner, R., N268
Feldman, H., N11
Fine, H. A., N2
Fishbane, M., N38
Fisher, R., N65
Fitzmyer, J., N305
Fohrer, G., 10; N318, N319, N321
Follis, E., N298
Forsyth, N., N37, N38, N45
Foster, F., N244
Fowler, J., N424
Frank, H., N65, N77, N86
Frankel, J., N134
Freedman, D. N., 88; N36, N230, N336, N411,
N460
Friedländer, I., N134
Fulco, W. J., N249

Gamaliel, R., N527
Gamaliel the Elder, R., N527
Garber, Z., N148
Gard, D., N494
Garr, W. R., N246, N247, N248
Gaster, T. H., N362, N365
Gehman, H., N494
Gemser, B., 104–5; N296, N298, N300, N308,
N331, N339, N351, N352, N353
Gerleman, G., N494
Gibson, J.C.L., N51, N398
Gingrich, F. W., N4, N6, N62, N63

Ginsberg, H. L., 10; N2, N51, N95, N96,
N246, N256, N362, N369, N398
Ginsburg, C. D., N463, N508, N511
Ginzberg, L., N19, N45, N145
Glatstein, J., N93, N140
Goedicke, H., N427
Goldin, J., N9, N14
Goldstein, J., N21
Golomb, D., N248
Good, E., 9–10; N*
Good, R., N51
Goodman, H., N65, N73, N74, N83
Gordis, R., 10, 53; N30, N38, N55, N116,
N223, N230, N250, N318, N352, N372,
N373, N403, N516, N518, N519, N521
Goshen-Gottstein, M. H., N512
Gray, G., 10; N235, N236, N237, N318, N373,
N380, N381, N431, N521
Gray, J., N262, N263, N268, N270, N271,
N275, N276, N277, N282, N283, N298,
N483
Green, D., N359
Greenberg, E., 68–71, 78, 79, 81, 97, 154,
157, 175; N65, N71, N72, N73, N76, N83,
N86, N90, N91, N93, N140, N144, N152,
N162, N163, N165, N166, N167, N169,
N170, N171, N172, N202, N206, N208
Greenberg, M., 139–140; N48, N427, N428,
N429
Greeven, H., N4, N5, N7, N63
Gregory the Great, N64
Guillaume, A., N244
Güterbock, H., N269

Haas, C., N4
Habel, N., 10, 114, 146–47; N67, N228, N230,
N231, N235, N298, N307, N315, N318,
N340, N342, N347, N348, N349, N352,
N355, N374, N375, N379, N384, N393,
N395, N397, N403, N407, N408, N409,
N414, N431, N433, N439, N440, N441,
N443, N447, N449, N454, N455, N456,
N463, N469, N470, N507, N521
Hackett, J., N248
Hadda, J., N65
Halafta, R., N527
Hallo, W., N47
Halpern, B., N248
Hanson, P., N256
Harrington, D., N45
Harvey, J., N332
Hatch, E., N62, N63, N515
Haussig, H., N361
Hautzig, E., 65, 67–68; N142, N147, N156
Hayes, J. H., N60
Hayward, L., N56
Heater, H., 167; N493, N496
Heller, C., N134
Henderson, R., N130
Herdner, A., N51, N362, N369

Index of Ancient Sources·

*Only texts that are actually cited are referenced in the index of ancient sources.